Francis Wright Beare

FROM
JESUS
TO
PAUL

Studies in Honour of
Francis Wright Beare

FROM JESUS TO PAUL

Studies in Honour of Francis Wright Beare

Edited by

Peter Richardson and John C. Hurd

Wilfrid Laurier University Press

Canadian Cataloguing in Publication Data

Main entry under title:
From Jesus to Paul

Includes indexes.
"Bibliography of Francis Wright Beare": p.
ISBN 0-88920-138-2

1. Paul, the Apostle, Saint — Addresses, essays,
lectures. 2. Jesus Christ — History of doctrines —
Addresses, essays, lectures. 3. Beare, Francis
Wright, 1902-   I. Beare, Francis Wright, 1903-
II. Richardson, Peter, 1935-   III. Hurd, John
Coolidge

BS2653.F76   1984   230   C84-098834-6

Copyright © 1984

WILFRID LAURIER UNIVERSITY PRESS
Waterloo, Ontario, Canada   N2L 3C5

84 85 86 87 4 3 2 1

Cover Design: Helen Lange

Contents

Tabula Patronorum   ix

Tabula Gratulatoria   xi

Introduction   xv

Francis Wright Beare: Cursus Vitae   xix

Bibliography of Francis Wright Beare
    JOHN C. HURD   xxi

Ma première rencontre avec le Professeur Frank W. Beare
    ADRIEN BRUNET, O.P.   xxv

Frank Beare at Trinity
    EUGENE R. FAIRWEATHER xxvii

1. From Jesus to Paul: The Contours and Consequences of a
   Debate
    S. G. WILSON   1

2. *Paulus alienus:* William Wrede on Comparing Jesus and
   Paul
    HANS ROLLMANN   23

3. Jesus or Paul? The Origin of the Universal Mission of the
   Christian Church
    CHARLES H. H. SCOBIE   47

4. Paul and Jerusalem
    LLOYD GASTON   61

5. "The Jesus Whom Paul Preaches" (Acts 19:13)
    JOHN C. HURD   73

6. The Thunderbolt in Q and the Wise Man in Corinth
    PETER RICHARDSON   91

7. Jesus as Lordly Example in Philippians 2:5-11
   L. W. HURTADO 113
8. Imitation in Paul's Letters: Its Significance for His Relationship to Jesus and to His Own Christian Foundations
   DAVID STANLEY, S.J. 127
9. "Kingdom of God" Sayings in Paul's Letters
   GEORGE JOHNSTON 143
10. The Spirit: Paul's Journey to Jesus and Beyond
    BENNO PRZYBYLSKI 157
11. "He who did not spare his own son . . .": Jesus, Paul, and the
    Akedah
    ALAN F. SEGAL 169
12. Musonius Rufus, Jesus, and Paul: Three First-Century
    Feminists
    WILLIAM KLASSEN 185
13. Marcion and the Critical Method
    ROBERT M. GRANT 207
    Notes on Contributors 217
    Index Nominorum 219
    Index Locorum 223

Tabula Patronorum

Knox College, Toronto
Oriental Club, University of Toronto
Presbyterian College, Montreal
Toronto School of Theology
Trinity College, University of Toronto
University College, University of Toronto

* * *

Professor Mary Beare
Mr. and Mrs. Samuel E. Beare
Mrs. Francis W. Beare
The Reverend Canon H. W. Buchner
The Most Reverend H. H. Clark†
Professor D. J. Conacher
Professor A. Dalzell
Professor G. Edison
Professor E. R. Fairweather
Professor G. G. Falle
Professor H. J. Forstman
Dr. Arthur Grenoble
Olaf and Anna Grobel
Professor G. M. A. Grube†
Professor F. K. Hare
Professor Walter Harrelson
Professor J. C. Hurd
Professor Sherman E. Johnson

Professor W. Stewart McCullough†
Mr. Maxwell Meighen
Dr. Stella G. Miller
Professor D. R. G. Owen
Principal G. P. Richardson
Mr. G. O. Shepherd
Professor Lou H. Silberman
Professor R. J. Williams
Professor F. W. Winnett

Tabula Gratulatoria

Charles P. Anderson, Associate Professor, Religious Studies, University of British Columbia, Vancouver, British Columbia.

Carl E. Armerding, Principal, Regent College, Vancouver, British Columbia

S. Murray Barron, Newmarket, Ontario.

B. Robert Bater, Principal/Professor, Queen's Theological College, Kingston, Ontario.

Schuyler Brown, Associate Professor, New Testament, Faculty of Theology, University of St. Michael's College, Toronto, Ontario.

D. A. Carson, Professor, Trinity Evangelical Divinity School, Deerfield, Illinois.

Anthony R. Ceresko, O.S.F.S., Associate Professor, Old Testament, Faculty of Theology, University of St. Michael's College, Toronto, Ontario.

Ernest G. Clarke, Professor, Near Eastern Studies, University of Toronto, Toronto, Ontario.

John H. Corbett, Associate Professor, Graduate Centre for Religious Studies, University of Toronto, Toronto, Ontario.

Guy Couturier, Professeur titulaire, Faculté de Théologie, Université de Montréal, Montréal, Québec.

Claude Cox, Chairman, Department of Religion, Brandon University, Brandon, Manitoba.

Peter Craigie, Dean, Faculty of Humanities, The University of Calgary, Calgary, Alberta.

Robert C. Culley, Professor, Faculty of Religious Studies, McGill University, Montreal, Quebec.

Paul E. Dion, Professor, Near Eastern Studies, University of Toronto, Toronto, Ontario.

Peter Fast, Assistant Professor, New Testament, Canadian Mennonite Bible College, Winnipeg, Manitoba.

J. T. Forestell, C.S.B., Professor, New Testament Studies, University of St. Michael's College, Toronto, Ontario.

Douglas J. Fox, Associate Professor, Hebrew and Old Testament, Huron College, University of Western Ontario, London, Ontario.

Daniel Fraikin, Associate Professor, New Testament, Queen's University, Kingston, Ontario.

Roman Garrison, Centre for Religious Studies, University of Toronto, Toronto, Ontario.

A. Kirk Grayson, Professor, Near Eastern Studies, University of Toronto, Toronto, Ontario.

Heinz O. Guenther, Professor of New Testament, Emmanuel College, Victoria University, Toronto, Ontario.

Melvyn R. Hillmer, Principal and Professor of New Testament, McMaster Divinity College, McMaster University, Hamilton, Ontario.

Raymond Hobbs, Professor, Old Testament Interpretation, McMaster Divinity College, McMaster University, Hamilton, Ontario.

Richard Hollingsworth, Social Development Manager, First-Pilgrim United Church, Hamilton, Ontario.

Ben T. Holmes, Toronto, Ontario.

R. W. Huebsch, Associate Professor, Early Jewish and Early Christian Literature, Department of Religious Studies, Niagara University, New York, U.S.A.

Edward Jackmann, O.P., Historian, Historical Institute of the Roman Catholic Archdiocese of Toronto, Toronto, Ontario.

Ian J. Kagedan, Lecturer, University of Winnipeg, Winnipeg, Manitoba.

John S. Kloppenborg, Toronto School of Theology, Toronto, Ontario.

Adrian M. Leske, Professor, Religious Studies, Concordia College, Edmonton, Alberta.

Richard N. Longenecker, Professor, New Testament, Wycliffe College, University of Toronto, Toronto, Ontario.

Gerd Luedemann, Professor, New Testament, Georg-August-University, Göttingen.

R. Sheldon MacKenzie, Associate Professor, Memorial University of Newfoundland, St. John's, Newfoundland.

Brice L. Martin, Pastor, Bedford Park Chapel, Toronto, Ontario.

Wayne O. McCready, Associate Professor, Religious Studies, University of Calgary, Calgary, Alberta.

Sean E. McEvenue, Principal/Associate Professor, Lonergan University College, Concordia University, Montreal, Quebec.

John W. Miller, Associate Professor, Religious Studies, Conrad Grebel College, University of Waterloo, Waterloo, Ontario.

Helen I. Milton, Associate Professor, retired, University of Windsor, Windsor, Ontario.

Michael Newton, Assistant Professor, Memorial University of Newfoundland, Sir Wilfred Grenfell College, Corner Brook, Newfoundland.

Barry N. Olshen, Associate Professor, Glendon College, York University, Toronto, Ontario.

R. E. Osborne, Professor, Religion, Carleton University, Ottawa, Ontario.

Harold Remus, Associate Professor, Religious Studies, Wilfrid Laurier University, Waterloo, Ontario.

John Rook, Assistant Professor, New Testament Interpretation, McMaster Divinity College, McMaster University, Hamilton, Ontario.

E. P. Sanders, Professor, Religious Studies, McMaster University, Hamilton, Ontario.

John Sandys-Wunsch, Vice-Chancellor and Provost, University of Thorneloe College, Sudbury, Ontario.

David Schroeder, Professor, Canadian Mennonite Bible College, Winnipeg, Manitoba.

R. B. Y. Scott, Professor Emeritus, Princeton University, Princeton, New Jersey, U.S.A.

V. George Shillington, Assistant Professor, New Testament, Mennonite Brethren Bible College and College of Arts, University of Winnipeg, Winnipeg, Manitoba.

Lawrence E. Toombs, Professor, Religion and Culture, Wilfrid Laurier University, Waterloo, Ontario.

Warren C. Trenchard, Professor, Biblical Languages and Religion, Canadian Union College, College Heights, Alberta.

Norman E. Wagner, President, The University of Calgary, Calgary, Alberta.

Ronald J. Williams, Professor Emeritus, University of Toronto, Toronto, Ontario.

Introduction

What follows is a "homage" to one of Canada's great scholars, certainly its greatest New Testament scholar. With the exception of Robert Grant, whose long friendship with Frank Beare gave us the opportunity of inviting him to participate, it comes from a collection of scholars all of whom work or have worked in Canada. However, apart from John Hurd and Eugene Fairweather, who have been colleagues of Frank's at Trinity College, none of the contributors has worked with him on the same teaching faculty, and none has been a student of his in a formal sense. This is unusual in a *Festschrift* and perhaps requires some explanation.

At the risk of oversimplification, Canada has had—at least in the biblical field—two kinds of scholars: Canadians who go outside the country to do their doctoral work, and non-Canadians who bring their training into the country to enrich it with their fresh approaches. At the time of Frank's retirement in 1968 doctoral work in New Testament in Canada was in its infancy. In Toronto neither the Toronto School of Theology nor the Centre for Religious Studies at the University of Toronto had been born. Hence, although almost all the contributors are now deeply rooted in Canada, their origins represent the diversity of Canada itself: England, Scotland, the United States, Poland—and within Canada both anglophone and francophone spread *a mari usque ad mare*.

The essays intend to open afresh the complexity of the Jesus-Paul issue, i.e., the question of Paul's dependence upon and continuity with Jesus. So much attention has been given in the past to this very difficult problem that fresh solutions are hard to find, and suspect when offered. One does not expect that a major breakthrough on this question will appear anywhere today, and this volume makes no such claim. On the contrary, these essays do not hew to a single line, but present considerable diversity of approach, stance, and conclusion—as Frank Beare would wish.

Wilson begins by providing an overview of the debate from Baur to the present, with a fresh analysis of the problems encountered in such a study and some acute observations on why some historical and theological options are not pursued as eagerly as they might be. Next, from almost completely unknown materials Rollmann examines the role of one important actor in this story: William Wrede. By analyzing Wrede's unpublished correspondence he helps to unravel the continental controversies over "anti-Paulinism," correcting a number of misconceptions along the way. Scobie maintains that the Hellenists are the link connecting Jesus and Paul, between whom there is considerable continuity. The Samaritan mission, he argues, is a middle term between Jewish and Gentile missions. By contrast and using a very different approach, Gaston concludes that the message of the Jerusalem Church and Paul's message were radically different. This conclusion he bases on a reading of Paul's explicit references to Jerusalem.

Hurd works from recent research on the Pauline letter-form and letter-sequence to an assessment of the similarity of Jesus' and Paul's eschatology. The earliest form of Paul's apocalypticism has important links with Jesus' futurist eschatology. Through an examination of the "Thunderbolt in Q" and 1 Corinthians Richardson traces connections between the conflicts in Corinth, especially that between Paul and Apollos, and the development of the gospel tradition, especially Q and, later on, Proto-Luke. The dominant view of Philippians 2:5-11, that no imitation of Jesus is in view, is contested by Hurtado's study of the structure and language of the hymn. He links the hymn with Paul's paraenetic purpose, the call to obedience. In a contrasting study Stanley argues that in general imitation language in Paul does not present Jesus as a model; rather he is presented as God's saving power. Like Stanley's paper, both Johnston's and Przybylski's contributions survey a particular facet of Paul's thought. Johnston sees parallels between Paul's use of the kingdom idea and Jesus', and brings to the fore its eschatological dimension. Przybylski ranges widely to show the measure of diversity in early Christianity on the issue of the finality of revelation. He suggests that there are three stages of revelation: Jesus, the Gospel from the risen Jesus, and revelation added to revelation in Paul's own ministry.

Segal tackles afresh the use of the Akedah—the tradition concerning the offering up of Isaac by Abraham—based upon three recent major attempts to settle the issue. He concludes that there was a pre-Christian Jewish exegetical tradition about Isaac which was more important to Christian thought than the frequently cited Isaiah 53 theme. Moving into the hellenistic world, Klassen compares Jesus,

Paul, and Musonius Rufus on the basis of their attitudes to women and to marriage. The paper argues that all three are frequently under-estimated, and that each might legitimately be viewed as a feminist. In the concluding essay Grant looks sympathetically at Marcion as a biblical critic, examining particularly Marcion's Gospel and his Pauline Prologues.

These essays often take issue with the results of current research—including also that of Professor Beare in whose honour they have been produced! They consider a broad range of the recent literature, and demonstrate that no satisfactory solution has yet been found to the Jesus-Paul question. Indeed, the debate may never be terminated. While the majority argue for a fair degree of continuity—at least historically—between Jesus and Paul, all show in varying degrees the theological tensions between Jesus and Paul.

Through them all comes a warm appreciation of the legacy that Frank Beare has left to his colleagues in his unusually productive career, spanning more than forty-five years since his first publication. His admirers in this volume look to him as a model of precision, fairness, and lucidity. Though at points we may have failed in this volume to live up to the standard he sets, we take it as our task to go beyond current positions—and even his work—to examine in our own ways some of the fundamental problems in the history and theology of early Christianity.

It remains for the editors to thank the contributors for their cheerful cooperation and hard work, the patrons for their support, and Wilfrid Laurier University Press for its careful professionalism.

John C. Hurd
Peter Richardson

Francis Wright Beare:
Cursus Vitae

1902   Born August 16 in Toronto, Ontario.

1925   B.A., University College, University of Toronto (Prince of Wales Scholar; Honour Classics: First Class, McCaul Gold Medal).

1925-26   Lecturer in Latin, Queen's University.

1926-28   Ontario Government Scholar: Ecole des Hautes Etudes, University of Paris.

1928-30   Lecturer in Greek, McMaster University, Hamilton.

1929   Graduated in Divinity, Knox College, Toronto (Testamur, First Class).
Ordained by the Presbytery of Toronto, Presbyterian Church in Canada.

1929-31   Assistant minister, St. Andrew's Presbyterian Church, Toronto.

1931-33   Studied (chiefly papyrology) as a foreign member of the Institut Français d'Archéologie Orientale, Cairo, Egypt.

1932   Carnegie Fellow, Royal Society of Canada.

1933-35   Lecturer in Church History, Presbyterian College, Montreal.

1935-46   Professor of Theology and Registrar, Presbyterian College, Montreal.

1942   President, Canadian Society of Biblical Studies.

1944-45   Visiting Lecturer in New Testament, Union Theological Seminary.

1945   Ph.D., University of Chicago.

1946-68   Professor of New Testament Studies, Trinity College, Toronto.

1947   Ordained Deacon by the Bishop of Toronto.

1948   Ordained Priest by the Bishop of Toronto.

1950   Visiting Lecturer in Divinity, University of Cambridge.

1951-62   Honorary Assistant, Church of the Holy Trinity (Anglican), Toronto.

1954-55   President, Oriental Club, University of Toronto.

1957-58   Senior Fellow, Canada Council.

1968-   Professor Emeritus, New Testament Studies, Trinity College, To-
          ronto.

1969   President, Society of Biblical Literature.

1969-71   Member, Council on the Study of Religion.

1972-73   Visiting Lecturer, Vanderbilt University.

1975   Visiting Theologian, College of Emmanuel and St. Chad, and Lec-
          turer in Classics, the University of Saskatoon.

1980   D. D. (honoris causa), Trinity College, Toronto.

Bibliography of
Francis Wright Beare

Compiled by
JOHN C. HURD

1937 "The Chester Beatty Biblical Papyri." *La Chronique d'Egypte* 23 (January), 81-91.

1938 "The Chester Beatty Papyri of the Old Testament in Greek." *La Chronique d'Egypte* 26 (July), 364-372.

1943 "Christianity and Other Religions." *Christendom* 8, 341-352.

"The Sequence of Events in Acts 9-15 and the Career of Peter." *Journal of Biblical Literature* 62, 295-306.

1944 "The Text of the Epistle to the Hebrews in P[apyrus] 46." *Journal of Biblical Literature* 63, 379-396.

"Note on Paul's First Two Visits to Jerusalem." *Journal of Biblical Literature* 63, 407-409.

1945 "Books and Publication in the Ancient World." *University of Toronto Quarterly* 14, 150-167.

"The Teaching of First Peter." *Anglican Theological Review* 27, 284-296.

1947 *The First Epistle of Peter: The Greek Text with Introduction and Notes.* Oxford: Basil Blackwell, x + 184.

1951 "The Parable of the Guests at the Banquet: A Sketch of the History of Its Interpretation." In S. E. Johnson (ed.), *The Joy of Study: Papers on New Testament and Related Subjects Presented to Honor Frederick Clifton Grant.* New York: Macmillan, 1-14.

1953 "The Epistle to the Ephesians: Introduction and Exegesis." In G. A. Buttrick (ed.), *The Interpreter's Bible.* 12 vols. New York and Nashville: Abingdon Press, 1951-57, Vol. 10, 595-749.

1955   "The Epistle to the Colossians: Introduction and Exegesis." In G. A.
       Buttrick (ed.), *The Interpreter's Bible*. 12 vols. New York and Nash-
       ville: Abingdon Press, 1951-57, Vol. 11, 131-241.

       "The Ministry in the New Testament Church: Practice and Theory."
       Anglican Theological Review 37, 3-19.

1958   *The First Epistle of Peter: The Greek Text with Introduction and Notes*. 2nd ed.,
       rev. Oxford: Basil Blackwell, xi + 213. (See 1947 above.)

       "The Risen Jesus Bestows the Spirit: A Study of John 20:19-23." *Cana-
       dian Journal of Theology* 4, 95-100.

1959   *A Commentary on the Epistle to the Philippians*. Black's New Testament
       Commentaries. London: Adam & Charles Black, xii + 182.

       "On the Interpretation of Romans 6:17." *New Testament Studies* 5, 206-
       210.

       "Jesus and Paul." *Canadian Journal of Theology* 5, 79-86.

1960   "'The Sabbath Was Made for Man?'" *Journal of Biblical Literature* 79,
       130-136.

       "A Symposium on Life and Death: A Study of the Christian Hope" (with
       E. Davies, J. C. McLelland, and J. S. Thomson). *Canadian Journal of
       Theology* 6, 3-14.

       "The Gospel According to Thomas: A Gnostic Manual." *Canadian
       Journal of Theology* 6, 102-112.

       "New Light on the Church of the Second Century: Gnosticism and the
       Coptic Papyri of Nag-Hammadi: A Review Article." *Canadian Jour-
       nal of Theology* 6, 211-216.

1961   "New Testament Christianity and the Hellenistic World." In *The Com-
       munication of the Gospel in New Testament Times*. Theological Collec-
       tions, Vol. 2. London: S.P.C.K., 57-73.

       "The Text of 1 Peter in Papyrus 72." *Journal of Biblical Literature* 80,
       253-260.

1962   "The Gnostic Gospels of Nag-Hammadi." *University of Toronto Quarterly*
       31, 362-377.

       "The First Letter of St. Paul to the Thessalonians." *Canadian Journal of
       Theology* 8, 4-11.

       "Christianity and Other Religions in the Graeco-Roman World." *Cana-
       dian Journal of Theology* 8, 197-207.

       St Paul and his Letters. London: Adam & Charles Black, and Toronto:
       Macmillan, 152. Reviewed by J. B. Corston in *Canadian Journal of
       Theology* 10 (1964), 212.

       *The Earliest Records of Jesus: A Companion to the Synopsis of the First Three
       Gospels by Albert Huck*. Oxford: Basil Blackwell, and New York and
       Nashville: Abingdon Press, 254. Reviewed by E. C. Blackman in
       Canadian Journal of Theology 9 (1963), 133-135.

       "Areopagite," "Artemis," "Atargatis," "Bible," "Canon of the New Tes-
       tament," "Dionysus," "Epicureans," "Religion and Philosophy of
       Greece," "Hermes," "Jupiter," "Mercurius," "Persecution," "Re-

phan," "Letter to the Romans," "Rome (Church)," "Stoics," "First Letter to the Thessalonians," "Second Letter to the Thessalonians," "Altar to Unknown God," and "Zeus." In G. A. Buttrick (ed.), *The Interpreter's Dictionary of the Bible*. New York and Nashville: Abingdon Press.

"Recent Trends in Life-of-Jesus Research." *Bulletin of Crozer Theological Seminary* 54/2 (January), 3-11.

1964 *The Earliest Records of Jesus: A Companion to the Synopsis of the First Three Gospels by Albert Huck*. 2nd ed. Oxford: Basil Blackwell, 254. (See 1962 above.)

"St. Paul as Spiritual Director." In F. L. Cross (ed.), *Studia Evangelica* II. Texte und Untersuchungen zur Geschichte der altchristlichen Literatur, Vol. 87. Berlin: Akademie-Verlag, 303-314.

"Speaking with Tongues: A Critical Survey of the New Testament Evidence." *Journal of Biblical Literature* 83, 229-246.

"Zeus in the Hellenistic Age." In W. S. McCullough (ed.). *The Seed of Wisdom: Festschrift for T. J. Meek*. Toronto: University of Toronto Press, 92-113.

1965 "Some Remarks on the Text of 1 Peter in the Bodmer Papyrus (P[apyrus] 72)." In F. L. Cross (ed.), *Studia Evangelica* III/2. Texte und Untersuchungen zur Geschichte der altchristlichen Literatur, Vol. 88. Berlin: Akademie-Verlag, 263-265.

"The Historical Truth of the Gospels: An Official Pronouncement of the Pontifical Biblical Commission." *Canadian Journal of Theology* 11, 231-237.

1966 "Linus," "Philippi," "Phoebe," and "Römerbrief." In B. Reicke and L. Rost (eds.), *Biblisch-historisches Handwörterbuch*. 3 vols. Göttingen: Vandenhoeck & Ruprecht, 1962-1966.

1967 "Sayings of the Risen Jesus in the Gospel Tradition: An Inquiry into their Origin and Significance." In W. R. Farmer, C. F. D. Moule, and R. R. Niebuhr (eds.), *Christian History and Interpretation: Studies Presented to John Knox*. Cambridge: Cambridge University Press, 161-181.

1968 "The Sayings of Jesus in the Gospel According to Matthew." In F. L. Cross (ed.), *Studia Evangelica* IV/1. Texte und Untersuchungen zur Geschichte der altchristlichen Literatur, Vol. 102. Berlin: Akademie-Verlag, 146-157.

"Concerning Jesus of Nazareth." *Journal of Biblical Literature* 87, 125-135.

1969 *A Commentary on the Epistle to the Philippians*. Black's New Testament Commentaries. 2nd ed. London: Adam & Charles Black, xii + 182. (See 1959 above.)

1970 *The First Epistle of Peter: The Greek Text with Introduction and Notes*. 3rd ed., revised and enlarged. Oxford: Basil Blackwell, x + 238. (See 1958 above. In comment see J. H. Elliott, "The Rehabilitation of an Exegetical Step-child: 1 Peter in Recent Research," *Journal of Biblical Literature* 95 [1976], 243-254.)

"The Mission of the Disciples and the Mission Charge: Matthew 10 and Parallels." Presidential Address to the Society of Biblical Literature. *Journal of Biblical Literature* 89, 1-13.

"Concerning Jesus of Nazareth." In R. Batey (ed.), *New Testament Issues.* London: SCM Press, 57-70. (See 1968 above.)

1971   *St Paul and his Letters.* Apex Books. New York and Nashville: Abingdon Press, 142, paper. (See 1962 above.)

1972   "The Synoptic Apocalypse: Matthean Version." In J. Reumann (ed.), *Understanding the Sacred Text: Essays in Honor of Morton S. Enslin.* Valley Forge, Penn: Judson Press, 115-133.

1974   "On the Synoptic Problem: A New Documentary Theory." In M. H. Shepherd, Jr., and E. C. Hobbes (eds.), *Gospel Studies in Honor of Sherman Elbridge Johnson.* Supplementary Series, Vol. 3, *Anglican Theological Review* (March), 15-28.

1981   *The Gospel According to Matthew.* Oxford: Basil Blackwell, and San Francisco: Harper & Row, 1982, ix + 550.

1982   "Jesus as Teacher and Thaumaturge: The Matthaen Portrait." In E. A. Livingstone (ed.), *Studia Biblica VII.* Texte und Untersuchungen zur Geschichte der altchristlichen Literatur, Vol. 126. Berlin: Akademie-Verlag, 31-39.

Ma première rencontre avec le Professeur Frank W. Beare

ADRIEN BRUNET, o.p.

Il n'est sans doute pas nécessaire, au début de ce Festschrift, de souligner la richesse de l'activité scientifique du Professeur Frank W. Beare et l'influence qu'elle a exercée depuis plus d'un demi-siècle. Les articles que ce recueil présente et qui veulent être un hommage à un grand scholar en sont déjà un éloquent témoignage. Toutefois, la personnalité de Frank Beare recèle davantage. Il fut et il demeure un chercheur et un exégète infatigable et rigoureux. Mais ces qualités universellement reconnues ne doivent pas nous faire passer sous silence *l'homme* qu'il est, avec ses préoccupations et ses convictions profondes. Si l'on voit en lui un scholar torontois, il est aussi un humain enraciné dans le milieu canadien (et j'emploie ce mot *canadien* dans son sens fort, sens qui ne s'enferme pas dans des frontières culturelles, linguistiques, et prétendument confessionnelles). C'est précisément sous cet angle que Frank Beare m'est apparu lorsque, pour la première fois, je l'ai rencontré à Toronto. Et c'est cette image que je retiens.

C'était au printemps de 1954 lors de la réunion annuelle de la Canadian Society of Biblical Studies tenue à l'Emmanuel College de l'Université de Toronto. Pour répondre à une invitation du Professeur F. V. Winnett, que je connaissais bien, j'avais accepté de devenir membre de l'Association, d'assister à son Congrès et même d'y faire une communication qui portait sur quelques points de mes recherches sur les livres des Chroniques. Après mon exposé, suivant le rituel reçu, une période était réservée aux échanges de vues avec l'ensemble des membres. Comme je venais à peine de terminer la présentation de mon travail, le Professeur Beare se leva spontanément, me remercia de ma collaboration, et improvisa un petit discours dont les idées maîtresses se

sont gravées dans ma mémoire et qui, à mon avis, manifestent tout un
aspect des convictions intimes de Frank Beare. En voici sommairement
la teneur:

Le geste que vient de poser le P. Brunet, disait-il, est un geste symbolique pour
nous! On sait que ce collègue est originaire du Québec et qu'il est dominicain,
par conséquent un catholique romain. Or notre association passe aux yeux de
la plupart des gens de notre entourage pour une association exclusivement
composée d'anglophones. Aucun de ses membres jusqu'ici n'est catholique. Et
pourtant, elle est une association *canadienne* et qui se range parmi les sociétés
savantes. ... Après avoir écouté le P. Brunet, je n'ai qu'un regret; c'est qu'il ait
cru bon de s'adresser à nous en anglais et non pas en français. Mais, il me faut
bien l'avouer, il en est beaucoup de ses auditeurs qui n'auraient pas pu suivre
son exposé.

Ce petit topo prononcé évidemment en anglais, le Professeur
Beare le répéta en un français impeccable, comme s'il avait voulu
donner lui-même un exemple de ce qu'il espérait voir se réaliser un
jour, dans la Canadian Society of Biblical Studies.

Nous étions donc en 1954, environ dix ans après la publication du
roman de Hugh MacLennan, *Two Solitudes*; et pourtant nous étions
transportés dans un climat bien éloigné de celui que nous présentait le
professeur de McGill. Frank Beare nous faisait oublier cet antagonisme
qui caractérisait les descendants des deux peuples fondateurs du
Canada. Il est vrai que déjà la Commission royale d'enquête sur
l'avancement des arts, lettres et sciences au Canada (la Commission
Massey-Lévesque) avait eu lieu (1949-51) et qu'elle avait émis le voeu
que se tiendrait bientôt une autre enquête, celle-là sur le biculturalisme
et le bilinguisme au Canada, voeu qui ne devait être exaucé qu'en
1965-67 (Commission Dunton-Laurendeau). On m'excusera de rap-
peler ici ces faits de l'histoire politique du Canada, qui évidemment
n'ont rien à voir avec l'oeuvre scientifique de Frank W. Beare. Toutefois, ils laissent bien entrevoir l'ouverture d'esprit qui l'a toujours
caractérisé, non seulement dans ses productions littéraires, mais aussi
dans les détails de la vie quotidienne.

Frank Beare at Trinity

EUGENE R. FAIRWEATHER

In the fall of 1946 Frank Beare joined the staff of Trinity College, Toronto, as Professor of New Testament Studies. It is no exaggeration to say that he blew into our Gothic halls like a fresh ocean breeze. As a large-minded scholar he made his chosen field of biblical studies an attractive area for study and debate, thereby enriching our intellectual life. As an energetic and outgoing personality he quickly found a place at the centre of our small but lively college community.

On the academic side, Frank played a major role in the renaissance of our faculty of divinity during the late 1940s and early 1950s. That renaissance did not begin any too soon, and in retrospect Frank's appearance on the scene seems nothing less than providential. The era of Provost Cosgrave—a notable period in Trinity's history—had ended in 1945. Within the decade before Frank's appointment no fewer than four divinity professors had left the college for prominent posts elsewhere. Two distinguished veterans had retired in 1945, and a third grand old man was soon to go. The teaching staff in divinity was obviously wearing very thin.

It is true that one survivor from pre-war Trinity, Lyndon Smith, was still fascinating and entertaining both his students and his colleagues with his learning and wit, and was to go on doing so for a good many years. Moreover, Charles Feilding was beginning his long and creative regime as dean of divinity, while Derwyn Owen, just returned from war service, was resuming the career which in due course was to make him an outstanding provost. But those notable contributions were still hidden in the future. What we badly needed in 1946, both for our academic quality and for our corporate morale, was a recognized "world-class" scholar. And that was just what we got in Frank Beare.

When Frank arrived at Trinity, his scholarly record was already a distinguished one, and his subsequent performance was to fulfill his early promise. The total volume of his published work is indeed small in comparison with the massive output of some of his peers—but then Frank has always been contemptuous of the *cacoethes scribendi*. He has consistently aimed at nothing less than excellence, and his aim has been consistently true. From his early commentary on First Peter to his recent major study of the Gospel of Matthew he has written succinctly and clearly, out of massive learning. I do not fear contradiction when I call him the most eminent scholar among those who have served our faculty of divinity during the past four decades of its history.

I should add that Frank has been an active promoter, as well as a remarkable example, of theological scholarship. During his teaching career at Trinity he constantly stimulated and provoked his colleagues to emulation. His known distaste for frivolous publication made his advice seem all the more weighty when (not too often) he said: "That idea sounds worth discussing; I think you should try to get it into print somewhere." To speak personally, I have valued no commission more highly than Frank's invitation to me to write a theological excursus for his commentary on the Epistle to the Philippians (1959).

On the social side, Frank—superbly supported by his wife Marion and her niece Marion Kerr—provided a hearth around which his colleagues happily gathered again and again. The much larger and more diffuse community which Trinity College now is falls naturally into various interest groups, and it is hard to explain to the Trinity of 1983 just what 122 Roxborough Drive meant to a smaller and more compact society. Nonetheless, many grateful memories impel me to record how, during their first two decades at Trinity, the Beares, through their unstinted and unaffected hospitality, made an immense and unforgettable contribution to our common life. Probably nobody could achieve the same result now, in greatly changed circumstances. But once upon a time a man and two women and circumstances combined to create something delightful, and that something should not be left unacknowledged.

So far I have said very little about my personal relationship with Frank Beare, but perhaps the time has come for me to declare my interest and claim my right to speak about him. When Frank came to Trinity, I had already been a divinity tutor for two years. I have now outstayed him as an active professor by fifteen years. Thus, in what I have said I have testified to what I know from an experience which more than covers the whole of Frank's teaching career in the college. Given that experience, I defy anyone to query my appraisal of his contribution to Trinity both as an academic institution and as a broadly human community.

But that appraisal is far from being the whole story. The tale of a great man cannot be exhaustively told in generalities, however well-founded. His concrete attitudes and interests and pursuits, not to mention his idiosyncrasies, are integral parts of his history. And so, from my own perspective and recollection, I want to add a few personal reminiscences of Frank.

Perhaps what strikes me most forcibly, as I look back over the years, is Frank's generosity to other (and especially to younger) scholars. As I have just recorded, I had been a divinity tutor for two years when he came to Trinity. During those years I had lived above my tutorial station, in an office vacated by Charles Feilding after the departure of the previous dean of divinity. When Frank joined our staff I was inevitably—and literally—kicked upstairs. Somewhat to my surprise, I never resented that move. (Of course, I should have had no right to resent it, but junior academics can sometimes be ultra-sensitive, especially if they have been spoiled.) I suspect that what effectively disarmed me was Frank's instant acceptance of me as a colleague—junior, indeed, in achievement and experience, but deserving respect in terms of competence and aims. I found myself responding instantly with deep regard for an able and confident scholar, generously appreciative of other people's gifts and skills.

To shift focus rather abruptly, I also recall Frank Beare as the coach of Trinity's water-polo team. I doubt that, in my time here, any divinity professor has played so large a part in college athletics. At any rate, I know that Frank is remembered with unusual fondness by generations of student athletes, who found in him both a warm friend and a highly efficient mentor.

And then I recall Frank Beare the investor. (Some "wets"—to borrow Prime Minister Thatcher's word—may view this part of the story as a sensitive area, better ignored, but I am trying to describe the complete personality.) During Frank's early days at Trinity most divinity classes were taught in two rooms, adjacent to a landing equipped with a communal telephone. His students enjoyed reporting the occasions when—perhaps, by a happy coincidence, in the midst of an exposition of the "Parable of the Unjust Steward"—Frank's signal would sound outside the room. He would respond promptly, listen briefly, and then say crisply, "Sell X and buy five hundred shares of Y," before returning to his class. It is interesting to note that his students (even marked left-wingers) tended to recount such episodes affectionately rather than maliciously. In fact, Frank's genial personality has rarely evoked malice from observers, however sharply they may have disagreed with him on matters of political and economic policy.

Incidentally, Frank's skill as an investor helped to make him a valued member of the Anglican diocesan synod of Toronto. For some years he served on that synod's investment committee. Given his marked financial skills, I can only suppose that his advice contributed effectively to the ongoing solvency of his diocese.

As I look back over almost forty years of association and friendship with Frank Beare, I find myself still pondering one question. It is this: Just what was it that brought him to Trinity and the Anglican Church in 1946 and has held him to that twofold allegiance ever since? A "cradle Presbyterian" turned Anglican, he has never displayed the obnoxious features of a "convert." On the contrary, he has maintained friendly relations with the Presbyterian community. And yet he has long been both a committed and a recognizable Anglican. What then, on the level of churchmanship, makes him tick?

My more or less educated guess is that what initially appealed to Frank and has continued to appeal to him in the Anglican tradition can be identified as its "liberal catholicism." Obviously, he could never have felt at home with the biblicism of conservative Reformed theology. Moreover, as he has frequently said to me, he has long regarded the typical Lutheran and Reformed emphasis on certain Pauline doctrines as promoting an unacceptably limited view of the Christian revelation and the New Testament witness. Finally, and more positively, he has consistently been faithful to the practice of catholic sacramentalism. These (and other) points considered, it is hardly surprising that he should have found in Trinity College, and in the Anglican Communion with which it is so closely linked, a congenial spiritual home.

Frank Beare retired officially in 1968, but he has remained a lively and welcome member of the Trinity community. Furthermore, since 1973 he has shared with us the friendly and engaging presence of his second wife Marianne. Frank's colleagues continue to enjoy their company and wish them both well in the months and years that lie ahead.

From Jesus to Paul: The Contours and Consequences of a Debate

S. G. WILSON

I've thought of following Christ many many times, but it would have to be the real thing—not this business going on in the Church. St. Paul altered, spoilt it all at the very start, didn't he? Yes, I'd certainly have a go at the original idea if I had the nerve, but I wouldn't waste my time on the rest of it.[1]

These words, recorded in the 1960s and attributed to a country doctor living in the heart of rural Suffolk, show the remarkable resilience in the popular mind of a view which most New Testament scholars would consider muddled and misleading. This scholarly judgment is to some extent justified, insofar as many such statements rest on a simplistic reading of the evidence or, more frequently, on the vaguely remembered slogans of an earlier era. Equally, however, it is difficult to deny that the "popular" view expresses the Jesus-Paul problem with a starkness and honesty which we look for in vain in many recent scholarly attempts to come to terms with it. That the issue survives in the "popular" mind at all is in part a hangover from the time when the Jesus-Paul problem was a matter of lively public debate as well as of serious scholarly discussion. It is no longer prominent in either sphere. That it is no longer in the public eye is the result of complex cultural and historical factors which, though we need not dwell on them, at least render the shift intelligible. That it has never again enjoyed among New Testament scholars the prominence it had around the turn of the century is perhaps more surprising. With the exception of a number of essays by Bultmann, which have justifiably received a great deal of

---

1 R. Blythe, *Akenfield* (London: Penguin Press, 1969), 63.

attention, discussion of the Jesus-Paul question has been a desultory affair and has not been conducted with the consuming passion of earlier days. This is surprising, not only because it is one of the most complex and intriguing issues facing the historian of early Christianity, but also because it has profound theological ramifications which go to the heart of the Christian faith.

A number of factors have contributed to this state of affairs. Most important is that the Jesus-Paul controversy has been subsumed under the broader question of the relationship between the historical Jesus and the kerygmatic Christ. These two issues are, of course, not identical, but there is sufficient common ground for us to suppose that the Jesus-Paul issue has been not so much ignored as it has been discussed under a somewhat different guise. Moreover, not only does the broader formulation include the narrower, it also implicitly corrects some formulations of the question by assuming the existence of non-Pauline kerygmata which contain much in common with Paul and thus refusing to isolate him artificially from the rest of early Christianity. We should not, of course, imagine that by so doing we have resolved any of the major issues; we have merely placed the problem in a broader and historically more realistic context. Yet there is good reason to insist that to formulate the comparison in terms of Jesus and Paul is to raise the issue in the sharpest possible fashion, not only because we know a great deal more about Paul than about other first-generation Christians but also because, as time has passed, Paul's understanding of Christianity has been immensely influential in the development of Western Christian beliefs.

Secondly, it might perhaps be felt that since all the evidence has been aired and the main positions staked out there is nothing much new to say. Thus among modern scholars Jeremias maximizes the continuity between Jesus and Paul,[2] Kümmel proposes a more modest list of common features,[3] Käsemann makes do with a minimal link[4] and Bultmann takes the more radical view that the search for continuity must be rejected in principle.[5] Faced with these alternatives, and varia-

---

2   J. Jeremias, "The Present Position in the Controversy Concerning the Problem of the Historical Jesus," *EvT* 69 (1958), 333-339. (Abbreviations in references are those used by the *Journal of Biblical Literature*. See *JBL* 95 [1976], 331-346.) Similar and more recent are J. D. G. Dunn, *Unity and Diversity in the New Testament* (London: SCM, 1977), 205-206; and F. F. Bruce, *Paul and Jesus* (London: SCM, 1977).

3   W. G. Kümmel, "Jesus und Paulus," the title of two different essays, one published in 1939 and the other in 1963; both are reprinted in *Heilsgeschehen und Geschichte: Gesammelte Aufsätze 1933-64* (Marburg: N. B. Elwert, 1965), 81-106, 439-456 respectively.

4   Especially in E. Käsemann, "Blind Alleys in the 'Jesus of History' Controversy," in his *New Testament Questions of Today* (London: SCM, 1969), 23-65. See also *Jesus Means Freedom* (London: SCM, 1969), 16-58.

5   R. Bultmann, "The Significance of the Historical Jesus for the Theology of Paul," in his *Faith and Understanding* (London: SCM, 1969), 220-246; "Jesus and Paul," in his

tions in between, it is natural enough for scholars simply to opt for that version which best fits their predilections about Jesus and Paul without feeling they have anything new to add.

I will venture a third explanation which cannot be documented and is therefore no more than a hunch. It sometimes seems that the topic is instinctively avoided because to pursue it too far leads to profound and disturbing questions about the origin and nature of Christianity—and it is felt, perhaps, that it is best to leave well enough alone. This suspicion may be entirely unjustified, and it is at any rate probably too baldly stated. That there is an element of truth in it, however, is suggested by the manner in which those who do discuss the problem frequently show a curious reluctance to reflect upon the theological consequences of their historical conclusions. What some of these conclusions might be is a theme to which we shall return later.

It is not my intention to provide either a chronological review of the Jesus-Paul debate or a discussion of the exegetical arguments on which different opinions are based. The latter would require something much longer than an essay, and the former is already available in convenient form.[6] Rather, I should like to stand back a little and consider the broad contours of the debate, the principles and assumptions which inform the various approaches, and the theological consequences which ensue. Before proceeding, however, a thumbnail sketch of the course of the debate will help to set the scene. There is, of course, a danger in telescoping the story in such a drastic fashion. Not only is there a degree of tendentiousness in the selection, but many minor and significant issues will inevitably be lost in the process. Nevertheless, the main developments are reasonably clear and will not arouse much controversy.

The Jesus-Paul debate can be divided conveniently into two main stages: from Baur to Wrede, and from Bultmann to the present. In elaborating his view of the course of early Christian history Baur explained Paul's apparent neglect of the historical Jesus by reference both to his bitter conflict with Jerusalem Christianity and to his own intense religious experience in which his view of Jesus was neither affected, nor in need of clarification, by historical data.[7] The emphasis

---

Existence and Faith (New York: Collins, 1960), 183-201. The first of these was originally published in 1929 and the second in 1936.

6 Most useful are V. P. Furnish, "The Jesus-Paul Debate: From Baur to Bultmann," *BJRL* 47 (1964-1965), 342-381, and D. Dungan, *The Sayings of Jesus in the Churches of Paul* (Philadelphia: Fortress, 1971), xvii-xxix. See also T. J. Keegan, "Paul and the Historical Jesus," *Angelicum* 52 (1975), 302-339, 450-484; and R. Regner, *"Paulus und Jesus" im neunzehnten Jahrhundert* (Göttingen: Vanderhoeck und Ruprecht, 1977).

7 The initial statement of the first point is in F. C. Baur, "Die Christuspartei in der korinthischen Gemeinde," *Tübinger Zeitschrift für Theologie* 4 (1831), 61-62; the second point is made in F. C. Baur, *The Church History of the First Three Centuries*, 2 vols. (London: Williams, 1878), 49-50.

on Paul's religious experience, beginning with his conversion, was to become a major theme—as, for example, in Wrede's assessment of the issue. Wendt's important contribution in 1894 introduced two further points: first, that Paul's Pharisaic learning led him to transform Jesus' simple teaching and piety into complex theology and speculation about the means of salvation; and second, if forced by major differences to choose between the two, Wendt emphatically preferred the teaching of Jesus as the more ennobling and potentially more vital influence on Christianity.[8] Wendt allowed an element of continuity between Jesus and Paul—their common belief in man's destiny as the child of a loving God—but Wrede, in his brilliant and incisive handbook on Paul, denied even this common assumption of the liberal theologians.[9] Wrede argued that the similarities between Jesus and Paul were superficial, that the distinction between Paul's religion and his theology (dear to the liberals) was false, and that the substitution of a religion of redemption for the simple ethical and eschatological teaching of Jesus was a novel and dramatic departure. Paul, the theologian and rabbi, introduced a religious system which created a much greater gap between himself and Jesus than there had ever been between Jesus and the other great teachers of Jewish piety. Thus Paul was, in Wrede's famous dictum, "the second founder of Christianity," who had had a stronger, though not necessarily a better, influence on Christianity than the first.

A considerable number and variety of responses followed on the heels of Wendt and Wrede. An earlier response to Baur by Paret had already introduced most of the arguments which were to become standard from that day to this among those wishing to forge strong and indissoluble links between Jesus and Paul.[10] One tack was to assert that Paul knew a great deal more about Jesus than he indicates in his letters; another was to insist that the differences between Paul and Jesus arise not as the result of the imposition of a novel and alien system of thought by the one upon the other but because of the inevitable, justifiable development and explication of what was implied in Jesus' teaching in the changed circumstances of Paul's day. A distinctive note was struck by Heitmüller who, against the general trend, played down the importance of Paul's conversion and Jewishness, and attributed his neglect of the historical Jesus to the influence upon him of a form of hellenistic Christianity in which that neglect was the norm.[11]

---

8   H. H. Wendt, "Die Lehre des Paulus verglichen mit der Lehre Jesu," *ZTK* 4 (1894), 1-78.

9   W. Wrede, *Paul* (London: P. Green, 1907), especially 155ff. A similar argument can be found in M. Brückner, *Die Entstehung der paulinischen Christologie* (Strasbourg: Heintz, 1903).

10 A point made by Dungan, *Sayings*, xviii-xix. See H. Paret, "Paulus und Jesus. Einige Bemerkungen über das Verhältnis des Apostels Paulus und seine Lehre zu der Person, dem Leben und der Lehre des geschichtlichen Christus," *Jahrbücher für Deutsche Theologie* 3 (1858), 1-85.

11 W. Heitmüller, "Zum Problem Paulus und Jesus," *ZNW* 13 (1912), 320-337.

A number of things stand out during this stage of the debate. One is the sheer intensity of the arguments both academic and popular—a feature which was not to be repeated. Another is that the majority of the participants, including Wrede who had already written his book on the Messianic Secret in Mark,[12] operated essentially with the "liberal" image of Jesus. It was used with remarkable confidence and remained more of a fixed point than their understanding of Paul. At this stage of the discussion, too, there was little agreement on the extent to which Jesus' teaching had influenced Paul, some finding Paul's letters littered with parallels and others finding virtually none. When differences between Jesus and Paul were recognized as they were by most parties, with the exception of Heitmüller they were usually ascribed to Paul's religious experience, his rabbinic turn of mind, and the changed circumstances of his day. The first of these found its most eccentric expression in Weiss's claim on the basis of 2 Cor. 5:16 that Paul had been impressed by the historical Jesus either through the reports of the earliest disciples or through his own first-hand experience.[13] Also interesting is the tendency among the minority who felt obliged to make a choice to opt for Jesus rather than Paul in line with the general tendency of "liberal" theology. In retrospect, while Baur, Wendt, Wrede, and Heitmüller did not go unchallenged and while their views have necessarily been modified in a number of ways, the central issues they raised and the conclusions they drew were never effectively countered in their time—and it is not clear that recent discussions have been much more successful.

With the appearance of Bultmann's article in 1929 the second phase of the debate was opened.[14] In this and subsequent essays Bultmann elaborated a stance which is rightly considered to be a classic of its kind. Through clearly dependent on earlier explorations, his unusual theological and philosophical interests enabled him not only to formulate some of the old issues with rare clarity and precision but also to introduce a number of new issues for consideration. With Heitmüller he argued that Paul knew Christianity in its hellenistic form and that in its essentials Paul's teaching shows neither an interest in, nor the influence of, the teaching of Jesus. Paul's teaching is thus in no way dependent on that of Jesus even though in a number of matters—law, man's sinfulness, God's transcendence, and God's rule—there is a material, and in some cases even a verbal, similarity. Two things, above all, separate Paul from Jesus: first, what Jesus waited for (the kingdom) Paul proclaimed as having occurred; and second, Paul showed no

---

12 W. Wrede, *The Messianic Secret* (Greenwood: S.C.: Attic Press, 1971; first published, Göttingen: Vandenhoeck, 1901).

13 J. Weiss, *Paul and Jesus* (London: Harper, 1909), especially 31-32.

14 Bultmann, "Significance," which originally appeared as "Die Bedeutung des geschichtlichen Jesus Für die Theologie des Paulus," *ThBl* 8 (1929), 137-151.

interest in the *how* or *what* of Jesus' life (his character, ministry, teaching, etc.) but solely in the *that*, the fact of it—for it was the fact of his life,
and especially his death and resurrection, which constituted the saving
events. It was Christ the living *kyrios* and not the historical Jesus with
whom Paul was concerned. In a later essay Bultmann broadened and
sharpened this difference.[15] He argued, first, that the only continuity
between Jesus and the kerygma is the identification of the historical
Jesus with the kerygmatic Christ, but that the kerygma does not and
need not go beyond the mere fact of Jesus' existence. Secondly, he
noted, the two ways of attempting to establish material continuity
between Jesus and the kerygma—either searching for the life and
teaching of Jesus in the kerygma or searching for the kerygma in the
life and teaching of Jesus—are unworkable because of the confluence
of fact and faith in early Christian writings (especially the Gospels) and
inadvisable because they tempt us to look for legitimation of the
kerygma in historical data. For even if it could be shown that Jesus'
message had a kerygmatic character, or implied a christology, this does
not establish its identity with the kerygma, since in the kerygma it is the
exalted Christ and not the historical Jesus who speaks. Put simply, the
disjunction is that the Christ of the kerygma does not teach about the
historical Jesus, and the historical Jesus does not teach about the
kerygmatic Christ.

Bultmann's views have been decisive not so much because they
have been widely accepted but because all subsequent discussions have
had to come to terms with his formulation of the issues. He also marks a
significant break with the earlier phase of the debate. Certainly, with
Wrede he refused to separate Paul's religion from his theology and with
Heitmüller he insisted on the importance of hellenistic Christianity in
moulding Paul's thinking. Yet for Bultmann, as for all others in the
second phase of the debate, it is not the liberal but the radical, eschatological Jesus who is to be compared with Paul—even though the
image of this Jesus has been subject to a great deal of variation and has
been, in contrast to the earlier stage of the debate, far less stable than
the image of Paul. Moreover, whereas earlier scholars rejected Paul in
favour of Jesus, Bultmann does the reverse—but out of necessity
rather than preference, since he believes that the only Jesus available to
us is irreducibly kerygmatic. Again, Bultmann separates Jesus and
Paul, not like his predecessors because of an absence of substantial
continuity between them, but because whatever continuity there is he
considers to be irrelevant.

In subsequent discussion one aspect of Bultmann's analysis has
won the day: few would now deny that Paul's interest in the person and

---

15   R. Bultmann, "The Primitive Christian Kerygma and the Historical Jesus," in C. E.
Braaten and R. A. Harrisville (eds.), *The Historical Jesus and the Kerygmatic Christ* (New
York and Nashville: Abingdon, 1964), 15-42.

teaching of Jesus is minimal, even though the reasons for and the significance of this interest remain a matter of some dispute. Even fewer, however, have felt able, with Bultmann, to align themselves with Paul in this matter. By far the majority opinion, it would seem, is that, if the Christian faith is not to lapse into docetism, we *must* enquire after the historical Jesus and that, if we follow with due honesty and caution the methods of modern historical criticism, we *shall* be able to retrieve him. We are now in a position to consider some of the recent discussions of these matters and it is convenient to do so in terms of three issues: first, the influence of the teaching and person of Jesus on Paul (Kümmel's problem of "continuity"); second, the similarity between the teachings of Jesus and Paul (Kümmel's problem of "identity");[16] and third, the consequences for Christian theology and belief.

THE INFLUENCE OF THE TEACHING
AND PERSON OF JESUS ON PAUL

A consensus of sorts has developed in recent years over the extent to which the life and teachings of Jesus influenced Paul's thought. That Jesus was born (Rom. 1:3; Gal. 4:4), had a brother (Gal. 1:19) and some disciples (1 Cor. 15:5), celebrated the Last Supper (1 Cor. 11; 23f), was crucified (Gal. 3:1; 1 Cor. 2:2; etc.) and was resurrected (1 Cor. 15; etc.) are the handful of facts about Jesus' life which can be gleaned from Paul's letters. They are never told simply for the sake of telling but always for some other purpose, and the two most frequently mentioned—crucifixion and resurrection—are viewed as eschatological rather than as historical events. Allusions to Jesus' meekness (2 Cor. 10:1) or humility (2 Cor. 13:12; Rom. 15:2-3) at best add an ounce of flesh to these otherwise bare bones.

References to Jesus' teachings are equally rare. 1 Cor. 11:23-25 recalls Jesus' words at the Last Supper but solely for paraenetic purposes. 1 Thess. 4:14-15 may recall a word of the historical Jesus, but it may equally well be a saying of the risen Christ. 1 Cor. 7:10 and 9:14 are the remaining and most interesting examples. Dungan has recently noted a paradox in Paul's use of these two sayings:[17] on the one hand, they show a remarkable conservatism in recording the Jesus tradition and may reflect closely the actual words of Jesus; on the other hand and even more remarkably, Paul in both instances is content to set aside these words of Jesus in order to establish regulations of his own (1 Cor. 7:11; 9:15-18). The claim that there are other allusions to the teaching of Jesus in the writings of Paul ranges from the more plausible references (e.g., 1 Cor. 13:12; Rom. 12:14; 13:9; 14:14) to the fantasies of Resch for whom there is scarcely a verse of Paul which does not contain

---

16 Kümmel, "Paulus" (1963), 447, thus reducing from three to two the issues outlined by Bultmann in "Significance," 220.
17 Dungan, *Sayings*, 33-36; 76-80; 100-101; 132-135.

such an allusion.[18] Dungan argues that the vagueness of the references to Jesus' teaching in 1 Cor. 7 and 9 indicates that it is Paul's habit to allude to, rather than to cite, Jesus' sayings and suggests that there may therefore have been a more extensive knowledge of the synoptic tradition among Paul and his readers than is usually supposed.[19] Unfortunately, apart from disowning the wilder extremes of Resch, Dungan does not specify what would be included on the basis of his argument. Unless we are to accept Dungan's view that in 1 Cor. 7:12-13 Paul in fact alludes to a saying of Jesus while claiming that he does not (which seems to me improbable), there remains an important distinction between the occasions when Paul *says* he is referring to Jesus' teaching even though the reference itself may be allusive, and those occasions when he *might* be alluding to Jesus' teaching but does not signal that this is the case.

The suggestion that Paul must have known more of Jesus' teaching than he mentions, or that he assumes a common knowledge shared by himself and his readers, are arguments from silence which have never been convincing. Indeed, the few references to Jesus' teaching we do find in Paul do not suggest that he had a more extensive knowledge of the synoptic tradition than he displays: 1 Cor. 11:23-26 is a liturgical snippet which Paul would have known from eucharistic worship, and 1 Cor. 7:10 and 9:14 are probably both "community rules," i.e., sayings of Jesus which had a wide and independent circulation because they had a direct bearing on the everyday lives of Christians.[20]

It is clear that the fact of Jesus' existence and thus the identity of the historical and the risen Christ is crucial for Paul, but beyond this bald statement it is difficult to go. It is almost impossible to forge significant links between Jesus and Paul on the basis of the sayings of Jesus which appear in the epistles: they are embarrassingly few in number, alluded to rather than quoted, perhaps known only because of their peculiar liturgical or legal status, and above all they are ignored by Paul when it suited his purpose. There is little to encourage links between Jesus and Paul here. Certainly we cannot argue, as some have done, that 2 Cor. 5:16 or Gal. 1:11-17 show that Paul had an aversion to information about the historical Jesus. Yet from the evidence of his letters we are bound to say that he showed little or no interest in him and that to this extent Bultmann's judgment that Paul was concerned with the *that* and not the *what* of Jesus' existence seems irrefutable.

Why was this so? Baur was the first to isolate two important factors. First, the nature of Paul's religious experience, beginning with his call, was such that his own first-hand knowledge was of the risen Christ and not the historical Jesus and accordingly his gospel was primarily about

---

18   A. Resch, *Der Paulinismus und die Logia Jesu*, TU, NF 12 (Leipzig: J. C. Hinrichs, 1904).
19   Dungan, *Sayings*, 93-94.
20   Bultmann, "Significance," 222, notes that they are "community rules."

the former and not the latter. He was interested in the historical Jesus only insofar as he was first seen as the risen Christ (the gist of 2 Cor. 5:16, as Bultmann points out, however we translate it). Secondly, Paul's access to the Jesus traditions may have been limited by, among other things, his strained relationship with the Jerusalem Church. The story of this conflict remains obscure, and it may well not have been as clear-cut as Baur would have us believe; but that there was a conflict and that it had a profound influence on Paul's life and thought can scarcely be doubted. If one of the things which his opponents held over him was their direct knowledge of the historical Jesus, it would not be surprising to find Paul tacitly playing down the importance of such links and emphasizing those things in which he was less disadvantaged.

To what extent Paul may have been influenced by a form of Christianity which also ignored the historical Jesus, as Heitmüller and Bultmann argue, is hard to say in view of the paucity of evidence for such groups apart from Paul's own letters. One might perhaps point to the sermons in Acts with their emphasis on the nodal points in Jesus' career as evidence for a view similar to Paul's. But quite apart from the problem of the provenance of these speeches, their telescoping of Jesus' career is almost certainly no more than a kind of shorthand which recalls to the reader the full account in the first volume. Apart from Paul's writings, the best evidence for other Christian groups is to be found in the evolving Gospel traditions; but the very existence and preservation of this material reveal a different order of interest in the historical Jesus from Paul, however much it may be refracted through kerygmatic faith. Thus while it might seem probable that Paul's views were shared by others, it is difficult to find any contemporaneous evidence to confirm this.

THE SIMILARITY BETWEEN THE TEACHINGS OF JESUS AND PAUL

If there is general agreement that little headway has or can be made in the attempt to discern the influence of Jesus' life and teaching on Paul, there is far less agreement on both the extent and significance of the substantial or material unity to be found in their teaching. Though many would agree essentially with Bultmann's analysis of Paul, unlike him they are not willing to adopt Paul's position. Perhaps the most pointed expression of this is to be found in Käsemann's argument that Paul's view, while adequate for its time, was open to the abuse of both legalism and enthusiasm and that the necessary antidote was to root Christian experience in the life of Jesus, as is done in the Gospels.[21] Most scholars rightly reject as an eccentricity Bultmann's view that we *should not* attempt to retrieve the historical Jesus because this somehow en-

---

21 Käsemann, *Questions*, 63-65; 82-107; 108-111.

dangers the principle of *sola fides*, for it is surely true that historical information per se neither creates nor destroys faith but is rather something to which we respond with or without faith. Bultmann's conviction that we *cannot* get back to the historical Jesus, that he is in principle beyond retrieval, is more difficult to refute. Yet the consensus seems to be that great advances have been made on this front and that a cautious and critical approach allows us to sketch at least the outlines of Jesus' teaching. Few would query the obvious differences—that there is a significant shift in terminology between Jesus and Paul, that Paul's teaching is more complex and argumentative, and that it is often expressed in hellenistic modes which take us beyond the horizons of Jesus' world. But many would maintain that a fundamental unity between Jesus and Paul can be discerned in a number of central themes and that these allow us to close the otherwise uncomfortable gap between them.

Above all, it is their eschatological convictions which are considered to unite them. Jesus preached the imminent arrival of God's kingdom and yet at the same time asserted that it had already arrived in connection with his ministry. Since a tension between the Already and the Not Yet is the dominant characteristic of Paul's teaching too, Jesus and Paul work with the same underlying eschatological scheme, and this agreement is for Kümmel and many others the firmest and most important bond between them. Yet, while few would doubt the significance of eschatology for either Jesus or Paul, it can and has been understood in radically different ways. Schweitzer and Bultmann, for example, believe that the dominant theme in Jesus' teaching is the imminent, future kingdom, while for Paul the important events are in the past—and while their view of both Jesus and Paul may seem lopsided a significant difference of emphasis is hard to deny.[22] Käsemann and Jüngel, on the other hand, expunge the futurist strand from the teaching of Jesus and find the fundamental unity between Jesus and Paul in their conviction that with Jesus the kingdom had already come.[23]

Closely allied to, indeed a consequence of, the emphasis on eschatology is the belief that an implied christology is contained in Jesus' conviction that his arrival and that of the kingdom were in some sense simultaneous, and that men's ultimate fate in the kingdom rests in part on their response to his message and presence. Jesus was not a mere prophet or preacher but one who believed that response to the messenger was part of the message. This could perhaps be described as the minimalist view of christological contact between Jesus and Paul. For

---

[22] On the eschatological tension see Kümmel, "Paulus" (1963), 448-449. On the difference of perspective see Bultmann, "Significance," 232-233, and A. Schweitzer, *The Mysticism of Paul the Apostle* (London: A. & C. Black, 1931), 113.

[23] Käsemann, *Questions*, 63-65; 82-107; E. Jüngel, *Paulus und Jesus* (Tübingen: J. C. B. Mohr, 1962).

some it is enough, but for others a number of other links are important too. Thus Kümmel believes that we can detect in Jesus' deliberate choice of the obscure title "Son of Man" not only a vision of his own role in the economy of salvation (as distinct from that expressed in more familiar Jewish categories) but also the underlying eschatological tension in his message in terms of the present and future roles of this "Son of Man."[24] To this Dunn would add that Jesus' experience and understanding of the Spirit resolves the eschatological tension for him in precisely the same way that it does for the early Church, including Paul, and that his profound filial consciousness (expressed above all in the term *abba*) which he attempts to share with his disciples comes close to Paul's assertion that Christians become the sons of God only through the unique Son of God (Rom. 8).[25]

The reaction of Jesus and Paul to the traditions and law of Judaism is also thought by many to place them in essentially the same fold. The similarity is usually thought to lie in their ambivalence towards the law—sometimes affirming it, at other times setting it to one side—which is rooted in a common eschatological conviction and a belief that in the person and teaching of Jesus the law has been superseded. The law is thus upheld as an expression of God's will, but discarded as a way of salvation. This is particularly important for Käsemann who in his attempt to delineate the distinctive traits in Jesus' teaching sets Jewish nomism over and against Jesus' radical demand for obedience and love and his clarion call to freedom.[26] Yet it can scarcely be denied that many of the most distinctive themes in Paul's critique of the law (law and sin, works of the law, etc.) find no echo in Jesus' teaching, and it can plausibly be argued that Paul does not refer to Jesus' teaching in his discussion of the law because little or nothing could be used to support his view and much could be arrayed against it—a contrast which holds even if we do not think, as Dungan does, that Paul had ready access to Jesus' teaching.[27]

The basis for critique of the law in Jesus and Paul is often thought to be their common conviction that the relationship between man and the divine rests solely on the character of God—a stern judge but also a gracious, loving and forgiving Father who welcomes the penitent sinner. Of course, this appears in Jesus' teaching in the form of parables and aphorisms while in Paul it is part of a more complex scheme of salvation, and it is clear that Paul works with a more pessimistic view of human nature and indeed of creation as a whole.[28] Yet, it is argued, the core conviction remains the same. Bultmann goes to some lengths to

24 Kümmel, "Paulus" (1963), 455-456.
25 Dunn, *Unity*, 211-215.
26 Käsemann, *Questions*, 64 and elsewhere.
27 Dungan, Sayings, 50, n.2.
28 Kümmel, "Paulus" (1939), 102.

defend this view, and it is one of the impulses behind the somewhat
eccentric argument of Jüngel that the theme of justification in Paul is
the necessary and inevitable explication of Jesus' preaching of the
kingdom.[29]

Common to all analyses of the problem is the recognition that
Jesus and Paul stand on opposite sides of a momentous divide, the
Resurrection, and that this marks a crucial distinction between them.
Paul looks back on the death and resurrection of Jesus as eschatological
events in the conviction that this same Jesus is now the heavenly Lord.
The consequence is an inevitable and profound change of perspective.
On this much all could agree. Some note the difference and view with
scepticism any attempt to show that Jesus sowed the seeds of later
interpretations of his death and resurrection. For others, however, a
link at this point is crucial to sustaining a significant connection between Jesus and Paul, and it is maintained that Jesus said enough about
his own death, its vicarious effects, and the ensuing resurrec-
tion/vindication that, without belittling the importance of the actual
occurrence of these events, he can be said to have anticipated all the
essential themes of the Christian kerygma.[30]

This sketch of the prominent themes in discussion of the thematic
unity in the teaching of Jesus and Paul will cause no surprise. No
attempt has been made to consider the exegetical details which form
the basis for the various views; they are as familiar to New Testament
scholars as the knowledge that more than one conclusion can legitimately
be drawn from the same body of evidence. The sketch thus serves
mainly as a reminder, but it also illustrates two rather obvious points:
first, that there is widespread agreement that Jesus and Paul share
some common ground and that this has a significant bearing on the
Jesus-Paul debate; and second, that there is almost no agreement as to
how much common ground is necessary, how much is provable, which
aspects are fundamental, and which are peripheral. I have a number of
comments to make about this aspect of the Jesus-Paul debate which
consist largely of misgivings about both the procedure and its results.
Some of them involve historical judgments where there is, of course,
always room for disagreement; others are of a more general nature and
lead naturally into the reflections in the concluding section.

First, it should be noted that the best, and theologically the most
significant, match between the teaching of Jesus and Paul is to be found
in those areas which are, in terms of historical analysis, the most
contentious. If it could be shown that Jesus anticipated the shift from
Proclaimer to Proclaimed, and most especially if he spoke of his own
death and resurrection in a manner which prepared for the role which

---

29   Jüngel, *Paulus*, especially 266.
30   For example, J. Jeremias, *New Testament Theology*, Vol. 1 (London: SCM, 1971), 250;
     Dunn, *Unity*, 210-211.

they have in Paul's preaching, we would have established a common conviction of considerable importance. Even if we allow that the conviction was not identical in all respects and that significant new perspectives were opened up by the Easter events, the preaching of Paul could be said to be rooted in the preaching of Jesus. Doubtless the belief that this should be the case to some extent colours the conviction of those who think that it is so. Yet it need scarcely be said that it is precisely Jesus' sayings about his own death and vindication which raise the problem of the kerygmatic nature of the Gospels in its most acute form, leaving many scholars deeply sceptical about the feasibility, not to mention the results, of any attempt to recover Jesus' teaching on this matter.

Second, if with Kümmel we emphasize the "implied christology" in Jesus' eschatological teaching and the identical eschatological tension to be found in Jesus and Paul, we must at the same time note the limitations of this line of argument—as, indeed, do some of those who use it. In the first place, the eschatological convictions of Jesus and Paul were not identical. Insofar as Jesus believed that the kingdom had dawned it was in connection with his teaching and healing, whereas for Paul it was Jesus' death and resurrection which marked the turn of the ages. Indeed, some would argue that the events which Paul associated with the dawning of the Age to Come may very well have been for Jesus the events which were supposed to mark its final arrival. Moreover, if Jesus' future expectations were centred on the arrival of God's kingdom, Paul's were centred on the return of Jesus. And if we try to forge a closer link by using Jesus' statements about his own vindication, which are mainly associated with the notoriously obscure and problematic phrase "Son of Man," we would have to recognize that while Jesus foresaw one vindication, Paul believed in two (Resurrection and Parousia). It is also probable that Bultmann is right in maintaining an important difference of emphasis between Jesus and Paul: what was for Jesus primarily a future expectation was for Paul primarily a thing of the past. It may be that they both exhibit a sense of eschatological tension, but the emphasis is significantly different: the difference between an overwhelmingly futurist conviction which contains an element of veiled anticipation and an overwhelmingly realized conviction which maintains an "eschatological reservation."

The very phrase "implied christology" strikes an appropriate note of caution, for it is a considerable step from this to the explicit christology of Paul, which is neither the necessary nor inevitable development of it. There is an important, indeed a radical, difference between the Proclaimer being part of his own message and being the whole of someone else's message. A similar observation holds for the postulated connection between Jesus' filial consciousness and the Pauline view that Jesus' unique sonship (and sacrifice) enables men to become the sons of God. The one need be no more than the teaching of an exceptional prophet or rabbi while the other, as Wrede noted long ago,[31] is locked into a scheme of redemption which moves in an altogether different world. And although in retrospect it might be argued that the explicit christology takes its lead from the implicit, it cannot confidently be asserted that the person responsible for the former either intended or foresaw what took place in the latter. This, I believe, creates a gulf between Jesus and Paul which it is difficult for either historical analysis or theological ingenuity to overcome.

There is another less frequently mentioned problem with declaring eschatology to be the fundamental bond between Jesus and Paul. If they both expected an early arrival of the kingdom or parousia, we must recognize that their expectations were not fulfilled. The end did not come nor has it yet. Moreover, if it is true, as both historical analysis and psychological probability would seem to suggest, that the conviction that eschatology was in the process of realization was tied intimately to the belief that this process was driving towards a rapid dénouement, the problem of coming to terms with the delay is then compounded. That the end (however precisely it is conceived) did not come is an embarrassment, and most attempts to come to terms with this, whether historical or theological, are in my view feeble and evasive. The harder it becomes to share this apocalyptic vision—and the passing of time has meant that all but a few Christians have effectively abandoned it—the harder it is to give credence to attempts to throw all the weight of Christian conviction back onto the events which have occurred. Viewed in this way eschatology is a problem not so much because of the differences (which are real enough) but because of the similarities between Jesus and Paul. There can surely be little comfort in maintaining the fundamental unity of Jesus and Paul only to have to admit in the same breath that it was based on illusory hopes and unfulfilled expectations.

Third, while it is clear that the issues already discussed most obviously have theological ramifications because they deal with the central christological issue, some would undoubtedly argue that Jesus' view of the law is also christologically significant and shows interesting parallels with the teaching of Paul. This is, however, a much more difficult case to make. It is not at all clear that Jesus significantly diverged from current Jewish legal practice and theory, and it is difficult to find parallels with Paul's characteristic statements about the law. Even if we allow that Paul's views fluctuated and were most negative when he and his gospel were seriously threatened, there are few if any precedents in the teaching of Jesus for either the substance of, or the rationale for, Paul's view of the law. And if Sanders is right, as I suspect he is, in thinking that for Paul the essential problem of the law

---

31   Wrede, *Paul*, 85, 155.

was that it was not Christ,[32] then far from helping to resolve the Jesus-Paul question the issue of the law restates it in the sharpest possible fashion.

Fourth, some of the more impressive parallels between Jesus and Paul are, with respect to the distinctive claims of Christianity, theologically the least significant, for, while all parallels are of interest, not all have the same importance. As has frequently been noted, much of their ethical teaching is similar and at times identical; and more recently emphasis has been placed on their common belief that sinful man depends on the grace of God for salvation. But it is precisely at these points where their common Jewish background is most obvious. This not only makes it difficult to argue for a genetic connection between their teaching, but it also shows that much that they held in common was not distinctively Christian. Some of the best parallels are not so much evidence for a connection between Jesus and Paul as for a connection of each of them with his Jewish environment.

Fifth, we must take full account of the differences as well as the similarities between Jesus and Paul. The reticence of Jesus about his own role, and especially about his messiahship, is in striking contrast to the bold use of messianic and other christological categories in the early Church. There is nothing in Jesus' teaching which comes even close to the christology of the hymns in Col. 1 and Phil. 2, except in its most embryonic forms. Paul's pessimistic view of the created world and his extreme view of human sinfulness find no real parallels in Jesus' teaching any more than do his views of baptism and the eucharist. Of crucial significance, too, are their different views of the timing and manner of the preaching to the Gentiles. What was apparently for Jesus one aspect of his apocalyptic vision of the future becomes for Paul overwhelmingly his most important activity in the present. In view of the degree to which Paul's theology springs directly from his experience of and reflection on the mission to the Gentiles, this can neither be dismissed as a minor difference nor adequately explained by reference to a mere change in the eschatological timetable.

There are few, if any, who would deny that there are some differences between Jesus and Paul. How are they to be assessed or explained? One approach is to suggest that many of the distinctive elements in Paul's teaching come from the form of Christianity he knew best. Yet, even when it is persuasive, this line of argument merely reformulates the question by making Paul representative of a larger group of early Christians. Another approach is to argue, with Kümmel, that the gap between Jesus and Paul caused by their differences is more than adequately bridged by their fundamental unity (based, in Kümmel's view, on their common eschatology). Yet this involves a value

---

32   E. P. Sanders, *Paul and Palestinian Judaism* (London: SCM, 1977), 442-447; 474-475.

judgment which can all too easily be based on wishful thinking and of necessity relies on scholarly fads. If, for example, it became apparent that Jesus and Paul agreed entirely on the question of the Gentile mission but disagreed rather obviously on eschatological matters, one can imagine only too easily how the case for their fundamental unity would be made—in precisely the same fashion as it is now, but by reversing the two themes! Again, it is commonly noted that some of the differences between Jesus and Paul result from the inevitable change of perspective brought about by Jesus' resurrection. This is undoubtedly true. But unless we can with some confidence suppose that Jesus had some inkling of this, it is more a restatement of the problem than an answer to it. It does have the advantage, however, of forcing us to attend to the christological significance of the disjunction between Jesus' expectations and developments in the early Church, including Paul. It is not difficult to make the case, and it is often enough made, that Jesus' view of, for example, messiahship, the law, and the Gentile mission were significantly different from those propounded by many early Christians. Indeed, one can only marvel at the unflinching honesty and rigour which characterizes critical analyses of these problems, even if one remains somewhat less impressed by reflections on their theological significance. Yet each time such a difference is noted it is potentially an embarrassment to christology, and the number of them merely compounds the problem. To admit to them is to admit that Jesus' unfulfilled expectations were "overwhelmed" or "corrected" by the resurrection and its aftermath. But how many such errors can the resurrection be asked to bear? And do we not move towards a subtle form of docetism as we increasingly assert the irrelevance of Jesus' views and emphasize the dramatic transformation caused by the resurrection? For the purpose of this line of argument is not, as it might have been, to draw attention to Jesus' frailty and true humanity but rather to subordinate his hopes and expectations to the overriding acts of God, and the effect is to evacuate his human existence of any real significance. Are we not then forced to resort to the view that it is the mere fact of Jesus' existence and not his own views and aspirations which is, in the last resort, significant—and not because, as Bultmann argued, the latter are irretrievable or threatening but because they so often turn out to be wrong?

Finally, it is necessary to stand back from these specific issues and address the broader question of principle. If we are to compare the teaching of Jesus and Paul we have to decide what it is that we are comparing. This immediately raises the fundamental question whether, even where there is consensus (and often there is not), there is any certainty possible in matters of historical reconstruction. Without being able to argue the point fully here, I take it as axiomatic that all forms of historical enquiry, indeed all acts of interpretation, are unavoidably limited, relative and partial. As is well known, the reconstruc-

tion of Jesus' career is made especially difficult by the avowedly kerygmatic nature of the Gospels. When we also bear in mind the waxing and
waning of scholarly and cultural trends, the plurality of defensible
interpretations which can be derived from the same body of evidence,
and the irreducible bias of individual interpreters, we cannot but be
deeply sceptical whether the Jesus-Paul question is in principle answer-
able, because lurking in the background there is always the question,
Which Jesus and which Paul? Two of the more obvious problems—the
evolution of opinions during the course of time and the plurality of
opinions at any given time—are readily illustrated. The decisive shift
from the "liberal" to the radical, eschatological Jesus, or from the
hellenistic Paul of the History of Religions School to the "rabbinic" Paul
of Davies and others, illustrates the former.[33] The contrast between the
Jesus of Käsemann and Jüngel and the common image of Jesus the
apocalyptic preacher, or the debate over the centrality of justification
by faith in Paul's theology, illustrates the latter. These are but the
obvious examples and countless others could be found. Moreover, that
this is the case is, in theory at least, widely recognized. In practice,
however, many discussions of the Jesus-Paul question are marked by an
unwarranted degree of optimism insofar as they suppose that we can,
and perhaps already have, overcome these limitations. Surely if we
have learned anything from Schweitzer it is that all our interpretations
of Jesus and Paul are to some extent time and culture bound.[34] Without
diminishing the genuine advances of scholarship in this century, can
we doubt that fifty or a hundred years from now our radical, eschatological Jesus will look as strange and as lopsided as the "liberal"
Jesus looks to us now? Or again, who can doubt the effect of temperament and circumstances on the various interpretations available at any
given time? Is it not clear, for example, that Käsemann's Jesus is to
some extent a reflection of his own radical temperament and of the
vicissitudes of political and ecclesiastical life in Germany through which
he has lived? It is, of course, one of the dilemmas of a self-conscious
hermeneutic that we can know that our view of things is limited without
knowing precisely how this takes effect, and an accompanying danger
is that we lapse into forgetfulness and place a quite unwarranted faith
in our own hermeneutical prowess. Neither theory nor practice, however, would encourage us to think that we are endowed with unique
hermeneutical skills or that we can overcome the limitations which we
so readily see in others.

There is a sense, therefore, in which any attempt to resolve the
Jesus-Paul issue in terms of the identity of their teaching is bound to
fail—not only because of the kerygmatic nature of the Gospels (which

---

33   W. D. Davies, *Paul and Rabbinic Judaism* (London: S.P.C.K., 1948).
34   A. Schweitzer, *The Quest of the Historical Jesus* (London: A. & C. Black, 1954); and
     Paul and His Interpreters (London: A. & C. Black, 1912).

causes problems enough) but because both the theory and the practice of interpretation would lead us to expect that the only certainty is that there is, and can be, no certainty, and that this is as true of our understanding of Paul as it is of our understanding of Jesus.[35] Neither Jesus nor Paul are stable entities and a definitive answer to the Jesus-Paul question, therefore, will always evade us. It can at best be answered by each generation and even then we cannot expect uniformity. It goes without saying that I am as subject to these limitations as anyone else, and it is clear from some of the arguments I have used earlier that as an average member of the scholarly community I have formed views about the teaching of Paul and Jesus which are both unremarkable in themselves and open to dispute. There is nothing illogical, however, in participating in the debate in terms of the current perceptions of Jesus and Paul, while at the same time maintaining that the arguments, conclusions, and even the very evidence are inevitably subject to change. And, of course, the debate will go on, for each generation of scholars will think that they can improve on the last and, if they are anything like us, they will be tempted by the illusion that the discipline has somehow reached its zenith in their time.

THE CONSEQUENCES FOR CHRISTIAN
THEOLOGY AND BELIEF

The following reflections have to some extent already been antici-pated. They concern a problem raised in one of its most acute forms in the Jesus-Paul debate, namely the relation between the historical Jesus and the Christ of faith. The traditional and implicit view of most major forms of Christianity has been to maintain a close connection between the two, usually by taking the Gospel narratives at their face value and thus supposing that Jesus anticipated in all essentials the beliefs of the early Church. For an incarnational religion which insists that God became man at one time and in one place it is difficult to imagine how else it could be. Once it is asserted that "the Word became flesh and dwelt among us" Christians are driven not only by simple curiosity to discover what the earthly existence of this Word was like but also by the theological necessity of avoiding docetism—a docetism that, according to Käsemann, leads eventually to enthusiasm and legalism and, perhaps more importantly, that evacuates the Christian call to decision of any tangible object. To insist that there must be at least a minimal knowledge of the *how* and the *what* of Jesus' ministry, which is probably the position of a majority of New Testament scholars, is, as Käsemann

---

35 Of course, in his many other writings Bultmann is more aware of the broader hermeneutical problem than any other New Testament scholar of this century. It would be pointless to try to list all those who have written on this topic, although H. G. Gadamer's *Truth and Method* (New York: Seabury Press, 1975) perhaps deserves special mention.

also notes, to depart not only from Bultmann but also from Paul. It is tantamount to declaring that the Pauline view, however satisfactory in its own day, is no longer adequate. It is true that Schmithals has argued that, with the exception of the Gospels, Paul's relation to the Jesus tradition was not much different from all other Christian writers up to the time of Justin. But even if this were the case—and it seems to involve a number of exaggerations—it would merely broaden the dilemma rather than solve it.[36]

It is often remarked that the "historical Jesus" is itself a modern, post-Enlightenment, historical-critical concept. Recognizing this, however, provides us with little comfort and less help. To know that we operate within a modern historiographic tradition does not make the awkward questions raised by this mode of discourse disappear. It may be that before the Enlightenment historical questions were not asked in the same way (and certainly not with the same urgency), in part because the historical Jesus and the Christ of faith, to use anachronistic terminology, were indissolubly blended and the Gospels were thought to give a wholly reliable account of Jesus' career. But once the distinction is made there is no going back. It may be a peculiarly modern concept to insist that the kerygmatic Christ bear some recognizable relationship to the historical Jesus but, unless the whole historical enterprise labours under an illusion, this does not resolve the dilemma for us. It might also be said that the dilemma is a peculiarly academic one and that it is likely to have little or no influence on popular Christian belief. But this is in no way unusual because, although there have been moments when academic disputes have filtered through to a wider audience, as we saw in the earlier stages of the Jesus-Paul debate, it is among scholars that these issues have had their most thorough airing—which is probably just as well for it would not do to have people's beliefs subject to the vagaries of scholarly fashion. To recognize this, however, in no way relieves scholars of the obligation to come to terms with what they do know.

The Jesus-Paul debate thus faces us with the most acute problem raised by historical study of the New Testament—the relation between history and faith, in this specific case in terms of the relation between the historical Jesus and the Pauline Christ. The options can be simplified roughly as follows: moving back from the Pauline Christ to the historical Jesus is something which, according to Bultmann, we should not and cannot do; Käsemann and Jeremias, who disagree on almost everything else, insist that we can and must proceed—Jeremias offering a "maximal" Jesus whose view of himself comes close to the view of him held by his followers after Easter, and Käsemann offering a "minimal" Jesus which gives to " 'the that of the coming of Jesus' certain

---

36   W. Schmithals, "Paulus und der historische Jesus," *ZNW* 53 (1962), 145-160; see the comments of Kümmel, "Paulus" (1963), 444-445.

unmistakeable traits of his individuality."[37] The dilemma, in my view, is that while Jeremias and Käsemann are right in saying that it should be done, Bultmann is essentially right in saying that it cannot be done. The reasons why it cannot be done are given in the previous section and they can be most succinctly formulated as follows: on the one hand, when we compare Jesus and Paul in terms of the current perceptions of them we find little that encourages an attempt to maintain their unity in this way; on the other hand, it is open to doubt whether this way of resolving the Jesus-Paul issue can in principle ever succeed. Perhaps the most poignant expression of the problem is to be found in Käsemann—so anxious to separate himself from Bultmann (and "docetism") and Jeremias (and "ebionitism"), so rigorous in his refusal to take the easy option, and so disappointing in the sketch he produces to flesh out the bare facts of Jesus' existence. For each element in his portrait of Jesus—"grouped round Jesus' message of the gracious God, his critique . . . of the law of Moses, his radical demand for obedience and love, and his death as the logical culmination of his ministry,"[38] and none of it coloured by apocalyptic expectations—can be, and has been, seriously challenged. He may well be right when he says of Jeremias that "it would be impossible to be more revolutionary in theory and more conservative in practice."[39] But it is equally clear that being revolutionary in theory and practice does not bring us much closer to a solution.

Exploring the Jesus-Paul problem thus provokes us to consider a number of thorny issues. Most important, perhaps, is that it brings us face to face with the problem of docetism. This form of docetism is not, like its ancient counterparts, based on resistance to the idea of Jesus' real humanity but on our ignorance of it. Driven by reflection on both the theory and practice of our historical craft to the view that there is little that we can confidently assert apart from the mere fact of Jesus' life and death, we are forced to fall back on a mythological figure (the Christ of faith, Pauline or otherwise) and adopt a position which verges on the docetic. This may not be what we would wish to be the case or what we think ought to be the case in terms of traditional Christian beliefs; it is, however, a conclusion which is difficult to avoid. That it diverges from the view to be found in most forms of Christianity need cause no great alarm, and at least it has the effect of placing us, for

---

37   Käsemann, *Questions*, 63.
38   Ibid.
39   Ibid., 39. Of course, many have written on the question of the historical Jesus since, but not, in my view, in a way which fundamentally alters the state of the question. See the useful discussion by L. E. Keck, *A Future for the Historical Jesus* (Nashville and New York: Abingdon, 1971). More recently B. F. Meyer, *The Aims of Jesus* (London: SCM, 1979), and E. Schillebeeckx, *Jesus: An Experiment in Christology* (London: Collins, 1979), have opened the historical and theological issues again in subtle and stimulating ways—though in the last resort they leave me unconvinced.

different reasons and perhaps against our wishes, in the same position
as Paul.

Paulus alienus: William Wrede on Comparing Jesus and Paul

HANS ROLLMANN

INTRODUCTION

On March 12, 1958, the scholar and theologian who is honoured with this *Festschrift* delivered a paper over the Trans-Canada network of the Canadian Broadcasting Corporation entitled "Jesus and Paul." In the published version Frank Beare expressed the following thoughts:

The notion of an undogmatic, non-sacramental faith which Jesus taught and which the early church maintained until St. Paul introduced his complications of sacrament and dogma is not based upon any historical evidence and cannot be scientifically deduced from analysis of the documents. It is a product of the imagination of scholars who hoped to show that Jesus taught the kind of moralistic religion which seemed to them appropriate for an enlightened and sensible person. In a way, it was the transference to a high level of the constant attempts which people make to remould Jesus in their own image, or rather in the image of what they themselves have come to regard as the highest and best. Jesus is not so easily brought into any image that we can form, even the highest and best.[1]

The scholars whom Professor Beare had in mind belonged to a long tradition of theologians and exegetes, notably of German origin, who alleged that there exists an irreconcilable gulf between the proclama-

---

1   *CJT* 5 (1959), 79-86; quote from 86. (Abbreviations in references are those used by the *Journal of Biblical Literature*. See *JBL* 95 [1976], 331-346.) Thanks are due to Professors John R. Williams and Sheldon MacKenzie for suggestions to the manuscript.

tion of Jesus and the theology of the Apostle Paul.[2] If anyone deserves a
position of pre-eminence in the history of the problem "Jesus and
Paul," it is William Wrede, the Breslau New Testament scholar, who in
the final chapter of his *Paulus* (1904) placed the Apostle to the Gentiles
within the history of early Christianity and stressed Paul's theological
and cultural distance from Jesus.[3] Wrede, in this popular yet thorough
book, raised to the level of general knowledge a problem that had
engaged European thinkers at least since Fichte. In the following
presentation I shall critically discuss the nature and aims of Wrede's
comparison and the influences that scholars allege to have acted upon
the mind of the German exegete.

---

2   For a comprehensive but misleading history of the problem see F. Regner, *"Paulus
    und Jesus" im 19. Jahrhundert: Beiträge zur Geschichte des Themas "Paulus und Jesus" in der
    neutestamentlichen Theologie*, Studien zur Theologie und Geistesgeschichte des
    Neunzehnten Jahrhunderts, 30 (Göttingen: Vandenhoeck & Ruprecht, 1977).
    Regner's claim that the "Paul and Jesus" topic was *the* unarticulated theme of New
    Testament theology in the nineteenth century is entirely untenable. Regner's fun-
    damental mistake lies in separating the "Paul and Jesus" issue from the larger
    context of Pauline research and from the history of biblical scholarship. He thus
    develops constructions and *geistesgeschichtliche* necessities unwarranted by the evi-
    dence. A knowledge of Wolfgang Wiefel's sober and most valuable sketch of the
    "Jesus and Paul" problem would have prevented Regner from conjecturing so wildly
    (Wiefel, "Zur Würdigung William Wredes," *ZRGG* 23 [1971], 60-83). Also a familiar-
    ity with the two important monographs on the *Religionsgeschichtliche Schule*, Ver-
    heule's *Wilhelm Bousset* and W. Klatt's *Hermann Gunkel* (see n. 7), would have shown
    Regner that his reconstruction of the scholarly development of the *Religionsge-
    schichtliche Schule* on pages 172-174 in untenable. See also the criticism of Regner's
    view of Holsten by Martin Rese in *ThLZ* 74 (1978), 380-383.
3   Wrede's *Paulus* is now conveniently reprinted in K. H. Rengstorf (ed.), *Das Paulus-
    bild in der neueren deutschen Forschung*, Wege der Forschung, 24 (Darmstadt: Wissen-
    schaftliche Buchgesellschaft, 1969), 1-97. In English see W. Wrede, *Paul*, trans. by
    E. Lummis (London: Philip Green, 1907; reprinted Lexington, Ky.: American
    Theological Association, 1962). In the following I refer to the 1969 German reprint.
    All translations are my own. I shall publish shortly a two-volume study in German on
    the life and work of William Wrede.
        Of special importance for the recent theological discussion of the "Jesus and
    Paul" problem is the following literature: R. Bultmann, "Die Bedeutung des
    geschichtlichen Jesus für die Theologie des Paulus (1929)," *Glauben und Verstehen*, 1
    (6th ed.; Tübingen: J. C. B. Mohr [Paul Siebeck], 1966), 188-213; cf. also
    R. Bultmann, "Paulus und Jesus [1936]," *Exegetica: Aufsätze zur Erforschung des Neuen
    Testaments*, ed. by E. Dinkler (Tübingen: J. C. B. Mohr [Paul Siebeck], 1967), 210-
    229; W. G. Kümmel's essays: "Jesus und Paulus [1939]," "Jesus und Paulus: Zu
    Joseph Klausners Darstellung des Urchristentums," "Jesus und Paulus [1963]," all
    reprinted now in Kümmel's *Heilsgeschehen und Geschichte: Gesammelte Aufsätze 1933-
    64*, ed. by E. Grässer, O. Merk, and A. Fritz, Marburger Theologische Studien 3
    (Marburg: N. G. Elwert, 1965), 81-106, 169-191, 439-456; Eberhard Jüngel, *Paulus
    und Jesus: Eine Untersuchung zur Präzisierung der Frage nach dem Ursprung der Chris-
    tologie* (3d ed.; Tübingen: J. C. B. Mohr [Paul Siebeck], 1967); Josef Blank, *Paulus
    und Jesus: Eine theologische Grundlegung*, SANT 18 (Munich: Kösel, 1968). The most
    significant Jewish voice on the topic is M. Buber, *Two Types of Faith: A Study of the
    Interpretation of Judaism and Christianity*, trans. by N. P. Goldhawk (New York: Harper
    Torchbook, 1961 [1951]).

WILLIAM WREDE ON COMPARING JESUS
AND PAUL

In the last chapter of his *Paulus* Wrede presents what he considers to be the decisive difference between the proclamation of Jesus—here conceived in curiously individualistic and ethical terms—and Paul's christological dogma.[4] For Wrede, Paul's distance from Jesus concerns the *Sache*, a difference in the meaning and intention between the proclamation of Jesus and Paul's theology. This *sachliche* difference reveals itself on the levels of form, content, and underlying religious experience. Wrede perceives the religious language of Jesus as direct and elementary, operating with only a few, but religiously effective, ideas, whereas Paul's letters are consciously reflective, employ concepts (*Begriffe*) and complex series of thoughts, and express religious life by means of general categories (e.g., "sin"). Complexity of thought and terminological differentiation are said to be absent from the proclamation of Jesus, while fixed religious concepts are grounded in the practical religious life and address not primarily the intellect but conscience and will.

To this difference in form and language corresponds, according to Wrede, a difference also in content in that the proclamation of Jesus is said to have as its supreme object the individual's relationship with God. The divine imperative throughout Jesus' proclamation indicates the seriousness of God's will and the requisite human responsibility. Paul's thinking, on the other hand, focuses upon faith and its grounding in supernatural salvific events. And since for Paul salvation is inseparably linked with Christ's salvific activity, it is largely in terms of christology that Paul differs from Jesus.

In Wrede's view, Paul sees in Jesus a metaphysical saviour figure who left his heavenly splendour, changed substantially his divinity, and became his opposite: a human being. Through an equally objective event, death and resurrection, he freed human beings from their enslavement to the "world," i.e., from the hypostatized powers of "flesh," "sin," and "the law." On the basis of Christ's salvific death and resurrection—his human life as such was of little significance, a mere episode—a person participates in the new being not only by image but "actually" (*eigentlich*). For Wrede, *pneuma*-existence conveys not only the supernatural power of transformation but also, by its religiously effective logic, is itself the agent effecting such change. In short, Paul's soteriology is all-comprehensive and is related to one theme: "Christ becomes what we are in order that through his death we become what he is."[5]

What distinguishes Wrede's interpretation of Paul's theology from his liberal predecessors is not only the consistency in Pauline

---

4 See Wrede, in *Paulusbild*, 83-90.
5 Ibid., 60.

soteriology[6] but also the alleged origin of the christological or
soteriological myth. The saviour myth is no longer explained as an
outcome of the conversion experience but existed, according to Wrede
and the *Religionsgeschichtliche Schule*, prior to Paul's conversion.[7] At the
time of his conversion Paul merely transferred the pre-Damascus
"christology" wholesale to Jesus. Wrede hesitates to specify more
closely the religio-historical background of that christology, but assumes as its origin and context Jewish apocalypticism.[8]

Wrede is in company here with his student Martin Brückner[9] and
his friend Hermann Gunkel, both of whom had already voiced similar
views on the origin of Pauline christology in the year prior to the
appearance of Wrede's *Paulus*. In Gunkel's agenda for the *Religionsgeschichtliche Schule, Zum religionsgeschichtlichen Verständnis des Neuen Testaments*, we read: "*All this* [the salvation myth of the incarnated, dying
and rising saviour] *has been transferred to Jesus, because it already belonged
previously to Christ; and that is . . . the secret of* New Testament *christology as
such.*"[10] And as early as 1900 Paul Wernle, a student of Wilhelm Bousset
who later dissociated himself from the *Religionsgeschichtliche Schule*, had
written in his *Anfänge unserer Religion*: "What Paul said of Jesus, it was
basically a myth, a drama, to which Jesus gave his name."[11]

What Wrede and the *Religionsgeschichtliche Schule* opposed was a
snug historical and *sachliche* continuity between Paul and Jesus, such as
they found expressed in the judgment of the two great liberal historians Wellhausen and Harnack, who saw in Paul "the theological in-

---

6 For Holtzmann even Paul's contemporaries had no access to his intricate web of
   personal experience, Jewish background, and Greek thinking. The only one who
   had understood Paul, Holtzmann maintained, was Marcion—and he had misunderstood him.

7 On the *Religionsgeschichtliche Schule*, the 1890s Göttingen circle of friends whose
   members, among others, were Ernst Troeltsch, Albert Eichhorn, William Wrede,
   Hermann Gunkel, and Wilhelm Bousset, see H. Gressmann, *Albert Eichhorn und die
   Religionsgeschichtliche Schule* (Göttingen: Vandenhoeck & Ruprecht, 1914); W. Klatt,
   *Hermann Gunkel: Zu seiner Theologie der Religionsgeschichte und zur Entstehung der
   formgeschichtlichen Methode*, FRLANT 100 (Göttingen: Vandenhoeck & Ruprecht,
   1969); A. Verheule, *Wilhelm Bousset: Leben und Werk: Ein theologiegeschichtlicher Versuch* (Amsterdam: Ton Boland, 1973). On Troeltsch see now H. Renz and F. W.
   Graf, *Troeltsch-Studien: Untersuchungen zur Biographie und Werkgeschichte* (Gütersloh:
   Gütersloher Verlagshaus Gerd Mohn, 1982); the article by Graf, "Der 'Systematiker'
   der 'Kleinen Göttinger Fakultät': Ernst Troeltschs Promotionsthesen und ihr Göttinger Kontext," 235-290, appears to me to be the best treatment so far of the
   theological profile of the *Religionsgeschichtliche Schule*, even if the negative criterion,
   the *Religionsgeschichtliche Schule*'s distance from Ritschl, is not entirely satisfactory in
   determining the position of a group whose main aim was historical-critical and not
   systematic-theological. On Wrede see my forthcoming Wrede monograph.

8 Wrede, in *Paulusbild*, 82.

9 See Brückner, *Die Entstehung der paulinischen Christologie* (Strassburg: J. H. Ed. Heitz
   [Heitz & Mündel], 1903); for Wrede's contribution to the work see the preface.

10 H. Gunkel, *Zum religionsgeschichtlichen Verständnis des Neuen Testaments*, FRLANT 1
    (Göttingen: Vandenhoeck & Ruprecht, 1903), 93.

11 Ibid. For Wernle's relationship to Bousset and Wrede see n. 36.

terpreter and successor of Jesus." Assuming instead a crucial *sachliche* difference between Paul's christological myth and Jesus' religiously direct piety, Wrede concluded that the Apostle to the Gentiles was not a successor and disciple of Jesus, but "the second founder of the Christian religion."[12]

The initial reaction to Wrede's book, especially among liberal exegetes and theologians, was severe and may have been partly the result of the offended liberal conscience, which had gone far out of its way to reconcile the "religion" of Jesus with the "theology" of Paul.[13] It had done this by assuming for Paul a substratum of religiosity identical with that of Jesus, covered only by temporally conditioned *theologoumena* and tradition, or by simply viewing Paul's theology as the correct "interpretation" of Jesus' proclamation.[14] For Holtzmann, the prince among the liberal interpreters of Paul, Pauline theology was "proof of the far-reaching spiritual power and pre-eminent vital power of Jesus himself."[15]

With the *Religionsgeschichtliche Schule*'s interest in the cultic elements of early Christianity, particularly with Heitmüller's *Taufe und Abendmahl bei Paulus* (1903), in which he demonstrated that for Paul redemption depended crucially on the sacraments, the liberal distinction between "theology" and "religion" lost much of its harmonizing qualities. As we shall see later, Wrede was to raise and radicalize these two modalities of the human social phenomenon of religion into a standard for comparison. In doing so, liberal theology was challenged to come to grips with the inseparability of religion from theology and with the alien character of Paul's theology. As Albert Schweitzer put it:

> To give up the [old liberal] distinction between "theological" and "religious" and to follow a purely historical method meant, as things stood at the beginning of the twentieth century, to be left with an entirely temporally conditioned Paulinism, of which modern ways of thought could make nothing, and to trace out a system which for our religion is dead.[16]

Methodologically the members of the *Religionsgeschichtliche Schule* were the successors of the "pure historians"—Harnack, Holtzmann, Weizsäcker, and Wellhausen—with whom they shared an ethos for

---

12   Wrede, in *Paulusbild*, 96.
13   An indication of the impact that Wrede's book had upon the theological left and right can be gained from the special section reserved for the topic "Jesus and Paul" during the years 1906 to 1909 in the German review organ, *Theologischer Jahresbericht*. Cf. also the relevant sections in A. Schweitzer, *Paul and his Interpreters: A Critical History* (London: A. & C. Black, 1956 [1912]).
14   See Bultmann, "Zur Geschichte der Paulusforschung (1929)," in *Paulusbild*, 314.
15   H. J. Holtzmann, *Lehrbuch der Neutestamentlichen Theologie* 2 vols. (2d ed.; Tübingen: J. C. B. Mohr [Paul Siebeck], 1911 [1897]) 2, 236; cf. Bultmann, "Zur Geschichte der Paulusforschung," 318.
16   Albert Schweitzer, *Paul and His Interpreters*, 166.

"presuppositionless" history.[17] They differed from them, however, in seeing more clearly the hermeneutical limits of a purely literary examination of sources and by being imbued with a greater reluctance to establish historical totalities beyond the tradition history of individual concepts or motifs. Theirs was the age of the historical monograph. And instead of availing themselves of Idealist categories of explanation, they forged and employed interpretative categories of a religiopsychological and sociological sort that are still with us today: eschatology, pneumatology, cult, and *Gemeindetheologie*. The *Religionsgeschichtliche Schule*, including Wrede, also drew more radical theological consequences than did their "liberal" predecessors Holtzmann, Harnack, Wellhausen, and Pfleiderer. Following the strict canon of contextuality, they focused attention upon the "alien" features of early Christianity and, unlike their mentors, tore down bridges that would have reconciled the chasm between the first century and the late nineteenth century.

In order to do justice to Wrede's *Paulus*[18] we have to view it as part of the *Religionsgeschichtliche Schule*'s quest to guard with suspicion against modern categories of explanation, speculative and historical wholes, and an all-too-smooth continuity among historical phenomena. In his introduction to Paul's doctrine, Wrede begs readers to take leave of their previous assumptions and declares categorically:

> Among the innumerable church-affiliated Christians who believe they share the views of Paul, there is not one today who would understand them truly as they are meant; and the same applies to those who raise their objections against the apostle.[19]

Wrede saw himself over against his own teacher Harnack[20] and Julius Wellhausen,[21] who, by making Paul the "disciple" and "successor" of

---

17 For the following, consult vol. 2 of my forthcoming book on Wrede. See also the following articles of mine: "Zwei Briefe Hermann Gunkels an Adolf Jülicher zur religionsgeschichtlichen und formgeschichtlichen Methode," *ZThK* 78 (1981), 276-288; "Duhm, Lagarde, Ritschl und der irrationale Religionsbegriff der Religionsgeschichtlichen Schule. Die *Vita hospitis* Heinrich Hackmanns als geistes- und theologiegeschichtliches Dokument," *ZRGG* 34 (1982), 276-279; "Theologie und Religionsgeschichte: Zeitgenössische Stimmen zur Diskussion um die religionsgeschichtliche Methode und die Einführung religionsgeschichtlicher Lehrstühle in den theologischen Fakultäten um die Jahrhundertwende," *ZThK* 80 (1983), 69-84.

18 A caveat is necessary at this point. Although the initial reaction to Wrede's *Paulus* was mainly a response to the alleged difference between Jesus and Paul, Wrede's book is much more than its last chapter. Besides the origin and character of Pauline Christology and the alleged distance between Jesus and Paul, it was especially the rejection of a modern, subjectivist interpretation of Pauline thought and the relegation of the doctrine of "justification by faith alone" to a polemical and transitional position within the whole of Paul's theology that can be seen as the main contributions of this book. The latter point did not emerge until the subsequent discussion of Wrede's book.

19 Wrede, in *Paulusbild*, 46.

20 See below.

21 For example, J. Wellhausen, *Israelitische und jüdische Geschichte* (Berlin, 1901), 392:

Jesus, had in Wrede's view violated the canon of historical particularity. We may also surmise that a similar incomprehension of Paul's views, attributed by Wrede in the preceding quote to "those who raise their objection against the apostle," refers to Lagarde and the anti-Paulinist tradition of which he was a part.

In evaluating the alleged difference between Jesus and Paul, Wrede's critics have considered the difference between the two not to be merely an historical judgment on Wrede's part but the result of his preference for the simple, ethical "religion" of Jesus over the supernatural, christological dogmatic of Paul. Consequently, Wrede is considered to be the apex of German anti-Paulinism, a latter day disciple of Fichte and a personal student of Paul de Lagarde.[22]

Central to this estimate of Wrede's comparison of Jesus with Paul is the distinction between "religion" (Jesus) and "theology" (Paul). Many interpreters of Wrede are confused in this matter, since "religion" for Wrede can mean both an over-arching classification of the human social phenomenon of religion (in the Western world predominantly represented by Christianity), *and* an experiential and ethical modality of this historical entity, side by side with the other rational one: "theology." And yet, this experiential-ethical modality called "religion," which in its ideal type is conceptually distinguished from "theology" by the absence of reflection, does not as such imply valuation. In stating that "the religion of the apostle is throughout theological, his theology is his religion,"[23] Wrede makes primarily a descriptive statement. He affirms the significant presence of discursive thought in Paul's "religion," and thus links reason with will/feeling in the human social phenomenon of religion.[24] The relative preponderance of the religious modality which aims at will, heart, and conscience characterizes Jesus' "religion," while the preponderance of (religiously charged) thought constitutes Paul's "theological religion."[25]

"Despite all remnants that remain attached to him, the man who wrote the letters to the Corinthians is truly the one who understood the Master and continued his work. Especially through him was the Gospel of the Kingdom changed into the Gospel of Jesus Christ, so that it is no longer the prophecy of the Kingdom, but the fulfillment of this prophecy, actualized through Jesus Christ." (Quoted in O. Kuss, *Paulus: Die Rolle des Apostels in der theologischen Entwicklung der Urkirche*, Auslegung und Verkündigung 3 (Regensburg: Friedrich Pustet, 1971), 445, n. 1.)

22 Representative of many is the judgment of Regner, *"Paulus und Jesus" im 19. Jahrhundert*, 187-188: "Wrede (with his *Paulus*) gave allegiance to this heritage of Lagarde. The times also made that easy. Nonetheless, he was the first one who openly introduced anti-Paulinism into theology."

23 Wrede, in *Paulusbild*, 42.

24 For the distinction between "religion" and "theology" as modalities of the human social phenomenon religion, see also the *Vita hospitis* of Wrede's friend Heinrich Hackmann, published in my "Duhm, Lagarde, Ritschl." Cf. also Bultmann, "Geschichte der Paulus-Forschung," 318-329.

25 The issue becomes even more complex where Wrede describes the coherence of Paul's soteriology on account of its *weltanschauliche* features as "myth." Cf. Wrede, in *Paulusbild*, 95-96.

Wrede always remains enough of an historian, however, to separate his own religious preferences from what he considers to be necessary religio-historical developments. Consequently, he understands
the movement from "religion" to "theology" (or "theological religion")
not merely as "damage," as Regner suggests, but as a religio-historical
necessity without which Christianity would not have continued.[26] He
writes:

> The step from religion to theology is always of fundamental significance. One
> perceives it first of all as a descent: from the simple, immediate, primitive life
> [*Urlebendigen*] to the complicated, mediated, reflected. But one also perceives it
> always as a necessity, as a condition for the maintenance of religion and thus as
> gain. The significance of a religion for culture depends on its assigning a role to
> *thought*, i.e., creating a theology.[27]

And it is precisely the transformation of Christianity into a religion of
"experienced salvation" that characterizes the change. Wrede questions whether this "myth" is still capable of being appropriated by
modern people and modern theology. But this question, which would
be asked with much more insistence by Bultmann, is something entirely
different from anti-Paulinism. Wrede felt that dogmatic christology,
especially the salvation myth and its *Weltanschauung*, was incapable of
being retained by modern men and women, and that the personalism
and ethical orientation in Jesus' proclamation was existentially more
relevant for moderns than the theology of Paul. Wrede expresses this
view, however, not only in connection with Paul but also in his treatment of John. In his book on *The Origin of the New Testament*, after an
appreciation of John's interpretative and literary achievements, he
writes:

> Of course we must today assign to the much simpler and less theological
> writings of his predecessors, the Synoptics, a higher, I think, a far higher value.
> For surely Christendom has to thank them for the best that it possesses, the
> picture, although frequently obscured, of the human personality of Jesus, and
> the knowledge of a great portion of His words full of spirit and life, full of
> power, depth, and simplicity.[28]

The vitalist criterion by which Wrede separates Jesus' ethical personality and message from Paul's soteriological myth is in our judgment
first and foremost a result of the psychological category formation of

---

26 Regner has Wrede judge Paul's contribution as "an enormous damage to Chris-
    tianity," a statement never made by Wrede. See Regner, *"Paulus und Jesus" im 19.
    Jahrhundert*, 186.
27 Wrede, in *Paulusbild*, 95.
28 Wrede, *Die Entstehung der Schriften des Neuen Testaments* (Tübingen: J. C. B. Mohr
    [Paul Siebeck], 1907 [posthumously]) is here quoted from its English translation: *The
    Origin of the New Testament*, trans. by J. S. Hill, Harper's Library of Living Thought
    (London & New York: Harper, 1909), 90.

the *Religionsgeschichtliche Schule* and has as *weltanschauliche* roots the anti-metaphysics of Ritschlianism and the religio-psychological vitalism of the late nineteenth century.[29] In addition, the canon of "vividness," a remainder from the liberal life-of-Jesus research where it served as criterion for establishing the veracity of an historical event, may very well have been influential here. Erhardt Güttgemanns, who first suggested this latter point in his *Der leidende Apostel und sein Herr: Studien zur paulinischen Christologie*,[30] has recently restated this view in *Candid Questions Concerning Gospel Form Criticism: A Methodological Sketch of the Fundamental Problematics of Form and Redaction Criticism* with these words:

Namely when Wrede, as did many of his contemporaries, misunderstood Paul's image of the "personality" of Jesus, this genial discoverer of the dogmatic tendencies of the gospels had to inquire where then anywhere in the N.T. an image of the "personality" of Jesus was to be found. But if there is nothing of the sort in the entire N.T., then it is not to be observed how this fact should be something specific to the Pauline Christology, unless the category of "vividness" normalized in the tradition of the gospels is surreptitiously used as a criterion for the comparative schema-like Jesus-image of Paul. We could also say that the antithesis of the non-graphic kerygma represented by Paul's theology, and the vivid tradition of the gospels is derived from a particular schematism in the history of research that is no longer a possibility for us today in this form.[31]

---

29 For an examination of the background of this category formation see my *William Wrede: Leben und Werk* 2.

30 E. Güttgemanns, *Der leidende Apostel und sein Herr: Studien zur paulinischen Christologie*, FRLANT 90, (Göttingen: Vandenhoeck & Ruprecht, 1966), 370-372.

31 E. Güttgemanns, *Candid Questions Concerning Gospel Form Criticism: A Methodological Sketch of the Fundamental Problematics of Form and Redaction Criticism*, The Pittsburgh Theological Monograph Series 26 (Pittsburgh: The Pickwick Press, 1979), 374-75; cf. the entire section 375-384.

The inadequacy of a comparison by means of a dated criterion of historicity does not necessarily preclude, however, the detection of radical change within history, or even of *sachliche* discontinuity between two systems of meaning. In the wake of the post-World War II interest in hermeneutical issues *Wirkungsgeschichte* has become a much more useful historical model by which to measure changes in meaning. And yet *Wirkungsgeschichte* is helpful only if its probative apparatus is specific enough to achieve an adequate differentiation of historical systems of meaning (e.g., the proclamation of Jesus and the theology of Paul *as wholes*). It will not suffice to rest assured in the assumption that all Pauline redactional modifications of Gentile- or Jewish-Christian traditions, as insignificant as these traditions may have been for the whole of Paul's theology, place the apostle harmoniously within the total picture of Early Christianity and link him (*eo ipso*) *sachlich* with pre-Pauline Jewish and Gentile Christianity, and thus ultimately with the historical Jesus. Tradition history of the Pauline letters, even where it takes account of the complexity in early Christian group formations, can only be a means, not the end, for determining the theology of Paul. Once one has determined the theology of Paul as a meaningful totality (not systematically tight, of course), one may even ask comparative questions as long as their heuristic nature is not forgotten. To rest content with the fact that Paul used traditions and to conclude (by a *wirkungsgeschichtliche* naiveté!) *eo ipso* his *sachliche* continuity with the past puts the interpreter one

Ironically, it was Wrede who in his study of the "Messianic Secret" in the Gospel of Mark rejected Holtzmann's canon of "vividness" as an indicator of historical bedrock. According to Wrede, Mark employed "vividness" (*Anschaulichkeit*) in the service of theological ideas (*Anschauung*).[32] In his *Paulus* Wrede reintroduced the category of vividness, or life, as a standard for comparing Jesus' religious immediacy with Paul's religiously charged reflection.

The hermeneutical inadequacy of Wrede's work lies in the univocal conception of historical knowledge. His historical scepticism is directed fundamentally only against a naive historical realism that sees an unambiguous correspondence between an historical event and its written account. Having considered critically the literary and *weltanschauliche* quality of the document, and barring inadequate sources, the historian, Wrede felt, is able to comprehend exhaustively and unambiguously the historical object under consideration. Wrede remained uncritical and non-historical regarding his category formation in assuming that these interpretative categories were unambiguously correlative to the historical object. By interpreting the "Messianic Secret" in Mark, for example, as an auxiliary construct mediating a pre-Easter, non-messianic historical Jesus with a post-Easter, adoptionist christology, he violated his own historicist canon of having recourse only to the historical object itself. Remaining unaware of the problem of subjectivity in historical interpretation, he assumed an "historical" awareness and subsequent dogmatization as constituitive of two phases in early Christian theology. In reality, by historicizing a literary motif in such a manner (not in his pointing out the motif!), Wrede projected into the Gospel of Mark the nineteenth-century issue of history and faith.

The separation of the ethical personalism of Jesus from the dogmatic Christ of Paul by means of a quasi-experiential, quasi-ethical, and quasi-aesthetic criterion is one more indication of Wrede's defective historiography—defective because it conceived historical knowledge ultimately as object-centred and thus permitted the surreptitious in-

---

step behind the *Religionsgeschichtliche Schule*, to the statistical levelling of the doctrinal concept (*Lehrbegriff*) method of a B. Weiss, W. Beyschlag, and, to a lesser extent, H. J. Holtzmann, who mistook the mere presence of *theologoumena* for a *significant* presence.

32 For Wrede, Mark's colourless and dogmatic life of Jesus makes his Gospel a document of the history of dogma, void of the "historical life of Jesus." See his *Das Messiasgeheimnis in den Evangelien: Zugleich ein Beitrag zum Verständnis des Markusevangeliums* (4th ed.; Göttingen: Vandenhoeck & Ruprecht, 1969 [1901]), 131. Even where the Gospel is truly vivid and graphic, the interpreter, according to Wrede, is not to take this (like Holtzmann) as an indication of historicity (ibid., 142-143). On Wrede's "Messianic Secret" see now the history of research by J. L. Blevins, *The Messianic Secret in Markan Research: 1901-1976* (Washington, D.C.: University Press of America, 1981); and H. Räisänen, *Das "Messiasgeheimnis" im Markusevangelium: Ein redaktionskritischer Versuch*, Schriften der Finnischen Exegetischen Gesellschaft 28 (Helsinki, 1976), 18-49.

troduction of a nineteenth-century *sachfremde* standard ("vividness" or "life") into his comparison. Wrede conceded subjectivity merely to the ancient writer. For him the critical task of the religious historian consisted in separating a complex historical document into true history, literary expression, and theological intention. Wrede's and the *Religionsgeschichtliche Schule*'s advance beyond the preceding generation (who cared primarily for "true history") consisted in seeing clearly the triple nature of such an interpretative task. But any future "critical historicism" will have to take seriously into account the historians' own positions and the historicity of their category formation.[33] This applies all the more to historical comparisons where one encounters not merely the problems of interpretation, but also the additional difficulty of choosing an adequate standard for comparison.

WREDE AND LAGARDE

If we keep in mind that Wrede's "preference" for the Synoptic Jesus is the result of a defect in his historical method, but not due to an anti-Paulinism, we shall have to be quite cautious regarding Paul de Lagarde's alleged influence upon Wrede. The influence is suggested in light of Lagarde's anti-Paulinism in his 1873 publication *Über das Verhältnis des deutschen Staates zu Theologie, Kirche und Religion.*[34] Being heir to the speculative anti-Paulinism of Fichte, Lagarde depicts Paul here very generally as the one who has changed the "pure Gospel of Jesus" (vaguely described by Lagarde as "a presentation of the laws of spiritual [*geistig*] life discovered by the religious genius") along Jewish-Pharisaic lines into a cult system of salvific facts and a theology of history.

Through Hans Walter Schütte's thorough study, *Lagarde und Fichte: Die verborgenen spekulativen Voraussetzungen des Christentumsverständnisses Paul de Lagardes*, we are in the fortunate position of having not only a commanding interpretation of Lagarde on Paul, Jesus, and Christianity, but also an examination of the German idealist presuppositions underlying Lagarde's view of early Christianity.[35] There are

---

33 For a "critical" historicism see T. Nipperdey's reflections on "Historismus und Historismuskritik heute," in his *Gesellschaft, Kultur, Theorie*, Kritische Studien zur Geschichtswissenschaft 18 (Göttingen: Vandenhoeck & Ruprecht, 1976), 59-73. On the observation that category formation in the historical disciplines, including the theological ones, is dependent upon the mutual relatedness of the historians with their historical *Gegenüber* see (besides the Dilthey-Bultmann-Gadamer discussion) K. Heussi, *Die Krisis des Historismus* (Tübingen: J. C. B. Mohr [Paul Siebeck], 1932), esp. 49-52. E. Güttgemanns questions the viability of even a "critical" historicism on account of the interrelatedness of historical realities, ancient and modern, with the "structural factors of the linguistic media" that represent these realities ("Sensus Historicus und Sensus Plenior: oder Über 'historische' und 'linguistische' Methode," *Linguistica Biblica*, 43 [1978], 75-112, esp. 90-100).

34 Reprinted in P. de Lagarde, *Deutsche Schriften*, Schriften für das deutsche Volk 1 (München: J. F. Lehmann, 1924), 45-90.

35 H. W. Schütte, *Lagarde und Fichte: Die verborgenen spekulativen Voraussetzungen des*

several material and formal similarities in Lagarde's and Wrede's views on Paul that invite speculation regarding an influence of Lagarde upon Wrede.

Wrede shares Lagarde's criticism of the Reformation hermeneutics which considers as "Gospel" the Pauline-inspired material principle of *sola fide*. But here Lagarde, unlike Wrede, adduces no historical reasons from Paul for questioning the historical legitimacy of such an emphasis. Rather he is content with pointing out that the Reformation view represents a temporally conditioned anti-Catholicism.[36]

Of greater weight is Lagarde's and Wrede's shared indictment of Paul's unreliability in understanding Jesus on the grounds that he was not an eye-witness.[37] And yet, this must not be indicative of an influence of Lagarde upon Wrede, since the historical correctness and consequences of Paul's vision of the resurrected Lord had been vigorously

---

Christentumsverständnisses Paul de Lagardes (Gütersloh: Gütersloher Verlagshaus Gerd Mohn, 1965). Unfortunately, Regner does not consult this book.

36   Ibid., 26-27. For the early Wrede note his licentiate thesis No. 7 of February 21, 1891, now published in H. Renz and F. W. Graf (eds.), *Troeltsch Studien*, 301. Note also that the second of three topics suggested by Wrede for his inaugural lecture at Göttingen (March 7, 1891) bore the title: "Similarity and difference of the Pauline and Lutheran doctrine of justification by faith." (*Aktennotiz* of February 23, 1891; Theol. 49: Wrede 1890-92 Universitätsarchiv Göttingen.) On Wrede's influence upon Wernle via Wernle's teacher Wilhelm Bousset, see Wrede's letter to Wernle of March 21, 1897, which contains the following statement: "And actually from the start of my teaching career I strongly emphasized that it contributes considerably to the correct understanding of Paul to contrast the Reformation understanding of Galatians and Romans with the Pauline thoughts themselves" (Universitätsbibliothek Basel). Cf. also W. Wrede, *Über Aufgabe und Methode der sogenannten Neutestamentlichen Theologie* (1897); reprinted in G. Strecker (ed.), *Das Problem der Theologie des Neuen Testaments*, Wege der Forschung 367 (Darmstadt: Wissenschaftliche Buchgesellschaft, 1975), 81-154, esp. 131, n. 58. A dissenting voice from among the members of the *Religionsgeschichtliche Schule* comes from Wrede's friend Eduard Grafe on a picture postcard from Luther's Wartburg. Grafe writes to Martin Rade: "In order to fully appreciate Paul, I first enthused myself for Luther" (Eduard Grafe and Albert Eichhorn to Martin Rade, February 25, 1888, MS 839 UB Marburg). From Wernle we also have the only unqualified negative reference of Wrede regarding Paul. Wernle writes in an autobiographical sketch: "I became acquainted with William Wrede during one of his visits to Göttingen (Wrede became *Extraordinarius* in Breslau in 1893) and received through a word, dropped by him in a hurried conversation about Paul as the spoiler (*Verderber*) of the Gospel of Jesus, an instigation for more serious reflection" (E. Stange [ed.], *Die Religionswissenschaft der Gegenwart in Selbstdarstellungen* 5 [Leipzig: Felix Meiner, 1929], 217).

37   Cf. Lagarde with Wrede in the following. Lagarde, *Deutsche Schriften*, 67: "Paul never saw Jesus, let alone have contact with him. His relations to Jesus are—on account of his hate towards Jesus' disciples and afterwards through his vision—surely the worst sources for historical knowledge that exist. . . . Everything that Paul says about Jesus and the Gospel has no assurance of reliability." Wrede, *Über Aufgabe und Methode der sogenannten Neutestamentlichen Theologie*, 142: "Only New Testament Theology can decide the question how much in the development of Christianity belongs to Jesus and how much to the apostle who had never seen Jesus and yet—what is contained in this fact!—became the first witness of the Gospel to the Gentile world."

discussed in German theology at least since Carl Holsten's 1861 study, *Die Christusvision des Paulus und die Genesis des paulinischen Evangeliums.*[38]

Other important views on Pauline theology held both by Wrede and Lagarde concern the origin of the idea of a supernatural Messiah in apocalyptic Judaism, the significance of the death of Jesus for salvation history, and, generally, Jesus' work and person as a fixed fact of established history, a history that—similar to the allegations levelled today against Luke[39]—was said to be incapable of generating life. But in all of these instances Lagarde's lack of historical perspective is striking. Lagarde's intricate linguistic argument that the term "Messiah" is non-Jewish and that the death of Jesus, viewed under the perspective of sacrifice, is grounded in Paul's own guilt would hardly find Wrede's assent.[40] The evidence from his writings overwhelmingly proves that Lagarde's historical reasons mustered in support of his estimate of Paul represent an artificial historical superstructure upon a mismatched speculative foundation. This suspicion becomes even clearer in those instances where Lagarde conceives Paul's rabbinic Judaism as an outright perversion of Jesus' gospel.

Any shadow of doubt regarding Lagarde's apriorism is removed when one ponders his historical violations in the service of establishing the Gospel of John (with its alleged pristine message of rebirth) as the central source for the proclamation of Jesus.[41] Also Wrede distinguishes Jesus' ethically motivated, evangelical antinomianism from Paul's cosmic universalism, but the Gospel of John is here as unyielding as Paul in the recovery of the proclamation of Jesus.[42] Lagarde's "Gospel" as a spiritual and ethical event free from any national particularity can be immediately verified by reference to its eighteenth- and nineteenth-century speculative presuppositions.

The same applies to particulars of Lagarde's and Wrede's views on the proclamation of Jesus. For Lagarde, eschatology is not a part of Jesus' "Gospel," not only because the conceptual apparatus of German Idealist historiography is ill-equipped to detect an otherworldly eschatology, but because the apriori that Jesus' "Gospel" is entirely novel and has no analogies in history whatsoever permits no link with Jewish apocalypticism. It must be admitted that Wrede's view on the proclama-

---

38 Güttgemanns, *Der leidende Apostel und sein Herr*, 331-335.
39 Cf. W. G. Kümmel, "Lukas in der Anklage der heutigen Theologie (1970-1972)," in: G. Braumann (ed.), *Das Lukas-Evangelium: Die redaktions- und kompositionsgeschichtliche Forschung*, Wege der Forschung 280 (Darmstadt: Wissenschaftliche Buchgesellschaft, 1974), 416-436.
40 Schütte, *Lagarde und Fichte*, 29-30.
41 On Lagarde about Jesus see ibid., 34-43.
42 For Wrede's views on the Gospel of John see especially his *Charakter und Tendenz des Johannesevangeliums*, Sammlung gemeinverständlicher Vorträge 37 (Tübingen: J. C. B. Mohr [Paul Siebeck], 1903; 2d ed., 1933), and Wrede's review of W. Baldensperger, *Der Prolog des vierten Evangeliums* (1898), in *Göttingische Gelehrte Anzeigen* 162 (1900), 1-26; also *Das Messiasgeheimnis in den Evangelien*, 179-206.

tion of Jesus in his *Paulus* is curiously psychological and ethical and
may, as we have already seen, be explained partly by a defective
historiography and its inadequate conceptual apparatus. It is hardly
informed, however, by Lagarde's speculative presuppositions.
Moreover, the soteriology in the religion of Jesus—as revealed in his
sayings and parables—has, according to Wrede, an eschatological dimension, but one that lacks apocalyptic urgency on account of its
emphasis upon the piety of the individual. In Paul, on the other hand,
"religion" is "acquired and experienced salvation," or to use a modern
term: "realized eschatology."[43]

In order to gauge Wrede's awareness of the eschatological dimension in Jesus' conception of the kingdom, one needs only to read
Wrede's 1892 study on "Die Predigt Jesu vom Reiche Gottes."[44] Like
Johannes Weiss's epoch-making book, this essay, too, served as a
religionsgeschichtliche corrective to Albrecht Ritschl's idea of the kingdom as an ethics of personal and cultural growth. Wrede takes pains to
distinguish the ethical heroism of abnegation of the individual in Jesus'
proclamation of the kingdom from Ritschl's heroism of culture.[45]

This does not mean to suggest that Wrede's interpretation of Jesus
in ethical terms was satisfactory. It merely indicates that the eschatological dimension of Jesus' proclamation was not foreign to Wrede, even in
the writing that neglects it most, his *Paulus*. The same cannot be said for
Lagarde.

As Hans-Walter Schütte has demonstrated, Lagarde takes over
Fichte's speculative critique of Protestantism and Paul and supplies
inadequate historical realia in support of his apriori. We can only agree
with Schütte's judgment of Lagarde on the issue of Jesus and Paul when
he writes:

Lagarde presupposes his judgment of Jesus and Paul as self-evident. What he
contributes towards a closer characterization are aphoristic particulars, which
stand in no essential relation to the evaluation of these persons. For him, the
historical perception is embedded in the contrast that understands the Johannine Jesus and the Paul who represents the Old Testament as the two mutually
exclusive fundamental expressions of a true and a false religion. The suppor-
tive material has, insofar as it fits into this scheme at all, the function of
illustrating this contrast.[46]

And on Lagarde's view of Paul:

Lagarde's view of Paul originates from neglect of all historical presuppositions,
under which the Pauline theology has developed. In light of the historical

---

43   Wrede, in *Paulusbild*, 95.
44   W. Wrede, "Die Predigt Jesu vom Reiche Gottes (1894)," in his *Vorträge und Studien*
     (Tübingen: J. C. B. Mohr [Paul Siebeck], 1907), 84-126.
45   For a study of the idea of "kingdom" in Albrecht Ritschl and Johannes Weiss see the
     Ritschlian apologia of R. Schäfer, "Das Reich Gottes bei Albrecht Ritschl und
     Johannes Weiss," *ZThK* 61 (1964), 68-88.
46   Schütte, *Lagarde und Fichte*, 62.

evidence it remains unclear how this judgment can be motivated. Lagarde's criticism of Paul makes it very clear that he is under the influence of a view of Paul that determines also his historical remarks. Objective scholarship is only an agenda.[47]

The same, and here we part company with Schütte, cannot be said of Wrede. In those instances where the historical Jesus is valued more highly for Wrede's contemporaries than Paul's christological myth, value judgments are always well separated from the historical argumentation. One can accuse Wrede of inadequate historical judgments on the basis of a defective hermeneutic and of inadequate standards for comparison, but not in the least of speculative presuppositions. Wrede's entire historicist agenda was devoted to undoing speculative presuppositions. The lasting achievement of Wrede and the *Religionsgeschichtliche Schule* lies precisely in the attempt to recreate history in its own terms even at the risk of severe challenges to theology and of developmental gaps, such as the ones between Jesus and Paul and between early Christianity and the nineteenth and twentieth centuries.

Regner and Wiefel also attempt to establish a biographical connection between Lagarde and Wrede by assuming with Jülicher[48] and Troeltsch[49] that Wrede was a student of Lagarde in Göttingen.[50] This assessment is clearly wrong. Jülicher, who knew Wrede personally but hardly the details of his education, must have assumed a connection between Wrede and Lagarde merely on the basis of Lagarde's presence in Göttingen while Wrede studied there, and perhaps from later presentations such as Reischle's *Theologie und Religionsgeschichte*, where Gunkel also is said to have been influenced by Lagarde. When Gunkel, who was a personal student of Lagarde, heard of this alleged influence, he angrily rejected any such insinuation and answered Reischle with these words:

It is just as groundless when R[eischle] wants to understand my judgment about the prehistory of Pauline theology as an after-effect of "Lagarde's fanciful judgment regarding Paul" (p. 40). That old talk, which attempts to make me a "disciple of Lagarde," should cease now that I have expressed myself so often on the most varied things in opposition to Lagarde. But like Hydra, such a thing hardly ever dies.[51]

---

47 Ibid., 64.
48 See Jülicher's article in the third edition of *Realenzyklopädie für die Protestantische Theologie und Kirche* (Leipzig: J. C. B. Mohr [Paul Siebeck], 1896-1913) 21, 507.
49 See Ernst Troeltsch, "Die kleine Göttinger Fakultät von 1890," *Die Christliche Welt* (1920), 283. Cf. also Troeltsch's letter to Hugo Gressmann of July 4, 1913, printed in Klatt, *Hermann Gunkel*, 23.
50 See n. 22 and Wolfgang Wiefel, "Zur Würdigung William Wredes," 69.
51 H. Gunkel, "Review of Max Reischle, *Theologie und Religionsgeschichte* (1904)," *Deutsche Litteraturzeitung* 25 (1904), 1103.

Wrede's independence from Lagarde is even more convincing. He was never a student of Lagarde, and Lagarde's influence upon Wrede's writings is clearly negligible. In three unpublished academic *curricula vitae* throughout his life Wrede names the men under whom he studied in Göttingen as: Duhm, Lotze, Reuter, Ritschl, Schoeberlein, Schultz, Wendt, and Wiesinger. The scholars in Göttingen who, according to Wrede, had a considerable influence upon him were his father-in-law Hermann Schultz and Albrecht Ritschl.[52] Also the unpublished correspondence available to us does not mention Lagarde a single time, although the letters discuss contemporary theology. The biographical evidence suggested in support of Wrede's dependence upon Lagarde is thus as wanting as the evidence from their writings. Our contention that Wrede's views on the difference between the theology of Paul and the proclamation of Jesus are the result of his historicist agenda and historical research is thus not contradicted and seems to distinguish him significantly from Lagarde's theological apriori.

WREDE, RENAN, AND HARNACK

If one wishes at all to assume an influence upon Wrede, it must come from outside German scholarship, namely, from Ernest Renan. Renan's historiographical notions coincide very much with Wrede's own. He intends to portray early Christianity in its living colours and differentiations. And he, too, has little use for logical categories of explanation. In his *Life of Jesus* Renan expresses the aims of the historical method as follows:

We should sin against the true historical method itself were we to follow our own aversions too far. The essential conditions of a true criticism are, first, the comprehension of the difference between eras, and then the ability to rise above our instinctive habits that are the fruit of a purely rational upbringing.[53]

In the methodological preliminaries to *Antichrist*, in volume four of his *Histoire des origines du christianisme*, Renan, like Wrede, criticizes the "doctrinal concept" (*Lehrbegriff*) method, a fruit of German speculative biblical theology, and anticipates Wrede's judgment that, if there was any adequate nineteenth-century understanding of primitive Christianity, it could be found in the naive faith of contemporary sectarianism. Renan held that the German theological faculties of his day were at their best in the recovery of sources. But because of their practical and theological preoccupation, they seemed less equipped to undertake the task of "a real history." Renan writes:

For history is the interpretation of an unfolding life, an expanding germ, while theology (so to speak) reads life backward. Attending merely to what confirms

---

52   For a documentation see my forthcoming Wrede monograph.
53   Quoted from E. Cassirer, *The Problem of Knowledge: Philosophy, Science, and History Since Hegel* (New Haven and London: Yale University Press, 1950), 306.

or invalidates his doctrine, even the most liberal of theologians is unconsciously an advocate: his aim is to defend or else refute. The aim of the historian is simply to tell the fact. He finds a value in what may be in substance false, in documents even spurious; for they paint the soul, and are often truer than barren fact. In his view it were the greatest of errors to regard as defenders of abstract opinions those good and simple-minded dreamers, whose dreams through all the ages have been a consolation and a joy.[54]

And with Wrede, Renan shares a disdain for dogma and an appreciation of "simple," ethical, and non-metaphysical religion, even if the background of Renan's critique of dogma has different roots: anti-Catholicism and French positivism.[55] It is undoubtedly true, however, that "religion" in Renan contains an artistic flavour, the nuances of which Wrede was incapable of appreciating. The only German who perhaps is akin to the "poetry" of Renan's presentation of early Christianity was Willibald Beyschlag, but he lacked historical rigour.[56] Ernst Cassirer is thus correct in writing of Renan's idea of primitive Christianity that it was "far more an aesthetic than a purely historical idea."[57]

In *Saint Paul*, the third volume of Renan's study on Christian origins, there are striking similarities with Wrede, although Renan takes less pain to separate value and aesthetic judgments from history. First of all, we find the same enormous difference between the synoptic Jesus and the metaphysical Christ of Paul, only accentuated in Renan's case by a unique aestheticism. Jesus, the "great poet," is less concerned with questions of the law than with "true religion," the knowledge and adoration of the heavenly father beyond institutional bounds—bounds relativized by Jesus' overriding concern with the "soul."[58]

Because Paul had not been an eyewitness, Renan thought him incapable of perceiving the true historical Jesus, whom the disciples had had the privilege of seeing. As in Wrede, a great gulf opens up between the visionary, the Jesus preaching the Sermon on the Mount, and the writer of Romans.[59] Renan contrasts effectively the Jesus of the Synoptics with the metaphysical christology of Paul when he writes:

---

54 E. Renan, *Antichrist*, trans. by J. H. Allen (Boston: Roberts, 1897), 2-3.

55 Cf., for example, ibid., 27, with Wrede in *Paulusbild*, 46.

56 I refer to the Renan-like quality of Beyschlag's *Neutestamentliche Theologie*, which even in its English translation preserves its artistic and nostalgic qualities. Cf. W. Beyschlag, *New Testament Theology*, 2 vols., trans. by N. Buchanan (Edinburgh: T & T Clark, 1908).

57 Cassirer, *The Problem of Knowledge*, 307. The most pertinent characterization of Renan's historiography and its destructive potential for theology can be found in Ernst Troeltsch, "Die theologische und religiöse Lage der Genenwart (1903)," in his *Gesammelte Schriften*, 2: *Zur religiösen Lage, Religionsphilosophie und Ethik* (Aalen: Scientia Verlag, 1962), 10-11.

58 E. Renan, *Saint Paul*, trans. by I. Lockwood (New York: G. W. Carleton, 1869), 72-73.

59 Cf., e.g., Renan, *Les Apôtres* (Paris: Michel Levy, 1866), iv: "Il n'a pas goûté l'ambroisie de la prédication galiléenne."

It was natural for Paul, who had not seen Jesus, that the entirely human figure of the Galilean master should transform itself into a metaphysical type, much more easily than for Peter, and the others who had conversed with Jesus. Jesus, in Paul's mind, is not a man who has lived and taught: he is the Christ who died for our sins, who saves us, who justifies us. He is an entirely divine being; we partake of him; we communicate with him in a wonderful manner. He is the redemption, the justification, the wisdom, the righteousness of man. He is the King of Glory. All power in heaven and on the earth is soon to be delivered up to him. He is only inferior to God the Father. Had this school alone transmitted us writings, we would not come into contact with the person of Jesus, and we might doubt that he ever existed. But those who knew him, and who kept the recollection of him, wrote, perhaps, already towards this period, the first notes upon which were composed those divine writings (I refer to the Gospels) which made the fortune of Christianity, and transmitted to us the essential traits of the most important character that there ever was to learn.[60]

Thus both suggest as reasons for the difference in theologies a spatio-temporal distance and differing societal and cultural backgrounds.[61] Whereas Paul's Christ myth is informed by Rabbinic wisdom, speculative apocalypticism, and hellenistic thought, Jesus represents for Wrede the "simple piety of simple societal circles."[62]

Although Renan would not call Paul the "second founder of Christianity"—that title is reserved for the Greek Gentile women proselytes hearing Paul's message[63]—his message is conceptually different not only from Jesus but also from Peter and Mary Magdalene by being a "theology." Paul's temper for individual freedom and his wrangling over dogma make him the "founder of Protestantism."[64]

Paul's dogmatic christology and soteriology is held responsible both by Wrede and Renan for the separation of Christianity from Judaism.[65] According to Renan, Paul's success, however, is quickly forgotten, since he left no outstanding disciples and the second century hardly speaks of him any longer.[66] Only from the third to the fifth centuries does Paul gain stature by becoming "the true president of those great councils which make Jesus the keystone of a system of

60   Renan, *Saint Paul*, 190-191; cf. 174-175, 203, 278, 326, and *Antichrist*, 88.
61   Wrede, *Aufgabe und Methode*, 14; also *Die Entstehung der Schriften des Neuen Testaments*, 18.
62   Wrede, in *Paulusbild*, 84.
63   Renan, *Saint Paul*, 126.
64   Ibid., 99, 183-184, 203, 286; *Les Apôtres*, 185-190, esp. 187: "Le protestantisme existe déjà, cinq ans après la mort de Jésus; saint Paul en est l'illustre fondateur. Jésus n'avait sans doute pas prévu de tels disciples; ce sont eux peut-être qui contribueront le plus à faire vivre son oeuvre, et lui assureront l'éternité."
65   Renan, *Saint Paul*, 286, 326; note on this question especially Renan's lecture before the "Société des études juives" on May 26, 1883, entitled "Identité originelle et séparation graduelle du judaïsme et du christianisme," in *Discours et Conférences* (Paris: Calman Lévy, 1887), 311-340.
66   Renan, *Saint Paul*, 327.

metaphysics."[67] Paul owes his current appreciation to the Reformation and Counter-Reformation.

Wrede also was convinced that a discontinuity existed for Paulinism within the second-century church—a fact that casts a dubious light on the claim that he be considered the "second founder" of Christianity. He is a founder without immediate historical continuity and effect. Only a later Paul-reception acquires his written thoughts for renewed ecclesiastical and dogmatic consumption.[68]

Renan is not content, however, with observing the difference between the person and proclamation of the historical Jesus and the dogmatic christology of Paul. He devalues Paul by comparing him unfavourably with Jesus and even with *homines religiosi* like Francis of Assisi and Thomas à Kempis. The theology of Paul is seen as the cause of a defect with which the entire history of theology is plagued. In the finale to his thirty-second chapter of *Saint Paul,* a chapter in which he outlines Paul's theological contribution, Renan writes:

The Son of God stands alone. To appear for a moment, to reflect a soft profound refulgence, to die very young, is the life of a God. To struggle, dispute and conquer, is the life of a man. After having been for three centuries, thanks to orthodox Protestantism, the Christian teacher par excellence, Paul sees in our day his reign drawing to a close. Jesus, on the contrary, lives more than ever. It is no longer the Epistle to the Romans which is the resumé of Christianity, it is the Sermon on the Mount. True Christianity, which will last forever, comes from the Gospels, not from the epistles of Paul. The writings of Paul have been a danger and a hidden rock, the causes of the principal defects of Christian theology.[69]

Regner does not mention Renan at all in his history of the problem of "Jesus and Paul" in the nineteenth century, while Wiefel sees a similarity between Renan's and Wrede's positions but then dismisses a possible influence upon Wrede on the basis of the alleged unfamiliarity of German Protestant scholarship with Renan's *Histoire des origines du christianisme*.[70] But already in 1886 Wrede was familiar with Renan's work—whose first three volumes had been translated into German in the 1860s. Wrede was especially aware of the difference that Renan saw between the Jesus of the Synoptic Gospels and the supernatural, metaphysical christology of Paul.

In a letter to Martin Rade of April 2, 1886, Wrede discusses the differences in the perception of early Christianity between Ritschl and Harnack. Ritschl's view of biblical theology, according to Wrede, is crucially dependent upon practical and dogmatic theology, unlike

---

67 Ibid.
68 Wrede, in *Paulusbild*, 90-93.
69 Renan, *Saint Paul*, 330.
70 Wiefel, "Zur Würdigung William Wredes," 69 and 76.

Harnack's, whose perception is fundamentally historical. Wrede
writes:

Harnack could have said any moment with Renan that Paul is the first corrup-
ter of Christianity [*Verderber des Christlichen*]. He would only need (which,
however, will not happen) to change his historical judgment. Ritschl would
have to change the formal basis of his theology if he wanted to consider even
the possibility of that opinion.[71]

Harnack himself shares this assessment of the difference between
Ritschl's and his own approach, but as we know from Harnack's later
statements, notably *Wesen des Christentums* (1900), he never seriously
entertained a change of historical judgment along the lines that Renan
had suggested and that Wrede espoused.[72]

   That Renan's *Saint Paul* remained an important book for Wrede is
indicated in his *Paulus* where, among the scholarly literature intelligible to the educated layman, the German translation of Renan's book is
listed in first place, followed by the studies of Weizsäcker, Pfleiderer,
and Wernle.[73]

   Regner's suggestion that Wrede was first led to the "Jesus and
Paul" issue through his methodological sketch *Über Aufgabe und
Methode der sogenannten neutestamentlichen Theologie* (1897) contradicts
not only his own assumption that Wrede was already influenced by
Lagarde as a student in 1879-1881 but also a host of other statements by
Wrede on the topic. Judging from the letter just quoted, Wrede knew
the "Jesus and Paul" problem at least since 1886. Again, the problem
was not the result of Lagarde's anti-Paulinism but an outcome of
Wrede's uncompromising historicism, especially his distrust of any
attempts to modernize Paul—an issue to which Renan's *Saint Paul* may
have directed his attention.[74]

---

71   The excerpt of this letter is printed in J. Rathje, *Die Welt des freien Protestantismus: Ein
     Beitrag zur deutsch-evangelischen Geistesgeschichte: dargestellt am Leben und Werk von
     Martin Rade* (Stuttgart: Ehrenfried Klotz, 1952), 38. The letter is now lost. It was not
     transferred with the Rade materials to the *Handschriftenabteilung* of the university
     library in Marburg.
72   On Harnack's judgment of Ritschl's "biblicism" see my "Theologie und Religions-
     geschichte: Zeitgenössische Stimmen zur Diskussion um die religionsgeschicht-
     liche Methode und die Einführung religionsgeschichtlicher Lehrstühle in den
     theologischen Fakultäten um die Jahrhundertwende," 73-74 n. 14, where a letter of
     Harnack about Ritschl is reproduced.
73   The bibliographical recommendations of Wrede are not included in the *Paulusbild*
     reprint.
74   As indicated above, we agree with Schütte that Lagarde's views about "Paul and
     Jesus" have a largely speculative foundation. An examination clarifying to what
     extent Lagarde's speculative Paulinism was rendered historically respectable by
     borrowing from Renan would be of great interest. Renan, according to Lagarde's
     own admission, was his personal friend (see Lagarde, "Konservativ? [1853]," in his
     Deutsche Schriften, 20). Lagarde at one time even announced that he was going to
     lecture on Renan (cf. L. Schemann, *Paul de Lagarde: Ein Lebens- und Erinnerungsbild*
     [Leipzig & Hartenstein: Erich Matthes, 1919], 75).

In the winter semester of 1892-1893 the young *Privatdozent* Wrede lectured in Göttingen "de Pauli apostoli theologia."[75] In a letter to Adolf Jülicher of December 3, 1892, he reveals that it is at times painful for him to show his students the great difference that exists between Paul and Jesus. He writes:

When I explain to my listeners how far distant Paul is from Jesus it cuts through my soul what burdens one can place especially upon the serious and honest [students] with such things. And yet one cannot and should not sweeten the bitter truths.[76]

The theme would occupy Wrede's thinking until his death, but only as part of his general attempt to present Pauline theology in its original emphases and colours.

The topic is also discussed in the unpublished correspondence with Harnack, especially after the publication of Wrede's *Paulus*. In a letter of January 2, 1905, Wrede objects to Harnack's lumping together Paul and the primitive church. Harnack had written in the third edition of his *Lehrbuch der Dogmengeschichte*:

The history of the Gospel contains two great transitions, both of which still fall within the first century: from Christ to the first generation of his believers *including Paul* [emphasis my own], and from the first (Jewish-Christian) generation of these believers to the Gentile Christians; expressed differently: from Christ to the church of the believers of Christ and from this to the emerging Catholic church.[77]

In his letter to Harnack Wrede insists that with Paul "a new division" be made "after the first significant transition from Jesus to the community of Christ's believers."[78]

In the same letter Wrede contrasts his own views on historical transitions with Harnack's "valuational" perceptions of the "essence" of Christianity. Wrede admits that if the goal of presenting the nature of Christianity aims at enucleating "a few simple truths and feelings," Paul and Jesus belong together. But such a viewpoint is to Wrede "a final value judgment about things, where we are actually indifferent toward historical *relationships* and where the thought continuity and development diminishes." On this level, Wrede maintains, Luther, Thomas, Bernard, Augustine, and Schleiermacher belong together. But if one asks the question of the historical relationship between two people,

---

75 *Index Scholarum . . . Semestre Hibernum*, October 15, 1892-March 14, 1893 (Göttingen: Dieterichiana Wilhelm Fr. Kaestner, 1893), 25.

76 Letter of Wrede to Jülicher, December 3, 1892 (UB Marburg, MS 695/1183), 2-3.

77 A. Harnack, *Lehrbuch der Dogmengeschichte.* 1: *Die Entstehung des kirchlichen Dogmas* (3d ed.; Freiburg & Leipzig: J. C. B. Mohr [Paul Siebeck], 1894), 69.

78 This and the following are from a letter of Wrede to Harnack dating from January 2, 1905 (Deutsche Staatsbibliothek, Berlin, German Democratic Republic).

then I think the differences become essential, and then Paul when compared to Jesus appears to me not as the interpreter and continuation, but as the essentially new beginning, only hidden by the fact that the second believes he is the proclaimer and interpreter of the first.

For Wrede Christianity appears as "a great conglomeration, in which new things always crystallize and where there can be noticed transition after transition on all sides." Consequently, Wrede cannot see in Paul the interpreter and continuation of Jesus, "as these predicates are commonly employed in historical writing."[79] Wrede expresses the same notion more fundamentally a little later on in his letter where he uses the model of a mineral rock to illustrate the difference between Harnack's view of early Christianity and his own. He writes:

Our difference appears to lie only in the fact that I find in Paul already a deposit of predominantly different chemical composition and that this deposit inaugurates then a wealth of formations, which—despite all peculiarities and differences—are after all related basically to the deposit, not to the bedrock.[80]

What Wrede argues against Harnack, whose *Hellenisierungsthese*[81] excepted Paul, Jesus, and early Christianity from any serious contrast and introduced radical change much later, is the possibility of novelty and qualitative change within the historical process. Wrede's objectivist hermeneutic considered the predication of difference to be inherent in the historical process itself and not merely an historical judgment on the part of the historian. Methodologically Harnack could have gone along with this had he not been heir to an idealist heritage that saw history in logically progressive terms and Paul's theology as the apriori legitimate continuation and interpretation of the proclamation of Jesus. Whenever the "liberals" did perceive a difference between Jesus and Paul, it was a difference in form only. It had little consequence in light of the assumed substratum of identical religiosity that was alleged to have existed between Jesus and Paul.

CONCLUSION

What Wrede and his fellow *Religionsgeschichtler* sought to safeguard with their historical "realism" was the autonomy and particularity of historical objects as totalities of meaning within the historical process. Wrede opposed a view of history that permits only relationships of

---

79   Ibid.; the background of this discussion is Harnack's lecture No. 10 of his *Wesen des Christentums* (1900). For an English translation see Adolf Harnack, *What is Christianity?*, trans. by T. B. Saunders, Crown Theological Library 5 (3d ed.; London: Williams & Norgate; New York: G. P. Putnams, 1904), 173-192.

80   Letter of Wrede to Harnack referred to in n. 78.

81   On this see Hermann-Josef Schmitz, *Frühkatholizismus bei Adolf von Harnack, Rudolph Sohm und Ernst Käsemann*, Themen und Thesen der Theologie (Düsseldorf: Patmos, 1977), 47-93, esp. 50-57 and 66-76.

agreement—a constant, self-same religious essence, which allows in its historical unfolding at most conceptual clarification or elaboration, but no true contrast or change. "Religion" and "theology," the two modalities of the historical and social phenomenon religion that had served the liberals as safety mechanisms in affirming historical continuity at any cost, Wrede redefined as indicators of a difference in meaning. In liberal category formation "theology" had only a formal and thus inferior role over against the more fundamental category "religion." By considering Paul's theology to be his religion and his religion theology, Wrede rejected the harmonizing qualities of the liberal distinction. At the same time he radicalized the distinction. By giving Paul's religiously charged reflection, his theology, equal status (in terms of category formation) with Jesus' "religion," he allowed the possibility of a radical difference between the two. For him, Paul's (religiously charged) theology as a totality of meaning is different from Jesus' "religion" because its soteriological mythology is the expression of a different mind and a different historical (Jewish apocalyptic) setting. By focusing in his comparison upon Paul's soteriology as an autonomous *totality* of meaning, and by denying that this *whole*[82] is exhaustively understood as the legitimate interpretation and succession of a previous totality of meaning, namely the proclamation of Jesus, Wrede sought to free historical research from an apriorism and—within the limits of their cultural conditions and previous history—reaffirmed the freedom of historical agents. That a defective hermeneutic hindered Wrede in successfully carrying out his historical comparison should not be confused with a speculative anti-Paulinism. In intention and scope Wrede remained thoroughly an historian.

---

82 Wrede writes (in *Paulusbild*, 42), "The Apostle has truly conceived a great total presentation (*Gesamtanschauung*), which includes entire riches of theological presupposition, statements, and conclusions. All of Christianity appears to him to a certain degree as an edifice of thought (*Gedankenbau*)."

Jesus or Paul? The Origin of the Universal Mission of the Christian Church

CHARLES H. H. SCOBIE

THE PROBLEM OF THE UNIVERSAL
MISSION

The missionary expansion of Christianity in the early centuries C.E. is a truly astonishing phenomenon.[1] The New Testament bears witness to the beginnings of this expansion and M. Hengel has rightly drawn attention to the emphasis on the rapid spread of the "pernicious superstition" in the earliest accounts of the Christian movement by Roman writers—the younger Pliny, Tacitus and Suetonius.[2]

The importance of Paul for the subsequent missionary expansion of the Church can scarcely be overemphasized. By his own extraordinary missionary activity concentrated into a relatively few years and by the theology worked out in his letters Paul laid the foundations for the later expansion in both practice and theory. He regarded himself as "apostle to the Gentiles" (Rom. 11:13), and did not hesitate to speak of his role as divinely predestined in terms which echo the calls of Jeremiah and the Servant of Deutero-Isaiah: God "who had set me apart before I was born, and had called me through his grace, was

---

1 Cf. A. Harnack, *The Mission and Expansion of Christianity in the First Three Centuries* (London: Williams and Norgate, 1908); K. S. Latourette, *A History of the Expansion of Christianity*, Vol. 1: *The First Five Centuries* (New York: Harper and Row, 1937).

2 M. Hengel, "Die Ursprünge der christlichen Mission," *NTS* 18 (1971), 15-38. (Abbreviations in references are those used by the *Journal of Biblical Literature*. See *JBL* 95 [1976], 331-346.) See Pliny, *Epistulae* 10:96; Tacitus, *Annales* 15:44; Suetonius, *Vita Claudii* 25:4.

47

pleased to reveal his Son to me, *in order that I might preach him among the Gentiles . . .*" (Gal. 1:15-16).[3]

What Paul preached and practised was a universal mission. It is of the essence of his position that the Gospel is not to be confined to Jews but is to be offered to the Gentiles. His mission was universal in a geographical sense also. Hints in his letters and the diary source employed in Acts allow us to appreciate the extent of his travels especially subsequent to the favourable outcome of the Apostolic Council in Jerusalem. By the time he wrote Romans Paul could claim to have "fully preached the gospel of Christ . . . from Jerusalem and as far round as Illyricum" (Rom. 15:19);[4] his plans were to visit Rome and then go on from there to Spain (Rom. 15:24, 28). Clearly, Paul sees himself playing the major role in proclaiming the Gospel throughout the whole *oikoumenē*.[5]

It is when we go back from Paul to the historical Jesus that serious questions arise. There is no evidence that Jesus conducted a mission to Gentiles, a fact to which Paul himself bears witness in passing when he remarks that "Christ became a servant to the circumcised" (Rom. 15:8). The only saying ascribed to Jesus which refers to Jewish proselytizing (Matt. 23:15) is highly critical in tone.[6] Moreover, Matthew's Gospel also records a quite specific instruction of Jesus to his disciples: "Go nowhere among the Gentiles, and enter no town of the Samaritans, but go rather to the lost sheep of the house of Israel" (Matt. 10:5-6; cf. 15:24). It is not uncommon to find Jesus presented as operating entirely within the framework of contemporary Judaism.

A major problem therefore presents itself in relation to the origin of the universal mission of the Christian Church. Was this most important development in any sense initiated or authorized by Jesus, or was it in fact quite contrary to his will and intention? We are faced here in effect with a form of the classic question, Who was the real founder of Christianity, Jesus or Paul?

THE HISTORY OF THE UNIVERSAL
MISSION

For our knowledge of the earliest period of the Christian Church during which the universal mission began, we are very largely dependent on Acts 1-12. The question of historical reliability is obviously a

---

3   See J. Munck, *Paul and the Salvation of Mankind* (Richmond: John Knox, 1959), 24-33.

4   Cf. J. Knox, "Romans 15:14-33 and Paul's Conception of His Apostolic Mission," *JBL* 83 (1964), 1-11.

5   This is certainly the view Paul had reached by the time of writing Romans, but it is quite possible that the conception of a world-wide mission was the result of a development in his thought. Cf. M. Hengel, "Die Ursprünge der christlichen Mission," 18, 21, 22.

6   See J. Jeremias, *Jesus' Promise to the Nations* (London: SCM, 1958), 11-19.

crucial one; despite the recent emphasis on Luke as a theologian there are no good grounds for denying that he made use of sources even if he felt free to edit and re-work these to a considerable extent.[7]

The great hero of Acts is Paul. Although care is taken to show that the Jews were given chance after chance to hear his preaching of the Gospel they did not respond, whereas the Gentiles did. The point is summarized in the closing verses of the book with the quotation from Isa. 6:9-10 and Paul's declaration "that this salvation of God has been sent to the Gentiles; they will listen" (Acts 28:29).[8] The three accounts of Paul's conversion in Acts 9, 22, and 26 all emphasize that God's purpose in calling Paul was that he might "carry my name before the Gentiles . . ." (Acts 9:15). Yet Acts does not depict Paul as engaged in any mission to Gentiles until Acts 13:48 and makes it clear that Paul was not the initiator of the Gentile mission.

The insertion of the Cornelius episode in Acts 10 and 11 prior to Paul's involvement in mission to Gentiles gives Peter a certain priority over Paul in this matter. The story is obviously very important for the author of Acts in demonstrating that the Gentile mission was no aberration but met with the approval of Peter, the leader of the original apostles,[9] but it can hardly be said to present Peter as the inaugurator of a mission to Gentiles. Peter does not take the initiative and is only led to accept the Gentile Cornelius because of a special divinely-granted vision. Moreover, Acts says nothing thereafter of any involvement of Peter in mission to Gentiles.

It must be regarded as a tribute to Luke's faithfulness to his sources that he ascribes the origin of preaching to Gentiles to neither Paul nor Peter but to members of the "Hellenists" who fled from Jerusalem following the martyrdom of Stephen and who "on coming to Antioch spoke to the Greeks also, preaching the Lord Jesus" (Acts 11:20). The context makes it quite clear that here "the Greeks" (*tous Hellēnas*) means Gentiles.[10] The ascription of this major breakthrough to an obscure group of anonymous Hellenists serves none of Luke's theological purposes and clearly indicates that we are dealing here with a historically reliable tradition. These Hellenists established the congregation at Antioch to which Paul attached himself: they therefore form the historical link between the earliest Jerusalem community and Paul.

---

7   For recent reassessments of the historicity of Acts, see W. W. Gasque, *A History of the Criticism of the Acts of the Apostles* (Grand Rapids: Eerdmans 1975); M. Hengel, *Acts and the History of Earliest Christianity* (Philadelphia: Fortress, 1979).

8   See J. Dupont, "Le Salut des Gentils et la Signification Théologique du Livre des Actes," *NTS* 6 (1959-60), 136, 137, cf. 149-154.

9   Cf. S. G. Wilson, *The Gentiles and the Gentile Mission in Luke-Acts* (Cambridge: University Press, 1973), 171-178.

10 Cf. F. F. Bruce, *The Acts of the Apostles* (2d ed.; London: Tyndale, 1952), 235-236; E. Haenchen, *The Acts of the Apostles* (Oxford: Blackwell, 1971), 365-366; H. Conzelmann, *Die Apostelgeschichte* (Tübingen: J. C. B. Mohr, 1972), 75.

There has been a growing appreciation of the key role of the Hellenists in early Christian history.[11] They were evidently Greek-speaking Diaspora Jews resident, for whatever reason, in Jerusalem, and they formed a distinct section of the early Christian community. The ferocity of the attack upon them—an attack which apparently left the "Hebrews" unscathed[12]—can hardly have been due to the fact that they spoke Greek; rather it must have been due to their distinctive beliefs which included a radical attitude towards both Torah and Temple.

A careful study of the traditions preserved in Acts indicates that the mission of the Hellenists developed in three stages. As Greek-speaking Jewish Christians they first of all shared their faith with their fellow Diaspora Jews: they "traveled as far as Phoenicia and Cyprus and Antioch, speaking the word to none except Jews" (Acts 11:19). Secondly, an important new stage is documented in Acts 8 where Philip preaches the Gospel to the Samaritans. Thirdly, in Acts 11:20 we have the further break-through with the preaching of the message to Gentiles.

Historically, this threefold development makes sense since the Samaritans served as a middle term between Jews and Gentiles. The Gospel having been extended to Samaritans and having been favourably received, it would then be much easier to take the next logical step and go to the Gentiles.

Luke's sources evidently suggested to him this threefold pattern of mission as a way of ordering the material of his second volume. Thus Acts 1:8 provides us with a rough table of contents:[13] You shall be my witnesses

(1) in Jerusalem and in all Judaea (Acts 1-7; 9-12);
(2) and Samaria (Acts 8);
(3) and to the ends of the earth (Acts 13-28).

While there is much that remains obscure, the information that we have on the threefold mission of the Hellenists does allow us, albeit in sketchy fashion, to trace something of the historical development from the earliest Jerusalem community to the Gentile-oriented congregation at Antioch as the representatives of which Paul and Barnabas set out on the so-called "First Missionary Journey."

---

11 See W. Grundmann, "Das Problem des hellenistischen Christentums innerhalb der Jerusalemer Urgemeinde," *ZNW* 38 (1939), 45-73; M. Simon, *St. Stephen and the Hellenists in the Primitive Church* (London: Longmans, Green, 1958); R. Scroggs, "The Earliest Hellenistic Christianity," in J. Neusner (ed.), *Religions in Antiquity* (Leiden: Brill, 1968), 176-206; O. Cullmann, *The Johannine Circle* (London: SCM, 1976), chap. 6; M. Hengel, "Zwischen Jesus und Paulus: Die 'Hellenisten,' die 'Sieben' und Stephanus (Apg 6, 1-15; 7, 54-8,3)," *ZTK* 72 (1975), 151-206.

12 Cf. W. Schmithals, *Paul and James* (London: SCM, 1965), 19; Hengel, *Acts and the History of Earliest Christianity*, 74; Conzelmann, *Die Apostelgeschichte*, 59.

13 Cf. P. H. Menoud, "Le Plan des Actes des Apôtres," *NTS* 1 (1954-1955), 44-51; Dupont, "Le Salut des Gentils," 135; Conzelmann, *Die Apostelgeschichte*, 27.

THE THEOLOGY OF THE UNIVERSAL MISSION

It is much more difficult to trace the theological development which must have lain behind the missionary outreach of the Hellenists for we know so little concerning their characteristic beliefs. Since the Hellenists and Paul were Diaspora Jews it could be argued that they represented a more open and liberal brand of Judaism: living in the Diaspora alongside Gentiles led them to emphasize the more universal aspects of the ethical monotheism of the Old Testament.

While elements of this type of universalism can be found in Paul,[14] such an approach ignores the most significant aspect of Paul's view of mission—its *eschatological* orientation.[15] The tremendous urgency of the missionary task for Paul is related to the limited time available before the Parousia. The Gentiles are converted "to God from idols" in order to "wait for his Son from heaven . . . Jesus who delivers us from the wrath to come" (1 Thess. 1:9, 10).

The presupposition of this view is the Old Testament concept of *the eschatological ingathering of the Gentiles*.[16] This can take a highly nationalistic form: one day all kings will fall down before the king of Israel and all nations serve him (Ps. 72:11). The Gentiles can be depicted coming to Jerusalem bearing tribute: "The wealth of the nations shall come to you. . . . They shall bring gold and frankincense" (Isa. 60:5-6). Isa. 2:1-4, however, introduces a different note: "many peoples" shall come to the mountain of the Lord in order to learn God's ways. For Second Isaiah the Gentiles come to the holy mountain in order to join in the worship of God (Isa. 56:6-7). The high point of this expectation is found in the appeal of Isa. 45:22-23: "Turn to me and be saved, all the ends of the earth! . . . 'To me every knee shall bow, every tongue shall swear.' " The nations will thus come to God by way of Israel (cf. Zech. 8:20-23). The eschatological ingathering of the Gentiles is found in the intertestamental literature though that period also saw a reversion to more narrowly nationalistic ideas.

14   Cf. D. G. Miller, "Pauline Motives for the Christian Mission," in G. H. Anderson (ed.), *The Theology of the Christian Mission* (New York: McGraw-Hill, 1961), 72-84.

15   See O. Cullmann, "Le caractère eschatologique du devoir missionaire et de la conscience apostolique de S. Paul," *RHPR* 16 (1936), 210-245; Munck, *Paul and the Salvation of Mankind,* chap. 2; J. H. Bavinck, *An Introduction to the Science of Missions* (Philadelphia: Presbyterian and Reformed Publishing Co., 1960), chap. 4.

16   On the Old Testament attitude to mission see Bavinck, *An Introduction to the Science of Missions,* chap. 2; G. E. Wright, "The Old Testament Basis for the Christian Mission," in G. H. Anderson (ed.), *The Theology of the Christian Mission*, 17-30; F. Hahn, *Mission in the New Testament* (London: SCM, 1965), chap. 1; J. Verkuyl, *Contemporary Missiology* (Grand Rapids: Eerdmans, 1978), "Significance of the Old Testament," 90-100. It is important to distinguish between the "universal" elements which are undoubtedly present in the Old Testament and "missionary" elements which are almost totally lacking; the distinction is brought out by J. Blauw, *The Missionary Nature of the Church: A Survey of the Biblical Theology of Mission* (London: Lutterworth, 1962), esp. chaps. 1-3.

None of this resulted in an actual mission to Gentiles in Old Testament times for three interlocking reasons. First, the ingathering of the Gentiles is an eschatological concept; the nations do not come to Zion now, but "in those days," i.e., at the end-time. Second, the ingathering will be the work of God, not of men. Third, Israel is not to go to the Gentiles, but rather the Gentiles are to come to Israel. Several writers, picking up on an idea of B. Sundkler,[17] have contrasted the *centripetal* movement in the Old Testament (a movement inward, from the Gentile nations to Zion), with the *centrifugal* movement typical of the New Testament (a movement outward, from Jerusalem to the ends of the earth).[18]

What comes to expression in Paul's theology is the conviction that with the Christ event the New Age has dawned. "Now is the acceptable time; behold, now is the day of salvation" (2 Cor. 6:2). Now, therefore, is the time for the eschatological ingathering of the Gentiles.

It is clear that Jewish resistance to the Christian mission created a major problem for Paul and we can see him wrestling with this issue in Rom. 9-11. The earliest Christian community seems to have worked with a timetable developed from the Old Testament teaching. Now was the time for the mission to Israel; before long would come the Parousia, to be followed by the ingathering of the Gentiles. But that was not the way things were working out! It was becoming increasingly apparent that now was the time of the ingathering of the Gentiles. Paul therefore was forced to alter the timetable: "I want you to understand this mystery, brethren: a hardening has come upon part of Israel, until the full number of the Gentiles come in, and so all Israel will be saved" (Rom. 11:25-26).[19] The order now is (1) the ingathering of the Gentiles, (2) the conversion of Israel, and (3) the Parousia.

It may be added that Paul's collection for the Jerusalem church to which he devoted so much time and thought is to be interpreted in part in eschatological terms. The delegates of the Gentile churches bearing their gifts to Jerusalem represent the fulfillment of the prophecies of the nations bringing their tribute to Zion.[20]

Paul's eschatological theology of missions was almost certainly taken over from the earlier Hellenists. It is noteworthy that the climax of Phil. 2:6-11, widely accepted as a pre-Pauline "Christ Hymn,"[21] is clearly modelled on the eschatological ingathering of the Gentiles (Isa. 45:23).

---

17   B. Sundkler, "Jésus et les païens," *RHPR* 16 (1936), 489, 492.

18   See Blauw, *The Missionary Nature of the Church*, 40; Jeremias, *Jesus' Promise to the Nations*, 60.

19   Cf. Munck, *Paul and the Salvation of Mankind,* 36-55; Hengel, "Die Ursprünge der christlichen Mission," 20, 21.

20   Cf. Munck, *Paul and the Salvation of Mankind*, 287-308; K. F. Nickle, *The Collection: A Study in Paul's Strategy* (London: SCM, 1966), 129-142.

21   See F. W. Beare, *A Commentary on the Epistle to the Philippians* (2nd ed.; London: Black, 1969), 73-88.

A more speculative question is how the Hellenists would have justified their preaching to Samaritans. Here we can draw attention to another series of Old Testament passages which express the hope of an eschatological reunion of North and South, i.e., of all the twelve tribes of Israel. Jeremiah's "Book of Comfort" (Jer. 30-31) is directed to both Israel and Judah, and a major theme is the ingathering and reunification of God's people. Ezekiel's concern for the North appears in chapters 33-37, especially in the vision of the two sticks in 37:15-23. In the ideal reallocation of the Holy Land (Ezek. 45:1-8, 47:13-48:35) equal portions are to be given to all twelve tribes.

Most Jews in later times refused to recognize the Samaritans as descendants of the old northern tribes. One approach was to develop the myth of the "lost tribes" still living in exile in a distant land; in the intertestamental literature this could still be combined with hope of an eschatological reunification. Another approach, however, was to ignore the whole idea of the exiled northern tribes and to regard the existing Jewish community as including representatives of all twelve tribes.[22]

The Hellenists apparently took neither of these views. The fact that following the death of Stephen and the ensuing persecution Philip made straight for Samaria indicates a much more favourable attitude to the Samaritans. It certainly would not be surprising if the Hellenists justified their missionary outreach to the Samaritans on the basis of the eschatological reunion of North and South.

Thus we suggest that a basic difference between the Hebrews and Hellenists lay in the area of eschatology. While the Hebrews accepted Jesus as the promised Messiah their eschatology was still essentially futurist. The Hellenists, on the other hand, grasped much more clearly the fact that the New Age had dawned with the Christ event and the position they arrived at was much more one of *inaugurated eschatology*. The end has already broken into history and the New Age had dawned. Now, therefore, was the time for the eschatological reunion of North and South, and if so, then indeed also the time for the eschatological ingathering of the Gentiles.

THE HISTORICAL JESUS AND THE UNIVERSAL MISSION

Having traced the development of the early Christian mission backwards from Paul through the Hellenists to the beginnings of the Church in Jerusalem the question remains as to how these develop-

---

22   See further C. H. H. Scobie, "North and South: Tension and Reconciliation in Biblical History," in R. J. McKay and J. F. Miller (eds.), *Biblical Studies in Honour of William Barclay* (London: Collins, 1976), 90-93.

ments were related to the teaching and practice of the historical Jesus. What was the attitude of Jesus to Samaritans and Gentiles?[23]

Jesus' position is known to us only through the Gospels which, of course, reflect the viewpoints of their authors and of the communities for which they were written. At first glance they seem to exhibit a bewildering variety of approach. With a degree of oversimplification the views of the Gospels in regard to the attitude of the historical Jesus towards Samaritans and Gentiles could be tabulated as follows:

Mark: an approach to Gentiles but not to Samaritans.
Matthew: no approach to Samaritians or Gentiles.
Luke: an approach to both Samaritans and Gentiles.
John: an approach to Samaritans but not to Gentiles.

It is possible here only to look briefly at each of the Gospels in turn.

Mark

Mark is the only Gospel to show no interest in the Samaritans from which we may conclude that the question of a Samaritan mission simply was not a live issue in the community for which Mark wrote. On the other hand, it is generally recognized that a major concern of Mark is the Gentile mission.[24] The Gospel depicts repeated excursions into Gentile territories on the fringes of Palestine. It has been argued that Jesus entered these areas only to seek out pockets of Jewish population, yet frequent encounters with Gentiles could hardly be avoided.[25] Examples are provided of contacts of Jesus with Gentiles in the healing of the Gerasene demoniac (Mark 5:1-20)[26] and of the Syrophoenician woman's daughter (Mark 7:24-30).

Mark recognizes that the universal mission comes only after the death of Jesus which is seen as a "ransom for many" (10:45; cf. 14:24); the climax of the Gospel comes with the words of the Gentile centurion at the cross, "Truly this man was Son of God" (15:39). Before the end comes "the gospel must first be preached to all nations" (13:10) and "in the whole world" (14:9). This is closely connected with another major theme in Mark: the Jews have had their chance and rejected it, therefore mission is directed to the Gentiles. The conclusion of the

---

23 See Sundkler, "Jésus et les païens," 462-499; T. W. Manson, *Jesus and the Non-Jews* (London: Athlone Press, 1955); Jeremias, *Jesus' Promise to the Nations*; Hahn, *Mission in the New Testament*, 26-46; D. Bosch, *Die Heidenmission in der Zukunftsschau Jesu* (Zürich: Zwingli, 1959); Bavinck, *An Introduction to the Science of Missions*, 29-36; Blauw, *The Missionary Nature of the Church*, chap. 5; Hengel, "Die Ursprünge der christlichen Mission," 35-37.

24 Cf. J. M. Robinson, *The Problem of History in Mark* (London: SCM, 1957), 63-67; Hahn, *Mission in the New Testament*, 111-120.

25 Cf. Hahn, *Mission in the New Testament*, 31; Jeremias, *Jesus' Promise to the Nations*, 35-36.

26 See F. Annen, *Heil für die Heiden: Zur Bedeutung und Geschichte der Tradition vom besessenen Gerasener (Mk 5, 1-20 parr.)* (Frankfurt: Josef Knecht, 1976).

Parable of the Vineyard makes this clear: "The owner . . . will come and destroy the tenants, and give the vineyard to others" (12:9).[27]

We have here a view of universal mission which is close to that developed by Paul, and many scholars would hold that the later situation has been read back into the life of Jesus, particularly in such passages as 12:9, 13:10, and 14:9. Yet we cannot but be struck by the general reticence of the Gospel.[28] Mark is doing his best to link the later Gentile mission with Jesus but appears to be working with a very limited range of material.

Matthew

The situation in Matthew is more complex. It could be characterized as "no approach to Samaritans or Gentiles" on the basis of the prohibition of 10:5-6, which appears at the outset of Jesus' charge to the Twelve. But this, of course, would be to ignore the strongly pro-Gentile attitude which permeates the Gospel.[29] Matthew reproduces the healings of Gentiles found in Mark—the Gadarene demoniac (8:28-34) and the Canaanite woman's daughter (15:21-28),[30] and adds from Q the healing of the centurion's servant which includes the saying on the ingathering of the Gentiles (8:5-13//Luke 7:1-10). His conclusion to the Parable of the Vineyard is even more pointed than Mark's: "The Kingdom of God will be taken away from you and given to a nation producing the fruits of it" (21:43). The Magi prefigure the ingathering of the Gentiles; they come bearing the gold and frankincense of Isa. 60:6. Matt. 12:18-21 quotes Isa. 42:1-4 concluding with the words, "in his name will the Gentiles hope." As with Mark, however, the Gentile mission is envisaged as occurring only after Jesus' death; only then will "this gospel of the kingdom be preached throughout the whole world, as a testimony to all nations; and then the end will come" (24:14; cf. 26:13). The basis for this outreach is found in the "Great Commission" of 28:18-20: "Go therefore and make disciples of all nations." Quite apart from serious questions of authenticity,[31] the command is clearly presented as one of the risen Christ not of the historical Jesus.

---

27   Such allegorizing of the parable is secondary; cf. J. Jeremias, *The Parables of Jesus* (London: SCM, 1963), 70-77.

28   Cf. Sundkler, "Jésus et les païens," 472.

29   Cf. K. W. Clark, "The Gentile Bias in Matthew," *JBL* 66 (1947), 165-172; G. Hebert, "The Problem of the Gospel According to Matthew," *SJT* 14 (1961), 403-413; L. Gaston, "The Messiah of Israel as Teacher of the Gentiles," *Int* 29 (1975), 24-40; D. E. Garland, *The Intention of Matthew 23* (Leiden: Brill, 1979).

30   Cf. H. J. Held, "Matthew as Interpreter of the Miracle Stories," in G. Bornkamm, G. Barth, and H. J. Held, *Tradition and Interpretation in Matthew* (Philadelphia: Westminster, 1963), 197-200.

31   See Hahn, *Mission in the New Testament*, 63-68; B. J. Hubbard, *The Matthean Redaction of a Primitive Apostolic Commissioning: An Exegesis of Matthew 28:16-20* (Missoula: Scholars Press, 1974).

How are the conflicting statements (1) prohibiting a Samaritan and Gentile mission, and (2) commanding a universal outreach, to be reconciled? A salvation-history approach is generally employed: 10:5-6 applies only to Jesus' lifetime which is the period of the mission to Israel; 28:18-20 applies to the post-Easter situation which is the period of the Gentile mission. Matthew himself probably reconciled the differing views in some such way.

Matt. 10:5-6, however, still raises problems. Matthew felt able to integrate this piece of traditional material into his gospel, but form criticism asks why the pre-Matthean community preserved and passed on such a saying. The historicity of the logion is disputed,[32] but whether it is a word of the historical Jesus or an utterance of an early Christian prophet it will only have been transmitted if it served a purpose within the community.[33] Now the threefold structure of the saying recalls in a remarkable way the threefold pattern of the mission of the Hellenists as a comparison with Acts 1:8 makes clear:

Matthew 10:5-6	Acts 1:8
Go nowhere	You shall be my witnesses
among the Gentiles	in Jerusalem and in all Judea
and enter no town of the Samaritans	and Samaria
but go rather to the lost sheep of the house of Israel	and to the ends of the earth

The one saying is almost an exact contradiction of the other and the conclusion is inescapable that the saying forbidding a mission to Samaritans or Gentiles was employed by a conservative Jewish-Christian community which stood in opposition to the outreach pioneered by the Hellenists.

This implies, what has in fact been recognized, that there are different levels of tradition within Matthew's Gospel: an earlier, conservative, Jewish-Christian stratum has been integrated with other material by a redactor who himself strongly supports the Gentile mission.[34]

Luke

Luke is unique in emphasizing Jesus' contacts with both Gentiles and Samaritans. It is widely recognized that a major theme of Luke-Acts is

---

32 The demonstration of Aramaic features is hardly decisive (cf. Jeremias, *Jesus' Promise to the Nations*, 19-20) since the saying could have originated from Aramaic-speaking, Jewish-Christian circles in the early church.
33 Cf. F. W. Beare, "The Mission of the Disciples and the Mission Charge: Matthew 10 and Parallels," *JBL* 89 (1970), 9.
34 Cf. E. L. Abel, "Who Wrote Matthew?," *NTS* 17(1970-1971), 138-152.

the development of the Gentile mission,[35] and to this end Luke adopts Marcan and Q material, adding an emphasis on the Gentile mission as the fulfillment of prophecy. There may be a further reference in the sending out of the Seventy (Luke 10:1-16), though the significance of this is disputed. Luke shares with Mark and Matthew the basic view that the Gentile mission is post-resurrection: 24:46-47 is a saying of the risen Christ and points forward to Luke's version of the missionary command in Acts 1:8 given by Christ at his Ascension.

In his special section, 9:51-18:14, Luke has included three passages which refer to Samaritans: the rejection of Jesus and his disciples by a Samaritan village (9:51-56), the Parable of the Good Samaritan (10:30-37) and the story of the ten lepers of whom only the Samaritan returned to give thanks (17:11-19). Since Luke uses the (1) Jews/ (2) Samaritans/ (3) Gentiles outline in Acts some scholars have long been suspicious that Luke has read back the later Samaritan mission into the Gospel. The most radical treatment of these passages is that of M. S. Enslin[36] who holds that the historical Jesus never had any dealings with either Samaritans or Gentiles. The rejection by a Samaritan village is a Lucan composition, as is the Parable of the Good Samaritan[37] and also the story of the Ten Lepers.[38]

The passages cannot be analyzed in detail here.[39] Suffice it to say that the presence of Lucan stylistic features and problems associated with the editorial introductions are not relevant to the question of whether Luke is employing earlier traditions. In relation to content, if Luke was trying to read back the later Samaritan mission he made a very poor job of it! Luke 9:51-56 tells not how Jesus was accepted by Samaritans but how he was rejected (contrast John 4:39-41!). The Parable of the Good Samaritan certainly portrays a Samaritan in a favourable light but totally lacks the theme of mission. The Thankful Leper also portrays a Samaritan in a good light; but the actual healing is on a par with Jesus' willingness on occasion to extend his healing ministry to Gentiles. The possibility of a historical core to these three passages cannot therefore lightly be set aside.[40]

---

35   See Wilson, *The Gentiles and the Gentile Mission in Luke-Acts*, esp. chap. 2.
36   "Luke and the Samaritans," *HTR* 36 (1943), 278-297.
37   Enslin draws here on a much earlier article by J. Hálevy, "Sens et origine de la parabole évangélique dite du bon Samaritain," *REJ* 4 (1882), 249-255.
38   Cf. in a similar vein, H. D. Betz, "The Cleansing of the Ten Lepers (Luke 17:11-19)," *JBL* 90 (1971), 314-328; W. Bruners, *Die Reinigung der zehn Aussätzigen und die Heilung des Samariters Lk 17, 11-19* (Stuttgart: Katholisches Bibelwerk, 1977), esp. 297-306.
39   For a recent discussion see I. H. Marshall, *The Gospel of Luke, NIGTC* (Grand Rapids: Eerdmans, 1978), 402-408, 444-450, 648-652.
40   O. Cullmann has supported the authenticity of all three passages; see "Von Jesus zum Stephanuskreis und zum Johannesevangelium," in E. E. Ellis and E. Grässer (eds.), *Jesus und Paulus* (Göttingen: Vandenhoeck & Ruprecht, 1975), 54-55. Cf. also Hahn, *Mission in the New Testament*, 30.

John

The Fourth Gospel says nothing about a Gentile mission.[41] The view
which holds that it does is based on later traditions which regard the
Gospel as very late, written in Ephesus, and dependent on the Synoptics, opinions which have been increasingly questioned in recent
Johannine research.

The healing of the official's son (John 4:46-54) can be interpreted
in terms of Jesus' acceptance of Gentiles only if such an idea is imported
from the Synoptics. The text itself gives no indication that the *basilikos*
(a soldier or government official in the service of Herod Antipas) was
a Gentile. The "Greeks" (*Hellēnes*) of 7:35 and 12:20 are frequently
supposed to be Gentiles but the Gospel itself says they were from "the
Diaspora of the Greeks" and had come to Jerusalem "to worship at the
feast," i.e., there is nothing to indicate that they were other than
Greek-speaking Diaspora Jews.[42]

On the other hand, the Fourth Gospel does very clearly depict
Jesus approaching Samaritans in John 4. At the level of the final
redaction the story serves as a framework for typical Johannine teaching on the Living Water and the True Worship, but behind this is a
stratum of tradition which is deeply interested in the mission to the
Samaritans[43] and which seeks to present Jesus as the initiator and
authorizer of such a mission. There are many indications that John's
Gospel originated in a community which ultimately went back to stages
one and two of the Hellenists' mission,[44] and this view is strengthened
by recent studies which suggest some Samaritan influence in the development of Johannine christology.[45] Here again, therefore, we catch
echoes of controversy, in this case over stage two, the mission to the
Samaritans. This, of course, raises the possibility that the narrative has
no historical basis but has been invented precisely in order to validate
the later mission. While some features of the passage, particularly the
glowing accounts of the conversion of "many" Samaritans (4:39-41),
may have been added in the light of later developments it is still possible
to side with those scholars who find a core of early tradition in the

---

41 On the attitude towards mission in general in John see F. N. Davey, "The Gospel
     According to St. John and the Christian Mission," in G. H. Anderson (ed.), *The
     Theology of The Christian Mission*, 85-93; J. Radermakers, "Mission et apostolat dans
     l'Evangile johannique," *Stud Ev* 11 (=TU 87 [1964]), 100-121.
42 Cf. J. A. T. Robinson, "The Destination and Purpose of St. John's Gospel," in *Twelve
     New Testament Studies* (London: SCM, 1962), 111, 112.
43 Cf. H. G. Kippenberg, *Garizim und Synagoge: Traditionsgeschichtliche Untersuchungen
     zur samaritanischen Religion der aramäische Periode* (Berlin: de Gruyter, 1971), 115-117.
44 See C. H. H. Scobie, "Rivers of Living Water: The Challenge of Johannine Studies,"
     Bulletin of the Canadian Society of Biblical Studies 41 (1981), 1-27.
45 See W. A. Meeks, *The Prophet-King: Moses Traditions and the Johannine Christology*
     (Leiden: Brill, 1967); C. H. H. Scobie, "The Origins and Development of Samaritan
     Christianity," *NTS* 19 (1972-1973), 390-414; J. D. Purvis, "The Fourth Gospel and
     the Samaritans," *NovT* 17 (1975), 161-198.

passage; the encounter of Jesus and a Samaritan woman in this account would be comparable to Synoptic stories of Jesus' willingness to reach out to those regarded by strict Jewish society as despised outcasts.[46]

CONCLUSION

Behind these varied presentations can we discern a consistent attitude on the part of the historical Jesus?

It is clear, in the first place, that Jesus confined his mission and that of his disciples to the people of Israel. The Gospels are generally agreed on this, and the explicit missionary commands in Matthew and Luke are ascribed not to the historical Jesus, but to the risen Christ. It is when John has Jesus winning large numbers of Samaritans as believers that the critical scholar has to become suspicious.

Secondly, Jesus affirmed the entry of non-Jews into the Kingdom, and their complete equality with Jews, as eschatological concepts. In so doing he rejected much of the narrowly nationalistic thought of his day and returned to the higher teaching of the Old Testament. His choice of twelve disciples and his promise to them that they would "sit on twelve thrones, judging the twelve tribes of Israel" (Matt. 19:28//Luke 22:28-30) indicates his acceptance of the eschatological reunion of all twelve tribes of Israel, both northern and southern. The saying of Matt. 8:11//Luke 13:29, the authenticity of which can be strongly defended,[47] combines the ideas of the eschatological ingathering of the Gentiles of Isa. 49:12 and the eschatological banquet of Isa. 25:6-8. Jeremias has shown how several other passages in the Gospels reflect the same cluster of ideas.[48] A similar emphasis is to be found in several passages which deal with the final judgment. In Matt. 25:32 "all the nations" are to be gathered before the throne of the Son of Man and the Parable of the Sheep and the Goats which follows spells out criteria for judgment that make Jewish descent irrelevant. Thus Gentiles like the men of Nineveh (Matt. 12:41//Luke 11:32), the people of Tyre and Sidon (Matt. 11:21-22//Luke 10:13-14), and even of notorious Sodom and Gomorrah (Matt. 10:15//Luke 10:12) may enter the Kingdom while unrepentant Jews will find themselves excluded.

In the third place, there were undoubtedly occasions when Jesus accepted both Gentiles and Samaritans and gave them a share in the coming salvation here and now. There are no good grounds for denying the historicity of Jesus' encounters with the Syrophoenician woman, the Gerasene demoniac, and the centurion of Capernaum. While it is true that in none of these cases does Jesus take the initiative,

---

46   Cf. R. Bultmann, *The Gospel of John: A Commentary* (Philadelphia: Westminster, 1971), 175-202. Bultmann finds "traditional material" especially in 4:5-10, 16-19, 28-30, 40.

47   See the discussion in Jeremias, *Jesus' Promise to the Nations*, 55-63.

48   Ibid., 62-70.

nevertheless he does accept Gentiles who approach him in faith. In the latter incident Jesus is moved to pronounce the verdict, "Truly, I say to you, not even in Israel have I found such faith" (Matt. 8:10). It is not just at the end time that Gentiles will be received on equal terms with Jews; that happens in Jesus' ministry. Similarly, a strong case can be made out for Jesus' having regarded the Samaritans in a favourable light (contrary to the prevailing view of his day) and for having healed and helped individual Samaritans.

This is consistent with the widely accepted view that we cannot eliminate the tension between present and future which exists in Jesus' sayings on the Kingdom of God. His position is best defined neither as a wholly futurist eschatology, nor a wholly realized eschatology, but rather as an inaugurated eschatology. For Jesus, God's rule still lies in the future; yet coming events cast their shadow before them and in his words and deeds the Kingdom is already breaking into history.[49] Thus Jesus not only affirms the future ingathering of those outside Israel; in his ministry he accepts Samaritans and Gentiles in addition to Jews.[50]

In the immediate post-resurrection period it was the Hellenists who saw the death and resurrection of Christ as the decisive event of salvation history. Perhaps it was above all their experience of the gift of the Holy Spirit which persuaded them that the New Age had now truly dawned. They were emboldened to preach to Samaritans and the success of that mission both confirmed their view that the time of the eschatological reunion of North and South had indeed arrived and prompted them to extend their mission to encompass the eschatological ingathering of the Gentiles.

Much in this earliest period of the church must remain shrouded in uncertainty. What has been attempted here is the sketching of a theory of the development of the universal mission of the early church which is consistent with the known evidence. This view suggests that while the attitudes of Jesus and Paul were certainly not identical, nevertheless there is a real continuity between their views. In bridging the gap between Jesus and Paul it is the Hellenists who provide both the historical and the theological link. Their key role in the development of the early church deserves greater recognition than has been granted to them.

---

49 Cf. J. Jeremias, *New Testament Theology, Part One* (London: SCM, 1971), 96-108; W. G. Kümmel, *The Theology of the New Testament* (Nashville: Abingdon, 1973), 32-39.
50 Cf. Hahn, *Mission in the New Testament*, 33.

Paul and Jerusalem

LLOYD GASTON

"There is nothing whatever to indicate that the primitive church in Jerusalem, or any elements in it, differed from St. Paul either in the matter of Christology or in sacramental practices and ideas." So wrote Professor Beare at the beginning of the supplementary note to his well-stated radio broadcast on "Jesus and Paul."[1] The attempt to separate Jerusalem and Paul stems from nineteenth-century liberalism, as he correctly points out. Sometimes it took the form of a dislike of Paul's "high" christology and ecclesiology coupled with a romantic longing for the simple piety and practice of the primitive church; sometimes it took the form of a dislike of the "Jewish legalism" of James coupled with a romantic admiration for Paul as the perfect hero of faith. It is also important to avoid a romanticism of the earliest church as a pure virgin, relegating all differences and "heresies" to the post-apostolic period. We will certainly try to avoid these extremes when expanding on and testing Beare's initial statement.

First, it is important to adhere to the language which says that this comparison is to be between Paul and the Jerusalem church[2] and not something called "Jewish Christianity." The latter term has been used in so many different senses as to make communication almost impossi-

---

1   F. W. Beare, "Jesus and Paul," *CJT* 5 (1959), 85. (Abbreviations in references are those used by the *Journal of Biblical Literature*. See *JBL* 95 [1976], 331-346.)
2   We could retain the term "primitive" if that meant nothing more than the Jerusalem church contemporary with Paul, but we will avoid it lest it imply that the church was primitive in comparison with Paul.

ble.[3] An influential book by J. Daniélou[4] uses it in a sense so broad as to be almost meaningless. He refers to the influence of Jewish ideas, particularly apocalyptic, on the entire Christian movement down to the middle of the second century. Another important book, by H. J. Schoeps,[5] studies only the pseudo-Clementines and other second- and third-century literature without making any explicit connection with the pre-70 C.E. period. To use specific Christian ideas, such as an Ebionite christology[6] or anti-Paulinism[7] and the exaltation of James[8] as criteria, raises the question of the meaning of the adjective "Jewish." Any attempt to try to understand a first-century phenomenon on the basis of second- or third-century sources completely begs the question of continuity.[9] B. Malina,[10] who advocates the term Christian Judaism, gives a conceptual definition but without any discussion of the sources. A minimal definition in his view should include at least circumcision[11] and enough relation to Torah as covenant and commandments to justify the noun and enough relation to Jesus to justify the adjective. We will try here to avoid confusion by not using the term "Jewish Christianity" at all and by limiting our inquiry geographically to Jerusalem and temporally to Paul's lifetime.[12]

---

3   Cf. R. A. Kraft, "In Search of 'Jewish Christianity' and Its 'Theology': Problems of Definition and Methodology," *Judéo-Christianisme* (= *RSR* 60 [1972]), 81-92; A. F. J. Klijn, "The Study of Jewish Christianity," *NTS* 20 (1974), 419-431; S. K. Riegel, "Jewish Christianity: Definitions and Terminology," *NTS* 24 (1978), 410-415.

4   J. Daniélou, *The Theology of Jewish Christianity* (London: Darton, Longman and Todd, 1964).

5   H. J. Schoeps, *Theologie und Geschichte des Judenchristentums* (Tübingen: Mohr, 1949).

6   So the tradition from Irenaeus to H. Lietzmann, *A History of the Early Church* (New York: Meridian, 1949).

7   Cf. G. Lüdemann, "Zum Antipaulinismus im frühen Christentum," *EvT* 40 (1980), 437-455.

8   The people who appealed to James in the second century may have had as little in common with the real James as many of the people who appealed to Paul had with the real Paul.

9   Cf. the statements by such different scholars as G. Strecker, *Das Judenchristentum in den Pseudoklementinen* (Berlin: Akademie, 1958), 214, and J. Munck, "Jewish Christianity in Post-Apostolic Times," *NTS* 6 (1960), 103-116. That the legend of the Pella flight cannot be used as a bridge has now been decisively demonstrated by G. Lüdemann, "The Successors of Pre-70 Jerusalem Christianity: A Critical Analysis of the Pella-Tradition," in E. P. Sanders (ed.), *Normative Self Definition*, Vol. 1: *The Shaping of Christianity in the Second and Third Centuries* (London: SCM, 1980), 161-173.

10 B. J. Malina, "Jewish Christianity or Christian Judaism: Toward a Hypothetical Definition," *JSJ* 7 (1976), 46-57.

11 Statements like: "They are not orthodox Jews, for they do not practice circumcision" (V. Corwin, *St. Ignatius and Christianity in Antioch* [New Haven: Yale University Press, 1960], 58) make it necessary to be explicit about this. Cf. my "Judaism of the Uncircumcised in Ignatius and Related Writers" (forthcoming).

12 Our limitation is very close to that of R. N. Longenecker, *The Christology of Early Jewish Christianity* (London: SCM, 1970), but when he speaks of Matthew, John, Hebrews, James, 1-3 John, 1-2 Peter, Jude, and Revelation as "addressed to Jewish Christians or to potentially interested Jews" (18), he introduces confusion by includ-

What are the sources that can be used to recover something of the theology of the Jerusalem church? To use material later than the first century raises the issue of continuity without any control, and therefore it must be completely put aside for the moment. If at one time the early chapters of Acts and particularly the mission speeches could be used for this purpose,[13] current scholarship on Luke would no longer allow it.[14] If at one time it was thought that the Synoptic Gospels could be used for this purpose, there is today a growing consensus that all three are not only addressed to Gentile Christians but were written by Gentile Christians.[15] The Synoptic Gospels must surely contain earlier traditions,[16] but contemporary study of the gospels with its concern for redaction criticism would need to develop criteria for distinguishing Jerusalem traditions from other traditions. I believe that in fact the synoptic traditions and traditions in Acts and even to a degree later Christian Judaism can be used to corroborate and fill out a picture drawn from other sources, but they certainly can no longer serve as a self-evident starting point. We are left then with Paul as our sole witness.[17]

The study of "Jewish Christianity" will always be associated with the name of F. C. Baur, who made extensive use of the Pauline epistles. He created a synthesis brilliant in its simplicity when he declared all of the opponents mentioned in Paul's letters to be identical and then connected them via Gal. 2 and Acts 15 with Jerusalem.[18] This thesis can no longer be a presupposition of our study, and we must develop a very cautious methodology. In the first place, we should confine ourselves to opponents who are explicitly mentioned and not confuse them with the congregation actually addressed. In the second place, we must refrain from the kind of mirror reading which assumes that whatever Paul affirms or denies, his opponents must have said the opposite.[19]

---

ing writings which in the opinion of most go far beyond his own definition. By no stretch of the imagination can 2 Pet. 1:4 be called "Jewish Christian"!

13 Cf. C. H. Dodd, *The Apostolic Preaching and Its Developments* (London: Hodder and Stoughton, 1936).

14 Cf. U. Wilckens, *Die Missionsreden der Apostelgeschichte* (Neukirchen: Neukirchener Verlag, 1961).

15 The fact that none (Mark 12:30, 33; Luke 10:27; Matt. 22:37) can reproduce the *Shema* accurately is but part of the evidence for this.

16 My attempt to reconstruct one such tradition in *No Stone on Another* (Leiden: Brill, 1970), 244-365, has not seemed convincing to many.

17 The only New Testament writings for which a convincing case can be made that they were written by and for Christian Jews or ex-Jews are Revelation, John, and 1-3 John. In none is there an obvious connection with Jerusalem, and all come from a period somewhat later than Paul.

18 I am convinced in general by the thorough refutation of his thesis by two such differing scholars as J. Munck, *Paul and the Salvation of Mankind* (London: SCM, 1959), and W. Schmithals, *Paul and James* (London: SCM, 1965).

19 This principle is well enunciated by H. D. Betz, *Galatians* (Philadelphia: Fortress, 1979), 6, but not always adhered to in his commentary (cf. e.g., 116).

The opponents are most clearly identified in 2 Corinthians. They are clearly Christian Jews in Malina's sense (11:22-23a), but Judaizing or the law are not issues at all. This is true also of 2 Cor. 3, where not Moses as law giver but Moses as a *theios anēr* model for ministry is the point of the discussion.[20] The Galatians were in danger of Judaizing, according to Paul, and the relation between the Galatians and the law is a major theme of the letter, but the identity of the troublemakers (1:6-9; 4:17, 30; 5:10-12; 6:12-13) is not at all clear. Paul says that they "do not keep the law," that is, are not Jews in his opinion.[21] It is now clear that the opponents in Colossians are in no sense Jews nor is the Jewish Torah in any sense an issue.[22] There is nothing to distinguish opponents referred to vaguely in Phil. 3 and Rom. 16 from those in 2 Cor. 10-13. In Rom. 1-15, 1 Corinthians, 1 Thessalonians, and Philemon there is no reference to opponents at all. In any case, Paul never connects any of his opponents with Jerusalem, and therefore we cannot take them as a starting point in our inquiry.

Paul always speaks of the Jerusalem church in positive terms.[23] He refers to two visits to that church (Gal. 1:18; 2:1) and a planned third visit (Rom. 15:25). The church was in existence then at least between the years 37 and 56. He mentions "the churches of Judea" (Gal. 1:22 [1 Thess. 2:14]), but the language of Rom. 15:31 may suggest that by that he means the church of Jerusalem; there is no hint of the possible existence of Christian communities in Galilee. Paul calls the Jerusalem Christians "the saints" (Rom. 15:25-26, 31; 1 Cor. 16:1; 2 Cor. 8:4; 9:1, 12), but one cannot be sure that this was their own self designation.[24] He mentions leaders of the Jerusalem church as "apostles" (1 Cor. 9:4; 15:7; Gal. 1:19; 2:8) and "brothers of the Lord" (1 Cor. 9:4), and he mentions by name James (1 Cor. 15:7; Gal. 1:19; 2:9, 12) and John (Gal. 2:9) and Cephas (1 Cor. 1:12; 3:22; 9:5; 15:5, Gal. 1:18; 2:7 *v.l.*, 8 *v.l.*, 9, 11, 14). Since Cephas is not a proper name but an Aramaic nickname ("Rock"),[25] we can conclude that the church spoke (also?) Aramaic. When we consider in addition that three leaders are called "pillars"

---

20 Cf. D. Georgi, *Die Gegner des Paulus im 2. Korintherbrief* (Neukirchen: Neukirchener Verlag, 1964), and J. F. Collange, *Enigmes de la deuxième épître de Paul aux Corinthiens* (Cambridge: Cambridge University Press, 1972).

21 One must distinguish between breaking certain commandments and not keeping the law at all. I would agree then with the thesis of J. Munck, *Paul*, and others about the Judaizing Gentile Christians. The most careful discussion is by J. G. Hawkins, *The Opponents of Paul in Galatia* (Ann Arbor: University Microfilms, 1971).

22 Cf. G. Bornkamm, "Die Häresie des Kolosserbriefs," *Das Ende des Gesetzes* (Munich: Kaiser, 1952), 139-156, and the recent commentaries by E. Lohse and E. Schweizer.

23 I have tried to show that this is true also of Gal. 4:25-31 in "Israel's Enemies in Pauline Theology," *NTS* 28 (1982), 400-423.

24 And they certainly did not call themselves "the poor"; cf. L. Keck, "The Poor among the Saints in the NT," *ZNW* 56 (1965), 100-129, and "The Poor among the Saints in Jewish Christianity and Qumran," *ZNW* 57 (1966), 54-78.

25 We see then how Paul can be used to identify such passages as Matt. 16:17-19 as traditions of the Jerusalem church.

(Gal. 2:9), and that the Jerusalem Christians may be referred to as "members of the house of faithfulness" (Gal. 6:10), the implications for their self understanding as God's temple are great.[26] If 1 Thess. 2:14 is not Pauline, as I believe, we know nothing of a persecution of the church, for Paul's own persecutions were not in Judea (Gal. 1:22-23). We do, however, hear of the possibility of persecution (presumably by Zealots) if "the saints" associate themselves too openly with Paul, who was suspected of causing Jews to become apostate (Rom. 15:31).[27] Exceedingly important to Paul was the collection from his churches for the Jerusalem church (Gal. 2:10; 6:6-10;[28] 1 Cor. 16:1-4; 2 Cor. 8-9; Rom. 15:25-33).[29] One of the motivations he gives for it is gratitude to Jerusalem for the "spiritual blessings" (Rom. 15:27) they have given to the Gentiles. When we add to all this Paul's statement of complete agreement with the gospel of Jerusalem—"whether it was I or they, so we preach and so you believed" (1 Cor. 15:11)—we could simply express complete agreement with the statement with which this paper began and stop here. Almost.

The account of the Jerusalem conference in Gal. 2:1-10 has been read for so long in the light of a theory about Paul's "Jewish Christian" opponents that it is difficult to confine ourselves to what is actually said there. Our proposal, however, is to learn as much as we can about the Jerusalem church from Paul alone as a control over any such theory. Paul says that when he outlined "his" gospel—the gospel which he "preaches among the Gentiles" (2:2; 1:16), "the gospel to the uncircumcised" (2:7)—for certain influential pillars, James and Cephas and John, they recognized that he had been entrusted with that gospel (by God) and acknowledged the grace (thereby) given to him. Paul also says that God "has been effective for Cephas for the apostolate to the circumcised" (2:8), so that the recognition was mutual. He claims that Titus, since he is a Greek, was not compelled to be circumcised (2:3), but he does not say that the "interloping false brethren" were members of the Jerusalem church at all (2:4). According to Paul, the idea of the collection from his Gentile churches for the Jerusalem church came about by mutual agreement (2:10). It may be that the tangled syntax in verses 4-6 indicates that perhaps things did not go as smoothly as Paul says, but let us remain with what is stated.

In the midst of all this mutual recognition we find astonishingly great theological differences between Paul and Jerusalem. Evidently they agreed on two gospels, one to the circumcised and one to the

---

26 Cf. my *No Stone*, 65-243, and for Gal. 6:10, L. Hurtado, "The Jerusalem Collection and the Book of Galatians," *JSNT* 5 (1979), 46-62.

27 That this passage does not indicate an antagonism between Paul and the Jerusalem church is argued by Schmithals, *Paul and James*, 79-84.

28 That these verses belong here, cf. L. Hurtado, "The Jerusalem Collection."

29 Cf. D. Georgi, *Die Geschichte der Kollekte des Paulus für Jerusalem* (Hamburg: Reich, 1965), and K. F. Nickle, *The Collection* (London: SCM, 1966).

uncircumcised, and on two apostolates, one to the circumcised and one to the uncircumcised. We can further infer an agreement that the circumcised would continue to obey the commandments of the Torah (cf. 5:3; 1 Cor. 7:18), while the uncircumcised would be responsible for none of them. Presumably this is what is meant by "nothing being imposed" and by "preserving our freedom" and "not submitting to the subjection" (2:5). The Jerusalem church is characterized by circumcision, by Torah, and by a mission restricted to Israel.[30] These are considerable differences indeed from Paul's own emphases. Since the incident at Antioch[31] did not occur in Jerusalem, we do not need to deal with it except to point out that, while Paul has harsh words for Cephas and Barnabas and the behaviour of certain Jews in Antioch, nothing whatsoever is said against James or the Jerusalem church. Nevertheless, must not differences in such vital areas as circumcision and Torah and mission have other theological consequences, even if they were not recognized by Paul?

We now go beyond specific references to Jerusalem to see if anything further can be gleaned about the theology of that church. There is considerable agreement today that it is possible to isolate certain formulae cited by Paul.[32] Often these are identified as being "Jewish Christian" in origin, although the criteria for this designation are seldom spelled out and rarely clear. We shall look briefly at a number of them without going into the complex issues of just how they are to be isolated.[33] We shall begin with those which most clearly can be identified with Jerusalem and use a kind of "criterion of coherence" to help us in other cases.

Most would say that 1 Cor. 15:3-7 contains a traditional formulation stemming from the Jerusalem church.[34] Not only does Paul specifically introduce it as tradition ("delivered ... received," 15:3), but he says in effect that this is the gospel preached by the people named, Cephas and James ("whether then it was I or they, so we preach," 15:11). There is also a fair amount of consensus on the extent of the formula:[35]

---

30 It was hoped that the Gentiles would come of their own accord to Zion once the redemption of Israel was final and visible. The classic statement of the distinction between a "centripetal" and a "centrifugal" concept of mission is by B. Sundkler, "Jésus et les païens," *Arbeiten und Mitteilungen aus dem neutestamentlichen Seminar zu Uppsala* VI (Uppsala, 1937), 1-38. Cf. also J. Jeremias, *Jesus' Promise to the Nations* (London: SCM, 1958) and Munck, *Paul.*

31 I would understand it along the lines of Schmithals, *Paul and James*, 63-78.

32 I have used as a convenient summary and control over the passages chosen P. Vielhauer, *Geschichte der urchristlichen Literatur* (Berlin: de Gruyter, 1975), 9-57.

33 Because of its complexity I have not included the hymn of Phil. 2:6-11 in this study, even though it was identified by E. Lohmeyer, *Kyrios Jesus* (Heidelberg, 1928), with the Eucharistic tradition of the Jerusalem church. He has not found many followers.

34 Cf. J. Jeremias, *The Eucharistic Words of Jesus* (London: SCM, 1966), 101-103.

35 I follow the most recent study by J. Murphy-O'Connor, "Tradition and Redaction in 1 Cor. 15:3-7," *CBQ* 43 (1981), 582-589.

died, for our sins, according to the Scriptures
was buried,
was raised, on the third day, according to the Scriptures
appeared   to Cephas,   then to the Twelve
               to James,   then to all the apostles.

If we look for specific aspects of the theology of the Jerusalem church,
we find the following. They had a concept of apostle which, especially if
it is understood to be parallel to the Twelve, differed from that of
Paul.[36] That the number twelve was chosen shows a claim of the group
on all of Israel but also only on Israel. Jesus' death and resurrection
were seen to be "according to the Scriptures," that is, as the climax and
culmination of the whole history of Israel which is the subject of the
Hebrew Bible. Insofar as these were understood as eschatological
events, we can assume an apocalyptic background to the entire conception. Finally, Jesus' death was seen to have expiatory significance: it was
"for (*hyper*) our sins."

Paul speaks of a tradition being received or delivered also in the
liturgical formula in 1 Cor. 11:23b-25, and the connection with the
Jerusalem church is indicated by the close parallel in Mark 14. If a
covenant theology was merely implicit in 1 Cor. 15, here it is explicit:
the cup is called "the new covenant." Jesus' death is referred to as his
"blood," which may well have sacrificial or even specifically covenantal
connotations (Exod. 24:8). The reference to a new covenant (Jer. 31:31)
is thus not one of contrast but of culmination and fulfillment. Some
have seen in *paradidōmi*, in connection with Jesus' death, traces of a
Dahingabeformel which may go back to the Jerusalem church (cf. Rom.
4:25, Gal. 1:4).[37] Jesus' death is said to be "for you" (11:24), and it is
probable that Matthew has correctly captured the sense of this statement in the Jerusalem church when he adds more precisely "for the
forgiveness of sins" (26:28).

W. Kramer identifies a pre-Pauline tradition in what he calls a *pistis*
formula, which is to be distinguished from a *homologia*.[38] Thus Rom.
10:9b would reflect a formula such as, "We believe that God raised
Jesus from the dead," a formula that goes back to the earliest church. If
it is true that this formula is older than the more complex one in 1 Cor.
15:3-5, then there may have been a stage in the Jerusalem church
during which the fundamental significance of Jesus was seen in his

---

36   Apart from himself, Paul names as Apostles Junia, Andronicus, Cephas, and proba-
     bly Barnabas, James, and Silvanus. Cf. W. Schmithals, *The Office of Apostle in the Early
     Church* (Nashville: Abingdon, 1969).

37   Cf. W. Popkes, *Christus Traditus: eine Untersuchung zum Begriff der Dahingabe im Neuen
     Testament* (Zürich: Zwingli, 1967).

38   W. Kramer, *Christ, Lord, Son of God* (London: SCM, 1966), 20-26; cf. Vielhauer,
     Geschichte, 13-16. Rom. 10:9a, on the other hand, "we confess that Jesus is Lord," is a
     homologia, which has a different origin and function.

resurrection as a revelation that his preaching of the Kingdom of God
was indeed true because the church was now living in the end times.

In its present form the formula in 1 Thess. 1:9-10 cannot come
from the Jerusalem church because that church did not engage in
Gentile mission.[39] Nevertheless, it is often referred to as "Jewish Christian,"[40] and the last three lines could represent Jerusalem theology.

> How you turned to God from idols to serve a living and true God
> And await his Son from heaven,
> Whom he raised from the dead,
> Jesus who delivers us from the coming wrath.

We have a *pistis* formula, a strong expectation of the parousia, and an
expectation of judgment. The way in which Jesus delivers from the
wrath is not stated, but it is presumably through the forgiveness of sin.

Gal. 1:4a has been identified as a pre-Pauline formula,[41] and it fits
in well with Jerusalem theology:

> who gave himself for our sins
> in order that he might liberate us from the present evil age.

Here again the *Dahingabeformel* expresses expiatory self-sacrifice for
sins. F. Bovon argues that the verb *exaireisthai* is to be connected in
particular with the Exodus tradition. Liberation in Christ is seen as the
new exodus through the forgiveness of sins.

The formula in Rom. 4:25 contains language which by now should
be very familiar to us:

> who was delivered up for the sake of our faults
> and raised up for the sake of our justification.

We have once more the *Dahingabeformel*, and the statement that Jesus'
death atones for our sins. In the light of the usage in the Qumran scrolls
we should not be surprised to find that justification is a concept of the
Jerusalem church and not unique to Paul.[42] Whether justification functions in the same way in the two theologies remains to be seen.

There are complicating considerations with respect to the formula
in Rom. 1:3-4. While the wording is easy to isolate from its Pauline
embedding, we have to reckon with Pauline additions within the formula itself. It seems clear that we should omit the words "in power," but
whether the contrast "according to the flesh—according to the Spirit of

---

39 Cf. U. Wilckens, *Missionsreden*, 80-82. It may be that from this formula and from the
    speeches in Acts 14 and 17 we can derive a pre-Pauline pattern of preaching in the
    Gentile mission. It is related to many of the motifs of Wis. 11-15. Cf. also Rom. 2:4.
40 Cf. Vielhauer, *Geschichte*, 29.
41 F. Bovon, "Une formule prépaulinienne dans l'épître aux Galates (Ga 1, 4-5),"
    Paganisme, Judaïsme, Christianisme (Paris: Boccard, 1978), 91-107. Cf. Betz, *Galatians*,
    42-43.
42 Cf. Gal. 2:16, where justification is presented as a concept common to Cephas and
    Paul, who are "Jews by birth."

holiness" was part of the original formula is disputed.[43] We use the shortest formula here for the sake of simplicity:

who was born of the seed of David ...

who was appointed Son of God ... since resurrection of the dead.

The Jerusalem church called Jesus "Messiah" in two senses. On the one hand he was the Messiah as son of David, but then later he became the Messiah as Son of God. The christology is adoptionist. We have until now avoided any discussion of christological titles which may have been associated with the formulae. Much work has been done on them by Kramer and Hahn,[44] but confidence in their solutions is not shared by all. To see that this particular formula is clearly messianic, whatever name or title be the antecedent of the relative pronouns, is enough for present purposes.

The formula most useful for our task, Rom. 3:24-26a, also presents the most difficulties and therefore has been kept to the last. First, Bultmann and Käsemann[45] were confident they could identify the text in 3:24-26a simply by omitting as Pauline additions "as a free gift by his grace" in 3:24 and "through faith" in 3:25. However, it has become increasingly difficult to show why 3:24 is not Pauline, with the possible exception of the word *apolytrōsis*, and it is hard to make sense of the supposed insertion in 3:25.[46] Second, the translation of 3:25b-26a is exceedingly difficult, and yet the sense of the whole formula depends on how these phrases are understood. We shall tentatively reconstruct and translate as follows:

whom God set forth as a means of expiation,
through [Jesus'] faithfulness at the cost of his blood,[47]
in order to demonstrate his righteousness,

---

43 That it was not is argued by R. Bultmann, *Theology of the New Testament* (New York: Scribner's, 1954), 1:49, and Vielhauer, *Geschichte*, 30-31. That it was is argued by E. Schweizer, "Röm. 1, 3f, und der Gegensatz von Fleisch und Geist vor und bei Paulus," *Neotestamentica* (Zürich: Zwingli, 1963), 180-89, and H. Zimmermann, *Neutestamentliche Methodenlehre* (Stuttgart: Katholisches Bibelwerk, 1968), 192-202.

44 Kramer, *Christ, Lord, Son of God*; F. Hahn, *The Titles of Jesus in Christology* (London: Lutterworth, 1969). It seems that in general the title which is the subject of the sentence could be changed more naturally than the formula which begins with the relative pronoun.

45 R. Bultmann, *Theology*, 1:46-47; E. Käsemann, "Zum Verständnis von Römer 3,24-26," *ZNW* 43 (1950/51), 150-154. The literature on this formula is extensive; cf. E. Käsemann, *Commentary on Romans* (Grand Rapids: Eerdmans, 1980), 91-92, and W. Wilckens, *Der Brief an die Römer* 1 (Neukirchen: Neukirchener Verlag, 1978). 182.

46 Cf. Wilckens, *Römer*, 183-184, and S. K. Williams, *Jesus' Death as Saving Event* (Missoula: Scholars Press, 1975), 11-16.

47 The translation of this line is based on Williams, *Jesus' Death*, 46-51. The best alternative would refer to God's covenant faithfulness, as argued by A. Pluta, *Gottes Bundestreue; Ein Schlüsselbegriff in Röm 3,25a* (Stuttgart: Katholisches Bibelwerk, 1969). There is no way grammatically to make the phrase mean "to be received by faith" as in the usual interpretations, even if it is a Pauline insertion.

because the prosecution of sins committed in the past was dropped in the forbearance of God.[48]

In his classic study of the formula Käsemann speaks of the righteousness of God as his *"Festhalten am Bunde"*;[49] it has to do with "the patience of God which demonstrates his covenant faithfulness and which effects forgiveness."[50] This is in the tradition of Exod. 34:6-7, "The LORD, the LORD, A God merciful and gracious, slow to anger, and abounding in covenant loyalty and faithfulness, keeping (LXX adds 'righteousness and') covenant loyalty for thousands, forgiving iniquity and transgression and sin."[51] Jesus' death is seen in cultic terms, and, whether or not we are to think specifically of the "mercy seat," it is clear that it replaces what would otherwise have been the function of the temple and its sacrifices. The righteousness of God is a concept also of Jerusalem theology, and it expresses itself in the forgiveness of sins. This formula is said by many to have its *Sitz im Leben* in the Eucharist.[52]

If we may summarize what we have learned about the theology of the Jerusalem church, it would be something like this: Jesus' resurrection was seen as the confirmation of his proclamation of the nearness of the Kingdom of God, as the revelation by God that Israel was living in the end time. In Bultmann's apt phrase, the church understood itself as the eschatological congregation.[53] The significance of this was expressed in terms of covenantal theology. What happened in Christ was God's act of eschatological righteousness in his faithfulness to the covenant made with Israel by providing a final means of atonement for the forgiveness of Israel's sins. Jesus' death signifies then the renewal of the covenant, the re-affirmation of the covenant and the commandments, the establishment of Torah. On the other hand, his death means the supersession and replacement of the temple and its sacrifices as a means of expiation. This atonement was celebrated in the Eucharist, now by the church but soon by all Israel. Then would come the final pilgrimage of the Gentiles to Mt. Zion. This is a clear "pattern of religion" to use the words of E. P. Sanders,[54] and it is clearly a different pattern from that of Paul.

---

48   The translation or paraphrase of this line is based on N. Dahl, "The Atonement—An Adequate Reward for the Akedah?," *The Crucified Messiah* (Minneapolis: Augsburg, 1974), 156. S. K. Williams, *Jesus' Death*, 27-34, makes a strong case for understanding this line with reference to the Gentile mission, in which case we would have a parallel to the expanded formula in 1 Thess. 1:9-10 (cf. n. 39). But I am not completely convinced.

49   Käsemann, "Verständnis," 153.

50   Käsemann, *Romans*, 100. Commentaries sometimes point to the contradiction between the forbearance of Rom. 3:25 and the wrath of 1:18-23, but of course the latter has to do with the situation of idolaters outside the covenant.

51   Cf. Wilckens, *Römer*, 197, and the references given there.

52   Cf. Käsemann, "Verständnis," and Pluta, *Gottes Bundestreue*.

53   Bultmann, *Theology*, 1:37-42.

54   E. P. Sanders, "Patterns of Religion in Paul and Rabbinic Judaism: A Holistic Method of Comparison," *HTR* 66 (1973), 455-478.

The Jerusalem church said that Jesus' death was "for our sins" (1 Cor. 15:3; Gal. 1:4a; Rom. 4:25; 3:25), but Paul speaks always of sin in the singular as a power and never of sins in the plural as guilt.[55] Paul also says that Jesus died (Rom. 5:6, 8; 14:15; 1 Thess. 5:10), was given up (Rom. 8:32; Gal. 2:20; Eph. 5:2, 25), was crucified (1 Cor. 1:13), was made sin (2 Cor. 5:21), was made a curse (Gal. 3:13) *for (hyper)*—but it is always for us, for you, for persons, and never for our sins. Rom. 8:3 says significantly that Jesus was sent for (*peri*) sin, not sins. Not only that, but Paul never speaks of forgiveness[56] and hardly ever of repentance.[57] The word atonement, for Paul, means not a way of dealing with sins but a one-time act of incorporating Gentiles into the body of Christ, the people of God, the giving of life to the dead. For Paul this takes place at baptism, when one participates in the death and resurrection of Christ. We know little of the significance of baptism for the Jerusalem church; it may even have consisted in repeated lustrations.[58] Though the Jerusalem church spoke in terms of the covenant and renewed covenant, Paul never uses this concept.[59] Though for Jerusalem the righteousness of God effects forgiveness of sins, for Paul it refers to the incorporation of Gentiles into the people of God. Though the Jerusalem church spoke of Jesus as the Messiah, Paul never does so.[60] For Paul, Jesus relates neither to David nor to Moses but to Adam and to Abraham. Jesus is not the climax of the history of Israel nor the fulfillment of the covenant but the one who overcomes the powers which enslave the creation by fulfilling the promises of God concerning Gentiles.[61] Paul's basic confession is "Jesus is Lord," and Jesus is infinitely more important to his theology than he ever could have been for Jerusalem. For Paul, Jesus is not only the revelation of God's eschatological activity but of God himself, and therefore the doctrine of the Trinity is a legitimate development from Pauline theology.

The theology of Paul and the theology of Jerusalem are completely different, and yet Paul can say they are the same (1 Cor. 15:11) and that each acknowledged the position of the other (Gal. 2:1-10). What makes them different is, of course, the fact that one gospel is addressed to

---

55 One function of footnotes is to list exceptions, in this case Rom. 7:5; 1 Cor. 15:17 (Rom. 4:7; 11:27 are quotations).

56 Rom. 4:7-8 is a quotation.

57 Here the exceptions are Rom. 2:4; 2 Cor. 7:9-11; 12:21.

58 Cf. Heb. 6:2 and Schoeps, *Theologie*, 202-211.

59 Rom. 11:27 is a quotation and 1 Cor. 11:25 is from the Jerusalem tradition. I would argue that in 2 Cor. 3:6, 14, both the "ancient" and the "renewed" covenant are the language of the opponents (cf. the works cited in n. 20). The word does not mean covenant in Gal. 3:15, 17; 4:24 (cf. n. 23) nor in Rom. 9:4 (cf. C. J. Roetzel, "Diathekai in Romans 9, 4," *Biblica* 51 [1970], 377-390).

60 Cf. the discussion in Kramer, *Christ, Lord, Son of God*, 131-150.

61 "Nicht die von Moses eingeleitete Heilsgeschichte Israels, sondern die Welt des gefallenen und unter dem Gotteszorn befindlichen Adam ist für Paulus das Gegenüber des gegenwärtigen Kairos" (Käsemann, "Verständnis," 154).

Gentiles and one to Israel. Yet there was such a common core of conviction that many of the differences we have outlined may not have been seen by the first-century participants. There is a real sense in which Professor Beare's statement with which we began is true. Perhaps we should speak of transmutations rather than differences. Paul pays tribute to the gospel of the Jerusalem church and is grateful to it for "spiritual blessings" which flow to the Gentiles (Rom. 15:27). At the same time, the common kerygma spoken in a different situation takes on a greatly transformed significance. The theology of the Jerusalem church had, of course, no future and certainly cannot be revived today, while the theology of Paul triumphed to such an extent that it is only with difficulty that we can recover the theology of Jerusalem. Nevertheless, I expect that in the Kingdom of God Paul and James will still be friends. If Paul can have such a different "pattern of religion" from that of the Jerusalem church, how much more different would his "pattern" be from the teaching of Jesus. And yet Paul was firmly and happily convinced that the gospel he preached among the Gentiles was given to him by a revelation of God in Christ (Gal. 1:15-16) and that he had the full approval of his Lord. Who is to say that he was wrong?

"The Jesus Whom Paul Preaches" (Acts 19:13)

JOHN C. HURD

In his 1958 radio broadcast our honoree said, "We need not hesitate to affirm that despite all the differences, Paul is essentially one with Jesus in the substance of the gospel which he preaches."[1] He therefore aligned himself firmly with those scholars who emphasize the continuity between the teachings of Jesus and of Paul and dissociated himself from those who speak mainly of discontinuity and difference.[2] And in the "Supplementary Note" to the published version of his address he commented, "The notion of an undogmatic, non-sacramental faith which Jesus taught and which the early church maintained until St. Paul introduced his complications of sacrament and dogma is not based upon any historical evidence."[3] Although the present writer's work on Paul has taken a somewhat different approach than that taken by Dr. Beare, or indeed most other Pauline scholars, it is interesting to see the extent to which a sequential use of the letters provides a picture of a dogmatic and sacramental church at a very, very early point, so early in fact that we may even speak in a limited sense of a dogmatic and sacramental Jesus.

---

1 F. W. Beare, "Jesus and Paul," *CJT* 5 (1959), 83. (Abbreviations in references are those used by the *Journal of Biblical Literature*. See *JBL 95* [1976], 331-346.)
2 A useful survey of the Jesus-Paul debate is provided by D. L. Dungan, *The Sayings of Jesus in the Churches of Paul* (Philadelphia: Fortress Press, 1971), xvii-xxix, who cites and supplements V. P. Furnish, "The Jesus-Paul Debate: From Baur to Bultmann," *BJRL* 47 (1965), 342-381.
3 Beare, "Jesus and Paul," 86.

ACTS AND THE STUDY OF PAUL'S
LETTERS

The first chapter of my book, *The Origin of 1 Corinthians*, was designed
to clear the way for an examination of that letter without the usual
preconceptions as to its relative or absolute date.[4] That chapter ended
by saying that its purpose had been

(i) To show how much the understanding of Paul's letters must rest on an
     understanding of the circumstances under which they were written.
(ii) To show how widespread among scholars today is a conventional recon-
     struction of these circumstances based on an uncritical use of the narrative
     of Acts.
(iii) To show how really unsound are the assumptions which underlie the usual
     dating and suggested sequence of Paul's letters.

To support this last assertion the chapter marshalled arguments to
show that

There is solid evidence that Acts is vague about chronological matters, incomplete in coverage, and built up of sources now probably beyond recovery. It
appears probable that its author had an incomplete knowledge of the events he
recounted, and, on the other hand, that he had a number of literary and
theological motivations which controlled the presentation of his materials.[5]

A set of extended footnotes and a special section of the bibliography
listed the dozens of scholars whose works exhibit this "unsound" use of
Acts as a basis for an interpretation of Paul.[6] I was therefore surprised
and a bit puzzled by the fact that reviewer after reviewer failed to take
issue with these basic assertions, either passing over them in silence or
indicating general agreement.

   I enlarged upon this theme in my contribution to the John Knox
Festschrift and argued that it is "an oversimplification to suggest that
scholars can be classified adequately simply by asking whether they
believe Acts to be (1) unreliable, (2) reliable, or (3) somewhat reliable"
as many scholars do.[7] There are many different ways by which historical value can be attributed or denied to Acts. For example, the reliability of the sequence of events in Acts may well be questioned but that of
individual pericopae maintained. No single credence quotient will do.
No single uniform attitude can be taken towards Acts any more than a
single index can control our use of the Synoptic Gospels.

   I argued further that a quantitative measure was in any case not
adequate to the problem, since there exists between Acts and Paul's

---

4 *The Origin of 1 Corinthians* (London: S.P.C.K., 1965), 3-42.
5 Ibid., 41-42.
6 Ibid., 299-305, 326-334.
7 "Pauline Chronology and Pauline Theology," in W. R. Farmer, C. F. D. Moule, and
   R. R. Neibuhr (eds.), *Christian History and Interpretation: Studies Presented to John Knox*
   (Cambridge: Cambridge University Press, 1967), 232.

letters a qualitative distinction: Acts is a secondary historical source whereas the letters are primary source material. What this distinction means is that we must hear the evidence of the letters first and from them try to recreate as comprehensive a picture of Paul as possible before turning to the evidence of Acts. The witnesses must be placed "on an agenda in such a way that the primary witnesses will give their evidence first, so that the evidence of the secondary witnesses will then be interpreted by it."[8] Between these two sections of the agenda should occur an intermission during which the primary evidence is examined, correlated, integrated, and synthesized as far as possible into an account of Paul's life and thought.

In the years since those words were published my gratification that the above arguments provoked no counterattack from reviewers has waned and my puzzlement has increased. It appears that, while there has been no disposition among scholars to contest these basic issues of method, neither has there been any inclination to abandon the traditional way by which Paul's life is understood on the basis of the narrative in Acts.[9] Books continue to appear on the chronology of Paul's life which base themselves almost entirely on the Acts narrative.[10] It seems as if the study of Acts by Acts scholars and the use of Acts by Pauline scholars have different goals and reach different conclusions![11]

The reason for insisting that Acts must be set aside while the evidence from the letters is fully examined is not because of any antipathy towards Luke, but because from the point of view of method it is the right thing to do. Scholars who hold a high view of the historical reliability of scripture should not object to this procedure, because they know beforehand that they will find Acts confirmed by Paul. My own reading of the letters, however, convinces me that taken alone the letters create a somewhat different picture than that provided by Acts.

---

8   Ibid., 233.
9   A recent example is J. A. T. Robinson, *Redating the New Testament* (London: SCM Press, 1976). He writes, "There can be no dispute that Paul writing in his own name is the primary witness, and the author of Acts, . . . a secondary witness" (33). He does not refer here to John Knox, myself, or C. H. Buck, but it is clear with whom he is in conversation, and their publications are cited in a general footnote two pages earlier. He continues, "When they conflict we are bound to prefer Paul. But most of the time they do not conflict." He then cites in support W. G. Kümmel, *Introduction to the New Testament* (2nd ed.; London: SCM Press, 1975), 254, and the latter's favourable citation of T. H. Campbell, "Paul's 'Missionary Journeys' as Reflected in his Letters" (*JBL* 74 [1955], 80-87), without any indication that the shortcomings of both Kümmel's and Campbell's position had been discussed in Hurd, "Pauline Chronology and Pauline Theology," 228-231 (which he cites in the note mentioned above). Robinson then concludes with the astounding words, "So we shall follow the procedure of trusting Acts until proved otherwise" (33-34)!
10   G. Ogg, *The Chronology of the Life of Paul* (London: Epworth Press, 1968); and J. J. Gunther, *Paul: Messenger and Exile—A Study in the Chronology of his Life and Letters* (Valley Forge, Pa.: Judson Press, 1972). Further, in spite of his protestations to the contrary, we should include R. Jewett, *A Chronology of Paul's Life* (Philadelphia: Fortress Press, 1979).
11   For bibliography see Dungan, *Sayings*, xxvii.

It is Acts and not the letters which creates the strong impression that
(*a*) all of Paul's letters were written relatively late in his career and that
(*b*) they were written in a relatively brief period. These chronological
conclusions are not harmless and do affect our understanding of Paul,
for they serve to justify and reinforce the assumption that Paul's letters
constitute a single pool of information from which we can draw out his
thoughts as required with little or no regard to the particular circumstances which occasioned each letter. Thus we turn to a consideration of the letters themselves.

PAUL'S WRITINGS AS LETTERS

As noted above, in my earlier work I took it as axiomatic that the
external and internal aspects of each letter should be related. In his
Chapters in a Life of Paul John Knox noted that writers about Paul's life
rely almost uniformly on the narrative of Acts and writers on Paul's
theology rely almost exclusively on his letters.[12] Further, as I noted in
my article on the sequence of Paul's letters, writers in these two areas
constitute two almost completely separate groups.[13] Writers on Paul's
life have a distrust of arguments based on development in his thought.
Writers on Paul's thought for the most part accept the chronological
impression created by Acts and show little concern for the circumstances surrounding the production of individual letters. As I said
in 1967, "At present it is as if there were in Pauline studies a wall
separating work on the 'introductory' matters and analysis of the
theological problems."[14] And I maintained, "The wall of separation
between Pauline chronology and Pauline theology must be breached if
the sources are to be studied with maximum results. . . . The outer and
the inner aspects of Paul's life must illuminate each other."[15]

Two years later the Society of Biblical Literature established a
five-year seminar to study the letter structure of Paul's writings. The
group addressed itself to the question, What does it mean for our
understanding of Paul that Paul wrote letters? The seminar gave birth
to a working group on epistolography, which has collected all examples
of Greek common letters and has continued the work begun by John
White in his published dissertation on the body of the Greek letter.[16]
The main seminar devoted its sessions to the analysis of five of Paul's
letters taken one at a time: Philemon, 1 Thessalonians, 1 Corinthians,
Galatians, and Romans. The seminar reached a consensus on a number
of points:

---

12 J. Knox, *Chapters in a Life of Paul* (New York: Abingdon-Cokesbury Press, 1950), 32.
13 "The Sequence of Paul's Letters," *CJT* 14 (1968), 193.
14 "Pauline Chronology and Pauline Theology," 247.
15 Ibid., 248.
16 J. White, *The Form and Function of the Body of the Greek Letter: A Study of the Letter-Body in
    the Non-Literary Papyri and in Paul the Apostle*, SBLDS 2 (Missoula, Mont.: Scholars
    Press, 1972).

(1) A number of epistolary formulae which served as conventional signals within the Greek common letter tradition reappear in Paul's writings. For example, the phrase *peri de* introduces the second and succeeding topics in the body of a letter dealing with a succession of issues.[17] Or again, *ou gar thelō hymas agnoein* indicates that the writer is introducing information which will be new to the recipients. There are formulae of introduction, thanksgiving, reproof, disclosure, request, transition, greeting, farewell—among others. Moreover, these formulae seem to have the same meaning for Paul as for other letter writers.

(2) Although Paul's letters are longer and more elaborate than most Greek common letters, they nevertheless exhibit many of the same structural features. The opening and the closing sections relate to past and future personal relationships. The central section is devoted to the business at hand. These major sections are themselves subdivided into elements that appear both in the common letter and in Paul. Thus the structure of Paul's letters reproduces the structure of the Greek common letter, although Paul has elaborated virtually every element to produce his own distinctive style.

(3) Further, the structural elements of the common letter have their own particular function and these functions also reappear in Paul's work. This fact means that an attempt to understand the meaning of a text from a Pauline letter must also include an analysis of its letter function. Thus the seminar was concerned not simply with "what" Paul said but also "how" he expressed himself.

(4) Just as each Greek common letter was part of a conversation between the sender and the recipient and reflected the immediate circumstances which caused the sender to write, so Paul's letters reflect an immediate occasion and conversational purpose. Thus external and internal matters are intimately connected. In addition to the "what" and "how" is the "why" of each letter.

Probably the most important implication of the work of this seminar is that each of Paul's letters must be considered individually. Each letter had a unique occasion. Each letter reflects a particular stage in the conversation between Paul and his converts. Thus the study of Paul's letters in the light of the common letter tradition leads us to the same conclusions maintained above that the inner and the outer aspects of Paul's writings must be kept together. The "why" and "how" are vitally important to the understanding of "what" Paul wrote.

THE SEQUENCE OF THE LETTERS

It may seem as though we have reached an impasse. On the one hand, it has been maintained that the historical reconstructions which have

---

17   Cf. C. E. Faw, "On the Writing of First Thessalonians," *JBL* 71 (1952), 221.

traditionally provided us with the external circumstances for the writing of Paul's letters are to be set aside. On the other hand, it is maintained that it is just these circumstances which are vitally necessary to an understanding of Paul's writing. The answer lies in the direction that John Knox has pointed. The letters taken individually and without reference to Acts must be examined for the information they can give us about events in Paul's career.[18] As is well known, Knox has identified two phases to Paul's work: (1) an extended missionary campaign which resulted in the foundation of the churches "from Jerusalem and as far round as Illyricum" (Rom. 15:19) and (2) a collection tour when he revisited his churches in the interest of "the poor among the saints at Jerusalem" (Rom. 15:26).[19] Knox locates the Apostolic Council between these two phases. As I pointed out in my article for the Knox *Festschrift*, his reconstruction taken as a whole is in many ways similar to other and more traditional reconstructions.[20] The vital difference, however, is the disappearance of Paul's "silent years," the eleven or fourteen years between Paul's first and second visits to Jerusalem. Instead, this period is filled with intense missionary activity.

Further, in my article, "The Sequence of Paul's Letters," I pointed out that when one summarizes the various suggestions by scholars based on evidence taken from the letters alone about the relative order in which two or more of Paul's letters were written, the result is a virtually unanimous sequence.[21] Paul's letters to the Thessalonians are taken to be his earliest surviving writings; then come the Previous Letter (see 1 Cor. 5:9), 1 Corinthians, Philippians, 2 Corinthians 1-9, Galatians, and Romans; his letters to Colossae, Philemon, and "Ephesus" are his last. The only substantial point of disagreement concerns the relative order of 2 Corinthians 1-9 and 10-13.[22]

There are, therefore, considerable grounds for confidence that the circumstances and contours of Paul's life can be recovered and that the occasions which immediately preceded the writing of his letters can be identified. Although the total reconstruction is not yet well advanced, it is not too optimistic to say (1) that the study of structure and letter occasions permits us to delineate the original letter units and (2) that these units, when read from the point of view of their relation to Paul's life, provide a more or less connected story. When we ask the letters to speak biographically, not just theologically, we are delighted to discover that answers do indeed appear.

---

18 *Chapters*, 47-60.
19 Ibid., 52-59.
20 "Pauline Chronology and Pauline Theology," 243-246.
21 "Sequence," 197-198.
22 There are also problems of genuineness for some scholars. Note that in the suggested sequence these problems occur at the ends, which is surely significant for further study.

THE THESSALONIAN LETTERS AND
1 CORINTHIANS

One of the most exciting aspects of the development sketched above is the freedom which it gives to the study of the Thessalonian letters. No longer is it necessary to think of 1 Thessalonians as having been written shortly after Paul founded the church in Thessalonica and escaped to Corinth. Once the impression created by Acts is removed, 1 Thessalonians can be treated on its own merits. The letter contains considerable evidence that significant time had elapsed between the founding of that church and the writing of the letter. As 1 Thess. 1:6-8 indicates, the Thessalonians had become missionaries both locally and in Achaia as well. Further, news of their work had travelled widely both within the Greek peninsula and elsewhere as well. In this period one or more members of the Thessalonian community had died, which created the pastoral problem to which Paul addressed himself in 1 Thess. 4:13-18. And there are other indications that time had elapsed.

Secondly, 2 Thessalonians is freed as well. The narrative of Acts does not seem to allow sufficient time between the founding of the Thessalonian church (Acts 17:1-10) and the ostensible point at which 1 Thessalonians was written (Acts 18:5) for any intervening correspondence. Therefore the general opinion is that 2 Thessalonians must have been written after 1 Thessalonians. Since 2 Thessalonians seems somewhat unlike Paul's later letters and since it has a number of points of similarity to 1 Thessalonians, it is generally believed that, if 2 Thessalonians is genuine, the interval between the two letters must have been brief. There have been, however, no satisfactory suggestions as to what led Paul to re-address the Thessalonians on many of the same topics but in such different tones. The dissimilarity of 2 Thessalonians to the other, later Pauline letters and its lack of obvious occasion have led some scholars to conclude that the letter is not Paul's. These scholars suggest that it is the work of a later writer who modelled it on 1 Thessalonians in order to arouse the apocalyptic fervour of a later generation. If, however, the Acts narrative is set aside, then the whole question of the meaning of 2 Thessalonians is reopened. Even when the hegemony of Acts was unquestioned, there were a number of scholars who had suggested that 2 Thessalonians should be understood as a letter written before 1 Thessalonians.[23] Now it is possible to examine this possibility afresh. It is the conviction of this writer that 2 Thessalonians was indeed written prior to 1 Thessalonians and that its dissimilarity to the later Pauline letters is due to its status as a primitive effort on Paul's part to administer his churches while absent. The apocalypticism which is characteristic of the letter can therefore be understood, not as a revival at a later time, but as evidence of the young

23   See *Origin*, 27, n. 1.

community's fervent expectation of an immediate end to this age. Paul attempted in 2 Thessalonians to clarify their expectations and account for the temporary failure of the Parousia to occur.

The effect of releasing 1 Corinthians from the Acts chronology is less dramatic than in the case of the Thessalonian letters. If 1 Corinthians is freed from the Gallio dating, it may drift somewhat earlier. Perhaps the collection is to be connected with the "famine in Judea" of 46 C.E.

More important, however, is the argument in my book which connects the Previous Letter of Paul to the Corinthians (1 Cor. 5:9-11) with 1 Thessalonians. The brief and pastoral affirmation of believers' resurrection at the time of the Parousia is just the sort of statement which we suggested was contained in the Previous Letter.[24] This statement then led to the objections and explanations which led to 1 Cor. 15. My identification of the stages which lie behind 1 Corinthians is in the main a codification of views which are widely held, although the reconstructed contents of these stages have by no means met with enthusiastic acceptance.[25]

When in my book I analyzed the structure of 1 Corinthians, I worked without the benefit of the insights gained by the SBL Paul Seminar. I hit on the expedient of separating the materials in 1 Corinthians on the basis of Paul's source of information, either oral reports or written communication. The result was a neat pattern: an introductory section (1:1-9), the treatment of a series of oral reports (1:10-6:11), a transition passage (6:12-20), responses to a series of matters raised by a letter from Corinth (7:1-16:12), and a final series of greetings (16:13-24). Within the Paul Seminar, however, my assignment was to examine the structure of 1 Thessalonians. To my surprise I discovered that this letter seemed to fit the same pattern as 1 Corinthians: an introductory section (1:1-10), a treatment of oral information (2:1-3:10), a transition passage (3:11-13), treatment of a series of more or less unrelated topics (4:1-5:11), and concluding exhortations and greetings (5:12-28). The similarity in the structure of 1 Thessalonians and 1 Corinthians led me to argue that 1 Thessalonians was, like 1 Corinthians, Paul's response to a letter he had received. Further, as C. E. Faw had already noted, the abrupt changes in topic in 1 Thess. 4-5 and the use of the *peri de* formula constitute a further similarity to 1 Corinthians and additional evidence that 1 Thessalonians is a reply letter.[26]

When we relate the sequence of stages which preceded 1 Thessalonians to those which preceded 1 Corinthians, we arrive at the following scheme:

---

24   *Origin*, 231-233.
25   For example, W. G. Kümmel, "phantastisch" (review of *Origin* in *TLZ* 91 [1966], 507a).
26   "Writing of 1 Thessalonians," 221.

Thessalonian Church	Corinthian Church
T-1 Founding Visit	
	C-1 Founding Visit[27]
T-2 *2 Thessalonians*	
. . . .	
T-3 Letter from Thessalonians	
T-4 *1 Thessalonians*	C-2 Previous Letter[28]
	C-3 Corinthian Reply Letter
	C-4 *1 Corinthians*

The Thessalonian data, therefore, serve to expand our knowledge of the events in the earliest period of Paul's missionary work.

WHAT DOES EARLY MEAN?

In *The Origin of 1 Corinthians* I argued that in 1 Cor. 15:51 Paul indicated his conviction that the death of Christians before the Parousia was exceptional and that the normal expectation for Christians was that they would survive to see the return of their Lord.[29] Whether or not this interpretation is accepted, the verse clearly falls within the first Christian generation. I argued further that 1 Thess. 4:13-18 is Paul's earliest surviving statement concerning the resurrection of Christians at the time of the Parousia and that his original preaching at Thessalonica and Corinth had not contained any such message.[30] Rather, it seems likely that Paul led his first converts in Macedonia and Achaia to expect that they would themselves survive to greet their returning Lord. It seems unlikely that a significant number of deaths had occurred in Christian communities founded prior to those in Macedonia and Achaia, for if so Paul could hardly have failed to anticipate the death of Christians in his original preaching in these provinces. We are therefore in a very early period of Christian history. The above table, therefore, may well go back to within a few years of Jesus' crucifixion.[31]

---

27 Phil. 4:15-16 seems to indicate that Paul's initial missionary tour progressed from Philippi to Thessalonica. Taken with 2 Cor. 11:9 the implication is that the original Corinthian mission followed his work in Macedonia.

28 The Previous Letter and 1 Thessalonians may be dated from the same general period on the basis of Paul's eschatology, but 1 Thessalonians contains no mention of the Collection and therefore should be placed a bit earlier than the Previous Letter. See *Origin*, 233, n. 2.

29 Ibid., 230, n. 1.

30 Ibid., 229-233, 282-283.

31 The early positioning of 2 Thessalonians makes it possible to re-open the question of the connection between the crisis which lies behind 2 Thessalonians and the events at the close of Caligula's reign (40-41 C.E.). Although occasionally such a connection has been suggested, the placing of 1 Thessalonians at Acts 18:5 and the dating of Gallio (Acts 18:12-17) in 51-52 C.E. have prevented serious examination of this possibility. See the discussion in M. Dibelius, *Die Geisterwelt im Glauben des Paulus* (Göttingen: Vandenhoeck, 1909), 57-61.

If early dates for the founding of Paul's congregations in Macedonia and Achaia can be considered a reasonable possibility, an interesting and important new prospect appears. In discussing the "Jesus-Paul" question David Dungan quite rightly notes that in attempting to relate Paul to Jesus the collecting of parallels between Paul's letters and the Synoptic Gospels is "no help, for it is plain that *they* [the Gospels] *also are records of the words and commands of the Lord* and not what we would term collections of the sayings of the historical Jesus."[32] Dungan finds that these two types of post-resurrection tradition illuminate each other and together help in the process of recovering the sayings of Jesus. It now appears possible, however, that Paul is more than a point of comparison with the developing Synoptic tradition: his writings may themselves form a bridge between the very earliest days and the period just prior to the Synoptic Gospels. Form critics recreate from these gospels the process by which the traditions about Jesus took the form in which we know them as they passed through the reconstructed life of the early church. If early dates for Paul's first letters are accepted, the Pauline corpus itself would then embody an independent and parallel line of development.

Since the chronological considerations outlined above affect most radically the early end of Paul's career, we turn now to consider Paul's earliest preaching and its implications for our knowledge of Jesus.

TOPICS IN PAUL'S ORIGINAL PREACHING

The final chapter of *The Origin of 1 Corinthians* deals with a series of matters which, I suggested, formed part of Paul's first preaching in Corinth. This material can now be amplified with the evidence of the Thessalonian correspondence.

Apocalypticism

The theme which most clearly belonged to Paul's primitive teaching is apocalypticism. The earlier one moves in the literary sequence outlined above the more apocalyptic is the material. It is clear, for example, that the Corinthians had been instructed by Paul on his founding visit that they would participate in the judgment of the world: "Do you not know that the saints will judge the world?" (1 Cor. 6:2). They are also to "judge angels" (6:3). Their expectation was that they would enter the Kingdom living and in this new age watch as their Lord destroyed "every rule and every authority and power" (1 Cor. 15:24) and put "all his enemies under his feet" (15:25). At the close of the Kingdom death would be destroyed (15:26) and the general resurrection would take

---

32   Dungan, *Sayings*, xxx (italics his).

place. Then the world would be judged. With this picture of the future we may compare Matt. 19:28//Luke 22:30, where the disciples will "sit on twelve thrones, judging the twelve tribes of Israel."

Further, the Thessalonians had originally been instructed that "the day of the Lord will come like a thief in the night" (1 Thess. 5:2). With this we may compare Matt. 24:43//Luke 12:39, "If the householder had known in what part of the night the thief was coming, he would have been awake and would not have let his house be broken into. Therefore you also must be ready; for the Son of Man is coming at an hour that you do not expect."

Although its authenticity is disputed, 2 Thessalonians fits well into this picture. If genuine, 2 Thess. 2:3-4, 9, 10 provides a snapshot of Paul's original teaching to the Thessalonians on these topics:

That day will not come, unless the rebellion comes first, and the man of lawlessness is revealed, the son of perdition who opposes and exalts himself against every so-called god or object of worship, so that he takes his seat in the temple of God, proclaiming himself to be God. . . . The coming of the lawless one by the activity of Satan will be with all power and with pretended signs and wonders, and with all wicked deception for those who are to perish.

The parallels with the synoptic apocalypse are obvious:

Take heed that no one leads you astray. Many will come in my name, saying, "I am he!" and they will lead many astray. And when you hear of wars and rumors of wars, do not be alarmed. . . . For nation will rise against nation, and kingdom against kingdom; there will be earthquakes in various places, there will be famines; this is but the beginning of the birthpangs. . . . But when you see the desolating sacrilege set up where it ought not to be . . . then let those who are in Judea flee to the mountains. . . . And then if anyone says to you, "Look, here is the Christ!" or "Look, there he is!" do not believe it. False Christs and false prophets will arise and show signs and wonders, to lead astray, if possible, the elect. . . .

But in those days, after that tribulation, the sun will be darkened, and the moon will not give its light, and the stars will be falling from heaven, and the powers in the heavens will be shaken. And then they will see the Son of man coming in clouds with great power and glory. And then he will send out the angels, and gather his elect from the four winds, from the ends of the earth to the ends of heaven (Mark 13:5-27).

At no point in his letters does Paul give a systematic account of his expectations for the end of the age and the ensuing Kingdom. There are, however, numerous allusions to such a picture. From them we may conclude that Paul preached an apocalyptic message that had parallels with and was dependent on traditions he had received and that was similar at many points to the teaching attributed to Jesus in the synoptic apocalypse. We will consider below the question of the extent to which that type of doctrine may be assigned to Jesus himself and content ourselves for the moment simply by noting parallels.

In-group vs. Out-group

The apocalyptic hope sketched above carries with it a sociological corollary: the believing community must distinguish itself from the general population. This need leads to a sectarian mentality in which the believers find their religious and social life in a more or less closed community. Their group cohesiveness is reinforced by real or imagined hostility from the world outside (cf. 2 Thess. 1:6-7; 1 Thess. 1:6; 2:14). This community consciousness is evidenced in Paul's outraged question, "When one of you has a grievance against a brother, does he dare to go to law before the unrighteous instead of the saints?" (1 Cor. 6:1). The functions of society are to be assumed by the community as far as possible. For example, the Thessalonian letters give evidence that some members of that church were not supporting themselves and were dependent on the community for support. Paul directed, "If anyone will not work, let him not eat. For we hear that some of you are living in idleness, mere busybodies, not doing any work. Now such persons we command and exhort in the Lord Jesus Christ to do their work in quietness and to earn their own living" (2 Thess. 3:10-12; cf. 1 Thess. 5:14). It appears that the primitive community had pooled at least a portion of its capital resources and had established its own charitable service for the benefit of its widows and poor. This charity was being abused by some who were able to support themselves but who had thrown up their jobs, presumably because of eschatological excitement. In this regard the Thessalonians were obeying gospel precepts, for the gospels abound with exhortations to poverty and the renunciation of everything for the sake of the Kingdom. Numerous synoptic sayings decry the possession of riches.

Lord's Supper

By the use of the formula, "I received from the Lord what I also delivered to you," Paul indicates that his tradition concerning the eucharist was part of his original preaching and antedated his own conversion (1 Cor. 11:23-26). Paul takes this practice to be in direct continuity with that of Jesus and his disciples. He indicates that he thinks of this remembrance as an eschatological proclamation of "the Lord's death until he comes" (1 Cor. 11:26).

The meal, therefore, was not only a memorial but also an anticipation of the Messianic Banquet to which "many will come from east and west and sit at table with Abraham, Isaac, and Jacob" (Matt. 8:11//Luke 13:28-29). In the Kingdom there will be no hunger (Matt. 5:6//Luke 6:21). Paul was incensed that the Corinthians had, as he believed, lost sight of this aspect of their common meal: "When you meet together, it is not the Lord's supper that you eat. For in eating, each one goes ahead with his own meal, and one is hungry and another is drunk" (1 Cor. 11:20-21).

We have no way of knowing whether Jesus was in the habit of gathering his disciples in meals having special significance, but he did so on at least one occasion. We find the same meal fellowship in Paul's early communities.

Ethics

Nothing is clearer than that the controlling principle for Paul's ethics in the early period was love. 1 Cor. 13 is simply one expression among many of this fact. The argument concerning the weaker brother in 1 Cor. 8 rests on love as the motivating principle. The triad, "faith," "hope," "love," appears in 1 Thess. 1:3, and 5:8. It is significant that Paul indicates that instruction on love was part of his earliest preaching when he says, "But concerning love of the brethren you have no need to have anyone write to you, for you yourselves have been taught by God to love one another" (1 Thess. 4:9). "Taught by God" is a unique expression in Paul's letters and points very probably to the summary of the law as found, for example, in Mark 12:31.

Paul's later attitude toward the Law as expressed in letters to the Galatians and the Romans is well known. But the germ of this freedom goes back to a very early point in Paul's preaching. In 1 Cor. 6:12; 10:23 Paul wrote, "All things are lawful." I have argued that this slogan is a quotation from the Corinthians' letter to Paul and is therefore correctly placed within quotation marks as in the RSV, for example.[33] And I have further argued that the Corinthians in turn were taught this slogan by Paul in his first preaching in Corinth.[34] Thus they quote Paul against himself in their opposition to any rule that they should avoid eating idol meat. By this slogan it is clear that Paul did not mean lawless behaviour but a higher state in which the law was, as it were, written on the heart and practised instinctively. He is far from believing that unethical or immoral behaviour is now to be condoned. So also in the gospels we find at many points Jesus making distinctions within the legal tradition by appealing beyond the law to God's intention or, we may say, the spirit of the law. Further there are many synoptic passages in which Jesus is criticized by religious leaders for his failure to observe the Law.

Immoral Men

Although Paul in his earliest preaching sharply distinguished the Christian community from the world around them, it appears that he did not fear contact with non-Christians. Indeed, he even seems to have allowed his converts to eat idol meat whether sold in the market place (1 Cor. 10:25) or served by a pagan host (10:27). He seems to have

---

33 *Origin*, 67-68, 119-126.
34 Ibid., 278-279.

believed that he and his converts were endowed with a certain immunity that would protect them from the immorality of the world, from hostile powers, and even from death itself. I have suggested that Paul considered that the regular reception of the Lord's body and blood constituted the "medicine of immortality" which would hold sin at bay and preserve the Christian until the Parousia.[35] Whatever the details, it does appear that Paul and his converts held a strenuous, enthusiastic form of faith supported, no doubt, by their apocalyptic hope. In parallel fashion we find in the Synoptic Gospels that Jesus is frequently criticized by his opponents for his seeming casualness about matters of purity, diet, and religious caste. "The Son of man came eating and drinking, and they say, 'Behold, a glutton and a drunkard, a friend of tax collectors and sinners!'" (Matt. 11:19//Luke 7:34).

Missionary Urgency

Coupled with Paul's belief in the nearness of the end of the age was his conviction that the time for the conversion of the Gentiles had arrived. Although a Jew by birth and training, he directed his missionary activity to the Gentiles, travelling through the main population centres within his ambit. To his converts he left the work of spreading the gospel into the surrounding countryside (1 Thess. 1:6-8). Later, as the Parousia tarried, Paul seems to have enlarged his endeavours. John Knox maintains that when Romans was written Paul intended to extend his missionary work beyond the quadrant stretching from Jerusalem to Illyricum and to travel to Rome, then Spain, and finally to return to Jerusalem through North Africa having reached the full number of Gentile nations.[36]

R. H. Lightfoot has argued that Jesus' cleansing of the Temple by expelling the money changers was his attempt to prepare a place for the Gentile nations to worship in anticipation of the end of this age.[37] In any case, the eschatological missionary fervour seems to be characteristic of the traditions attributed to Jesus: "You will not have gone through all the towns of Israel, before the Son of Man comes" (Matt. 10:23).

Life in the Kingdom

Paul and his early converts seem to have believed that in a preliminary fashion they were living as though in the Kingdom. As noted above, their common meal was in anticipation of the messianic banquet. It has also been suggested above that they considered that the power of death had been abolished within their own number. Further, it appears that

---

35   Ibid., 286.
36   "Romans 15: 14-33 and Paul's Conception of His Apostolic Mission," *JBL* 83 (1964), 1-11.
37   *The Gospel Message of St. Mark* (Oxford: Oxford University Press, 1950), 60-69.

sexual distinctions were set aside. Women as well as men exercised leadership in these early communities. At a later point (1 Cor. 11:5-10) Paul criticized the failure of some Corinthian women to wear veils while praying or prophesying, but he assumed the validity of their ministry. In his discussion of marriage Paul exhibits a balance between the rights of husband and wife remarkable for his time (1 Cor. 7:2-4). Further, I have argued that there was a considerable amount of marital asceticism in Paul's earliest communities, both as a form of discipline for those already married at the time of their conversion and in the form of spiritual marriages for those who married afterwards.[38] With his attitude may be compared the saying, "When they rise from the dead, they neither marry nor are given in marriage, but are like angels in heaven" (Mark 12:25).

Words of the Lord

Twice in his letters Paul uses the expression, "I delivered to you . . . what I also received," quoted above. It is interesting to notice that both occurrences are in 1 Corinthians (1 Cor. 11:23; 15:3). Further, Paul at four points in his letters refers to sayings "of the Lord" (1 Thess. 4:15; 1 Cor. 7:10; 9:14; 11:23). Clearly, he must have known more such traditions, and indeed in 1 Cor. 7:12 and 7:25 he specifically prevents any possible assumption on the Corinthians' part that his advice on mixed marriages and on virgins was part of the tradition he inherited. Notice again that these six references are all in 1 Thessalonians and 1 Corinthians. A. M. Hunter adopts the suggestion of H. A. A. Kennedy that this concentration occurs because 1 Corinthians is "the only letter in which a number of practical questions affecting the life and organization of the church were dealt with."[39] This explanation is hardly satisfying, however. Church organization is hardly a prominent topic in the tradition stemming from Jesus. Moreover, all Paul's letters deal with the life of the church. Some at least of the many implicit parallels that Hunter and others have collected between Paul's letters and gospel tradition are occasions on which Paul could have cited the authority of his Lord directly. Why only in 1 Corinthians and 1 Thessalonians?

In addition, we may recall the major parallels between 2 Thessalonians and the synoptic apocalypse. Paul specifically designated this material as given to the Thessalonians on his founding visit. Moreover, we may note the formula *ouk oidate hoti* used six or seven times in 1 Corinthians to remind the church of his original preaching and never

---

38 *Origin*, 274-278.
39 Hunter, *Paul and His Predecessors* (rev. ed.; London: SCM, 1961), 51, citing Kennedy, *The Theology of the Epistles*, Studies in Theology (London: Duckworth, 1919), 103.

used in this way in any later letter.[40] In 1 Thessalonians Paul repeatedly said, "You yourselves know," to remind them of his first teaching.[41]

It seems best to say simply that these are the early letters and in them Paul is more conscious of the tradition he received from those who were in Christ before him and more aware that his own first preaching was in direct continuity with theirs.[42]

DISCONTINUITIES AND DIFFERENCES

We must not close without considering the major difference between the situation of Paul and that of Jesus' first followers. The major event which separated them is the experience by the early church of Jesus' resurrection. The early church believed that in this event God had revealed the identity of his "Son of Man," who was to bring in the new age. The Son of Man eschatology of the synoptic tradition becomes in Paul the expectation of the Parousia of the Lord Jesus Christ. The clouds, the angels, and all the rest of the imagery is the same in both expectations. But there is an important difference. Sayings are repeatedly attributed to Jesus that "no sign will be given to this generation" (Mark 8:12; Matt. 16:4; 12:39; Luke 11:29). Paul, on the other hand, explicitly listed the signs which must precede the advent of the Lord. Jesus' futuristic eschatology has become in Paul a full-blown apocalypticism. What has caused the change? It seems reasonable to assume that the earliest church understood the resurrection of Jesus to be the great sign that God had at last initiated the final sequence of events which would culminate in the arrival of the Lord Jesus Christ from heaven. Jesus' resurrection had its impact on the early church, not because the idea of resurrection was unexpected but because the time of his resurrection was unexpected. Jesus was resurrected ahead of time, that is, ahead of the general resurrection. The reason for this anticipation, the earliest Christians concluded, was because God had designated Jesus as the one who was to bring in the new age. The victory of his enemies was only temporary. At this moment he was gathering reinforcements and would return with an army of angels to wreak vengeance on those who had oppressed him and his followers. In this context it was only natural for at least some of the traditional apocalyptic signs of the end to be included in the expectations of the young communities. Thus, prior to the apocalypticism of Paul the apostle stands the futuristic eschatology of Jesus. The major difference

---

40 See *Origin*, 85. The only reference outside of 1 Corinthians is Rom. 6:16, which refers to a matter of common knowledge.
41 1 Thess. 2:1; 3:3; 5:2; cf. 4:2, 9.
42 Hunter also called attention to what he called the "guarded tradition" and from Paul's letters he cited 2 Thess. 2:15 and 1 Cor. 11:2 (*Paul*, 22). We may contrast Phil. 3:16, "Let us hold true to what we have attained." The guarded tradition may not have lasted as long as Hunter hoped (23).

between the two is the conviction on Paul's part that the identity of the mysterious "Son of Man" is now known to be "the Lord Jesus Christ."

CONCLUSION

The traditional use of Acts as the historical background to Paul's letters has caused the letters to be thought of as a more or less unified corpus of texts written within a relatively brief span of years. The effect has been to submerge the distinctive characteristics of Paul's earliest thought and writings. When the letters are allowed to speak individually and in an open sequence, a picture of Paul's earliest communities arises which is strikingly similar in many ways to the practices and teachings of Jesus as remembered by his earliest followers.[43] In particular, Paul provides important evidence of the futuristic nature of Jesus' eschatology. Taking account of the difference noted above, the eschatology of Paul and his converts on the one hand and of Jesus and his followers on the other are continuous. Further, a notable number of beliefs and practices—dogmas and sacraments, if you will—in Paul's earliest communities show signs of being in conscious continuity with those of Jesus. It is noteworthy that these signs of continuity occur in the earlier Pauline letters. Later events caused Paul to modify and refine his early beliefs, and as a result the specific dependence on Jesus' teaching no longer lies on the surface. Thus we may view Paul's writings, not as an island located rather closer to the synoptic authors than to Jesus, but as an isthmus which in a real sense connects the period of Jesus' ministry with the theologies of the synoptic authors and of the later church.

---

43   It is ironic that J. A. T. Robinson, *Redating*, has argued for earlier dates for all the NT writings *except* Paul's letters (if we exclude the Pastoral epistles)! He has missed the major weakness of the prevailing NT chronology.

The Thunderbolt in Q and the Wise Man in Corinth*

PETER RICHARDSON

In his recent *magnum opus* on Matthew, Professor Frank Beare comments on the development of gospel sources as follows:

It is likely that notes of some kind were prepared for the use of teachers and preachers as they moved from place to place to spread the gospel message. It is not too bold a conjecture that the need of written materials increased as the mission spread beyond the ranks of the Jewish people into areas of Gentile population, and especially to Greek-speaking people who would not be acquainted with the Aramaic of Palestine.[1]

This is a lucid and probably correct statement of conditions in the earliest Christian period. To this I wish to add one other conjecture, perhaps also not too bold, that early Christian teachers and preachers differed in their view of those sayings. This conjecture is developed by looking at the relationship between one synoptic pericope and an important section of 1 Corinthians. Some peculiarities in 1 Cor. 1:17-2:16, and its place in the letter body (1:10-4:21) had attracted my attention in the course of a larger study of that letter. This paper focuses upon the relationship between that section and Luke 10:21-

* Research on this paper was begun with the assistance of a grant from the Social Sciences and Humanities Research Council of Canada that allowed a stay in Israel and Greece. The facilities and co-operation of the Ecole Biblique et Archéologique in Jerusalem and of the American School of Classical Studies in Athens are gratefully acknowledged.

1 F. W. Beare, *The Gospel According to Matthew: A Commentary* (Oxford: Basil Blackwell, 1981), 44.

24//Matt. 11:25-27 plus Matt. 13:16-17, which I shall for convenience refer to as the *Jubelruf* or the thunderbolt.

In the study of the gospels, particularly the formation of the gospels in successive layers, the question of their development within the context of the mission of the Church is often neglected. There is a rather strong tendency to separate epistolary developments and the history reflected there from gospel developments. While there is some evidence of interest in the integration of gospel and epistolary history, it is by no means a dominant concern today.[2] To put the question too baldly: Did the circumstances of the Pauline mission, about which we know a good bit, have any bearing on the development of gospel traditions? The usual answer, of course, is no.

Professor Beare summarizes the situation well: "There is nothing in the Letters of Paul, the only literature that survives from the first Christian generation, to suggest that he ever heard of such a collection" (viz. of sayings of Jesus).[3] If one presumes the spread of written materials, Paul's presumed lack of knowledge of such collections would need an explanation. If by this statement Professor Beare means that Paul does not allude to the availability of a collection of Jesus' sayings, he is absolutely correct. But if he means that there is no evidence of Paul having some knowledge of sayings of Jesus, perhaps in a collected form, Professor Beare's conclusion is not quite so sure, for, as he goes on to point out, Paul occasionally refers to a word of the Lord—whatever that may mean.[4]

Professor Beare notes specifically the "parallel thought" between the *Jubelruf* in Matt. 11:25-26 and Paul's statements in 1 Cor. 1:20, 26-29.[5] Matt. 11:27, the "meteorite from the Johannine heaven . . . is undoubtedly a theological (christological) composition from the hand of an unknown mystic of the early church" and is likely a fragment of incipient Gnosticism.[6] He does not, however, hint at any explicit connection between 1 Corinthians and the Q tradition.

There is a general willingness (at least among those who accept the Q-hypothesis) to believe that Q shows a particular concern for—or,

---

2 See, for example, J. P. Brown, "Synoptic Parallels in the Epistles and Form History," *NTS* 10 (1963), 27-48. (Abbreviations in references are those used by the *Journal of Biblical Literature*. See *JBL* 95 [1976], 331-346.) H. Koester ("The Structure and Criteria of Early Christian Beliefs," in *Trajectories Through Early Christianity* [Philadelphia: Fortress, 1971], 205-231) makes a suggestive association between wisdom, Q, Paul, Apollos, Corinth, and 1 Cor. 1-4 (222-223). From a different perspective D. L. Dungan, *The Sayings of Jesus in the Churches of Paul* (Philadelphia: Fortress, 1971), makes a major contribution to this question; see especially his conclusions, pp. 139-150.

3 Beare, *Matthew*, 20.

4 Ibid.; cf. also P. Richardson, "'I say not the Lord': Personal Opinion, Apostolic Authority and the Development of Early Christian Halakah," *Tyndale Bulletin* 31 (1980), 65-86.

5 Beare, *Matthew*, 265-266.

6 Ibid. The famous phrase is von Hase's.

perhaps better, acceptance of—the gentile mission of the Church, and that Q's view of Israel presupposes the acceptance by a number of Gentiles of the good news of Jesus.[7] Is it possible to go beyond that descriptive statement and claim that Q is in some sense or other a "gospel" to the Gentiles and was used in the gentile mission? If that were the case it would neatly fit the situation described so well by Professor Beare (above). It may not be accidental, for example, that Q's way of relating Gentile acceptance of Jesus and Israel's rejection resonates with Paul's, at least as that is expressed in Romans 11.

But Q is only one early stage in the development of the Gospels. Another stage may be represented by what Streeter dubbed Proto-Luke—the view that this Q material was combined with other Lukan material to form a coherent Gospel.[8] Such a resultant "gospel" would have combined an existing catechetical collection of Jesus' sayings with other important narrative and polemical material. In particular it would have included, perhaps for the first time, a passion narrative and resurrection account to form a more "balanced" record of what Jesus said and did. Such a thesis should, as Streeter long ago claimed, be able to be substantiated or falsified, though it seems to have been more neglected than refuted, no doubt because of the important agenda of Form and Redaction criticism.[9] Perhaps it should be examined again in the light of the developments since Streeter and Taylor.[10]

That is not the purpose here. But the questions bear tangentially on this contribution to the debate on the relation of Jesus and Paul. One possible motive for a revised "gospel" such as Proto-Luke would represent is the perceived deficiency of Q as an authoritative collection of material about Jesus. If the author of Proto-Luke were Luke, Paul's companion, its major difference from Q is readily explicable: he incorporates the passion narrative with its strong testimony to the cross and resurrection, an element essential to the Pauline "gospel." What is

---

7 See especially P. D. Meyer, "The Gentile Mission in Q," *JBL* 89 (1970), 405-417. For a broad survey of studies in Q, see R. D. Worden, "Redaction Criticism of Q: A Survey," *JBL* 94 (1975), 532-46, and literature cited there.

8 B. H. Streeter, *The Four Gospels: A Study of Origins* (London: Macmillan, 1924), especially 199-222. The hypothesis originally appeared in the *Hibbert Journal*, October, 1921.

9 Much the most interesting recent study is by Lloyd Gaston, *No Stone on Another: Studies in the Significance of the Fall of Jerusalem in the Synoptic Gospels* (Leiden: Brill, 1970), esp. 224-256.

10 V. Taylor, *Behind the Third Gospel: A Study of the Proto-Luke Hypothesis* (Oxford: Clarendon, 1926), was Streeter's most important follower. It would seem that the hypothesis came at exactly the wrong moment to be considered seriously. Frequently alluded to, it has not been thoroughly examined, for it came at the tail end of the concern for source critical questions, when that approach had been exhausted, and in the midst of the excitement over form criticism. Perhaps it is time to return to some of the source critical questions, for fresh attention to these might change significantly the way in which some of the redaction critical studies are being pursued. Specifically, consideration of the Proto-Luke hypothesis might call for a fundamental revision of Lukan redactional studies.

more, in a few detailed features, at least, these accounts are distinctly "Pauline" (especially in the institution of the last supper and the absence of resurrection appearances to women).

These questions about the development of the Gospels shape the paper that follows, though they will not be attacked directly. What follows approaches one Q pericope and one important section in 1 Corinthians to see how far there might be evidence for some influence of Q in 1 Corinthians. It builds especially upon, but diverges from, a recent study of 1 Corinthians by Biörn Fjärstedt.[11]

We may begin by noting three important factors, factors which I dare to think are interlocking and significant. First, there are obvious points of contact between Paul's discussion of wise men—and wisdom—in Corinth and the famous meteorite from the Johannine sky. This similarity is particularly noteworthy in the opening parts of Paul's discussion in 1 Cor. 1:17-25.[12] Second, the immediate context of this discussion in 1 Corinthians is Paul's analysis of the divisions in Corinth and his identification of important differences between himself and others, differences that focus on baptism and the cross. The question of "wisdom" follows directly on from those emphases and is the major item on Paul's agenda as he carries on a dispute with his "opponents." Third, the foremost "opponent" in the Corinthian context is Apollos. It appears from the Acts evidence that Apollos is baptized by John, and Acts implies that Apollos fits into the wisdom tradition. The context of the thunderbolt—in Matthew at least—is other Q material dealing with John the Baptist and Jesus.[13] So one question that prompts itself is whether the material in 1 Cor. 1-2 overlaps with the thunderbolt in Q because that tradition is known and used by both Paul and Apollos. To put it more bluntly, is it possible that Q, which has a special interest in John the Baptist and in wisdom questions and has, it appears, no passion narrative, has reached Ephesus and has influenced the group with which Apollos was as-

---

11   B. Fjärstedt, *Synoptic Tradition in 1 Corinthians: Themes and Clusters of Theme Words in 1 Cor. 1-4 and 9* (Uppsala: Uppsala Teologiska Institutionen, 1974).

12   See the suggestive analysis by M. Jack Suggs, *Wisdom, Christology and Law in Matthew's Gospel* (Cambridge, Mass.: Harvard University Press, 1970), esp. 71-86. He quotes Harnack approvingly: "Whenever I read 1 Cor. 1:19, 21 . . . I am ever again struck by the coincidence here, both in thought and vocabulary, with [Mt. 11:25-26] though all of course has been passed through the crucible of Paul's mind" (Harnack, *Sayings of Jesus*, 301). Cf. also A. M. Hunter, "Crux Criticorum—Matt. 11:25-30—A Reappraisal," *NTS* 8 (1961-62), 241-249; F. W. Beare, *Earliest Records of Jesus* (Nashville: Abingdon, 1962), 89-90.

13   In the Matthean order of Q, Matt. 11:2-6//Luke 7:18-23 raises the question, asked by John's disciples, whether Jesus is the Coming One. It includes the statement "blessed is he who is not scandalized by me" (cf. 1 Cor. 1:23). The following pericope, Matt. 11:17-19//Luke 7:24-35 and 16:16, deals with Jesus' view of John, containing the important statement that "there is no one greater in the Kingdom of Heaven than John" (cf. 1 Cor. 4:20?). It also includes references to "children" and to "wisdom." Then come the Woes (Matt. 11:20-24//Luke 10:13-15) with the reference to "mighty works" (cf. 1 Cor. 4:19-20; 2:4-5; 1:18, 24).

sociated in ways that run contrary to Paul's understanding of the gospel?

To put this essay in context, it might be noted that recent studies of 1 Cor. 1-2 have tended increasingly to see these chapters as fitting into the conceptual world of hellenistic Jewish wisdom speculation.[14] Other recent studies have sought, on the contrary, to demonstrate that some of the concepts of these chapters are drawn from the teaching of Jesus, especially from the Q-traditions.[15] Both claims may well be true, and for two quite different reasons. On the one hand Jesus may himself be influenced by the speculations about wisdom in hellenistic Judaism. On the other hand—and more relevant to this paper—there may be a connection between the use of the Q-traditions and Jewish wisdom speculation in the person of Paul's opponent.

<hr>

LINKS BETWEEN 1 CORINTHIANS 1-2 AND THE *JUBELRUF*

<hr>

In a sometimes-too-clever piece of detection Fjärstedt has analyzed two large sections of 1 Corinthians and has conjectured that Paul "knows a type of tradition which has been handed down in an early church context and got its final place in the present synoptic gospels."[16] To a large extent, he claims, what Paul knows is the Q-tradition. Fjärstedt's method involves the preparation of tables showing the overlapping of theme words in 1 Corinthians with specific synoptic pericopes. The clusters of words are often impressive, and his conclusion (to his analysis of 1 Cor. 9) is that they "must point to some shared knowledge," specifically to synoptic-like traditions which need to be sufficiently well known for the allusions Paul makes to them to be understood. He believes that Paul uses this allusive form to raise question marks in the hearers' mind which will prompt them to discover—in the synoptic materials—Paul's meaning.[17]

When he turns to 1 Cor. 1-4, Fjärstedt first analyzes the relation between 1 Cor. 4 and Luke 16:1-5,[18] as well as Luke 12:35-38, Matt. 25:31-46, and Matt. 5:1-16. He then compares 1 Cor. 1:17-2:16 with Luke 10:21-24,[19] and following that with Matt. 12:38-42. He concludes:

<hr>

14 In several articles this point has been developed by R. A. Horsley (especially his "Wisdom of Word and Words of Wisdom in Corinth," *CBQ* 39 [1977], 224-239), who sees Apollos as a rather important factor in the Corinthian setting.

15 For example, Fjärstedt, *Synoptic Tradition*.

16 Ibid., 173.

17 Ibid., 96-97.

18 Ibid., chap. 6. He has a unique solution to the troublesome phrase "not beyond what is written" on pp. 118-119, where he relates the phrase to the Parable of the Unjust Steward. It demonstrates clearly the weakness of relying as much as he does on hints and allusions to synoptic passages to reveal Paul's *true* meaning.

19 Ibid., 139-153. He argues, convincingly I believe, that the connection between Paul and the *Jubelruf* is not just a common reference to the Hebrew scriptures (146).

The stream of information runs very fast with new images, significant words and combinations of words. There is no argument, really, in spite of the fact that very essential subjects are touched upon. . . . The vocabulary can in many cases be found to have a background in well known OT passages, but a closer look at the passages reveal [sic] that the synoptic type of material already has similar collocations of words and that Paul, in fact comes close to passages in the synoptics.[20]

Following that he compares 1 Cor. 3 with Matt. 21:33-46 and with 1 Peter 2:1-12, then with Luke 6:47-49, Matt. 10:40-42, Luke 17:22-37, and Matt. 13:24-30, 36-43.

Fjärstedt's tables of comparisons, amended here for easier comparison, includes the following points of contacts between 1 Cor. 1:17-2:16 and Luke 10:21-24, which he feels is the closer connection.

Luke [Matthew]	1 Corinthians
sophōn	*sophian tōn sophōn* (1:19)
sunetōn	*sunesin tōn sunetōn* (1:19)
eudokia	*eudokēsen* (1:21)
oudeis [epi]ginōskei	*ouk egnō* (1:21)
nēpiois	*teleiois* (2:6)
apekrupsas [ekrupsas]	*apokekrummenēn* (2:7)
apekalupsas	*apekalupsen* (2:10)
ophthalmoi/blepontes	*ophthalmos* (2:9)
idein	*eiden* (2:9)
akousai	*ēkousen/ous* (2:9)

To this list of similarities might be added a few more. (*a*) The intent of *nēpioi* in the synoptic pericope is very similar to the force of 1 Cor. 1:27-28: God chooses the foolish, weak, low, and despised (*mōra, asthenē, agenē, exouthenēmena, ta mē onta*).[21] (*b*) Luke's introduction to the pericope draws attention to Jesus' rejoicing in the Spirit, and that same attention to Spirit runs through 1 Cor. 2:10-16. (*c*) The structure of one part of the pericope—"no one knows . . . except"—is almost identical to the structure of 1 Cor. 2:11—"who knows . . . except" (*oudeis ginōskei . . . ei mē*, cf. *tis gar oiden . . . ei mē*).

There are three main difficulties with Fjärstedt's thesis. On the one hand, he relies far too heavily on the supposition that the congregation in Corinth must know the synoptic material in question: on his view the readers must discover and appreciate the hints in order to explain the relation of Paul and Apollos in the church. This strains too much one's historical sense of the extent of general knowledge of synoptic traditions in the middle fifties; it seems unlikely that written

---

20 Ibid., 152-153.
21 S. Légasse, "La revelation aux NĒPIOI," *RB* 67 (1960), 321-348, concludes, however, that no light is shed on the problem of the synoptic pericope by the group in 1 Cor. 1:26-29.

collections of sayings would be widely available to congregations, though more plausible that itinerant preachers might have access to them. Fjärstedt's view also makes the letter a much more contrived vehicle of communication than the passionate character of 1 Corinthians itself suggests.

The second problem is that the force of Paul's remarks is not precisely similar to the force of the *Jubelruf*. Despite the many impressive and, in my opinion, undeniable similarities, the words are being used in somewhat different ways. The *Jubelruf* is a thanksgiving to God for the hiddenness of revelation to the wise—presumably the scribes—and its openness to the innocent—presumably Jesus' followers. Everything—including the Father—is revealed to the Son and to whomever the Son selects. The related pericope (Luke 10:23-24/Matt. 13:16-17) compares the disciples' blessedness because they see with prophets and kings (Matthew: righteous men) who did not see or hear. In 1 Corinthians Paul contrasts his preaching of the cross with eloquent wisdom, a wisdom that is destroyed and made foolish by God. The desire for wisdom and signs is fulfilled only in Christ who is both the wisdom and power of God. To the lowly Corinthian congregation Paul brings the powerful message of a crucified Christ. But then he changes tone and admits to a kind of wisdom focusing on the Spirit, yet it is a message the Corinthians could not receive adequately because they were too much babes in Christ! So in the *Jubelruf* the focus is on the Son and the revelation to those not wise, while in 1 Corinthians the focus is on the folly of wise men[22] preaching wisdom rather than the cross of Christ, with a revision to this that admits to a proper sort of wisdom for the truly spiritual.

The third difficulty is that the christology is different. The synoptic pericope is almost entirely a Father/Son christology, in which the references to the Son stand out from the rest of the synoptic materials. This Son christology is not altogether absent from 1 Corinthians: it appears in an intriguing fashion both in the thanksgiving (1 Cor. 1:9) and in an important portion of the chapter on resurrection (1 Cor. 15:28). But as compared with, say, Romans and Galatians the role of the Son is muted in both 1 Corinthians and 2 Corinthians. The primary christological emphasis of 1 Cor. 1-2 is on "Christ."

In the light of these three difficulties it seems impossible to claim that the relationship of 1 Cor. 1-2 to the *Jubelruf* is as simple as Fjärstedt claims, yet it seems impossible to deny that there is a bearing of one text upon the other, for at the decisive points in Paul's argument (1:17-21; 2:6-10; 3:1-4) the similarities are strongest.

---

22   The use of *sophos* as a substantive noun is limited in Paul to Rom. 1:14 (probably from the same period as 1 Corinthians) and to 1 Cor. 1 and 3, plus 6:5. It may be that in 6:5 the tone is derogatory and is intended to be a sarcastic reference to the person animating this dispute. See, for an earlier view, my paper "Judgment in Sexual Matters in 1 Corinthians 6:1-11," *NovT* 25 (1983), 37-58.

A COMMON BACKGROUND?

The points of contact between 1 Corinthians and the *Jubelruf* concentrate in two verses, 1 Cor. 1:19 and 2:9, each of which purports to be a quotation. Clearly 1 Cor. 1:19 is a citation of Isa. 29:14 with one small verbal alteration. But 1 Cor. 2:9, which has an almost similar introductory formula, is not a quotation of anything we now know. According to Origen it is a quotation from the lost Apocalypse of Elijah; according to most commentators, it is likely to be a combination of Isa. 64:3 and 65:16.

It could be argued, of course, that the closest parallels between the *Jubelruf* and 1 Cor. 1-2 are in these two quotations simply because both depend upon some common background: canonical texts, non-canonical texts, or merely a generalized wisdom tradition.[23]

The question is a complicated one, and cannot be dealt with here. There is, however, a growing consensus that the background of the *sophia* speculation in 1 Corinthians is not to be found in gnostic speculation but in the hellenistic-Jewish wisdom tradition.[24] In 1968 Baumann made an important suggestion, that Paul uses *sophia* not *gnōsis* deliberately in order to be able to invoke the Old Testament wisdom teaching.[25] He went on to argue this in some detail for 1:26-31, claiming, contrary to Cerfaux (who saw 1:18-3:23 as a florilegium of scripture citations)[26] and contrary also to E. Peterson and H. J. Thackeray (who saw 1:18-31 as based on Baruch 3:9-4:4),[27] that this section of 1 Corinthians has a "wisdom scheme of thought" (*ein weisheitliches Denkschema*).[28] He argued in a similar fashion with respect to 2:6-3:4.[29] Much the same ground was covered by Felix Christ's important volume *Jesus Sophia*,[30] but in a more comprehensive fashion he surveyed the most important texts of the Jewish wisdom tradition as a background to his study of "Jesus as Wisdom." Because he was interested primarily in the theological dimensions of the problem he tended to overlook the

---

23 On the wisdom tradition, see B. L. Mack, *Logos und Sophia: Untersuchungen zur Weisheits-Theologie im hellenistischen Judentum*, SUNT 10 (Göttingen: Vandenhoeck und Ruprecht, 1973).

24 See B. A. Pearson, *The Pneumatikos-Psychikos Terminology in 1 Corinthians*, SBLDS 12 (Missoula: Scholars Press, 1973); Horsley, "Wisdom of Word." Contrary, U. Wilckens, *Weisheit und Torheit: eine exegetisch-religionsgeschichtliche Untersuchung zu 1 Kor 1 und 2*, BHT 26 (Tübingen: J. C. B. Mohr, 1959).

25 See R. Baumann, *Mitte und Norm des Christlichen: eine Auslegung von 1 Korinther 1:1-3:4*, NTAbh, n.F. 5 (Münster: Aschendorff, 1968), 78-79.

26 L. Cerfaux, "Vestiges d'un florilège dans 1 Cor. 1:18-3:23," in *Receuil Lucien Cerfaux, II* (Gembloux: Duculot, 1962), 319-332.

27 See especially E. Peterson, "1 Kor. 1:18f und die Thematik des jüdischen Busstages," *Fruhkirche, Judentum und Gnosis* (Rom/Freiburg/Wien: Herder, 1959), 43-50.

28 *Mitte und Norm*, 124-148.

29 Ibid., 171-209.

30 F. Christ, *Jesus Sophia. Die Sophia-Christologie bei den Synoptikern*, ATANT 57 (Zürich: Zwingli Verlag, 1970).

similarities of the *Jubelruf* with 1 Cor. 1:19. In his analysis, however, he paused briefly to ask if Paul knew Q? or if both 1 Cor. 2:6ff. and Q go back to a word of Jesus? or if Q has used Paul? He concluded that it is likely that both go back to a broader *Revelationsschema*, with no *literary* relationship between 1 Cor. 2:9 and any of the possible backgrounds,[31] and that the Q text also presupposes a generalized Sophia-christology. Christ argued that such a Jewish form of speculation existed not only in Alexandria but in Palestine.

Siegfried Schulz, in a more broadly conceived study of Q, has examined the *Jubelruf* as well and emphasized how much it is coloured by the wisdom tradition of late Judaism, including (as Christ also suggests) Qumran.[32] Schulz finds the origin of the saying not in a Palestinian setting,[33] that is not in the earliest layer of the development of Q originating from a community living in the Palestinian-transjordanian area. He claims that the enthusiastic-apocalyptic kerygma of the oldest Q-community stood diametrically opposed to Pauline preaching of justification and did not know the central place of the pre-Pauline passion kerygma.[34]

It matters little whether the *Jubelruf* is an authentic word of Jesus.[35] Nor does it matter greatly whether that particular pericope is from an early and Palestinian strand of Q or from a later, perhaps Christianized, hellenistic-Jewish strand. But that it stands in Q, with its apocalyptic and wisdom emphases, and that the theology of Q is in some respects—but only in some—in conflict with the theology of Paul, are important points.[36]

It is also important for this paper to decide whether Paul and Q are both simply independent recollections of earlier sources or patterns of

---

31 Ibid., 82, n. 298; 83; cf. 93.

32 S. Schulz, *Q. Die Spruchquelle der Evangelisten* (Zürich: Theologischer Verlag, 1972). See also W. D. Davies, " 'Knowledge' in the Dead Sea Scrolls and Matthew 11:25-30," *HTR* 46 (1953), 113-139, and also in *Christian Origins and Judaism* (London: Darton, 1962), 119-144.

33 Schulz, *Q*, 213-228, especially 217. W. Grimm concluded ("Der Dank für die empfangene Offenbarung bei Jesus and Josephus," *BZ*, n. F. 17 [1973], 249-256) that there is a tradition-history line from Ethiopic Enoch through 1 QH and Matthew to Josephus (251).

34 Schulz, *Q*, 165-175, esp. 167. H. C. Kee, *Jesus in History* (New York: Harcourt, Brace, Jovanovitch, 1977), describes the Q community as falling in the tradition of charismatic prophets, with little concern about ethical issues, sharply dualistic, and open toward Gentiles.

35 For a defence of its authenticity, see H. Mertens, *L'hymne de jubilation chez les synoptiques: Matthieu XI, 25-30 – Luc X, 21-22* (Gembloux, 1957). For its inauthenticity, see T. Arvedson, *Das Mysteruim Christi Eine Studie zu Mt. 11:25-30*, Arbeiten und Mitteilungen aus dem neutestamentlichen Seminar zu Uppsala 7 (Leipzig: Lorenz, 1937).

36 See, in *Neutestamentliche Studien. Georg Heinrici zu seinem 70 Geburtstag, dargebracht von Fachgenossen, Freunden und Schülern*, UNT 6 (Leipzig: J. C. Hinrichs, 1914), the essays by J. Weiss, "Das Logion Mt. 11:25-30'l' (120-129), and especially H. Windisch, "Die göttliche Weisheit der Juden und die paulinische Christologie" (220-34).

thought. The view of the majority of scholars just cited suggests this, and their cumulative weight is almost compelling. Against them, however, must be placed a few other considerations, which may be listed briefly.

(1) The association of the *Jubelruf* with 1 Cor. 1:17-2:16 is often undervalued, primarily because concern focuses on the christological implications of the *Jubelruf* and of wisdom speculation generally. Paul's concern is not primarily christologized wisdom theology but wisdom teaching and wise men generally, as is shown by 1 Cor. 1:20-21; 2:1-5; 2:14-3:4; and 3:18-23. Hence the similarities between the *Jubelruf* and, especially, 1 Cor. 1:19 are doubly important.

(2) It is not generally recognized that the similarities between Paul and Q concentrate in the two quotations in 1 Cor. 1:19 and 2:9. These two quotations—while clearly not quotations of Q—follow closely the *pattern* of Q, so that 1 Cor. 1:19 reflects closely Luke 10:22, while 1 Cor. 2:9 reflects just as closely the thrust of Luke 10:23. A table will show this clearly.

1 Corinthians 1:19	Luke 10:22
gegraptai gar	*hoti*
apolō tēn sophian tōn sophōn	*ekrupsas tauta apo sophōn*
kai tēn sunesin tōn sunetōn	*kai sunetōn*
athetēsō	*kai apekalupsas auta nēpiois*

1 Corinthians 2:9	Luke 10:23, 24
alla kathōs gegraptai	*humōn de makarioi*
ha ophthalmos ouk eiden	*hoi ophthalmoi hoti blepousin*
kai ous ouk ēkousen	*kai ta ōta humōn hoti akousousin*
kai epi kardian anthrōpou ouk anebē ha hētoimasen ho theos tois agapōsin auton	

(3) In both cases, in 1 Cor. 1:19 and 2:9, the similarities are extended by new resemblances to the *Jubelruf* as Paul develops his argument in the surrounding materials (see Fjärstedt's table, above). These similarities extend to include several examples of wording, an example of identical structure, and certain basic ideas.

It seems likely, then, that the similarity between Paul's treatment of wisdom in 1 Cor. 1-2 and the *Jubelruf* in Q is not merely dependent on common background materials, but rather that Paul makes a deliberate attempt, as Fjärstedt has suggested, to reflect upon a Q saying which he knew in roughly the form it now has. Paul's recollection of the Q saying, however, goes behind that saying itself to an Old Testament text (1:19, citing Isa. 29:14) and to a mixed recollection, probably, of two other Old Testament texts (2:6, drawing upon Isa. 64:3 and 65:16). He is driven back to these scriptural texts because of the disagreements over wisdom in Corinth. In doing so, however, he is not mysteriously alluding to these disagreements, as Fjärstedt suggests, but trying to present a correct understanding of wisdom on the basis of conveniently chosen Old Testament texts.[37]

THE POLEMIC IN 1 CORINTHIANS 1-4

If Paul is reflecting on the *Jubelruf*, the most likely explanation for his needing to do so is buried in 1 Cor. 1-4. As Dahl has correctly observed, no fully satisfactory solution has yet been found, assuming the integrity of the letter, for the relation of 1 Cor. 1-4 to 5-16.[38] It is easy enough to see that the general purpose of 1 Corinthians is to answer a Corinthian letter, but it is not so easy to describe the relation between Paul's response to the oral information contained in Chapters 1-4 (plus 5-6?) and his response to the written questions in Chapters 7-16. Dahl tries to supply such an explanation, most of which is very helpful. But he underestimates, as many do, the degree of polemic in 1-4 and the specific sources of the trouble against which Paul argues.[39] Dahl's basic explanation is that "the quarrels and the slogans at Corinth were related to the assumption that the apostle would not return." This is probably correct so far as it goes. In fastening on this as the reason for the trouble Dahl almost eliminates any sense of opposition between Paul and the others. For him the problem is found among the Corinthian Christians.[40]

This will not do. As Dahl recognizes, the concluding paragraph to the letter body (4:16-21) indicates best of all the situation.[41] Here the polemic does not bear only on travel plans, but on superiority, on "power" as opposed to "word," on questions of the Kingdom of God.[42]

---

37   It is barely possible that it is this type of issue that lies behind Paul's very difficult exhortation in 1 Cor. 4:6 ("in order that you should follow the not-beyond-what-is-written things"). In other words, he may be insisting on driving back behind the Jesus-collection to the Hebrew scriptures. For a different possibility, see M. D. Hooker, "'Beyond the Things which are Written': An Examination of 1 Cor. 4:6," *NTS* 10 (1963-1964), 127-132.

38   N. Dahl, "Paul and the Church at Corinth," in *Studies in Paul* (Minneapolis: Augsburg, 1977), 40-61, originally published in 1967. He criticizes John C. Hurd, *The Origin of 1 Corinthians* (London: S.P.C.K., 1965), for not providing a "reasonable explanation of the function of the first major section" (43). See also J. Munck, *Paul and the Salvation of Mankind* (London: SCM, 1959), 135-167.

39   Dahl's "principles" ("Paul," 44-45) provide a good methodological starting point.

40   Dahl, "Paul," 46, 51-52. This is one way to resolve the problems of the text. Another way has been cogently argued by John C. Hurd: Paul has changed his mind (*Origin*, 242-246, 294-295; cf. 214-215).

41   Dahl, "Paul," 48, n. 21. W. Wuellner, "Haggadic Homily Genre in 1 Corinthians 1-3," *JBL* 89 (1970), 199-204, analyzes the bickerings in Corinth on the basis of Halakic and Haggadic discussions. This is, I suspect, partly true but undervalues the importance of the more clearly stated reasons for controversy. See also his article in the *Daube Festschrift* (Oxford: Clarendon, 1978), 165-184 ("Ursprung und Verwendung der *sophos-, dunatos-, eugenēs-* Formel in Kor. 1:26").

42   This major section both opens and closes with references to "wisdom" and "power"

As Dahl hints, it is also a question of who should stand in as the appropriate model for the Corinthians' imitation of Paul (4:16). He says here (4:17) that he has sent Timothy who is his beloved and faithful child in the Lord (contrast 3:1 where the Corinthians are "babes"). Timothy will remind the Corinthians of Paul's ways. It is difficult not to connect this with the conclusion of 1 Corinthians where Paul reverts to his travel plans (16:1-9) and in the process again commends Timothy to the Corinthians (16:10-11). He finds it necessary to request the Corinthians to "put him at ease," "not to despise him," and to "speed him on his way." Paul implies that Timothy might not be well treated. By contrast, Apollos ("Now concerning Apollos . . . ," 16:12) refuses to go to Corinth despite Paul's urging. It is striking that the conclusion to the letter body and the concluding response topic both appear to bear directly on the contrasting relationships of Timothy (hence Paul) and Apollos to the Corinthians. Both underline the nature of the real difficulty.

The difficulty is that Apollos was preferred by some of the Corinthians to Timothy and even to Paul; so, as Dahl suggests, Paul's travel plans *are* a part of the quarrels. Some want him back and others do not. It would seem that Apollos hovers over the difficulties in Corinth to a very much larger extent than many recent commentators allow.[43]

This will be argued in two ways, first of all by assessing the shape of the conflict in 1 Cor. 1-4, and then by looking at the figure of Apollos.

There is no fully satisfactory way to recover and describe the position of Paul's opponents. It is notoriously difficult to go behind the material to the dispute itself, but it is possible to start from the view that, in many cases, when Paul is negating something he does so because it is a part of the position he is countering. We must depend upon the likelihood that at least some of Paul's readers will know these opponents—perhaps even be among them—so that Paul will be likely to be honest in his descriptions.[44]

(1) 1:12-17. There is a dispute about baptism and the close link between baptizer and baptized. Paul tends to undervalue baptism, wants it clear that he baptizes seldom, and stresses that the cross might be emptied by this controversy. The other position seems to stress baptism and its importance, and undervalues the cross.[45]

(1:17; 1:22-24; 4:19-20). The main point of the letter body is to ventilate these important differences of opinion, differences which have themselves given rise to the paraenetic issues in chapters 5-16.

43 The reluctance of both Dahl and Hurd, for quite different reasons, is typical of many others. Cf. also H. Koester, "Gnomai Diaphoroi: The Origin and Nature of Diversification in the History of Early Christianity," *Trajectories*, 114-157, esp. 149.

44 See the discussion in Hurd, *Origin*, 61-62, 112, 268; he refers to Olof Linton, "The Third Aspect: A Neglected Point of View: A Study in Gal. 1-2 and Acts 9 and 15," *ST* 3 (1950), 79-95.

45 It is remarkable how seldom in the NT a person is identified as a baptizer. Here in 1:16 Paul uses the form "I baptized." In Acts only John the Baptist and Philip are identified as baptizers. In every other case a passive is used, as if it were of no

(2) 1:17-25. The undervaluing of the cross touches a raw nerve in Paul, both in terms of the place of the cross and how he preaches it. Its place is fundamental despite the views of the wise, whom God will destroy.[46] The preaching of it is foolishness, because it cannot be done eloquently, or with wisdom. The other position would appear to elevate wisdom and eloquence, and downgrade the offence of the cross.

(3) 2:1-5. For his part, Paul did not proclaim the mystery eloquently or wisely; he proclaimed only Christ crucified so that the Spirit's power would be clear. His opponents must have claimed that Paul's preaching was not intellectual enough, that wisdom has a proper place and ought to be included.

(4) 2:6-16. Aware of the objection, Paul modifies what he says about wisdom, granting that he does speak a kind of wisdom—but not one amenable to this age. The others' message must be interpreted by Paul as "of this age," presumably because they have made God's wisdom too accessible, too human, not sufficiently dependent upon the role of the Spirit. In other words, Paul seems to charge his opponents both with being too popular and being too élite at the same time.

(5) 3:1-3. Paul still has to treat the Corinthians as babes, not as spiritually mature. The opponents seem to claim that they deal with their fellow Corinthians as mature people while Paul talks down to them.

(6) 4:1-13. Paul rejects the judgment being made upon him—that he is not fully equipped as a servant and steward—because it is premature. In Paul's view the opponents are puffed up; they claim to be filled, rich, ruling, wise, strong, worthy. Why, they even go above-what-is-written. Their view seems to be that they are superior interpreters, who have already begun to reign.[47]

(7) 4:14-20. When Paul arrives in Corinth himself, he will determine how powerful these puffed-up people are. Talk is cheap, but the Kingdom of God comes not in talk nor in wisdom but in power. The Corinthians, apparently, value some one else's speech more than Paul's.

---

importance who does the baptizing. Perhaps, despite what he says here, baptism is important for Paul as a church-building function. Might he be referring, somewhat sarcastically, to Apollos' role as a baptizer of many when, in 3:6, he refers to "watering." Against this somewhat fanciful possibility is the basic meaning of *potizō* ("drink") but note the close association between *potizō* and baptism in 1 Cor. 12:13 (*Baptizō* appears in Paul, apart from 1 Cor. 1:13-17, only in 1 Cor. 10:2; 12:13; 15:29; Rom. 6:3; Gal. 3:27. *Hudōr* never appears in Paul (cf. Eph. 5:26).

46 It seems altogether likely that the quotation in 1:19 is a deliberate pun on the name of Apollos (*apolō tēn sophian tōn sophōn*). If so, the connections between the parties in 1:10-13, the question of baptism in 1:13-16, the cross in 1:17-25, and Apollos is made still closer. When in 1:20 Paul asks "where is the wise man . . . the scribe . . . the debater?" it is probably pointed against Apollos.

47 One of the issues is an over-realized eschatology, where some are claiming to reign, to be able *now* to judge. One is reminded of the Q saying in Matt. 19:28//Luke 22:30, cf. 1 Cor. 4:5; 5:3; 6:2-3; etc.

This rather sketchy outline of the opposing position in 1 Cor. 1-4 can be put in a yet more cursory fashion. Baptism and the attachments it creates are apparently overlooked by Paul; but baptism is a fundamental feature of the Christian life. When Paul denigrates baptism and exaggerates the cross he creates intellectual difficulties for the Corinthians. Emphasis should be placed on "wisdom," as many synagogues in the hellenistic world do, for strategically wisdom is more persuasive among the "right" kind of people. Paul's work was, therefore, not entirely adequate. The mature teaching of others has proved to be more attractive then Paul's.

The teaching of one person, Apollos, seems to have been especially helpful (see 3:5-9 particularly) as a way of reconciling this Christian message with "wisdom" (cf. 3:18-23). His way of exegeting scripture was fresh and illuminating; it allowed the Corinthians to go beyond Paul's rudimentary stress on the cross (4:6-7; cf. 1:18-19).

A few more remarks on Paul and Apollos are now necessary. To begin with, it is clear that Paul and Apollos are still talking, still interested in their complementary roles. Paul explicitly underlines their complementarity in 3:21-4:2; 3:5-6; and in 16:12 it is obvious that Apollos and Paul are within easy distance.

Having said that, it is still highly likely that the relationship between the two men is very strained. When in 2 Cor. 1:19 (while describing his travel plans) Paul refers to his preaching in Corinth, he associates with himself Silvanus and Timothy and overlooks completely what he has already admitted to the Corinthians—that Apollos has assisted in bringing Corinthians to belief (e.g., 1 Cor. 3:5). The omission of Apollos from 2 Corinthians must be more than merely accidental. Paul chooses not to negate Apollos' role, but he is totally silent about it. Why?

The reason seems obvious from 1 Cor. 1-4. Though Paul acknowledges in 1:11-13 and in 3:3-4 that a large part of the problem arises from incorrect attachments, and in 3:5-9 that he and Apollos are equal (*hen eisin*) and fellow-workers (*sunergoi*), it is nonetheless important to Paul to stress that he is the only founder of the congregation (3:10) and the father who gave it birth (4:16). He appears to resent that others—or another?— have come along behind him (4:16 "a myriad of tutors"; cf. 3:10, "another builds upon"; cf. also the temporal priority of planting to watering in 3:6-8). This resentment, generated by another (*allos*), is developed in 3:10-15 in heavily loaded eschatological terms. Each is to "take care" (or "beware"—*blepetō*—3:10) how he builds, because "the Day will disclose . . . what sort of work each one has done." Some work will survive; but some will be burned up with fire. Nevertheless, even though the work of some will be destroyed at the End, the person in question will be saved, but as through fire (3:15).

This aggressively antagonistic passage follows from his description of himself and Apollos in 3:4-6. It develops into another reference to the problem of wisdom—focused on "someone (*tis*) [who] thinks himself to be wise among you" (3:18-19)—and goes straight back to the problem of Paul, Apollos and Cephas, this time not under the guise of parties as in 3:4 but more nearly with respect to the persons themselves (3:22, *eite Paulos . . . Apollōs . . . Kēphas*).

Paul takes care in 4:1-2 to say that "we" are "servants of Christ and stewards of the mysteries of God," but he demands that servants be "faithful" (*pistos*) and may imply that not all are (4:2). That introduces one of his complaints against the Corinthians: they are judging him before the time (4:3-5). When judgment is rendered by the Lord, "each" (*hekastō*) will receive from God his due (4:5).

That might seem an inoffensive enough comment were it left there: "each" would then refer to those in Corinth who were judging Paul before all the evidence was in. But in a curious phrase Paul goes straight on to say that he has applied all these things to himself and Apollos (*tauta . . . meteschēmatisa eis emauton kai Apollōn di humas*, 4:6). Where does one find the antecedent for *tauta*, and in what way does the verb (*metaschēmatizō*) illuminate Paul's meaning? The nearest antecedent of "these things" is the "dark things" or "purposes of the heart," but the reference to Apollos and Paul makes this unlikely. If the antecedent is slightly more remote, it is either the "judging" being done in Corinth on Paul's work or the question of "wisdom" (3:18-23) or the "planting over" and "building over" (3:5-15). But whichever the antecedent (the likeliest is the previous reference to Apollos and Paul in the context of wisdom in 3:18-23), it is nearly certain that "these things" are "bad" in Paul's view, something against which he needs to contend.

The verb *metaschēmatizo* supports this interpretation. It is not used by Paul in exactly this way again; in the other instances the word has its more usual meaning of "change" or "transform" (Phil. 3:21; 2 Cor. 11:13, 14, 15). But it is worth noting, in order to help to recover the tone if not the precise meaning of this verb, that in every other case the context is explicitly opposition to Paul.[48]

In 1 Cor. 4:6 also the "tone" is opposition, both before it (see above) and after it, where Paul emphasizes the danger of spiritual superiority (*physiousthe . . . diakrinei . . . kauchasai . . . eploutēsate . . . ebasileusate*) apparently in connection with some form of scriptural interpretation (4:6).

When one turns to the first mention of Apollos and Cephas, in 1:12, the emphasis is on those forming the parties. But Paul's defence quickly moves away from people's perception of him to his actions: "I am thankful that I baptized none of you" (1 Cor. 1:14; cf. 1:15-16);

---

48 Thus, in 2 Cor. 11:13-15 he is dealing with "false apostles" who transform themselves into "apostles of Christ . . . servants of righteousness" just as Satan transforms himself into an angel of light. In Phil. 3:21, while it is the body which is transformed, the immediate context deals with enemies of the cross of Christ who will be destroyed (3:18-19); cf. also 4 Macc. 9:22.

"Christ did not send me to baptize but to preach" (1:17). This defence, which focuses immediately on the question of baptism and Paul's reticence about baptizing, shades off just as quickly into the question of wisdom, a subject that stands front and centre for two chapters. The minimum conclusion that should be drawn is that the party divisions in Corinth are intimately related to Paul's reticence on two questions— baptism and wisdom—and that they involve major differences between Paul and Apollos (with Cephas in the wings).[49]

One other piece of evidence makes inescapable, in my view, this conclusion that Apollos is much more than a passive bystander whose position is being pushed too far by some group of Corinthian Christians. This evidence is the well-known description in Acts 18:24-19:7. The following points should be noted briefly:

(1) Apollos is an eloquent man (*anēr logios*) powerful in the scriptures (*dunatos... en tais graphais*), who confutes the Jews from the scriptures (18:28). Paul, however, has to withdraw from the synagogue in Ephesus because of opposition (19:8-9).

(2) Apollos, who has been working in Ephesus (18:24), has only the baptism of John (18:28); when Paul goes to Ephesus from Corinth, he finds a group of "disciples" who have only the baptism of John (19:1-4). Paul corrects their deficiency, baptizing them into the Lord Jesus so that they receive the Spirit (19:5-6). When he subsequently has trouble in the synagogue, he withdraws taking the "disciples" with him (19:9).

(3) The thrust of Apollos' message in Corinth, after being properly instructed by Priscilla and Aquila in the way of God (18:26), appears to be the demonstration that the Messiah is Jesus (18:28). On the contrary, Paul's message in Ephesus is described in terms of baptism, charismatic experience, and the kingdom of God (19:4, 6, 8).[50]

The fit between this description in Acts and 1 Corinthians is significant. First of all, Paul and Apollos have for some period of time exchanged fields, so that Apollos has been in Corinth on Paul's territory and Paul is in Ephesus on ground Apollos first ploughed. Second, baptism is an issue; Paul is pleased that he did not baptize in Corinth but in Ephesus, according to Acts, he re-baptizes. Third, Apollos is described in Acts in terms that fit closely the problems to which Paul refers in 1 Corinthians (*logios... dunatos... en tais graphais*). Now Paul in his defence (1 Cor. 1:17; 1:23-24; 2:8) is careful to emphasize that the

---

49   3:4-6; 4:6-7 refer only to Paul and Apollos. In 3:22 Cephas is again in view. It is possible that this happens because 3:10-15 (the "foundation" passage) refers to Cephas' role as the foundational apostle, while 3:5-9 (the "planting/watering" passage) refers to Apollos' role. The primary opposition is between Paul and Apollos; the analogy of 3:5-9 deals with that question but prompts a similar analogy in 3:10-15 dealing with Paul and Cephas, after which Paul remarks in 3:22 on the three leaders.

50   Note that it is Paul, not Apollos, who is described in Acts as the "charismatic"; cf. Paul's emphases in 1 Cor. 12, 14, and 2:4-14.

distinctive issue between him and his opponents is the cross on the one hand, and the role of "wise words" on the other. What is more, he emphasizes a christology focused on "Christ" (cf. Apollos in Acts 18:28).

We should not, of course, interpret 1 Corinthians through the eyes of the secondary evidence in Acts. Still, it is surprising how good a match there is between the inferences from 1 Corinthians and the statements of Acts. Though Acts (typically) overlooks any hint of controversy, when one reads between the lines of Acts 18:24-19:10 there is considerable potential for difficulty.

We may go one step further: 1 Corinthians presupposes that Apollos is not in Corinth but somewhere near Paul (1 Cor. 16:12). If so, we might wonder whether Apollos went back to Ephesus to attend to the dificulties Paul was creating for his followers in Ephesus, just as Paul sends a letter along with Timothy to attend to the problems Apollos has created in Corinth. The difficulty has arisen, we may surmise, from two sides: on the one hand is the territorial imperative—each is working in the other's field;[51] on the other is the theological distinctive—Paul stresses "cross" and Apollos stresses "wisdom." In addition, there are tensions created by baptism: someone (probably Apollos) has baptized some of Paul's converts in Corinth; Paul, for his part, has re-baptized some of Apollos' converts in Ephesus.

Such a reconstruction illumines the situation reflected in 1 Cor. 1-4.

Q'S BEARING ON PAUL AND APOLLOS

What has all this to do with the question of the thunderbolt in Q and 1 Corinthians? It may be readily granted that there are tensions between Paul and Apollos, perhaps even opposition. But in what way does this shed light on the growth of the gospel traditions in a missionary situation?

We may begin by noting again that Q has certain distinct emphases.[52] First, and most important, Q not only lacks a passion narrative, in fact it lacks altogether any reference to the suffering and death of Jesus. It also has neither resurrection accounts nor birth narratives. It stresses the role of the earthly Son of Man and his future coming, so that the tension is resolved between the future and present Kingdom of God.[53] Q also has a tendency to associate Jesus with personified wis-

---

51   See my article, "Pauline Inconsistency: 1 Corinthians 9:19-23 and Galatians 2:11-14," *NTS* 26 (1980), 347-362.

52   On Q's Theology see P. Hoffmann, *Studien zur Theologie der Logienquelle*, NTAbh, n.F. 8 (Münster: Aschendorff, 1972). He deals with the *Jubelruf* on pp. 118-124 but does not mention 1 Corinthians. See also A. Polag, *Die Christologie der Logienquelle*, WMANT 45 (Neukirchen: Neukirchener Verlag, 1971).

53   See H. E. Tödt, *The Son of Man in the Synoptic Tradition* (London: SCM, 1965), esp. 268-269.

dom,[54] to stress in general a role for wisdom consistent with late Jewish wisdom speculation, though it incorporates—in the *Jubelruf* in particular—criticism of the wise men.[55] It gives considerable visibility to John the Baptist and tends to associate him with Jesus, contrasting Jesus (and John) with "this generation."[56] For Q the Gentile mission is a legitimate *fait accompli*; Israel has rejected Jesus' message and God has turned to the nations.[57] The work as a whole is permeated by eschatology.[58]

The most provocative contribution to the story of Q is the analysis by J. M. Robinson of the *Gattung* of Q. He argues that Q stands in a particular tradition, one that is on its way to developing from Jewish wisdom literature to the later developments of Gnosticism: it is a collection of sayings of wise men or "sayings of the sages."[59]

Q is then a collection of the sayings of Jesus (and of John) in which the following distinctive emphases occur:

(1) no passion
(2) no resurrection
(3) no birth narrative
(4) stress on the Son of Man
(5) stress on eschatology and the resolution of tension between present and future
(6) emphasis on wisdom both with respect to Jesus and in general
(7) emphasis on John the Baptist
(8) contrast with this generation
(9) stress on the Gentile mission.

Many of the above are relevant for the question of Paul and Apollos: only items 3 and 4 play no role in 1 Corinthians or in Paul generally. Concerning item 9 we may hypothesize that both Paul and Apollos agree on the nature of the Gentile mission and perhaps also on the place of Israel.[60] The rest are remarkable. Item 6 has been dealt with sufficiently in the above. The stress on John the Baptist in Q (item 7) bears directly on the differences between Paul and Apollos: Apollos knew only John's baptism and he was associated with others in Ephesus who shared only that baptism. Further, Paul, defends himself against

---

54 See M. J. Suggs, *Wisdom, Christology and Law*, who argues that in Q Jesus is only wisdom's envoy.
55 See J. M. Robinson, "*Logoi Sophon*: On the Gattung of Q," in *Trajectories*, 71-113, esp. 112-113; and cf. H. C. Kee, *Jesus*, 81.
56 See D. Lührmann, *Die Redaktion der Logienquelle*, WMANT 33 (Neukirchen-Vluyn: Neukirchener Verlag, 1969), 31.
57 Meyer, "The Gentile Mission in Q."
58 Kee, *Jesus*, 84, 91-117.
59 Robinson, "Logoi Sophon."
60 Hence, one might speculate, there is no need in 1 Corinthians, given its role as polemic between Paul and Apollos, to deal with these questions. An earlier attempt to resolve this question, entitled "On the Absence of Anti-Judaism in 1 Corinthians," is soon to be published in P. Richardson (ed.) with D. Granskou, *Anti-Judaism in Early Christianity* (Waterloo: Wilfrid Laurier University Press, 1984).

misunderstandings of his baptizing practices (1:13-17) and reverts to baptism again in 12:13 and 15:29-34.[61] With the defence of his baptismal role goes a defence of his stress on the cross (item 1) in 1:17-25, and a defence of his view on the resurrection (item 2) in chapter 15.[62] The question of present and future (item 5) pops up a number of times in 1 Corinthians, most noticeably in 4:6-8, 4:19-20, and 15:12-19 (cf. also, inter al., 5:1-5, 11:17-37). And the contrast with this generation (item 8) weaves through chapters 1-2, especially.

This is not to suggest that either Apollos or Paul had any hand in collecting the Q-materials! But it is possible, if the consensus on dating Q about 50 C.E. is correct, that both Paul and Apollos were familiar with Q, and that some of the differences between Paul and Apollos were heightened by their different perceptions of the importance and authority of Q. Paul's emphasis on Jesus' suffering, death and resurrection, and his denigrating of baptism and wisdom, might well be related to the particular characteristics of Q. And Apollos' background as a follower of John the Baptist, together with his interest in wisdom might suggest a closer dependence on Q and help to account for his lack of interest in the passion and his tendency (if it is his?) to see the resurrection as past.

Earlier it was suggested that there were several important issues if it were the case that Paul is referring in 1 Cor. 1-2 to the *Jubelruf* (pages 96-97). In the first place, the difference between the "Son" christology of the thunderbolt and the "Christ" christology of 1 Corinthians would be a part of Paul's desire to assert a distinction between himself and Apollos. Someone who knew only John's baptism and who preached "Jesus" might be in danger of devaluing the messianic role of Jesus.[63] In the second place Paul's use of the *Jubelruf* allowed him to refer to a part of the Q tradition that was itself critical of the wise man. For Paul, the wise man was quintessentially Apollos; since Apollos had some support in Q for a "wisdom" approach, it was doubly useful for Paul to fasten on the one Q saying that undercut that approach. In the third place, far from simply pointing to Q as the place to go to find out how to interpret Paul's and Apollos' dispute (as Fjärstedt suggests), Paul directs attention back to the scriptures that undergird the Q saying. And in so doing he deliberately cites Isa. 29:14 which begins

---

61 The number of references to baptism in 1 Corinthians is uncharacteristic; Paul seldom refers to baptism elsewhere.

62 Note that 1 Cor. 15 is the only major topic in the paraenetic section of 1 Corinthians not introduced by *peri de*. It may be that this topic is dealt with not because it is raised by the Corinthians but because it relates directly to the differences between Paul and Apollos and represents an important aspect of his teaching that Paul has not yet commented on. It is suggestive that it comes immediately before his travel plans (16:1-11) and his final reference to Apollos (16:12). To put it differently, 1 Corinthians begins with the cross and ends with the resurrection.

63 For this reason Luke tries to bridge the gap between Paul and Apollos by having Apollos (in Acts 18:28) argue that the Messiah is Jesus.

with the word *apolō*. It seems he has Apollos in mind, and he suggests that Apollos' kind of wisdom will be destroyed (1:19; 3:15; 3:19; 4:19).

Paul, then, appears to be involved in a dispute with Apollos that is directly related to the nature of the gospel (baptism, cross, resurrection, wisdom) and tangentially related to a collection of sayings of Jesus, sufficiently close to Q that we have simply called it Q. Much in the paper is speculative, so it would be unwise to claim too much for it. It ought not, for example, to be claimed that Paul is opposed to Q; but it may be tenable to argue that he does not favour Q because it is deficient in certain important respects, and because some of those deficiencies play into Apollos' hand in the controversy between the two of them.[64]

If this be approximately correct the very form of the Gospel was an issue in Ephesus and Corinth. The questions were more than questions of travel plans, ethical standards, the Jerusalem decree—though all of these are important. The underlying question was the adequacy of a collection of Jesus-sayings to shape the Church, a collection which provided only sayings and did not present the sacrifice of Christ and his triumph over death.

The mission of Paul was based on a view of the gospel rooted in death and resurrection. The mission of Apollos was rooted in the wisdom tradition and his experience of John's baptism. Between these two men the role of Q became an issue, for Q tended more to Apollos' side than to Paul's.

AN APPENDIX IN PLACE OF A
CONCLUSION

If the above speculation concerning the role of Q in the debate between Paul and Apollos in Corinth is correct, one further speculation is in order. It is likely, in my view, that there is a first edition of Luke in which Q is combined with L-material. It may have been a quite finished work with its own distinctive beginning in 3:1. Such a work would have to be relatively early (say the 60s) and, *ex hypothesi*, be independent of Mark. Luke would be a prime candidate as author.

The distinctive features of this hypothetical Proto-Luke cannot be considered in detail.[65] Proto-Luke almost surely, though, included the passion narrative, resurrection accounts, and much polemical material, some of it in parables. It also seems to have included some editorial revisions that tended to the subordination of John the Baptist (especially Luke 3:19-20 which, together with the alteration to 3:21, effectively remove John from the scene and avoid naming him as the

---

64   Is it remotely possible that it is deficient in concept, because it deals with sayings of Jesus? Paul's difficult saying in 2 Cor. 5:16 ("from now on we know no one according to flesh; even though we knew the Messiah according to flesh, now no longer do we know him") might bear on this question.

65   See Taylor, *Behind the Third Gospel*, especially his conclusions on pp. 273-274.

baptizer of Jesus). Much more would need to be considered, especially the distinctive features of Luke's accounts of the Last Supper, the Trial, Death, and Resurrection. The above observations are consistent with the hypothesis that Luke was prompted to write a gospel himself, partly as a result of Paul's conflicts with Apollos in Corinth and Ephesus. In doing so he sought to modify some of the deficiencies of Q.[66]

If Koester is correct[67] that Luke and Acts show the victory of Paul's Corinthian opponents (and I am not sure he is) that victory would need to be understood in terms of the final edition of these works. The Gospel of Luke, as we know it, has on the above showing incorporated the Gospel of Mark (to some degree Petrine) with an earlier (somewhat "Paulinized") gospel—Proto-Luke. The Gospel of Luke in its present form has already bridged the Peter/Paul conflict.[68] It may be that the same could be said of Acts. Without commenting on the thorny question of sources in Acts, the source of the latter half with its attachment to Paul has been amalgamated with a source or sources focusing on Peter and the Jerusalem Church. Might it be that a Proto-Acts lay behind the last half, and that the earlier Petrine materials have been added to Acts in order to alter it in somewhat the same way that Markan materials are added to Proto-Luke?[69]

---

66 It is noteworthy that he does not (perhaps in the interests of bridging the differences between Paul and Apollos?) remove the wisdom emphasis in Q.

67 In "Gnomai Diaphoron."

68 One very important question, untouched here, is the question of the relationship between Cephas and Apollos.

69 See already V. Taylor, *Behind the Third Gospel*, 198-201.

Jesus as Lordly Example in Philippians 2:5-11

L. W. HURTADO

Whoever takes pen in hand to comment on such a frequently-studied passage as Phil. 2:5-11 must offer some justification to readers who already have access to the learned commentary by our honoured colleague, Professor Beare,[1] as well as the contributions of many other scholars. In partial justification, one can say that the very volume and continual flow of scholarly studies on this passage make it evident that the discussion has by no means reached a consensus and that more study is required.

Further, in light of the fact that this volume of essays is devoted to the topic "From Jesus to Paul," it seems legitimate to give attention to this passage where Jesus is so obviously the centre of attention (though what is said about him is very much still under dispute!). It should also be noted here that for many English-speaking students, including the present writer, Professor Beare's commentary has served as a major tool in wrestling with the significance of the Philippian letter in general and this passage in particular. If in the following pages I take views in disagreement with some of his, nevertheless I offer this treatment of Phil. 2:5-11 with acknowledgement of the stimulus his commentary provided and in tribute to his distinguished example as a New Testament scholar.

The intensity of scholarly labour expended on the study of Phil. 2:5-11 is impressive, the web of issues involved complex, and the mountain of publications on the passage daunting. The limits of this

---

1 F. W. Beare, *A Commentary on the Epistle to the Philippians*, Black's NT Commentaries (London: A. & C. Black, 1959).

essay make it impossible to review all the issues or to mention all the contributions, and the valuable monograph by R. P. Martin makes this unnecessary.[2] Though scholars have debated questions about the origin and authorship of the passage (pre-Pauline, Pauline, or post-Pauline?), its form and structure (hymnic? the number of stanzas?), the conceptual background of the passage (Old Testament, Gnostic myth, general Hellenism, wisdom speculation?), and detailed issues involving its interpretation, the questions before us in the present essay are whether Jesus is cited as an example for Christians in Phil. 2:5-11, and, if so, how his example is described. In what follows we shall first examine major studies that have contributed to the present climate of opinion on these questions, and then we shall consider the evidence afresh, noting reasons for viewing Jesus in Phil. 2:5-11 as the "lordly example."

LOHMEYER AND KÄSEMANN

In his 1959 commentary on Philippians Professor Beare acknowledged as crucial investigations of 2:5-11 the work of Lohmeyer and Käsemann, and at this point, many years later, this judgment still must be echoed.[3] It was Lohmeyer's work that made it practically a scholarly commonplace that the passage exhibits hymnic characteristics and that it was likely a liturgical piece from some setting in the early Christian church. Käsemann made two main contributions: his case for the Gnostic-mythic background of the passage and his interpretation of the passage as a soteriological drama. The argument for a Gnostic background helped to make the study of the conceptual background of the passage a major line of investigation, and his interpretation of the passage secured followers, whether or not they agreed with his position on the background of the passage. For example, in his valuable treatment of the history of interpretation of the passage, Martin adopted with enthusiasm Käsemann's interpretation[4] and has repeated this position in his recent commentary.[5] Since Käsemann's interpretation of Phil. 2:5-11 is the major case against any notion that Jesus is presented as an example there, it will be important to examine his work more closely before venturing to offer a dissenting view.

---

2   R. P. Martin, *Carmen Christi: Philippians 2:5-11 in Recent Interpretation and in the Setting of Early Christian Worship*, SNTSMS 4 (Cambridge: Cambridge University, 1967). (Abbreviations in references are those used by the *Journal of Biblical Literature*. See *JBL* [1976], 331-346.)

3   Beare, *Philippians*, 74. Ernst Käsemann, "Kritische Analyse von Phil 2:5-11," *ZTK* 47 (1950), 313-360; the English translation referred to in this essay is "A Critical Analysis of Philippians 2:5-11," in *God and Christ: Existence and Province*, JTC 5 (New York: Harper and Row, 1968), 45-88.

4   Martin, *Carmen Christi*, 90-92, 177-182, 287-292.

5   R. P. Martin, *Philippians*, New Century Bible (London: Oliphant's, 1976), 92-93.

Käsemann's famous essay on Phil. 2:5-11 included a critique of what were then more recent German studies of the passage, and in this critique the work of Lohmeyer was prominently featured. Though Käsemann acknowledged Lohmeyer's contributions to the modern study of the passage, he nevertheless took issue at important points. For example, he challenged Lohmeyer's view concerning the Semitic and Old Testament background of the description of Christ in this hymn.[6] The major objective that Käsemann was trying to achieve, however, was clearly to refute any idea that Christ was presented as an example in the Philippians "hymn." While his exegetical examination involved arguments on several continuing philological and historical issues, these were but troops he marshalled for the main task. One of the enduring qualities of all Käsemann's work is that, for all his obvious learning in the technical matters of historical-critical exegesis, he always is concerned with the theological meaning of a passage, and in the essay in question here Käsemann clearly was motivated by theological concern. It is not always recognized how very prominent in Käsemann's essay are indications that theological matters heavily determined his interpretation of Phil. 2:5-11. The opening comments express his concern that "the guideline of a firm doctrinal tradition in the church has been increasingly abandoned by Protestant exegesis,"[7] and the following pages of his essay are studded with indications of what was at stake theologically for Käsemann. Again and again his comments make it plain that the major reason he opposed any of the varieties of interpretation that presented Christ as an example in Phil. 2:5-11 was that to him they all smacked of "ethical idealism," which seems to be his label for the theology of Old Liberalism.[8] That is, his real problem with the examples that he cites of "ethical" interpretation of the passage is that they all reduce the work of Christ here to being a representative of a generally valid norm of conduct, an example that lowliness and service will be rewarded. Thereby, the soteriological nature of Christ's work is lost from view, and the Christian message of justification for sinners is changed into mere moral exhortation.[9]

Käsemann's description of those he criticizes for this type of interpretation seems accurate, and it is true that Lohmeyer, for example, was a theological heir of nineteenth-century Liberalism. This being so, it is not out of the question to suggest that Lohmeyer's theological position influenced his interpretation of the passage.

But if Käsemann was right in accusing Lohmeyer and others of a reductionist interpretation of the passage on account of their theological tendencies, this properly raises the question of whether his in-

---

6 Käsemann, "A Critical Analysis," 46-48.
7 Ibid., 45.
8 Ibid., 46-59, *passim.*
9 Ibid., 50, 57.

terpretation was itself unnecessarily constricted on account of his theological commitments. For example, is it possible that in his justifiable rejection of the "ethical idealism" of Old Liberalism he came close to rejecting any sort of ethical appeal as a legitimate part of the NT message? With regard to Phil. 2:5-11 specifically, did his commendable kerygmatic theological tendencies make him unnecessarily resistant to indications that Christ may be held forth here in some kind of exemplary role? That his theological reaction against Liberalism (as a representative of the kerygmatic theological emphases made famous by Bultmann and Barth) may have skewed his reading of Phil. 2:5-11 is rendered more likely by the fact that from the Reformation on the passage had been seen as referring to Jesus as a model for Christian life. Only with the kerygmatic theology movement of this century did this view of the passage come under heavy attack.[10]

Though further discussion of these matters might prove interesting, the only purpose here has been to describe briefly the theological viewpoint that may help account for some of the exegetical positions taken in Käsemann's influential essay. Others have insisted, against Käsemann, that Jesus is portrayed as an example in Phil. 2:5-11, and have expressed dissatisfaction with his exegesis of this passage on several points,[11] but I do not believe that other critics have seen how prominent the theological concerns are in Käsemann's essay and how much they seem to have shaped his interpretation of the passage. If I am correct that Käsemann's theological views predisposed him against seeing Jesus as an ethical example in Phil. 2:5-11 and that his views were formed in reaction against the moralizing tendencies of Liberal theology, we may be justified in undertaking a re-examination of the question of whether Jesus is presented as an example in this passage. Of course we must have more substantial reasons for disagreeing with Käsemann's view than simply the suspicion that certain *a priori* theological views skewed his interpretation, and in the following pages I offer what I hope will be seen as reasons of sufficient weight for taking another view of Phil. 2:5-11.

THE QUESTION OF BACKGROUND

We must begin this section of our study by noting that Käsemann placed great importance on a purported Gnostic-myth background for the hymn as the clue to its meaning, and that for him the primary

---

10 Note that Käsemann applauds Barth's rejection of any idea that Christ is an example in Phil. 2:5-11, though Käsemann differs with him on other matters (ibid., 50-52).
11 For example, note E. J. Tinsley, *The Imitation of God in Christ* (London: SCM, 1960), 134-165; W. P. De Boer, *The Imitation of Paul: An Exegetical Study* (Kampen: J. H. Kok, 1962), 58-71, 212-216; E. Larsson, *Christus als Vorbild* (Uppsala: Almquist and Wiksells, 1962), 232-270; G. N. Stanton, *Jesus of Nazareth in New Testament Preaching*, SNTSMS 27 (Cambridge: Cambridge University Press, 1974), 99-110.

source for this Gnostic background was the Hermetic material. Most importantly, the overall structure of the events in Phil. 2:5-11 was interpreted on the analogy of the descent and ascent of the Gnostic "*Urmensch*-Saviour,"[12] and the Gnostic world view was seen as determinative for every item in the passage. Thus, 2:6-8 refers to the steps in which Christ became subservient to the hostile cosmic powers,[13] and 2:10-11 refers to the conquest of these hostile powers and their recognition of their defeat.[14] Repeatedly Käsemann appealed to this Gnostic background as the proper context in which to interpret Phil. 2:5-11, and argued that the proper context was crucial for the right interpretation of the passage.[15] In this view, the passage makes no reference to the personality or deeds of the earthly Jesus, but is wholly a recital of a cosmic drama of salvation. Because this is so (per Käsemann) the events of the drama, such as the humiliation and servitude of 2:6-8, can have no use as ethical example.

In view of the emphasis upon the Gnostic background of the passage in Käsemann, it cannot be without significance to note that this now seems to be a highly untenable position. In general, and for reasons sufficiently well known as to require no explanation here, the appeal to a pre-Christian Gnostic redeemer-myth has fallen on hard times in recent years; and, with specific reference to Phil. 2:5-11, Käsemann's Gnostic background is now generally denied.[16]

Though he expressed agreement with the basic drift of Käsemann's interpretation of the passage, Beare preferred to describe the religious background as simply the syncretism of the hellenistic world.[17] But in general the drift of opinion has been away from analogies in the pagan religious movements of the ancient world and toward preferred roots in Jewish religion of the hellenistic period.[18] Thus Georgi referred to the background of hellenistic-Jewish wisdom literature and the figure of the righteous sufferer.[19] J. A. Sanders criticized Georgi's proposal as too narrow, and argued that the proper background was in a wide array of Jewish sectarian literature, in which he found ideas similar to those in texts such as the Hermetica.[20]

---

12 Käsemann, "A Critical Analysis," 63-67.
13 Ibid., 67.
14 Ibid., 78-80.
15 Ibid., 62, 66, and 72, "Everything depends upon the context into which the exegete places this term."
16 See C. Colpe, *Die religionsgeschichtliche Schule* (Göttingen: Vandenhoeck und Rup-recht, 1961); E. Yamauchi, *Pre-Christian Gnosticism: A Survey of Proposed Evidences* (Grand Rapids: Eerdmans, 1973). On Phil. 2:5-11 see J. T. Sanders, *The New Testament Christological Hymns*, SNTSMS 15 (Cambridge: Cambridge University Press, 1971), 58-70.
17 Beare, *Philippians*, 30-32, 74-75, 76-78.
18 So also the survey of recent opinion in Martin, *Philippians*, 112-114.
19 D. Georgi, "Der vorpaulinische Hymnus Phil 2:6-11," in E. Dinkler (ed.), *Zeit und Geschichte* (Tübingen: Mohr, 1964), 263-293.
20 J. A. Sanders, "Dissenting Deities and Philippians 2:1-11," *JBL* 88 (1969), 279-290.

Although the exact description of the religious background for Phil. 2:5-11 remains disputed, two things about the recent scholarly discussion seem worth noting. First, as already pointed out, there is wide agreement that the most important texts and the most likely religious atmosphere have to do with the Judaism of the Graeco-Roman period.[21] This, however, sugests a second noteworthy point, not so well recognized. The various Jewish materials now pointed to all reflect an interest in ethical matters. Jewish wisdom literature, for example, such as Wisdom of Solomon, is concerned mainly with the cultivation of behaviour that reflects the divine will, and the righteous figure of Wisdom of Solomon seems to be a role model for the readers. The Jewish literature preferred by J. A. Sanders also reflects ethical concerns. The fallen watchers in Enoch, or the rebellious angels of *Vita Adae et Evae* function as examples of the traits to be avoided in the readers and not just as mythical explanations of evil in the world.[22] It is clear that the overall purpose behind the writing of the pseudepigraphical literature of ancient Judaism and the literature of the Qumran community was to secure a style of religio-ethical response, and not just to tell tales of origins. Now, if what is regarded these days as the general background of Phil. 2:5-11 reflects ethical concerns, and if the figures in this literature that are offered by scholars as analogies or contrasts for the description of Christ so function in the Jewish literature as to include their being positive or negative ethical examples, then this raises the question of whether Jesus too so functions in this passage.[23] To say that the figures in the Jewish literature, so often pointed to as the background of the passage, reflect paraenetic concerns is not to suggest that they are nothing but moral examples. Also, to suggest that the description of Jesus in Phil. 2:5-11 includes a description of him as an example for Christian response does not mean that Jesus' actions of self-humbling and obedience are seen as nothing but illustrations or examples of Christian ethical ideals. All that is being claimed at this point is that the nature of the Jewish literature thought to be behind the description of Jesus in Phil. 2:5-11 is such as to suggest that paraenetic concerns may have been involved in Jesus' description.[24]

---

21 Thus, e.g., J. T. Sanders, *The New Testament Christological Hymns*, SNTSMS 15 (Cambridge: Cambridge University Press, 1971), 73-74, who expresses some reservations about Georgi's view but agrees that, whatever the ultimate origin of the ideas that may be reflected in the passage, the immediate background is probably Jewish.

22 See the examples cited in J. A. Sanders, "Dissenting Deities," 284-288.

23 It is strange that J. A. Sanders thought that his argument that Jesus in Phil. 2:5-11 is contrasted with the rebellious angels of Jewish literature rendered it *less* likely that Jesus functioned in the passage as an example (ibid., 289). He seems to have been unable to see that a description of the actions of beings such as watchers, though "mythical," could be intended to reflect real ethical values and could include an intention to provide good or bad examples of these values.

24 Other examples of recent attempts to locate the background of Phil. 2:5-11 in Jewish materials include J. Murphy-O'Connor, "Christological Anthropology in Phil. 2:5-

But even more important than the fact that the particular background proposed by Käsemann seems incorrect, we must ask whether his whole emphasis that Phil. 2:5-11 must be interpreted solely on the basis of a pre-Christian background of myths and images is not a serious mistake in exegetical method. What is implicit in the exegesis of Käsemann is raised to the level of an explicit principle in Martin's otherwise valuable study when he urges, "It is of the utmost importance to isolate the meaning of the terms in the hymn from the use which is made of them by Paul in the verses which precede and follow."[25] What this kind of exegesis amounts to is the ignoring of the context of a passage and the use of hypothetical constructions of the "background" of thought to interpret what the passage means. With all due appreciation for the necessary historical-critical task of reconstructing the thought-world of the Graeco-Roman era as an aid to exegesis, surely one must insist that such background information must not be used as a basis for ignoring the context of a NT passage. Whatever the origin of imagery, terms, or concepts, the crucial step in exegesis is seeing how such matters are treated in the context of a given NT document and of early Christianity. It is a useful work of historical hypothesis-making to detach a formula expression or a credal or hymnic passage from its present context in the attempt to describe its "tradition-history," its origin and usage previous to its use in its present location, but such a procedure cannot be called complete exegesis of the present text of Phil. 2:5-11, and it does not necessarily tell us very much about what Paul intended by including this passage in his letter.[26]

Whether prompted by theological concerns (as I suggest above may have been the case with Käsemann) or by an enthusiasm for tradition-historical inquiry (as may have been the case with Martin), setting aside the immediate context of Phil. 2:5-11 with its obvious paraenetic concerns works unnecessary mischief upon the exegetical enterprise. In what follows, then, let us take note of some major evidence from the context and from within Phil. 2:5-11 itself that Paul's description of Jesus in this passage is intended not only to inspire an ethical response but also to give an authoritative example for that response.

11," *RB* 83 (1976), 25-50; and J. D. G. Dunn, *Christology in the Making* (London: SCM, 1980), 114-121.

25 Martin, *Carmen Christi*, 215. Cf. 289, "Once the hymn's significance in its original form is detached from the use Paul makes of it, we are relieved of these irritating difficulties of interpretation"(!), referring to the evidence that the passage carries a paraenetic function in its present context.

26 G. Strecker, "Redaktion und Tradition im Christushymnus Phil 2:6-11," *ZNW* 55 (1964), 63-78, helpfully distinguishes between the previous use of the hymn and its present function, which is clearly paraenetic. I was not able to consult R. Deichgräber, *Gotteshymnus und Christushymnus in der frühen Christenheit* (Göttingen: Vandenhoeck und Ruprecht, 1967), but I understand he makes a similar point. Martin formally allows for the distinction, but seems to ignore it in practice (cf. *Carmen Christi*, 287).

THE QUESTION OF CONTEXT AND
TEXT

As we enter upon this section of our discussion, in which we will examine the passage in question in some greater detail, it may be useful to give first some brief attention to the question of whether Paul elsewhere cites the example of Jesus in paraenetic exhortation. This may be a particularly worthwhile step in view of the fact that it is urged, as an argument against the view that Jesus is cited here as an example, that "Paul never uses the earthly life of Jesus as an *exemplum ad imitandum*."[27] If this rather astonishing statement means what it appears to say, it goes against evidence in the Pauline letters, as others have shown already.[28] It is true that Paul's references to the example of Jesus are almost always specifically references to his death, and it is true that, for Paul, Jesus' death had eschatological and cosmic significance and was therefore not *simply* an exemplary event. Nevertheless the crucifixion was for Paul a real historical event, the most illustrative event to be sure, in the earthly ministry of Jesus. So, though Paul's references to Jesus as example in Rom. 15:3, 8; 1 Cor. 11:1; 2 Cor. 4:8-11; 5:14; and 1 Thess. 1:6 all have to do mainly with the death of Jesus, they are nonetheless evidence that the earthly Jesus in his self-sacrifice could be cited by Paul as pattern for behaviour. The observation, so often urged, that Paul did not distinguish the earthly Jesus from the heavenly Lord is true, if it means that Paul saw the earthly Jesus as in some way the incarnation of the pre-existent and now exalted Son of God, and therefore never *merely* as a heroic human example. But it is incorrect to think that Paul's awareness of the heavenly significance of Jesus prevented him from citing Jesus as an inspiring example for believers.[29] With this in mind, let us turn directly to Phil. 2:5-11.

Käsemann proposed the view that *en Christō Iesou* (2:5) was not a personal reference to Jesus but in effect a circumlocution for the circle of Christian fellowship, a view that has been taken up with approval by many.[30] This understanding of the phrase is disputed by others,[31] but

---

27 Martin, *Carmen Christi*, 288.
28 Cf. J. Weiss, *Earliest Christianity* (New York: Harper & Row, 1959 [German, 1914; ET, 1937]) 2:448-458. On Jesus as example in Paul see W. Michaelis, *TDNT* 4:666-673, but his rather arbitrary treatment of the evidence makes his conclusions problematical. Cf. E. J. Tinsley, *The Imitation of God in Christ*, 134-165; W. P. De Boer, *The Imitation of Paul*; G. N. Stanton, *Jesus of Nazareth in New Testament Preaching*, 99-110; M. S. Enslin, *The Ethics of Paul* (New York: Abingdon, 1957), 107-119; V. P. Furnish, *Theology and Ethics in Paul* (Nashville: Abingdon, 1968), 216-223 (and his references).
29 Cf. W. D. Davies, *Paul and Rabbinic Judaism* (London: S.P.C.K., 1955), 147-196.
30 Käsemann, "A Critical Analysis," 83-84. See, e.g., Beare, *Philippians*, 75-76; Martin, *Carmen Christi*, 289-291.
31 E.g., Larsson, *Christus als Vorbild*, 232-233; Stanton, *Jesus of Nazareth*, 101; I. H. Marshall, "The Christ-Hymn in Philippians 2:5-11," *Tyn Bul* 19 (1969), 118. Cf. the careful analysis of W. Kramer, *Christ, Lord, Son of God*, SBT 50 (London: SCM, 1966), 141-146.

even if we allow it to stand, this does not settle the question of how the following verses are to be understood. In fact, however, even in Käsemann's interpretation of *en Christō Iesou*, a personal reference to Jesus cannot be excluded, for the next words take up events directly connected with Jesus, and the church is in Paul's writings always the circle grounded upon the personal work of Christ. However we translate the somewhat elliptical *ho kai en Christō Iesou*, the following verses determine more fully the interpretation to be given to the passage as a whole.

Though the more popular view that 2:6-7 refers to the pre-existent Christ has been challenged of late, for the present purpose it is not necessary to debate this issue, and we shall assume that the dominant view is correct.[32] On the basis of this view, it is rightly objected both that it is not the earthly Jesus but a heavenly figure who is here described, and that it is difficult to see how the action of such a figure could be an example for believers.[33] In reply, two points must be made. First, while there can be no direct duplication by mere humans of the action of a heavenly being who is seen as enjoying quasi-divine status, it is not impossible that such an action might be described so as to make it exemplary for earthly behaviour, the differences notwithstanding.[34]

Second, in the present instance, though it may be the action of the pre-existent, heavenly one that is referred to in 2:6-7, this action is directly linked with the action of the earthly Jesus in 2:8, for surely *morphēn doulou labōn* is intended to correspond to *etapeinōsen heauton* and *genomenos hypēkoos*. That is, the unseen and ineffable action of heaven is described after the fashion of the observed, historical action.[35] And here again the limited usefulness of the supposed mythological parallels for interpreting this passage is apparent, for surely in Paul's mind it was the action of the earthly Jesus in submitting to crucifixion that provided basis for describing him as a *doulos* and as *hypēkoos*, and not some previous mythic pattern.

Further, it is of great importance that this vocabulary used to describe Jesus' actions in 2:7-8 has such obvious connections with two other bodies of teaching: Pauline paraenesis and the Jesus tradition of

---

32 See recently J. Murphy-O'Connor, "Christological Anthropology"; and J. D. G. Dunn, *Christology in the Making*, 114-121, who argue that the earthly Jesus is here likened to Adam in being *en morphē theou*. If this view is correct, then it would make the case even stronger that Paul is citing Jesus here as both basis and pattern for Christian existence.

33 Thus, e.g., Käsemann, "A Critical Analysis," 64-65.

34 Does not Käsemann come close to admitting this when he says that, though Jesus is not a *Vorbild* in Phil. 2:5-11, he is the *Urbild* (ibid., 74)? There are valid differences between the two words but, though *Urbild* connotes something not merely illustrative but constitutive and foundational, there is a certain correspondence between an *Urbild* and what comes after it.

35 *Thanatou de staurou* makes it plain that 2:8 refers to the earthly Jesus and to the nature of his actions!

the Gospels. As is well known, Paul describes himself as a *doulos* of Christ (Rom. 1:1; Gal. 1:10; Phil. 1:1) and himself and others as *douloi* of the churches (2 Cor. 4:5; Col. 4:12). In addition, he uses the term in moral exhortation of the Roman Christians (Rom. 6:19), and the verb form is a common description of Christian life (Rom. 7:6, 25; 12:11; 14:18; 16:18; Gal. 5:13; Phil. 2:22; Col. 3:24; 1 Thess. 1:9).

Although the terms *diakonos, diakonia, diakoneō* can be distinguished from the *doulos* word group (in the latter group there is comparatively more emphasis upon the subjected status of the servant/slave in relation to the one being served)[36] the two word groups are used in such close association that it is legitimate to cite the use of the *diakonos* word group as background for the word *doulos* in Phil. 2:7.[37] Thus, Paul describes Christ as having become a *diakonos* (Rom. 15:8) in the service of God, and often uses members of this word group to describe himself and others in their work among the churches (e.g., 2 Cor. 3:6; 6:4; Col. 1:7, 23, 25; 1 Thess. 3:2; Rom. 16:1).

All of this means that, when Paul describes Jesus as having taken the role of a *doulos* in Phil. 2:7, he is using language with rich positive overtones for him and his readers.[38] While it is not expressly stated in 2:7 that Jesus was *doulos* to God, neither is it expressly stated that Christ became *doulos* to evil powers (as Käsemann suggests), and there are better reasons for taking the former meaning than the latter. First, as shown above, the *doulos* word group is used more frequently in Paul with reference to Christian life and service than with reference to the unredeemed condition of humans and is *never* used to mean human existence as such.[39] Second, in the immediate passage the contrast

---

36 H. W. Beyer, *TDNT* 2:81. Cf. G. Abbot-Smith, *A Manual Greek Lexicon of the Greek New Testament* (Edinburgh: T & T Clark, 1950), 108. A feature distinguishing the *doulos* group from the *diakonos* group that has not been pointed out, so far as I know, is that in Paul the latter group most frequently refers to activities like preaching and other church service, while the *doulos* group is characteristically associated with general Christian life and obedience. In this light, the reference to Jesus as *doulos* in Phil. 2:6 is all the more interesting. Cf. Rom. 15:8.

37 Cf. Col. 4:7 where Tychicus is called both *diakonos* and *doulos*, or 1 Cor. 3:5 and 2 Cor. 4:6 where Paul uses the terms of himself and others as if they are almost interchangeable. The same association of the terms appear in Mark 10:43-45// Matt. 20:26-28.

38 Though Paul uses *doulos* in a negative way in Gal. 4:7 and Rom. 6:17, 20, the verb form negatively in Rom. 6:6; Gal. 4:3, 8, 9, 25, and *douleia* negatively in Gal. 4:24; 5:1; Rom. 8:21, these must be set over against the heavier and more widespread use of these terms positively in Rom. 7:6, 25; 12:11; 14:18; 16:18; Gal. 5:13; Phil. 2:22; Col. 3:24; 1 Thess. 1:9; Rom. 1:1; 6:19 (twice); 2 Cor. 4:5; Gal. 1:10; Phil. 1:1; and Col. 4:12. By "positive" I do not mean to minimize the contrast between *morphē doulou* in Phil. 2:7 and *morphē theou* in 2:6 or *Kyrios* in 2:11. I mean only that the primary *Pauline* association of the term was not bondage to evil powers but servitude to God and to others for his sake.

39 Käsemann wished to have *morphē doulou* mean human existence as such, and argued that the *en homoiōmati anthrōpōn genomenos* should be taken as a fully synonymous phrase ("A Critical Analysis," 66-67). This is not quite correct, however, for the latter phrase functions rather to explain the medium taken by Jesus in carrying out the

between the *harpagmos* put aside or rejected, *to einai isa theō*, and the path chosen, *morphēn doulou*, suggests that what is meant is service toward God, or for his sake. Third, and crucially I think, the striking *dio* of 2:9, and the fact that God is the actor in 2:9-11, show that the service of 2:7-8 must be seen as offered to God, and that 2:9-11 is the divine response. Paul does not just contrast God's act with Christ's (as *alla* would have implied), but makes God's act of exaltation a consequence of Christ's obedience.

The terms used in 2:8, *etapeinōsen heauton* and *hypēkoos*, are also attested in Paul's writings with reference to Paul and the churches. Thus, Paul says he humbled himself (!) in the service of the Corinthians (2 Cor. 11:7; cf. Phil. 4:12), and refers to the present vehicle of Christian life as *to sōma tēs tapeinōseōs hēmōn* (Phil. 3:21).[40] A cognate term, *tapeinophrosunē*, is urged in Col. 3:12 and Phil. 2:3. The noun "obedience" and the verb "obey" are widely used Pauline terms for Christian existence.[41]

Now the point of all this is that the description of Jesus' actions in Phil. 2:6-8 is replete with terms whose most customary usage is in connection with paraenesis and references to Paul's own ministry. The most reasonable conclusion, therefore, is that Jesus' redemptive work is so described as to make it at the same time something of a pattern for those who call him Lord. If Paul intended the words to be taken in a sense different from their usual Christian semantic associations, why did he not insert modifying phrases to make this plain, especially since, in the opinion of many, it appears that he may have felt free to add other phrases to this "hymn" (e.g., *thanatou de staurou*, 2:8)?

This brings us to another matter of greater significance than is usually recognized. The easily observable lack of typical Pauline redemptive terminology (e.g., *hyper hēmōn*) is frequently cited mainly as evidence that 2:6-11 was not originally written by Paul. However correct this inference may be, the absence of such language may also imply something about Paul's purposes in this passage. That is, the fact that Paul did not use specifically redemptive language (or did not add it to this "pre-Pauline hymn") when he apparently did make at least one insertion in 2:8b may signify that Paul's interest in reciting the acts of Jesus in 2:6-8 was simply to give their dimensions and quality so as to provide both a basis and a pattern for the paraenesis that surrounds the passage and that is its obvious context. Käsemann's emphasis that the absence of references to the church in 2:6-11 is evidence that every-

---

role of servant. That is, Paul is not saying that human existence in this world is *douleia* as such but that in Jesus' case the decision to take a servant's position found expression in his human life of obedience.

40   1 Pet. 5:6 and Jas. 4:10 exhort Christians to humble themselves to God in trust that he will exalt them (*hypsoō*!), further evidence that the terms in Phil. 2:8 bore widely-known semantic association with Christian paraenesis.

41   "Obedience," Rom. 1:5; 5:19; 6:16; 15:18; 16:19, 26; 2 Cor. 7:15; 10:5, 6; Phlm. 21; "obey," Rom. 6:17; Phil. 2:12; 2 Thess. 1:8; 3:14.

thing in the passage has to do with Jesus and the cosmic powers not only flies in the face of the evidence amassed so far about the ordinary Pauline use of the language of the passage, but also lifts the passage from its present paraenetic context in Philippians and reads into the passage references to beings that may at most be alluded to in 2:10-11 as partaking in the acclamation given by all creation.[42]

In addition to the evidence that the description of Jesus in 2:6-8 draws upon the vocabulary of early Christian paraenesis, there is also evidence that Paul may be reflecting here the Gospel tradition of Jesus' earthly ministry. In all the Synoptic Gospels there is the tradition that Jesus commanded his disciples to be servants of one another after the analogy of his own role (Mark 10:43-45/Matt. 20:25-28/Luke 22:24-27; Mark 9:35; Matt. 23:11).[43] Further, in the well-known foot-washing episode in John 13:5-17 a similar tradition appears, where Jesus uses *doulos* imagery. We may even note Heb. 5:8-9, where the obedience of Jesus is referred to, as a possible echo of this same sort of tradition. When, therefore, Paul refers to Jesus as he does in Phil. 2:6-8, he may have been drawing upon traditional descriptions of the role of the earthly Jesus, and this tradition is far more likely to have informed Paul's use of the key terms *doulos, tapeinoō, hypēkoō*, than the sources proposed by Käsemann or the "hellenistic background" invoked by others. The obedience of Phil. 2:8 is not the obeying *of* death, as if death were one of the cosmic powers here, but obedience to the *extent* of death (*mechri thanatou*, not *thanatōi*!).[44] What is emphasized is the quality of Jesus' action; the action is not limited to the experience of death, but includes a larger obedience that remains steadfast even to the point of death. This being so, it is not strictly true that Paul refers *only* to death in the earthly career of Jesus, for in this passage Paul seems to reflect traditional language in a summary description of the contour of the earthly career of this obedient one.

Up to this point we have been examining 2:6-8 in the attempt to understand the actions of Jesus described there. It is a major point in Martin's case against the view that Jesus is referred to as an example that 2:9-11, which is crucial for the passage, is not done justice.[45] Now it is undeniably true that 2:9-11 is the climax of the whole passage and that any interpretation of 2:5-11 must not minimize the significance of these verses. But, in order to give 2:9-11 its proper importance, one

---

42 This is not to deny that "cosmic powers" or angel-beings figured prominently in Paul's thought, or that he saw Christ's death as a deliverance from such powers elsewhere (Col. 2:13-19; Gal. 4:3, 8-10). The present point is that there is inadequate reason to see these cosmic powers as implicitly referred to in Phil. 2:6-8, and that the obedience of Christ here is more likely with reference to God.

43 In these passages *doulos* and *diakonos* are used synonymously.

44 Cf. Martin, *Carmen Christi*, 227-228, who seems insensitive to the syntax here and reads colourful meaning into the statement, which unfortunately does not support his notion.

45 Ibid., 288.

need not deny that Jesus' actions in 2:6-8 are exemplary and thus
fitting for the paraenetic context of the letter. Nor, in order to hold that
Phil. 2:5-11 serves Paul's paraenetic purpose, need one advocate some
version of "naive ethical idealism," or suggest simplistically that "all that
a Christian has to do is to follow in the Master's footsteps."[46] Contrary to
Martin's claim that 2:9-11 has "no relevance to Paul's ethical admonition,"[47] these verses show that the actions of 2:6-8 received divine
vindication and approval, and that the one who took the role of slave is
now *kyrios*, to whom all owe reverence. This means that 2:9-11 is not an
epilogue to 2:6-8, but rather serves to evaluate Jesus' obedience in the
highest terms. Further, the fact that Jesus is now *kyrios* (2:9-11) means
that his action of self-humbling and obedience has not just exemplary
but also fully authoritative significance. What Paul calls for is obedience
(2:12), as Christ was obedient (2:8), and the authority of his call to
obedience (as the *hôste* of 2:12 indicates) rests on the fact that the one to
whom his readers are summoned to conform is now the *kyrios*. For
Paul's readers the acclamation of Jesus as *kyrios* was to have defin-
ite ethical implications, for the connection between kerygma and
paraenesis is clear in Paul.

   The interpretation of the passage advocated here is one in which
the themes of obedience (2:6-8) and vindication (2:9-11) are both done
justice. Neither the simplistic ethicizing interpretations rejected by
Käsemann and Martin nor their own "cosmic drama" interpretations
are capable of doing justice to the full import of 2:5-11. Here Jesus is
certainly presented as the triumphant Lord who now bears cosmic
authority and whose humiliation and obedience was unique in kind
and soteriological in effect. But here also Jesus' own action in 2:6-8 is
described in language designed to ring familiar tones with Paul's
readers, language that attributes to Jesus' action the character the
readers were to exemplify in their own lives. The unique nature of
Jesus' obedience and its cosmic consequences (2:9-11) mean that his
action is foundational for all Christian obedience and that the Christian
cannot simply replicate the obedience of 2:6-8. To borrow Dahl's
terms, it is not strict *imitatio* but rather *conformitas* that the passage
promotes, by which the believers are called to see in Jesus' action not
only the basis of their obedience but also its pattern and direction.[48]

---

46   Ibid.
47   Ibid., 289.
48   N. A. Dahl, *Jesus in the Memory of the Early Church* (Minneapolis: Augsburg, 1976), 34;
     cf. 20. This "pattern" involves self-humbling service and obedience, based on Jesus'
     authoritative example and in trust that God will vindicate those who acclaim Jesus as
     Lord in their obedience. Martin (*Carmen Christi*, 289) suggests that if Jesus is
     portrayed as an example to the believers his exaltation in 2:9-11 would have pro-
     moted "false motives and the acceptance of unworthy ends," but this is not necessar-
     ily so. First, the divine action in 2:9-11 is as unique in significance and nature as Jesus'
     actions in 2:6-8, and Paul's point is that Jesus was not just lifted from his humiliation
     but was made *Kyrios*. Thus, Jesus is not just example but is Lord of the Christian life

CONCLUSION

We have by no means dealt with all the issues pertaining to Phil. 2:5-11 but have organized our discussion around the question of what Paul's purpose was in citing Jesus in this passage. In summary, it may be helpful to list briefly the conclusions put forth in this investigation.

(1) There is reason to think that Käsemann's influential analysis of the passage was an overreaction against particular examples of "ethical idealism" and pietism, so that he was unable to do justice to the evidence of Paul's paraenetic purposes in including this passage in his letter.

(2) The primary consideration in determining the meaning of Jesus' actions in 2:6-8 must be the use of the language in early Christianity. While the larger Graeco-Roman context must not be ignored, the immediate early Christian context of language and ethos is most important.

(3) The language used to describe Jesus' actions qualitatively in 2:6-8 is drawn from the language of early Christian paraenesis and possibly from the Jesus tradition of the Pauline period. This suggests that the tradition of the earthly Jesus was influential in shaping both this description of his actions, and possibly early Christian paraenesis. Further, this evidence suggests strongly that Jesus' actions are so described as to present them as a pattern to which the readers are to conform their behaviour.

(4) The soteriological and cosmic effect of Jesus' actions of obedience *en morphē doulou* is not to be denied, and indeed the climactic verses 9-11 show that Jesus is presented here as more than simply a role model or pioneer, for he is *kyrios* to whom all must bow. But these verses do not forbid one to think that Paul presents Jesus as the authoritative pattern for Christian existence. In fact, these crucial verses emphasize that Jesus' actions were foundational for Christian existence, and at the same time show that his self-denial and obedience have received divine vindication, making Jesus' pattern of service the Lordly example to the readers who acclaim him now.

To conclude, Paul's picture of the cosmic Lord to whom all shall bow is informed by the shape of the ministry of Jesus who was *hypēkoos mechri thanatou*. In 2:5-11 there is not only his ultimate glory and authority but also the echo of the tradition of his historical service, to which the Christian, the subject of this Lord, is called to be conformed.

---

and indeed of the universe. That is, the Christian is called to conform to Jesus' pattern of obedience and service not on the basis of some general moral appeal but on the basis of his present authority. Second, while Jesus' exaltation was unique, it was also cited as a pattern for early Christian hope (Phil. 3:21; Rom. 8:11, 17; cf. 2 Tim. 2:12), and if this hope for a divine vindication as encouragement for service and patience in humiliation be regarded as "unworthy," that is a judgment apparently not shared by Paul!

Imitation in Paul's Letters: Its Significance for His Relationship to Jesus and to His Own Christian Foundations

DAVID STANLEY, S.J.

Some reflections on Paul's notion of imitation find an appropriate place in a volume of essays, gathered around the theme of the relation of Paul to Jesus, and presented to our distinguished colleague, Dr. Frank W. Beare. Because this imitation of himself "and of the Lord" (1 Thess. 1:6) appears to have been original with the Apostle[1] and related to his self-understanding as one called by God "to preach the gospel among the pagans" (Gal 1:16), it may be expected to shed light on his own view of his personal relation to Christ. As a review of the relevant texts will disclose, the recommendation of his own manner of life "in Christ Jesus" (1 Cor. 4:17) is intimately linked with "the gospel," a distinctively Pauline word for the Christian message.[2] Moreover, the novelty of the proposal that his hellenistic Christians imitate himself is cause for surprise in one who repudiated the insinuation of his opponents that he was seeking to make disciples for himself. "We do not proclaim ourselves but Jesus as Lord, with ourselves as your slaves for the sake of Jesus" (2 Cor. 4:5).[3]

---

1 *Mimeisthai* is elsewhere in the New Testament found only in Heb. 13:7 and 3 John 11, *mimētēs* in Eph. 5:1 and Heb. 6:12.
2 J. A. Fitzmyer, "The Gospel in the Theology of Paul," *Int* 33 (1979), 339-350. (Abbreviations in references are those used by the *Journal of Biblical Literature*. See *JBL* 95 [1976], 331-346).
3 Paul never employs *mathētēs, mathēteuein* or other gospel terms for discipleship in his letters.

The curious phenomenon of setting his own living of the gospel before his converts as exemplary (2 Thess. 3:9; Phil. 3:17; 1 Cor. 4:16; 11:1), while rarely referring to the example of Jesus (Rom. 15:3; Phil. 2:6-11), may well indicate a concern to adapt the Jewish-Christian proclamation to the very different culture of those "Greeks and barbarians" (Rom. 1:14) he was sent to evangelize. This sensitivity to the need for acculturation is attested by his innovative development of the ancient letter-form, which for centuries had remained bound by convention in the hellenistic world.[4] Under the impulse of Paul's genius it was forged into a medium for continuing his proclamation of the gospel by clarifying for his Christian communities the significance for their life of faith of Jesus' earthly history. It would not then be entirely implausible to view the Pauline letters as the initial phase in a process that would lead to the creation (by Mark) of the uniquely Christian form of literature, the written Gospel, concerning which redaction criticism has proved so enlightening.

And here I venture to suggest that a discussion of the meaning of imitation in Paul is particularly relevant in a *Festschrift* designed to honour Professor Beare. For in my judgment the distinctive feature of his long, scholarly career lies in the unwavering conviction, to which he witnessed both in the lecture hall and by his many writings, that rigorous adherence to the demands of critical biblical scholarship remains an indispensable means to a solid formation of his audiences and readers in a genuinely Christian spirituality. His academic life thus illustrates a courageous commitment to the Anselmian principle, *fides quaerens intellectum* (faith that seeks understanding). In his characteristically forthright manner, Professor Beare waged relentless war against what is known as "biblicism," or scriptural fundamentalism, because he so clearly saw it to be a shoddy substitute for the authentic message of the Christian gospel. One instance of this unflagging commitment must suffice here.

Some years ago Dr. Beare wrote a thoughtful, sympathetic evaluation of a document issued by the Pontifical Biblical Commission, April 21, 1964, entitled "The Historical Truth of the Gospels."[5] He took issue with a *caveat* it contained for preachers and "those who write for the Christian public at a popular level" as regards the divulging of the recent findings of Gospel criticism. He observed that

What is needed . . . is to make the results of scholarly investigation known far more widely, and to show that the continued use of the biblical writings for the nourishing of the spiritual life is not at all dependent on the maintenance of obsolete and untenable notions of their character. . . . It is time for us all to grasp the nettle, to cease trembling for the ark of the Lord, and to show that the modern critical understanding of the Scriptures makes them not less but more

4   B. Rigaux, *Les Epîtres aux Thessaloniciens* (Paris: J. Gabalda, 1956), 357.
5   The text is found in *CBQ* 26 (1964), 305-312.

"profitable for teaching, for reproof, for correction, and for training in righteousness."[6]

THE IMITATION OF CHRIST IN
CHRISTIAN SPIRITUALITY

Before we explore the sense of imitation in Paul's writings it may be well to advert at least in passing to the position of honour in which the imitation of Christ was held in Christian spirituality.[7] In the sixteenth century Martin Luther reacted against some excesses in the mediaeval devotion to the humanity of Christ. While admitting that Jesus was exemplar as well as gift, he came more and more to underscore the latter aspect, and ultimately viewed the imitation of Christ as an attempt by human pride to acquire merit. Yet, to avoid any misunderstanding of what such imitation should mean for Christian spirituality, it may be helpful to cite the eminent Roman Catholic theologian, Karl Rahner. "The imitation of Christ does *not* consist in the observance of certain moral maxims which may be perfectly exemplified in Jesus, but which have an intrinsic value in themselves independently of him . . . [but] in a true entering into *his* life and *in him* entering into the inner life of the God that has been given to us." He adds, "The call to follow Christ does not reach us in words that come from outside. . . . Ultimately, this call is the necessary development and unfolding of what we have always been: free persons determined by our very nature to live with Christ."[8]

The thought expressed here in existentialist terms is reminiscent of Paul's understanding of his own relationship to Christ. "For me living means Christ" (Phil. 1:21a). "It is no longer I that live—Christ lives in me. As regards my present bodily existence, I live my life by faith in the Son of God, who loved me and handed himself over for me" (Gal. 2:20). In addition, Paul describes the ongoing development of the Christian life as a "remoulding," a *transformation* into Christ. "All of us while, with unveiled face, we behold as in a mirror the glory of the Lord are being remoulded into the same image from glory to glory by the Lord [who is] Spirit" (2 Cor. 3:18). It is in these same terms that Paul describes the divine plan of redemption: "Those he [God] knew beforehand he destined to be remoulded in the image of his Son, in order that he might become firstborn of many brothers" (Rom. 8:29). This transforming action of God, which accompanies the believer through life, can be denominated "a new creation" (2 Cor. 5:17; Gal. 6:15), and in this characteristically Pauline conception the risen Christ appears as

---

6   F. W. Beare, "The Historical Truth of the Gospels: An Official Pronouncement of the Pontifical Biblical Commission," *CJT* 11 (1965), 237.

7   See the article "Imitation du Christ," in *Dictionnaire de Spiritualité* 7 (Paris: 1971), 1536-1601.

8   K. Rahner, *Spiritual Exercises* (New York: Herder & Herder, 1965), 118.

"the last Adam" (1 Cor. 15:45).[9] As "image of God" (2 Cor. 4:4; see Col. 1:15) the Son of God, made fully human through death and exaltation (Phil. 2:6-11), has become *the* exemplary model for the Christian, who through his own life, death, and resurrection is destined to enter God's family. To help his "Greeks" grasp the gospel message, Paul does not hesitate to borrow the hellenistic legal term *hyiothesia*.[10] "But when the time reached its fulfilment, God sent forth his Son, born of woman, subject to law, in order that he might redeem those under law, that we might receive adoptive sonship." Yet, while the believer has been numbered among "God's sons" through faith and baptism (Gal. 3:26-27), this sonship is but inchoate, to be fully realized only by "the redemption of our body" (Rom. 8:23).

We may pause to note the concern of Paul to adapt the gospel to the culture of his Christians by employing terminology with which they are familiar. Indeed, this procedure may be said to be a practice of his. Yet, it is crucial to realize that such words or phrases are employed *analogously*. This is especially clear in the case of *mimeisthai, mimētēs*, which betray no influence by Xenophon, Plato, or Aristotle.[11] It is largely his failure to perceive the new Christian sense which appears in Paul's usage of this terminology that has led W. Michaelis to misconstrue the meaning it has in the Pauline letters.[12]

THE MEANING OF "THE GOSPEL" FOR PAUL

To appreciate the new meaning which imitation has acquired in Paul's letters, it is necessary to recall the radical insight he expressed through the term gospel. He always regarded his preaching of it as the quintessential feature of his apostleship (1 Cor. 1:17). "For if I go on preaching the gospel, that is nothing for me to boast of—I am constrained to do so, since I am lost if I stop preaching the gospel" (1 Cor. 9:16). However, Paul never thought of this apostolic activity merely in terms of "communications," as a skill to be credited to himself (1 Cor. 9:16-18). "Our gospel reached you not as a matter of words only, but also by the power of the Holy Spirit" (1 Thess. 1:5; see 1 Cor. 1:18). In its deepest reality, the gospel is nothing less than "God's dynamic power leading to

---

9   See my article, "Paul's Interest in the Early Chapters of Genesis," *AnBib* 17 (1963), 241-252.

10 Here, as elsewhere, Paul gives a Christian meaning to the term: see, for example, *ta diapheronta* (Phil. 1:10), *to epieikes* (Phil. 4:5), borrowings from popular philosophy.

11 See the article *"Mimeomai*, etc." by W. Michaelis in *TDNT* 4, 659-663 for usage of the term in secular Greek.

12 Ibid., 671-672, where Michaelis categorizes Pauline usage of *mimeomai, mimētēs* as simple comparison (1 Thess. 2:14, possibly also 1 Thess. 1:6), following of an example (2 Thess. 3:7, 9; Phil. 3:17), obedience (1 Cor. 4:16; 11:1; 1 Thess. 1:6). H. Schlier, *Der Brief an die Epheser* (Düsseldorf: Patmos-Verlag, 1957), 231, n. 1, as also C. Masson, *Les deux épîtres de saint Paul aux Thessaloniciens* (Neuchatel-Paris: Delachaux & Niestlé, 1957), 21, n. 2, takes exception to the interpretation of Michaelis.

salvation for those who believe" (Rom. 1:16). Yet Paul remains cogniz-
ant that *what* he proclaimed, even "the form" in which he proclaimed it,
was of weighty, if secondary, importance (1 Cor. 15:1-2). He appears to
have been content to allow these two aspects of the gospel to stand in
tension, because each in its own way reflected the influence of the two
most important relationships in his apostolic career, that to Christ and
that to his communities.

PAUL'S UNDERSTANDING OF HIS RELATIONSHIP WITH CHRIST AND HIS OWN CHURCHES

How did Paul view his relation to Christ? The most revealing metaphor
occurs in his self-description as "a slave of Christ Jesus" (Phil. 1:1; Gal.
1:10; Rom. 1:1). While in the ancient world the slave could attain
positions of eminence in city government, among the literati or men of
wealth, he was never his own man: his entire existence was ordered
necessarily to his master.[13] For Paul, such a total orientation of himself
to the risen Lord was also the determining factor in his relationship to
those Christian communities he founded (2 Cor. 4:5). The obligation
he felt to make them see him as "an imitator of Christ" (1 Cor. 11:1)
governs his practice of providing his addressees with frequent notices
about his experiences (Phil. 1:12-20; 1 Cor. 4:1-14; 2 Cor. 10:3-6). His
impassioned *apologia* against an insinuation of fickleness by some Corinthians is comprehensible only as a defence of himself as imitator of
Christ Jesus. "You surely did not find him wavering between 'Yes' and
'No': with him it has always been 'Yes'" (2 Cor. 1:17-20a).

Paul's consciousness of his relation to Christ is to be explained
chiefly through four formative experiences on which he reflects in his
letters: the initial confrontation with the risen Lord, his own baptism,
his reception of the evangelical traditions learned in his early instruction in the faith, and the vicissitudes of his career as apostle. These
require some amplification.

Paul considered the foundational experience, which made him at
once a Christian *and* apostle (*klētos apostolos*: Rom. 1:1), worthy to rank
with those post-resurrection appearances of Christ listed in the primitive tradition (1 Cor. 15:5-8). He saw this momentous meeting as the
result of God's gracious decision "to reveal his Son in me, that I might
gospel him among the pagans" (Gal. 1:15-16); he compared it to the
divine creation of light (2 Cor. 4:6; Gen. 1:3). Hence he describes his
(and others') relationship with Christ as "a new creation" (2 Cor. 5:17;
Gal. 6:15).

We find Paul employing a new way of expressing his belief that he
is an imitator of Christ, when he describes the baptismal experience in

---

13 See S. Scott Bartchy, *First-Century Slavery and I Cor 7:21* (Missoula: Scholars Press,
1973).

writing to the church in Rome.[14] "Surely you are aware that each of us who has been baptized into Christ was baptized into his death? Thus we were buried together with him (*synetaphēmen*) through baptism into his death, in order that, just as Christ was raised from death by the glory of the Father, so we in turn might live a completely new kind of life" (Rom. 6:3-4). Where in his earlier letters Paul speaks of imitation, it appears characteristic of his maturer thought (2 Corinthians, Galatians, Romans, Colossians) to use a series of neologisms, verbs compounded with the preposition *syn*, which he appears to have created,[15] to express what he meant by declaring himself to be an imitator of Christ by being united with him in the twofold event proclaimed by the gospel, death and resurrection.

Since Paul, like the evangelists at a later date, did not know Jesus during his earthly life (2 Cor. 5:16), he received the Christian traditions about what Jesus said and did from others (Gal. 1:18; 2:2; Acts 22:14-16). He continually attested to the high value he set on them (1 Thess. 1:13, 15; 4:1-2; Phil. 4:9; 1 Cor. 11:23; 15:1-3). He took care to distinguish dominical sayings from his own injunctions (1 Cor. 7:10; 9:14), and moreover denominated the former "sayings of *the Lord*" (1 Thess. 4:2, 15; 1 Cor. 9:14; Rom. 14:14).[16] This use of the resurrection-title to designate the risen Christ as source of the tradition shows that for Paul his reception of that tradition was something more than data-gathering. It involved for him an experience of the action of the exalted Lord. This appears to be the sense of the difficult text (Gal. 1:11-12), which must be understood in the light of Paul's repeated assertions of receiving the traditions about Jesus, and his claim that "There is no other gospel" (Gal. 1:7; 2 Cor. 11:4).[17]

---

14   See P. Adnès, "Réflexions Théologiques," in "Imitation du Christ," *Dictionnaire de Spiritualité* 7, 1587-1597, who points to the Christian baptismal experience as the initiation into the imitation of Christ.

15   The impressive list of these verbs, all of which deal with the new life brought by Christ through the cross and resurrection, appears to have ultimately replaced the imitation theme. If this surmise is correct, it is an additional indication that the example of Paul and the imitation of himself he proposes must be reckoned as more than a merely moral influence. See *syzēn* (2 Cor. 7:3; Rom. 6:8); *syzōpoiein* (Col. 2:13); *sympaschein* (Rom. 8:17); *synapothnēskein* (2 Cor. 7:3); *syndoxazesthai* (Rom. 6:4; Col. 2:12); *systaurousthai* (Gal. 2:19; Rom. 6:6). Where these terms imply the divine activity in the Christian's assimilation to Christ, the imitation-vocabulary includes the mediation of Paul as founder of the community.

16   Paul speaks in a similar way in attributing the actions and words of Jesus at the Last Supper to "the Lord Jesus" (1 Cor. 11:23). He asserts that the Jews "killed the Lord Jesus" (1 Thess. 2:15), the powers of evil "crucified the Lord of glory" (1 Cor. 2:8). The divine dynamism unleashed in history through the resurrection of Jesus, operative in the gospel (Rom. 1:16), is what, in Paul's view, has given relevance and authority and power to the Christian *anamnēsis* of the earthly history of Jesus.

17   G. Bornkamm, *Paul*, trans. by D. M. G. Stalker (New York: Harper & Row, 1979), has perceptively observed that to make out from Gal. 1:11-12 that Paul depended for his knowledge of Jesus only upon his visionary experiences is tantamount to saying that "for the primitive Church's traditions about Jesus, Paul substituted his own vision of

Finally, an insight into Paul's understanding of himself as an "imitator of Christ" is provided through his assessment of his experiences in the apostolate (see 2 Cor. 1:17-20a). "Yet I carry this treasure in a vessel of clay, which proves that its transcendent power belongs to God, not to myself. Harried on all sides, I am never cut off; at a loss, yet never driven to despair; routed, still never abandoned to my fate; struck down, but never finished off. Always I carry about in my bodily person the dying of Jesus, that Jesus' life may in its turn be revealed in my person. For every day I live I am being handed over to death like Jesus, so that the life of Jesus may radiate through my mortal flesh" (2 Cor. 4:7-11; see also Phil. 3:10-11).

We must now turn to the texts which exhibit imitation-terminology, all of them occurring in Paul's earlier letters (1 Thessalonians, Philippians, 1 Corinthians). With these we also consider 2 Thess. 3:6-9, prescinding from the question of that letter's authenticity. There is no mention of the imitation of himself by Paul in letters to churches he did not found, with which he was in consequence not personally familiar (Romans, Philemon, Colossians).

THE THESSALONIAN ACCEPTANCE OF PAUL'S GOSPEL

The first two references to imitation occur in the extraordinarily lengthy thanksgiving (1 Thess. 1:2-3:13), which is a peculiar feature of Paul's first extant letter. The so-called Pauline thanksgiving was an innovative development of the conventional introduction to the hellenistic letter. In reality it is an account for his addressees of the prayer of petition as well as of gratitude Paul made for them before writing.[18] Thus it attests Paul's conviction that his own intercession was in fact a significant part of his apostolic responsibility.[19] As he narrates how he gratefully reminisced at his prayer and his own part in the Thessalonians' acceptance of his gospel, he describes the event as their imitation of himself "and the Lord" (1 Thess. 1:6). Somewhat later he thinks of the same happening as an imitation of the experience of Jewish-Christians in Palestine (1 Thess. 2:14). Thus these first instances of Paul's use of imitation exclude any notion of a deliberate or extrinsic copying of an example: the term denotes a deeply religious Christian experience of conversion to the faith.

Christ. . . . In this case . . . he would have been a disruptive, 'enthusiastic' crank who, for the sake of his own experience, jeopardized the unity of the church" (20). I should differ from Bornkamm in his assumption that the initial experience of Paul near Damascus could be counted—in the mind of the apostle—among his other "visions and revelations" (2 Cor. 12:1).

18   See my reflections on the thanksgiving in Pauline letters in *Boasting in the Lord: The Phenomenon of Prayer in Saint Paul* (New York/Toronto: Paulist Press, 1973), 134-164.

19   See J. D. Quinn, "Apostolic Ministry and Apostolic Prayer," *CBQ* 23 (1971), 479-491; also K. Stendahl, "Paul at Prayer," *Int* 34 (1980), 240-249.

We keep giving thanks to God always on account of all of you as we make a memento of you in our prayer, because unceasingly we remember the activeness of your faith and the labour of your love and the endurance of your hope in our Lord Jesus Christ in the presence of our God and Father, because we recognize, brothers beloved by God, his election of you, since our gospel did not reach you merely as a matter of words, but also through the power of the Holy Spirit and because of [our] complete conviction—you know what manner of life we led among you for your good. And you, for your part, became imitators of us and of the Lord by accepting the Word amid great tribulation with joy from the Holy Spirit, so that you yourselves became an example for every believer in Macedonia and Achaia. For from your community the Word of the Lord rang out—and that, not only in Macedonia and Achaia. Everywhere in fact your faith in God has travelled, so that there is no need at all for us to mention it (1 Thess. 1:2-8).

Paul begins (somewhat breathlessly)[20] by gratefully recalling the quality of the new life given by God to his converts in terms of the triadic description of Christian existence familiar to the addressees from his previous teaching: faith, which directs their Christian living; love that inspires difficult tasks for others; hope in the Parousia that enables them to bear up under the severe testing of persecution.

This heroic manner of life demonstrates the authentic character of their "election" by God, a traditional biblical term for vocation, which underscores the divine initiative and the untrammelled freedom exercised by God in calling them to the gospel. Their acceptance of the gospel was governed primarily by "the power of the Holy Spirit": it was not simply the force of the words in which Paul and his companions expressed their message. Yet their own "complete conviction" and "manner of life" were a contributory factor to the conversion of the Thessalonians (1:5). The transcendence and dynamism of God's invisible, inaudible activity did not, however, render superfluous Paul's preaching (Rom. 10:14) and his own living of the gospel.

The acceptance of the gospel by these neophytes is presented through a metaphorical use of imitation: "And you for your part became imitators of us and of the Lord." For, as Charles Masson observes, the passive force of the verb (*egenēthēte*) implies that God, not these new Christians, is the principal agent of this event.[21] The remarks of some commentators apply more properly to some of the later imitation-texts. Béda Rigaux considers that this imitation of Paul appears in his later conduct of the community after its foundation.[22] The same is true of Leander Keck's comment that Paul wished "his life to be transparent enough that his hearers could glimpse the power of the

---

20   It will be noticed that vv. 2-5 in the Greek text form one overcharged sentence.
21   Masson, *Thessaloniciens*, 21, n. 4.
22   Ibid., 383.

gospel. This transparency is what Paul wants the believers to imitate."[23] Here there is no mention of a wish or command, but a statement of fact.

In addition, Paul characterizes this imitation as having been principally "of the Lord," since they accepted "the Word amid great tribulation with joy from the Holy Spirit," as Jesus himself had taught (Matt. 5:13; Luke 6:23). The Jesus proclaimed by Paul was the One "having been crucified" (1 Cor. 2:2): though risen, he represents for Paul the crucified majesty of God.[24] Thus the experience of the cross is the authenticating mark of Christian living.

It is the following verse which describes the subsequent living of the gospel by these recent converts: they "became an example for every believer in Macedonia and Achaia" (1 Thess. 1:7). As Paul's living out of the gospel had, under God and Christ, been efficacious in bringing the Thessalonians to the faith, their existence as a community of faith in its turn served as a means of spreading the gospel, since from it "the Word of the Lord rang out" (1:8). This implies that the word example expresses something more than a moral influence. As in the case of Paul himself the lives of these believers have played an effective part in the communication of the gospel.

The second pertinent text (2:13-16) parallels the first in certain respects and confirms what has already been said about imitation and example.

And for the following reason also we keep giving thanks to God unceasingly, because in receiving the Word of God from our lips you accepted it not as a human word, but as it is in truth, God's Word, which is moreover actively at work in you as believers. For you became imitators, my brothers, of the churches of God in union with Christ Jesus in Judaea, since you suffered in your turn the very things from your own countrymen which they suffered from the Jews, who killed the Lord Jesus and the prophets, and persecuted us. They are in no way pleasing to God as enemies of the entire human race, by trying to hinder us from addressing the pagans that they may be saved (2:13-16).

In the verses immediately preceding this paragraph Paul described his conduct towards the Thessalonians as their apostle and founder in terms of paternity (see 1 Cor. 4:15): "As you know, [I conducted myself] towards each one of you as a father towards his children, exhorting, encouraging, adjuring you to lead lives in a manner worthy of the God who is calling you into his own Kingdom and glory" (2:11-12). Paul thereby indicates the distinctive character of his gospel, adapted to Greek-speaking peoples, and his personal way of dealing with them.

---

23   L. E. Keck, "The First Letter of Paul to the Thessalonians," in *The Interpreter's One-Volume Commentary on the Bible* (Nashville/New York: Abingdon Press, 1971), 867.

24   This is the force of the Greek perfect *estaurōmenon*. For Paul and the author of the Fourth Gospel (John 20:20), Jesus' resurrection has not blotted out the effects of his Passion.

This adaptation of his message to individuals of a different culture and language he knew to be of the utmost significance for his task of converting non-Jews, even though he realizes that in its most radical sense his gospel "is in truth God's Word . . . actively at work in you as believers." At the same time, we recall Paul's insistence upon the uniqueness, in fact the *unicity* of the gospel (Gal. 1:7-9), despite the cultural variants in its presentation and practice. He sets great store by the traditions and credal formulae (1 Thess. 4:14; 1 Cor. 15:3-8) he himself had received from Jewish-Christianity, as his two visits to Jerusalem indicate (Gal. 1:18; 2:1-2). Accordingly, just as Paul can describe the Thessalonian acceptance of the gospel from him as becoming imitators of himself, he can also rightly describe it as an imitation of those Jewish-Christians, to whom Paul knew himself to be indebted for the evangelical traditions. In his proclamation of the death of "the Lord Jesus" he undoubtedly mentioned the part played by some of his own people; he had indicated how Jesus had truly been prefigured by the martyred prophets of Israel; and from his own experiences as apostle of the pagans he recounted instances of persecution by Jews of the Diaspora (2 Cor. 11:24) and their attempts to hinder his mission (Phil. 3:2). Consequently it would be both meaningful and consoling for these suffering Thessalonians to learn that they were being given the same destiny as their Palestinian brothers, whose Christian traditions about Jesus they now shared through the mediation of Paul's gospel. Moreover, *pace* Michaelis,[25] it is a question of more than a comparison with the Jewish-Christian endurance of persecution, as Paul's repetition of *mimētai egenēthēte* shows, for the equivalent passive indicates the action of God.

IMITATION IN 2 THESSALONIANS 3:6-9

Allusion is made to this instance of imitation, because—despite the debated authenticity of the entire letter—the passage advances a principle dear to Paul as a sign of apostolic frugality and simplicity (1 Cor. 9:3-18; 2 Cor. 11:7-10). The problem addressed arose from the clash between the Greek attitude to manual labour and that exhibited by the more religious Jewish culture. Paul's solution represents one of the rare occasions on which he refused to yield to the demands of acculturation.

Now we charge you, brothers, in the name of the Lord Jesus Christ, to have nothing to do with any brother leading an idle existence, an attitude contrary to the tradition we passed on to you. For your part you know how necessary it is to imitate us, inasmuch as we did not live idly among you, nor did we eat anyone's bread gratis. No, we kept working hard and long, day and night, in order not to burden any one of you. It was not that we did not have the right, but in order that we might present ourselves to you as an example for imitating us (3:6-9).

---

25 Michaelis, "Mimeomai," 668-669.

The solemn tone of the intervention leaves no doubt concerning the seriousness with which the command is issued, and at first sight it might seem that imitation is now used in a sense different from the two preceding examples to designate obedience to Paul. However, the appeal to "the tradition we passed on to you" shows it is rather a question of complete fidelity to the living of the gospel, which Paul has taken great pains to inculcate through his own example. He considers his conduct while at Thessalonica a concrete illustration of Christian love in two ways: "in order not to burden any one of you" (3:9), and to "present ourselves to you as an example." This vehement correction of a misunderstanding of his gospel by some believers, the result of an incorrect surmise about the imminence of the Parousia, is precious evidence that Paul did not entertain the notion of an "interim ethic."

IMITATION OF PAUL, A WAY TO UNIFYING THE CHURCH OF PHILIPPI

The main thrust of Philippians, as it now stands in the Pauline epistolary collection,[26] is seen in the urgent appeals for unity within that Christian community. If it be taken also as a "thank you" note, it is remarkable that Paul never directly thanks these beloved Christians for their support of himself during his incarceration, but reminds them that their generosity is a gift from God, to whom his gratitude is addressed. For it is God who has made "all of you sharers in the grace that is mine, as I lie in gaol or take the stand to defend and affirm the gospel" (1:7). The source of unity is found in "living your lives as citizens (*politeuesthe*) in a way worthy of the gospel of Christ" (1:27), since "our *politeuma* lies in heaven" (3:20). The gospel inculcates mutual love, humility, esteem of others and concern for their best interests, for it provides from the Redeemer's example "encouragement in Christ" and "sharing in the Spirit" (2:1-11). It is then obedience *to the gospel* that will assist them to realize their salvation as a community, "for the One who puts power in you, both as regards the willing and the execution, is God!" (3:12), who graciously imparts that power by the gospel.

The immediate context of the verse containing Paul's exhortation to imitate himself as a means to fellowship is autobiographical (3:2-16). Whether or not this section belongs to a different letter need not concern us. Paul seems to have been aware, when citing the hymn extolling the career of Christ as redeemer (2:6-11), of the impossibility of its imitation by any human being. Thus he was careful to propose only the humility (2:3) and the obedience (3:12) of Jesus as exemplifying the communitarian aspects of Christian living. In chapter 3, he recalls the story of his momentous meeting with Christ, which revolu-

---

26   While the commentators are divided on the question of the unity of Philippians, it is the text as it now stands which demands the attention of the interpreter.

tionized his religious ideals. His new attitude, first described in forensic terms as "that righteousness through faith in Christ, which is from God, based on faith" (3:9), is further depicted with reference to the twofold event announced by the gospel. His new aim is "to know him, that is, the power of his resurrection and fellowship in his sufferings by being remoulded together [with him] to his death, that somehow I may attain to the resurrection from the dead" (3:10-11). Through the rest of the paragraph Paul insists that, far from considering himself "perfect," he realizes that the course of his life has been set upon a never-ending quest for deeper union with Christ. In 3:12 he employs a metaphor from the foot-race (*katelemphthēn*: see 1 Cor. 9:24): he was "overtaken by Christ in the race."

No, brothers! I do not judge myself to have reached the goal. One thing only I bear in mind: forgetting what lies behind, I press on eagerly to what lies ahead. I run hard towards the goal for the prize [announced by the gospel], the call heavenwards by God in Christ Jesus. Hence, this is the attitude for those of us who are 'perfect'; accordingly if any of you have a different attitude, God will also reveal this to you (3:13-15).

As his final conclusion Paul states, "Unite together [as a community] in becoming imitators of me, brothers, and keep your eyes on those who so live according to the example you have in us" (3:17). In his commentary on this letter Dr. Beare appositely remarks on the problems faced by a Christian minority in a wholly pagan society of which the apostle is well aware. "The new life cannot be wholly set forth by precept; it must be embodied in the lives of Christ's ministers."[27]

The concern of Paul in the letter to inculcate a deeper sense of Christian fellowship and the immediate context, which describes the ideal governing his own life as a consuming desire for an ever closer communion with Christ, suggest that the variant expression *symmimētai* is intended to convey a special nuance. Observance of the ideals by which Paul lived the gospel will strengthen their sense of community. They will achieve this goal by imitating "the example you have in us."

HEALING THE DIVIDED COMMUNITY
OF CORINTH

In the first of his extant letters with the refractory church of Corinth Paul begins with what he considers its gravest problem: the threat to Christian unity from partisan factions. In fact, to emphasize the high priority he places on this union of minds and hearts, he mentions it at the very end of his account of the prayer he made for this foundation before writing, where he had renewed his own belief in the fidelity of

---

27   F. W. Beare, *A Commentary on the Epistle to the Philippians* (2nd ed.; London: A. & C. Black, 1969), 135.

the God "by whom you were called into the fellowship of his Son Jesus Christ, our Lord" (1 Cor. 1:9).

Paul analyzes two causes of the disunity that reigns among these Christians of Greek culture: (1) misunderstanding of the true character of the gospel as "the word of the cross" (1:18), because of a tendency to view it in terms of rhetoric and popular Greek philosophy (1:18-2:16), and (2) partisan loyalties to various apostolic leaders, Cephas, Apollos, himself, the source of which is a false notion of the preacher's role in propagating the gospel (3:1-4:21). In reality, men like Paul himself or Apollos are "subordinates of Christ and stewards of God's mysteries" (4:1). To illustrate the meaning of this characterization, Paul points to the presence of the cross in their living of the gospel, which constitutes a shocking rebuke to the airs of his deluded Christians, who have failed to see that all they have and are is God's gift (4:6-13). As a conclusion to this whole development, Paul urges them to imitate himself.

I am not trying to shame you by writing this, but I am attempting to put some sense in you as my dearly loved children. For while you may have ten thousand guides in Christian formation, you do not have a plurality of fathers—in this matter of union with Christ Jesus, it was I myself through the gospel who fathered you. Consequently, I am urging you, "become imitators of me!" Here is the reason I am sending Timothy to you—he is my beloved child and worthy of trust as a Christian, and he will recall for you my manner of life in Christ, as I teach everywhere in each congregation (4:14-17).

Paul had earlier employed the metaphors of father and child to describe his moral influence with the Thessalonians: "I used to urge, encourage, implore you to lead your lives in a manner worthy of the God who is calling you into his Kingdom and glory" (1 Thess. 2:11-12). He makes use of the same figure of speech again in a moral sense in recalling Timothy's co-operation with himself. "Like a child he slaved with me for the gospel" (Phil. 2:22).

When in the present paragraph he calls himself "father," he points to a relationship he considers more than moral, one issuing from his role as founder of Christian Corinth. He contrasts this with the moral influence of those who are "guides (*paidagōgous*) in Christian formation." In Greek society the *paidagōgos* was a household slave, charged not with the child's instruction but only his training in behaviour and etiquette. Paul compares his unique role as apostle-founder to the paternal generation of a child (4:15; elsewhere only at Phlm. 10), because he knows himself (and his colleagues)—paradoxically because of the utter weakness he has so dramatically pictured in 4:9-13—to have been God's instruments for communicating his divine power deployed "through the gospel." It is this complementarity, rather than tension, between the apostle's weakness and God's dynamic power which has established these believers "in union with Christ Jesus." J. H. Schütz suggests not implausibly that it is this truth that Paul claims to "teach everywhere in each congregation."[28] Accordingly, to reduce imitation here to obedience to Paul's injunctions is to trivialize his metaphor and equate his concern for the community's interior growth in Christ with an authoritarian defence of his own leadership.[29]

Somewhat later (8:1-11:1) Paul deals with another cause of division between some at Corinth, who considered themselves enlightened and defended their new freedom to eat meat offered in pagan sacrifices, and others, whose scrupulous conscience made them "insecure" (8:7). The specific issue has long ceased to be of concern to Christians, but the passage deserves attention as a valuable contribution to a contemporary problem, the formation of the Christian conscience. Paul, who himself possessed a robust conscience,[30] displays assurance and great sensitivity in correcting what is faulty in both points of view. His concern throughout is with what "builds up"—fraternal love (8:1, 10; 10:23). He agrees with "the robust," in his defence of Christian liberty with respect to food, that "certainly food will not bring us into God's presence," but warns such a one to "Be careful that this freedom of yours does not become a stumbling block (*proskomma*) for the insecure" (8:8-9). For there is a danger that "This knowledge of yours means utter disaster for the insecure, the brother for whom Christ died. In thus sinning against your brothers and wounding their conscience, you sin against Christ" (8:12). Israel's disastrous presumption during the wandering in the desert (10:1-11) illustrates negatively, as Paul's own practice (9:3-23) shows positively, that reliance upon self or one's "rights" in the sight of God imperils one's salvation. The scrupulous person, on the other hand, has not found true freedom in the gospel, and his insecurity stems from his refusal to believe in God's irrational love for himself as "the brother for whom Christ died," or in the goodness of the entire creation which remains God's possession (10:26).

To both groups Paul addresses this final advice, "Therefore, whether you eat or drink or whatever you do, perform everything for God's glory. Learn to be no cause for stumbling (*aproskopoi*) to Jew or Greek or the church of God, just as I myself try to please everyone, refusing to seek my own advantage but that of the majority, in order

---

28   See J. H. Schütz, *Paul and the Anatomy of Apostolic Authority* (Cambridge: Cambridge University Press, 1975), 228-229.

29   As Michaelis does, "Mimeomai," 668; Schütz, *Paul*, 228, points out an objection to Michaelis's view: "The difficulty . . . is that what Paul teaches is not clear. Nor does Paul elsewhere demand this kind of obedience. The Christian is obedient to the gospel, not to the apostle or the apostle's rules."

30   See K. Stendahl, "The Apostle Paul and the Introspective Conscience of the West," in S. H. Miller and G. E. Wright (eds.), *Ecumenical Dialogue at Harvard: The Roman Catholic-Protestant Colloquium* (Cambridge, Mass.: Harvard University Press, 1964), 236-256.

that they may be saved. Become imitators of me, just as I am of Christ" (10:31-11:1).

The principle Paul seeks to inculcate is one he had learned some years before when he prayed earnestly to "the Lord" to be delivered from some mysterious affliction he considered a serious impediment to his own apostolic ministry. The answer given him by Christ he never forgot, "My graciousness is enough for you: for [my] power is brought to fulfilment through weakness" (2 Cor. 12:7-9). This refusal to rely upon himself Paul here describes as seeking "to please everyone in all I do by refusing to seek my own advantage." He knows that he himself can do nothing "that they may be saved," except to give full play to the divine power of Christ. Thus his final statement on imitation is the result of an antithetical parallelism between what his weakness and selflessness achieve, and Christ's power to save. Just as he did not cite the career of Christ as redeemer for imitation by his Philippians (Phil. 2:6-11), so here he does not propose that Christ, as a source of salvation, is to be imitated by the Corinthians. He sets himself forth as an example to them by living the gospel with unwavering confidence in God's power which it communicates and without any reliance upon self. He wishes them to experience personally the grace bestowed upon himself as their apostle by realizing how the power of Christ is fulfilled through weakness "that they may be saved."[31]

CONCLUSIONS

The examination of the Pauline texts in which imitation and example appear has made it evident that they are employed in a sense only analogous to ordinary usage. They are intended to point to a reality transcending merely human exemplarity, moral influence, or external simulation. Nor can Pauline imitation be reduced to obedience to the apostle's authority. Paul's singular use of imitation and example is the result of his radical insight into the gospel as the communication of God's saving power in Christ and his total awareness of human impotence vis-à-vis that divine power. In urging the imitation of himself upon his own Christian foundations, he endeavours to lead them to share his own experience of man's need to rely with full confidence on the divine power graciously offered through "his gospel."

---

31 F. W. Beare, "St. Paul as Spiritual Director," in F. L. Cross (ed.), *Studia Evangelica* 2 (Berlin: Akademie-Verlag, 1964), 312, observes that for Paul "the life that is worthy of God is a life that is being transformed into the likeness of Christ . . . a process that goes on within us day by day, and continues as long as we live. We are made one with Christ, and his life flows into us and becomes the spring of our lives."

"Kingdom of God" Sayings
in Paul's Letters

GEORGE JOHNSTON

On March 12, 1958, Dr. Frank Beare, whom we honour in this volume as a distinguished Canadian New Testament scholar, teacher and Churchman, addressed the public through the facilities of the C.B.C. on the subject, "Jesus and Paul." Revised, the address appeared in the *Canadian Journal of Theology* in 1959,[1] and it is well worth reading still. At one point he writes:

Naturally, he [Paul] sought for ways of making his gospel intelligible to Greeks; he makes no bones about borrowing words and phrases and good ideas from the religions and philosophies of the Greek world, if only he could bring them into the service of the gospel. The kingdom of God, of which Jesus spoke so often, meant nothing to a Greek; and so Paul hardly ever makes use of the phrase when he is writing to Greeks. . . . All this, and much more in his teaching is nothing but the transposing of the gospel into the language and the thought-forms of another people, the kind of adjustment that was needed if the gospel of Jesus was to be brought effectually into the Greek world.[2]

Unfortunately, the gap in my quotation was not devoted to telling us Paul's equivalent for "the kingdom of God"; rather, he speaks about "Messiah" and a Greek substitute, *kyrios*.

I think that Beare is basically correct in affirming Paul's usage in transposing from Hebrew, or Aramaic, modes to Greek for apologetic

---

1   F. W. Beare, "Jesus and Paul," *CJT* 5 (1959), 79-86. (Abbreviations in references are those used by the *Journal of Biblical Literature*. See *JBL* 95 [1976], 331-346.)
2   Ibid., 84.

and missionary purposes. But one really needs to examine afresh the eight kingdom-of-God texts in Paul's letters, set down in Greek and sent to congregations that contained a large element of Greek-speaking converts.

One possible clue to a substitute for "the kingdom of God" could be found in Luke 19:9 concerning the change in Zacchaeus, "Today salvation has come to this house." Compare the M saying, "The tax collectors and harlots are preceding you into the kingdom of God," and the word to the scribe in Mark 12:34, "You are not far from the kingdom of God." For there is plenty of evidence that one meaning of the kingdom is that it denotes the Age to Come, the time of final deliverance for the people of God, a time of hope fulfilled. It is, however, not by any means clear whether the fulfillment can be on earth or must be in a new world or *aiōn* beyond death and time; hence kingdom texts in Jesus' teaching are ambiguous, or must relate to various tenses and to an eternal order.

Now "salvation" occurs in Paul a dozen times, and just over a half of the references are to future blessedness (2 Thess. 2:13; 1 Thess. 5:8-9; 2 Cor. 1:6, with 1:14, 4:14, 17; Rom. 10:1, 10; 13:11; and Phil. 1:28). A few of them must refer to the present life of converts, as well as their ultimate hope: 2 Cor. 7:10; Phil. 2:12 (cf. Rom. 14:17); and possibly Rom. 11:11 (salvation has passed to the Gentiles; it is open to them now, perhaps, as well as in prospect).

The idea of salvation was quite familiar in the Graeco-Roman world, frequently with the hope of immortality in the foreground. We may therefore expect that, if "kingdom of God" carries the freight of religious deliverance, it could be employed sometimes without unduly straining the Greek capacity for understanding.

I undertake this fresh examination of the Pauline texts partly because I am on record as holding that the kingdom of God in Paul "is always futurist, for salvation is basically eschatological."[3] That is too simplistic a judgment, though it has the support of C. F. D. Moule in his commentary on Col. 1:13-14.[4] W. D. Davies also, in his magisterial study, *Paul and Rabbinic Judaism*, cites six of the eight texts to demonstrate that "whenever Paul speaks of a kingdom that is to come," he thinks of a kingdom of God.[5] The fact that in 1 Cor. 4:20 and Rom. 14:17 "kingdom of God" is not easily susceptible of a future reference should raise doubts about the exclusively futurist slant of the other six texts. Can we show that?

3   G. Johnston, *Ephesians, Philippians, Colossians and Philemon*, NCB (London: Oliphants, 1967), 69.
4   C. F. D. Moule, *The Epistles of Paul the Apostle to the Colossians and to Philemon* (Cambridge: Cambridge University Press, 1957), 57-58.
5   W. D. Davies, *Paul and Rabbinic Judaism* (2nd ed., London: S.P.C.K., 1955), 295.

THE KINGDOM AS A FUTURE
INHERITANCE

I begin with a group of texts that appear at first sight to concur in regarding the kingdom as a state or a life or a blessedness into which the faithful can expect to enter at the End or goal to which present time is but preliminary.

A. 2 Thess. 1:5-12, and specifically verse 5. *This is evidence of the righteous judgment of God, that you may be made worthy of the kingdom of God, for which you are suffering.*

When Paul writes that the Thessalonians are suffering now for the sake of God's kingdom (*basileia*), he might, I suggest, just as well have said, "for God's sake," because they are a community of those who hope to enjoy the blessings of God's New Age; they have been chosen and called (2:13); they bear the mark of the new state as baptized men and women, and they claim its representative Jesus as their Lord (*kyrios*, 1:1). This community is an *ekklēsia* that can be defined as a congregation "in God our Father and Jesus Christ (our) Lord." Clearly this "in" refers to the present condition of the believers. Grace is with them, and it will keep coming to them, provided they persevere in well-doing (3:13, 18).

For Paul, Jesus Christ is a reality of faithful life today, and that is why his encouragement (*paraklēsis*) bears "the mark of the Eternal": it is *aiōnios*, belonging to the Age to Come; or it is ageless. The *hope* Christ brings is good, that is, it can be relied on.

In other words, the present tense of "you are suffering" in 1:5 is grounded in past events of redemption (note the verbs in 2:13, 14, 16), and this necessarily points to a future consummation. It may not be wise, then, to interpret the kingdom of God here wholly as a futurist concept. For Paul has had to compress its tenses into a single religious experience, into a time that is already trans-temporal. The key to his meaning must be found in the faith that *Jesus Christ is now the Lord who is to come in power and judgment*, so that the wicked will be destroyed and the faithful be glorified (1:12). A classic passage from Paul's maturity may be adduced to support our view: Rom. 8:12-17, where it is said, God's children live day by day as Spirit-guided people who are the "heirs of God and joint-heirs with Christ." If now in this age they share the Messiah's tribulations, they too will be glorified. Such a doctrine has parallels in the teaching of Jesus.

B. 1 Thess. 2:11-12. *We exhorted ... and encouraged you ... to lead a life worthy of God, who calls you into his own kingdom and glory.*

This letter quickly comments on the past conversion of the Thessalonians and their present condition: *to be* the servants of God (1:9) and *to await* the *parousia* (advent or coming) of the Lord Jesus, God's Son (1:10; 2:19). Indubitably it is the latter aspect that is the focus of the apostle's pastoral concern (1:2-3; 3:2-6, 13; 4:3-12; 5:6, 12-22). He is also worried about whether these recent converts can "take it" in difficult circumstances; and at Salonica questions have been raised about the Parousia itself: Will it come indeed like a thief in the night? What is the fate of converts who have died already, and what will be that of those who are alive at the moment of the coming? (4:13-18; 5:2-3).

It is essential, but in fact all too easy, to underline the "adventism" of 1 Thessalonians and peer beneath the surface for an anxious concern with a future kingdom, future glory, and future salvation (2:12; 5:9). "You see, a visible hope is not really hope . . . (and therefore) we are expecting it in an attitude of patient endurance" (Rom. 8:24-25). Of course, this is partially correct exegesis, and Jesus' message contains similar ideas.

One may enter and inherit God's kingdom (e.g., Matt. 5:20; 6:10; 7:21; 18:3; 19:23-24; 25:34; 26:29). There is going to be a great table-feast and fellowship "in God's kingdom," from which the unresponsive will be excluded with weeping and wailing and gnashing of teeth, but into which the patriarchs, prophets and representatives "frae a' the airts"[6] will be happily ingathered. A harassed missionary like Paul could not have failed to kindle and keep alive this marvellous expectation during a career of calumny, desertion, and partial triumph. The hope is for real.

On the other hand, Paul in 1 Thessalonians has his feet on earthly ground. His converts are commended for a *faith* that has achievements to its credit;[7] a *love* that is being manifested in activity, however trying the environment;[8] and a *hope* that is steadfast only because it is the sister of faith and love, only because the Christians are in truth living in a spiritual glow, in a "joy that is inspired by God's Spirit" (1:6). No wonder, in that case, that their apostle girdles them in exclamations of pride: "As for you, aren't you my hope, my joy, my crown and pride, my glory and joy [his ecstasy has to be multiplied by tautology!]—all that I shall have to show when the Lord comes?" (2:19-20; cf. 2 Thess. 2:16). One is reminded of the Scots mystic of Charles I's time, Samuel Rutherford, who overwhelmed his correspondents with similar outbursts of love and hope.[9] Paul says that he can carry on with his living and working for the Lord, if the Thessalonians will keep up their good work and maintain the glow (3:8-10), though they are not yet perfect (4:4-8; 5:13-15).

We must look for the secret of this man's pastoral oversight and his agonizing over the spirituality of himself and the members of local churches. It is to be found, most scholars would agree, in his ecstatic

---

6   Scots for "from every quarter."
7   *Ergon* in 1:3 is dynamic, giving practical proof of a religious profession.
8   *Kopos* must echo Paul's own toil in the midst of adversity: cf. 2:9 with 2:6 and 2:10-12.
9   Andrew A. Bonar (ed.), *Letters of Samuel Rutherford* (Edinburgh and London: Oliphant, Anderson & Ferrier, 1891), *passim*.

communion with the resurrected Lord (Gal. 2:20); in the *serenity* that resulted from the assurance that his errors and trespasses had been justly but lovingly dealt with here and now by the God who in Christ crucified was the Redeemer (e.g., Rom. 3:21-26; 5:1-5); and his *commitment* in response to a vocation, that he would always and everywhere declare the goodness of God (1 Cor. 1:22-25; 2:1-5; Phil. 1:21-28; Col. 1:28-29). To direct him, he had sometimes direct revelation (2 Cor. 12:1-10), sometimes only the apostolic traditions (1 Cor. 11:23; 15:3-11; 2 Thess. 2:15); but sometimes also specific words of Jesus his Lord (1 Cor. 7:10; 9:14).

C. Gal. 5:21. *I warn you, as I warned you before, that those who do such things shall not inherit the kingdom of God.*

D. 1 Cor. 6:9-10. *Do you not know that the unrighteous will not inherit the kingdom of God?* (Details in verse 10.)

E. 1 Cor. 15:50. *I tell you this, brethren: flesh and blood cannot inherit the kingdom of God, nor does the perishable inherit the imperishable.*[10]

The theme of heirship and inheritance has a long history in the Old Testament: e.g., Gen. 31:14; Num. 18:20; Isa. 57:6. It relates to Yahweh's apportionment of Canaan to the children of Abraham, but it offered a way of thinking about the deliverance of exiles or of captives, either in a renewed kingdom of David or in some supernatural form of the divine rule over Israel and the nations of the earth (cf. Dan. 7:14-27). In one way or another this hope informs what we call the messianic expectation, though there was no single accepted form in the time of Jesus and Paul.

In the Synoptic teaching of Jesus there are a few examples of the inheritance theme: Mark 12:1-9, and parallels, is primary; see also Matt. 5:5 (quoting Ps. 37:11, and therefore it may be an editorial gloss); Matt. 25:34, 46, where the kingdom assigned to the just at the Last Judgment is equated with the life of the Age to Come, as probably in Mark 10:17; Luke 10:25; Matt. 19:29; and compare John 3:3, 5, 15.

What to do about the original wording and intention of the Parable of the Wicked Husbandmen (Mark 12:1-9) has provided much toil to recent interpreters. Perhaps, though one writes with caution, the most likely point is not "eschatological" but polemical. The blessings of God are to be removed from the nation Israel and its chieftains and transferred in revolutionary fashion to the landless poor: a view that would justify the gloss of Ps. 37:11 (note Luke 1:51-55).

To take such a line means that one agrees with the thesis that in the phrase "the kingdom of God" the operative word is "God," not "kingdom."[11] Jesus' message was about God as *Abba* (Father) and King, and

10 Cf. also Gal. 3:18; Col. 1:12; 3:24; Eph. 1:14, 18; 5:5.
11 Note B. D. Chilton, "Regnum Dei Deus Est," *SJT* 31 (1978), 261-270; and the

about his shameless merciful care for outcasts and sinners, as well as his threat to dispossess the proud and self-righteous (compare Luke 4:16-21, which may not be historically the text for Jesus' sermon in Nazareth, but if not is still true to his mission). It is nevertheless no easier on this view to discover precisely what Jesus expected for the destiny of Israel and the world after he had suffered the fate of a prophet (compare Mark 13 and parallels).

Paul, it seems, did worry about a new world and an Age to Come beyond resurrection, beyond the arraignment of all mankind before the judgment seat of Christ (2 Cor. 5:10; cf. Phil. 2:16; Rom. 2:1-11).

Paul can employ allegory to convey his hopes: Jewish and gentile Christians, the Israel of the Spirit, and no longer Abraham's natural descendants, have become, by adoption, the children of God, the seed of Abraham, and the heirs to the promises (Gal. 3:23-4:7; Rom. 8:14-17). But these promises cannot be fulfilled in this life only. The redemption of the body demands resurrection (Rom. 8:19-23; 1 Cor. 15:50). So "kingdom life" is indeed life in the Age to Come. It is ageless and eternal. And one guarantee for all this is quite simply the resurrection of Jesus (1 Cor. 15:12-28).

In this way, it may be argued, the apostle has had to go some way beyond Jesus' own teaching, and yet his confidence is placed in exactly the same reality, the love of that Father who is now to be defined as "the God and Father of our Lord Jesus Christ." Jesus' own submission to death, obedient to the Father's will, rather than his explicit words as the Evangelists have retained them for us, is the basis for believing that Jesus too entertained a genuine hope that beyond his own death God will still be God, always the *Abba*, always the invincible One who makes all things new. That confidence was inherited by the apostle from the Church's *kērygma* (gospel).

Given all that, it is no aberration when Paul warns sinners that they cannot share the inheritance (1 Cor. 6:9-10)[12] and assures the faithful that they are to share "the inheritance of the saints in light" (Col. 1:12; 3:24).[13]

In summary, these texts certainly tell us that Paul did not minimize the hope of a new world and that, for at least the early period of his career, he often emphasized the expectation of the Parousia or glorious coming of the Christ. At the same time, it is clear that a new life began with conversion and baptism, and it was possible to describe it in terms of the kingdom of God, as other texts will prove.

---

summary in H. Küng, *On Being a Christian* (Garden City, N.Y.: Doubleday, 1976), 214-216, 636.

12   He is using the old Kingdom idiom, but clearly not with reference to an earthly monarchy and so not to any dominion that might rival the Roman Empire.

13   Cf. Eph. 1:18; 5:5. "The Kingdom of Christ and of God" is a non-Pauline expression.

LIFE IN THE SPIRIT IS KINGDOM LIFE

F. 1 Cor. 4:20-21. *For God's kingdom (is not displayed) in speech but in power [dynamic action]: so what do you want? Am I to come to you with a rod, or in loving-kindness and a spirit of gentleness?*

In the early chapters of this letter Paul is still teaching converts about the coming Day of Christ (1:8) and the spiritual power that flows from the cross (1:17). God has planned to deliver those who believe in him as One who was active in Christ crucified (1:21) and so Christ can be called at once God's "power" and his "wisdom." The new vitality and the spiritual endowments of converts demonstrate the divine power at work in this present age and world (2:5).

Because that is the context, 4:20 may be interpreted as affirming that God has truly initiated a process of redeeming his people (1:18) through the gospel which finds its centre in the sacrificial death of Jesus (2 Cor. 5:18-6:1). In that process God exercises sovereign authority, attacking the evil powers of sin and death and offering here and now a way of escape and hope for a glorious future; Isaiah 49:8, in particular, could be quoted as a word of the Lord fulfilled in the Christ event (2 Cor. 6:2):[14] "The hour of favour has now come; now, I say, has the day of deliverance dawned."

Of course, for a Christian apostle this wonderful fact did not mean that there would be a new exodus and conquest for Israel; there would be no Israelite empire on earth, as the poet-prophet of the Exile and other prophets had expected. Rather, there is to be something far more radical, "a new creation." C. K. Barrett's discussion of this deserves careful scrutiny, and he may be quoted:

It is not true that the material creation has been swept away, or that history has been annihilated. . . . To know one's environment in a new way, and to be newly related to God through justification, is to live in a new world; a new set of relationships has come into being. . . . (The saved man's) relation to God . . . now stands on a different basis. . . . Christian existence means that by faith one lives in the midst of the old creation in terms of the new creation that God has brought about through Jesus.[15]

Yet, as we shall see, even that does not go far enough in telling us what life in the Spirit, the life "in Christ" fully meant for Paul.

Nor is K. L. Schmidt's paraphrase of 4:20 very helpful: "We catch the sense if we paraphrase: The kingdom of God does not consist in the power of man but in the Word of God."[16] For that sounds very like a Reformed Churchman's attempt to interpret Paul along a single line. It is the *power of dynamic action* that we have to investigate.

---

14   See C. K. Barrett, *The Second Epistle to the Corinthians* (London: A. & C. Black, 1973), 183-184.
15   Ibid., 174-175.
16   K. L. Schmidt, *"Basileia,"* TDNT 1:583, n. 76.

To do so in detail would require a full examination of 2 Cor.
3:1-7:16, where the apostle writes extensively about the activity of God's
Holy Spirit in the life of Christians and the Church (3:6). Its effect is
their transfiguration (3:18), and ultimately will lead to their resurrection to stand with their Lord in God's presence (4:14). That is why a
Christian's attention is not to be directed primarily to this temporal,
mortal world whose time is short (1 Cor. 7:29-31), but to the eternal and
unseen (4:18). Here one lives in a world of ambiguity and trouble:
abuse, contempt, jail and all manner of tribulation is an apostle's lot
(4:7-12; cf. 1 Cor. 4:8-13; 2 Cor. 11:16-12:13). It is a world of corruption
and death (4:16a), and even the non-human *kosmos* is in bondage (Rom.
8:21). So Paul can speak of Christians as those upon whom the *telē*
(ends, i.e., End) of the ages (*aions*, literally) have fallen (1 Cor. 10:11).[17]

Amidst circumstances like that, with that imminent goal almost in
sight, the mystery is proclaimed and is *already in part realized* that a new
humanity is emerging. It is part of the Christ who is the last Adam and a
life-giving Spirit (1 Cor. 15:45). The process of inner renewal goes on
day by day (2 Cor. 4:16b). The outcome is sure, because God is supernatural power. It is certain: provided Christians continue to be loyal
and trusting. And it will be what Paul calls "an eternal glory," something that outweighs all the perils, nuisances, demonic temptations,
treachery, arrogance and secular persecutions that are thrown at believers in "this short-lived age" (4:17). (He was wrong about its being
short-lived, as men measure time!)

Who revealed that mystery? God. He who was in Christ at his
reconciling work (2 Cor. 5:19). That God whose speech is heard even
from a timid, stuttering, unworthy spokesman like Paul of Tarsus, the
Christian Jew (1 Cor. 2:3-4).

How does God intend to enable converts to outlast trouble, keeping their eyes on the unseen and eternal, and persevering until the Day
of universal Judgment (5:4, 10; 6:1)? It is by granting them as a guarantee and first installment his own Holy Spirit (5:5). One cannot emphasize enough that Paul fully believed in this gift, this *arrabōn*, of the
Spirit, the first-fruits of the new creation (Rom. 8:23, and the whole
chapter). To live under the rule of God as a believer, as a disciple of
Jesus, as a member of the Body of Christ which is the Church, is to be
spiritually alive and under the discipline of divine love (*agapē*; cf. Gal.
5:22-23). "Kingdom of God" in 1 Cor. 4:20 is thus a shorthand for this
marvellous new reality, for this divine activity to redeem and also to
sanctify. Long before Judgment Day, and without special reference to
its distance or imminence, life in the Spirit means acquiring a new
disposition and mind, concentrating on the honourable, the pure and
attractive, the gracious (Rom. 8:5-8; Phil. 4:8). That breeds a life of

---

17 See Hans Conzelmann, *1 Corinthians*, Hermeneia (Philadelphia: Fortress Press,
    1975), 168.

serenity (Rom. 8:6; cf. Rom. 5:1 with 5:3-5). It is my thesis that in the last analysis the so-called "eschatological" dimension of the kingdom idea has been relegated to a fairly minor place, and its present fact has been translated instead into the great concept of spiritual life.

Paul was a realist, and he knew perfectly well that converts did not in fact allow the enabling power of God to work in their lives, except in piecemeal fashion. He was a pastor to ex-perverts and to schismatic Christians (1 Cor. 6:9-11; 1:10-12). His painful task was to discipline them when they fell from grace, to provoke them to godly grief and its fruit, repentance (2 Cor. 6:1; 7:10). In doing so he did not always express the gracious manner himself, so there was bitterness at Corinth with which the peacemaker Titus had to deal.

Enough has been elucidated, I hope, to show that, although he and his disciples felt the force of exile from heaven and though they longed for the blessedness to come,[18] anxiety took second place to a sense of wonder that God had already released the supernatural powers of his Spirit for the benefit of each member and the entire Body (1 Cor. 12 *passim*).

Moreover, it can be shown that this translation coheres with known elements in the teaching of Jesus:

(1) Luke 11:13; Matt. 7:11. Israel's God gives good gifts, or gives his Spirit, to those who ask him.

(2) Luke 11:20; Matt. 12:28. Jesus' exorcisms were performed by divine power, "the finger of God" (compare Exod. 8:19).

(3) Mark 3:29 and parallels. The New Age has come within hearing and hailing range,[19] and some men and women perceive the saving presence of God in Jesus (Matt. 21:31; Luke 19:10; 7:48). For Jesus is clothed in the Spirit of God.

(4) Mark 13:11 and parallels. God will not desert the disciples of Jesus in future times of trial and sorrow, for his Spirit will assist them to bear witness.[20] This means that the "God" of the commonplace "kingdom of God" idiom is One who has chosen to act savingly and decisively in the Jesus-event.

Jesus, like his later disciple Paul, does not appear to make any radical distinction between God's royal presence as Saviour and his gift of salvation in a life beyond tribulation and death. The present and the

---

18 Note 2 Cor. 5:2, "we groan" and "we are oppressed" or "heavy-laden"; 2 Cor. 5:7, "we walk by faith and not by sight"; and Phil. 1:24, "I would rather depart and be with Christ, . . . but there is a more compelling need for me to remain in this life."

19 Based on C. H. Roberts in *HTR* 41 (1948), 1-8, "within your reach" or "within your grasp." By 1961 this had been accepted by C. H. Dodd: see his *Historical Tradition in the Fourth Gospel* (Cambridge: Cambridge University Press, 1963), 401, n. 1.

20 Cf. Acts 14:22 and the comment of E. Haenchen: " 'Enter the kingdom of God' seems to imply that for the Christians this is accomplished in their death (cf. Luke 16:19ff. and 23:43)." In the footnote, however, he takes this view to be Lucan interpretation. "Luke had abandoned expectation of the imminent end" (*The Acts of the Apostles* [Philadelphia: Fortress Press, 1971], 436).

future are convoluted in the past acts of his revealing, redeeming, creating work, so that there is never a time when he is not a very present help in time of trouble. Paul's ground of faith and hope was the resurrection of the crucified Jesus with its immediate effect in the outflow of the powers of the Holy Spirit. Jesus becomes the Prince Viceroy until the End (1 Cor. 15:24). And at the Lord's Supper the Church waits "until he comes" (1 Cor. 11:26). Futurist ideas are never discarded altogether.

W. L. Knox, like Frank Beare, suggested long ago that Paul was faced "with the necessity of reconstructing the Gospel, if he was to appeal to the intellect of the Gentile world."[21] He probably had to meet accusations that he was a subversive, anti-Caesar (Acts 17:7; probably Acts 19:8; 20:25 and 28:31 employ the phrases "the kingdom" and "the kingdom of God" as simple summaries of the Pauline gospel). He may indeed have limited his use of kingdom of God language lest he be misunderstood by the authorities and by his Gentile audiences. But he was perfectly capable of conveying otherwise the major themes hidden in that phrase: (a) the sovereign work of God in human history; (b) the blessed future awaiting the faithful; (c) the place of Jesus in the divine mission; e.g., as power and wisdom (1 Cor. 1:24); as the *eikōn* of God (his image in human shape, 2 Cor. 4:4; Col. 1:15); as the firstborn Son (Rom. 8:29; Col. 1:15, 18); as last Adam (perhaps a translation of "Son of man," 1 Cor. 15:45); as Lord and Christ (*kyrios*, the Messiah of the Jews but also the Saviour of mankind, Phil. 3:20).

One might echo the judgment of Vincent Taylor about Paul's christology: "However far he may rise on the wings of speculation, and no matter how ecstatic his utterances may sometimes be . . . he is always in closest touch with the brown earth of common Christian belief."[22]

If our argument is sound, they are correct who insist that there is an essential continuity between the kerygma of Jesus and Paul's kerygma about Jesus. For both, God is all in all. God is the supreme reality. God rules over the cosmos and over mankind.

G. Rom. 14:17. *For the kingdom of God does not mean eating or drink-ing; it means justice [goodness?], peace, and joy that is inspired by a holy spirit.*

The second half of this verse is difficult to translate: "Justice" is *dikaio-sunē*, "righteousness," used here, as several commentators agree, not in its technical sense but more generally. Again, the phrase, "inspired by a holy spirit" may refer to God's Holy Spirit and if so there should be capitals, the Holy Spirit. But does this qualify only "joy," as Sanday and Headlam, and more recently Matthew Black think; or all three nouns,

---

21 W. L. Knox, *St. Paul and the Church of the Gentiles* (Cambridge: Cambridge University Press, 1939), 26.
22 V. Taylor, *The Person of Christ* (London: Macmillan, 1958), 37.

as in William Barclay's version, "It consists in justice and peace and joy—and all in the atmosphere of the Holy Spirit"? Probably it belongs with "joy." The Spirit is less an atmosphere than a dynamic personal force, operating on Christians with a view to harvesting in them a life that is godly. In fact, it is the immanence of the all-holy, almighty transcendent God lovingly at work to influence the meek and the faithful.

Here, if anywhere, one must not minimize the emphatic present tense implied in the Greek, even though Aramaic would have been more dubious. The context concerns interpersonal relationships within a local church (or any church), and Paul reminds his readers of what it means to live under God's rule. Black quite rightly says that "'Kingdom of God' is virtually here *regula dei* (like *regula fidei*), as in the rabbinical idea of taking on oneself the 'yoke' of the *malkuth* of God. In other words, it is here a spiritual absolute, though naturally also eschatologically conceived."[23]

That being so, it would not be hard to discover parallels in Jesus' message, expressed in a different vocabulary:

(1) For the general theme, note the great Q passage Luke 12:22-31/Matt. 6:25-33, "Do not seek what you are to eat or drink, and don't be worried. . . . Seek rather your Father's kingdom."

(2) For the "yoke" theme, compare Matt. 11:29-30 (M).

(3) "Justice" or "goodness" can be summed up in keeping the commandments of God, as in Judaism (Mark 10:19). Significantly, this is put in terms of the weightiest of all the commandments, again as in Judaism. One is to love God, the neighbour, and (in Jesus' new statement of Lev. 19:33-34) the enemy (Mark 12:29-31, 34). Yet another summary is given in the Golden Rule of Q (Luke 6:31//Matt. 7:12a) in the positive form, not, as in Judaism and in some early Christian versions, in the negative. In spite of many severe modern attacks on the value of this Rule,[24] it should, in my judgment, be interpreted with approval as a major though not necessarily a unique contribution by Jesus to a religious ethic. A good man produces good, says the cliché of Luke 6:45a//Matt. 12:35. But is this perhaps more than simply a preacher's cliché? Pharisees, probably not without some justification, are condemned for neglecting justice and the love of God.

To these Markan and Q sayings we may add from M material: Matt. 5:20, practise a superior goodness to that of the Pharisees, e.g., in secret almsgiving (6:2-4), which will be rewarded, presumably at the Last Judgment. Matt. 20:15b, in the Parable of the Labourers in the

---

23   M. Black, *Romans*, NCB (London: Oliphants, 1973), 168-169.
24   I. Abrahams, *Studies in Pharisaism and the Gospels* (Cambridge: Cambridge University Press, 1917; New York: KTAV, 1967), 1:21-28. R. Bultmann, *History of the Synoptic Tradition* (2nd ed.; Oxford: Blackwell, 1968), 103. K. Stendahl, "Matthew," in M. Black and H. H. Rowley (eds.), *Peake's Commentary* (London: Nelson, 1962), 780a. There is a useful note in David Hill, *Matthew*, NCB (London: Oliphants, 1972), 149.

Vineyard the owner retorts: "Because I am [unexpectedly] generous, must you be cantankerous?" Justice in this story is transformed into a moral from a legalistic category.

Matt. 25:46, at the Judgment kindly folk will enter into life eternal, i.e., the kingdom in one of its aspects. The ethical imperative that imposes itself on the hearer is that the duty to be kind to the poor, the outcast, the prisoner, and the disadvantaged is for this present life. For in Jesus' mission the future really does exercise its power upon the present, but this must not be stated in the prosaic fashion of much twentieth-century New Testament scholarship as "the *eschaton* has come." No, it is always God who comes, the same God who will deal justly with his people at the *telos* of history, in the fulfillment of his purpose in the creation of the world and of humanity. Of that *telos*, no one can tell the date, says Jesus (Mark 13:32). Everyone of us knows that as of today that *telos*, that *eschaton*, has certainly not arrived!

It is seldom that Jesus put any of this in Spirit terms, if we can trust our gospels: we noted earlier almost every saying that can be accepted as authentic. He may well have said more. At any rate, he requires a goodness that springs from the inner self, that is motivated by *agapē* rather than obedience to legislation.

(4) "Peace": the saying in Mark 9:50, "be at peace with one another," may have no integral connection with the ideas about life or about entering the kingdom of God (Mark 9:43-47). But the Q passage of Luke 10:5-6//Matt. 10:13, 7 (where each Evangelist has modified in some way the original saying) calls on disciples when they go out on a mission to offer the *shalom* (peace) in the Name of God and the context that "God's kingdom has become present" to their hearers, as in Mark 1:15 and Luke 11:20.

In the L tradition we may cite Luke 7:50, "go in peace" (cf. 8:48; Mark 5:34). As Creed says, "faith" is used here in a Pauline sense to mean "the human response which appropriates forgiveness of sin."[25] When the penitent of Luke 18:14 went home "justified," he went as a man at peace with God, and, we may assume, as one who would henceforth live more peaceably with his family and neighbours: if not, justification would be empty of real significance. The cry of Luke 19:42, "Would that even today you knew what would make for (your) peace, O Jerusalem," may refer to conditions that lead to peace with God (so Klostermann).

In the M tradition there is the beatitude of Matt. 5:9, where peacemakers are God's children; compare the admonition of Matt. 5:24, "first be reconciled with your brother" before you attempt to worship God. This fits in with other teaching about forgiveness, e.g., Luke 11:4; Matt. 6:12: "Pardon our offences as we now pardon those who have offended us" (here I am indebted to J. Jeremias).

---

25   J. M. Creed, *The Gospel According to St. Luke* (London: Macmillan, 1942), 112.

(5) "Joy" is a recurring refrain of the parables about finding the lost (Luke 15:6, 9, 24, 32; compare Matt. 18:13). "Rejoice . . . and leap for joy," since God's ultimate reward for his humble poor ones is certain (Luke 6:20-23). A similar lesson is explicit in the parable of the Pearl of Great Price (Matt. 13:44): for here it is suddenly, unexpectedly discovered that God in the power of his saving work is a person's ultimate concern and that a life of ageless quality begins now and continues in the Age to Come. Godliness is the bedfellow of joyfulness.

Perhaps one should combine Paul's "justice, peace and joy" into the tight articulation of a complex but integrated sentiment of love. It is such a sentiment that produces a godly character, and both Jesus and Paul seem to agree that it is dependent on the immanent power of God, which brings illumination, encouragement and the deepest spiritual satisfaction. Johannine teaching, if it is true to Jesus' mind (as it probably is) might also be adduced to give further support to the position adopted in this essay. Kingdom life is life in the Spirit, within the company of disciples, a community of the loving and faithful.

KINGDOM AND COVENANT

H. Col. 4:10-11. *Aristarchus, Mark, and Jesus Justus are the only Jewish converts sharing with Paul his mission "for the kingdom of God"* (compare Acts 28:31).

This seems to be a quite general way of describing what Paul was up to in the Roman Empire: he preaches God, the God of Israel, as active to fulfill his promises through Jesus, Israel's Christ and Lord of the Gentiles (2 Cor. 1:20; Rom. 9:4f.; Phil. 2:10-11). It may be, as R. P. Martin suggests, that these men were eager like Paul "to bring the gospel to Israel and to point to the hope of the Jewish people in their Messiah (Rom. 1:16; 9:1-5; 10:1)."[26] Yet it is to be noted that these words are included in a letter to people who had formerly been heathen.[27]

More specifically, one may add that the Pauline mission—and that of colleagues like Epaphras—was directed to God's inauguration of the New Covenant through the crucified Jesus (Messiah, Lord) who is remembered at every eucharist (1 Cor. 11:25). There it is very relevant that God did this at a precise historical moment and in Galilee and Judaea (and Samaria?); and that he is now leading the faithful to life beyond death, in essence the same kind of life that the baptized live in the Body of Christ on earth (see Rom. 1:3-4; 3:24-26; 5:21a, 21b; 6:11 and 8:14-18). Thus all the tenses of time coalesce at the Sacrament.[28] "Kingdom of God" means God in his royal redeeming work in each of

---

26 R. P. Martin, *Colossians: The Church's Lord and the Christian's Liberty* (Grand Rapids, Mich.: Zondervan, 1973), 143.

27 E. Lohse, *Colossians and Philemon*, Hermeneia (Philadelphia: Fortress Press, 1971), 2.

28 Cf. C. H. Dodd, *The Apostolic Preaching and its Developments* (London: Hodder & Stoughton, 1936), 234-235.

the tenses; it should not be confined to ideas of future salvation in the resurrection life. "Salvation, then, is past, present, and future," as George Caird writes in his brilliant summary of Pauline theology.[29]

It is not difficult to understand why Paul goes farther, to teach his converts that in this present age, while men and women must live in hope of God's final victory, Jesus Christ reigns as Prince or Viceroy (1 Cor. 15:24-25; Col. 1:13). Yet such a concept is rare: Christ is the *Head* of the Body, and the Body is a Spirit-filled organism rather than a "nation" or the like. Thus, as John put it, Jesus' kingship is not of this world (John 18:36). Today one may well ask whether "kingdom of God" and "kingship of Christ" are not better avoided. For they tend to mislead men and women who have grown accustomed to national imperialism; they speak of "realms" and areas of sovereign power of which the sanctions are weapons of universal devastation. The modern Church may therefore have to seek ways to liberate itself even from what C. H. Dodd called "the least inadequate myth of the goal of history." It is that myth "which moulds itself upon the great divine event of the past, known in its concrete actuality, and depicts its final issue in a form which brings time to an end and places man in eternity—the second Coming of the Lord, the Last Judgment."[30] What Christians have to affirm, on the basis of the teaching of Jesus about God ever just, ever holy, and ever loving, is that this God is today and always present to men and women in their own time. That, whatever they may do foolishly with the forces of Nature and whatever devastation they may plan with neutron bombs and hydrogen bombs, the divine purpose to recreate humanity after the likeness of the good Man Christ Jesus can never be finally thwarted. This gospel stands or falls with the victory of Jesus over death, with the transfiguring work of his Spirit in his disciples, with the hope that the covenant God of Israel and the Church will overcome all the ambiguities and contradictions of our existence, because he is the God and Father of the Lord Jesus Christ.

29   G. B. Caird, "Paul's Theology," in J. Hastings, *Dictionary of the Bible*, rev. ed. by F. C. Grant and H. H. Rowley (New York: Scribner, 1963), 739a.
30   C. H. Dodd, *The Apostolic Preaching*, 240.

The Spirit: Paul's Journey to Jesus and Beyond

BENNO PRZYBYLSKI

It has often been noted that Paul's extant writings contain relatively few explicit appeals to the teaching of the pre-resurrection Jesus. This observation coupled with 2 Cor. 5:16-17 ("Even though we once regarded Christ from a human point of view, we regard him thus no longer.... The old has passed away, behold, the new has come") has led some interpreters to contend that Paul not only drew a sharp distinction between the pre-resurrection Jesus and the resurrected Lord, but indeed that he had no interest in the former.

W. Wrede, for example, saw Paul as "the second founder of Christianity,"[1] and viewed Paul's message as unrelated to that of the pre-resurrection Jesus. R. Bultmann notes that Paul's "letters barely show traces of the influence of Palestinian tradition concerning the history and preaching of Jesus,"[2] and he concludes that "in relation to the preaching of Jesus, the theology of Paul is a new structure."[3]

Other interpreters have arrived at a position diametrically opposed to that of Wrede and Bultmann. These scholars stress the fact that Paul's letters are occasional writings prompted by particular circumstances. As such, they presuppose a knowledge of the crucial facts concerning the life and teaching of the pre-resurrection Jesus. They contend that there are numerous implicit references to the pre-resurrection Jesus in Paul's letters. Concerning 2 Cor. 5:16 they argue that it is ambiguous and open to various interpretations. C. H. Dodd[4]

---

1 W. Wrede, *Paul* (Lexington: American Theological Library Association, 1962; rpt. of 1908 trans. by E. Lummis), 179.
2 R. Bultmann, *Theology of the New Testament* (New York: Scribner's, 1951), 1:188.
3 Ibid., 189.
4 C. H. Dodd, *History and the Gospel* (Digswell Place: James Nisbet, 1938), 53ff.

and F. F. Bruce[5] are prime examples of interpreters who advocate this general view. Professor Beare would also appear to align himself with this view, for he has stated that "Paul is essentially one with Jesus in the substance of the gospel which he preaches."[6]

It is beyond the scope of this paper to attempt an overall evaluation of the relative merits of the opposing views in the Jesus-Paul debate. The intention of this paper is more modest: to show what bearing Paul's view of the Spirit has on his depiction of Jesus.

J. D. G. Dunn has aptly noted that "Paul takes it wholly for granted that possession of the Spirit is the hallmark of the Christian."[7] This conclusion is substantiated by passages such as Rom. 8:9, 14; 1 Cor. 12:3. Indeed, according to Paul the Christian life is depicted as life according to the Spirit (Rom. 8:4-5, 13; Gal. 5:16, 18).

Juxtaposed to life according to the Spirit is life according to the flesh (Rom. 7:5; 8:4-9; Gal. 3:3; 5:16-17). Flesh leads to death while Spirit leads to life. In essence, the terms "flesh" and "Spirit" designate two diametrically opposed spheres of reality,[8] death and life. While it is true that Paul also uses other terminology, especially that derived from the concepts of law and slavery, it appears that the polarity of flesh versus Spirit is at the heart of Paul's soteriological theology.

Does Paul's stress on the distinction between life according to the Spirit and life according to the flesh have any bearing on his portrayal of Jesus? I would suggest that it has a major influence. Paul maintains that the distinction between flesh and Spirit is grounded in nothing less than the life of Jesus Christ. Man should progress from the sphere of flesh to that of Spirit in conformity to the example of Jesus Christ. According to Rom. 8:3, God sent his "Son in the likeness of sinful flesh." Similarly, Paul does not refer to a virgin birth but without explanation states in Rom. 1:3 that Jesus Christ "was descended from David according to the flesh" and in Gal. 4:4 that he was "born of woman." Even if the hymn to Christ in Phil. 2:5-11 rests on a *Vorlage*,[9] a passage such as 2:8, "And being found in human form he humbled himself," clearly fits into Paul's view.

But Jesus Christ did not remain in the flesh. With reference to the time after the resurrection, Paul emphasizes the spiritual dimension. In 2 Cor. 3:17-18 it is stated twice that "the Lord is the Spirit." While there

5 F. F. Bruce, "Paul and the Historical Jesus," *BJRL* 56 (1974), 317-335. (Abbreviations in references are those used by the *Journal of Biblical Literature*. See *JBL* 95 [1976], 331-346.)

6 F. W. Beare, "Jesus and Paul," *CJT* 5 (1959), 83.

7 J. D. G. Dunn, *Jesus and the Spirit* (London: SCM Press, 1975), 142.

8 This phrase is used by P. W. Meyer, "The Holy Spirit in the Pauline Letters. A Contextual Exploration," *Int* 33 (1979), 15.

9 Thus F. W. Beare, *A Commentary on the Epistle to the Philippians* (London: A. & C. Black, 1959), 73-78.

has been some scholarly controversy[10] whether this passage points to an actual identity between the Lord who is Jesus Christ (2 Cor. 4:5) and the Spirit, it is safe to say that Paul points to the closest of possible affinities between the two. References to the Spirit of Christ (Rom. 8:9), Spirit of Jesus Christ (Phil. 1:19), and the Spirit of his Son (Gal. 4:6) must also be viewed in this light. In fact, Rom. 8:9-10 even indicates that the Spirit of God is at the same time the Spirit of Christ.[11]

That Paul indeed sees a direct, logical development from flesh to Spirit with respect to Jesus is clearly evident from Rom. 1:3-4. According to this passage Jesus Christ "was descended from David according to the flesh and designated Son of God in power according to the Spirit of holiness by his resurrection from the dead." Also, 2 Cor. 5:16-17 must be seen as pointing to this logical development. The natural corollary to no longer regarding Christ from a human point of view is to regard him from the perspective of Spirit.[12] This Pauline teaching is also reflected accurately in 1 Tim. 3:16, "He was manifested in the flesh, vindicated in the Spirit."

The turning point in proceeding from flesh to Spirit, from one sphere of reality to the next, is death itself. Paul insists that he preaches the crucified Jesus (1 Cor. 1:23; 2:2) and that man must be willing to die with Christ (Rom. 6:6-8). Only if man dies with Christ will he be able to live with him. Indeed, 1 Cor. 15:20-24 argues that the resurrection of Christ is the first-fruits of the resurrection of all believers.

Thus for Paul the life, crucifixion, and resurrection of Jesus serve as the perfect analogy for the soteriological process for man. With respect to the specific interest of the present study it must be noted that Paul's apparent negative portrayal of the pre-resurrection life of Jesus must be viewed first and foremost as a necessary counterfoil to the Spirit-nature of the post-resurrection Lord. The apparent relative superiority of the post- over the pre-resurrection Jesus must be seen as governed by the theological consideration that Spirit is of greater importance than flesh. After all, while flesh leads to death, Spirit gives life.

It might be suggested that Paul's discussion of Jesus in terms of the soteriological scheme outlined above can be utilized to show that, from a strictly historical perspective, Paul drew a sharp distinction between the pre-resurrection Jesus and the resurrected Lord, and indeed that he had no interest in the former. But this is to disregard the contextual nature of Paul's thought. Paul's comparison between the pre-resurrection Jesus and the resurrected Lord is governed by theological

---

10   Cf., for example, the discussion by H. Ridderbos, *Paul: An Outline of His Theology* (Grand Rapids: Eerdmans, 1975), 88, 543.
11   Beare, *Philippians*, 71.
12   Ibid., 112.

rather than by historico-biographical considerations. The fact that
Paul's letters are occasional writings must be taken into account.

Of course, it should also be noted that the data discussed up to this
point in no way suggest that Paul had a great historical interest in the
life of the pre-resurrection Jesus. All that has been shown is that the
data discussed simply have no direct bearing on the question of
whether or not Paul had such an interest; Paul viewed life in the Spirit
as being of greater importance than life according to the flesh and he
used Jesus as an example.

Having indicated how the concept of the Spirit affects Paul's discussion of the life of Jesus, we can now consider the question of the
Spirit's role in Paul's view of the teaching of Jesus.

To begin with, Paul leaves room for a link with the teaching of the
pre-resurrection Jesus by way of the mechanism of tradition. The best
example is provided by 1 Cor. 11:23-25, where Paul relates the tradition
concerning the Last Supper. While the expression "from the Lord"
could conceivably refer to special revelations which Paul received directly from the resurrected Lord,[13] it is much more likely that Paul is
here referring to a passing on of tradition. Moffatt's explanation that
"*From* indicates the source of the tradition, not the means by which it
reached him,"[14] is convincing. Insofar as the Spirit is involved in the
knowledge of truth (1 Cor. 2:10-13) in general, the Spirit is not to be
completely dissociated even from the concept of tradition. Nevertheless, the emphasis in the concept of tradition is on the human transmission of the teaching of the pre-resurrection Jesus.

While it is clear that Paul in no way rules out the concept of
tradition as a link with the teaching of the pre-resurrection Jesus, the
emphasis in his extant writings is by no means on this particular
connection. Rather, Paul stresses that he received the Gospel of Christ
(Gal. 1:7) not from man but directly through a revelation of Jesus
Christ (1:12). In this direct revelation the Spirit played an important
role. Paul makes the general assertion that God reveals things to us
through the Spirit (1 Cor. 2:10-13), and that the resurrected Lord is the
Spirit (2 Cor. 3:17-18).

At this point a word of caution must be inserted. The relative stress
in the extant Pauline letters on direct revelation by the resurrected
Lord, as opposed to the normal transmission of tradition, must not be
exaggerated; it does not govern Paul's overall thought. The fact that
Paul's letters are occasional writings precludes such a conclusion. On
the other hand, it is instructive to pursue the question of why Paul
stresses what he does in the writings which we have at our disposal:
what is the particular motivation for Paul's seeming emphasis on the

13   Cf. Gal. 1:11-12.
14   J. Moffatt, *The First Epistle of Paul to the Corinthians* (London: Hodder and Stoughton,
     1938), 167; O. Cullmann, *The Early Church* (London: SCM Press, 1956), makes the
     same point.

gospel received by revelation through the resurrected Lord rather than on the teaching of the pre-resurrection Jesus by way of tradition?

Before dealing with Paul, it may be of some benefit to look briefly at this question from the broader perspective of first- and second-century Christianity as a whole, though no attempt will be made to establish lines of possible influence.

It appears that only two major movements in early Christianity viewed the teachings of the pre-resurrection Jesus as an essentially complete and sufficient revelation of truth. According to Jewish Christianity, as shown by the Kerygmata Petrou[15] source underlying the Pseudo Clementines, it is clear that Jesus, the True Prophet, prior to his crucifixion had perfect knowledge and transmitted it to his followers in a direct way.[16] Similarly, in Marcionite Christianity the pre-resurrection teaching of Jesus was viewed as the final revelation of truth. Man's task was simply to preserve this truth properly. No new revelation was necessary.[17]

Other streams within early Christianity saw the revelation of truth as being still incomplete at the point of the crucifixion of Jesus. According to the Gospel of John, it appears that Jesus had perfect knowledge (16:12, 14-15), but this knowledge was not internalized by the disciples prior to his resurrection. Whether the reason for this lack of understanding was a failure on the part of the disciples to comprehend the truth (e.g., 16:25), or a failure on the part of Jesus to communicate the whole truth (e.g., 16:12), is immaterial. The fact remains that according to the Gospel of John a full comprehension of the truth by the disciples was possible only with the help of the Spirit after the resurrection of Jesus (16:13).

While there is no absolute consistency in the Gnostic literature, the dominant view is that of the resurrected Saviour imparting a secret tradition to his disciples, a teaching that goes beyond that of the pre-resurrection Jesus.[18]

Irenaeus pinpoints the revelation of the final truth yet more exactly. He states in *Adv. haer.* 3.1.1 that it was at Pentecost that the apostles received perfect knowledge through the mediation of the Holy Spirit. This truth was then transmitted by way of the Church and the Scriptures.

It should not be supposed, however, that those who thought it necessary to complete or clarify the teaching of the pre-resurrection Jesus were necessarily opposed to this teaching. There was no emphasis on this teaching being of little significance or in need of correction. No,

---

15 The Kerygmata Petrou source is here used as reconstructed by G. Strecker, *Das Judenchristentum in den Pseudoklementinen*, TU 70 (Berlin: Akademie Verlag, 1958).

16 Cf. *Rec.* 6.4, 8.59; *Hom.* 3.20, 11.19; Strecker, *Judenchristentum*, 151-153.

17 Cf. E. C. Blackman, *Marcion and His Influence* (London: S.P.C.K., 1948), 42ff.

18 E.g., *The Apocryphon of John* (II, 1), 1:2-3, 31:28-31.

the teaching of the pre-resurrection Jesus was deemed important, but, for one reason or another, needed clarification or completion.

Did Paul view the teaching of the pre-resurrection Jesus as complete or as incomplete? Judging from his insistence that he received his gospel by way of a revelation by the resurrected Lord (Gal. 1:7-12) it appears that Paul placed great importance upon the clarification that such revelation brought.

What was Paul's rationale for insisting that the teaching of the resurrected Lord was essential? It appears that his primary concern in this regard was the authentication of the Gentile mission.

On the basis of Rom. 15:8 it is clear that Paul viewed the ministry of the pre-resurrection Jesus as confined to the circumcised, that is, the Jews. As Professor Beare has pointed out, this passage may indeed accurately reflect the earliest tradition.[19] After all, in the Gospel of Matthew the ministries of Jesus (15:24) and of the disciples (10:5-6) are confined to the house of Israel. It is only the resurrected Jesus who commands the disciples to embark on the mission to the Gentiles (28:19).

That the tradition regarding the initial confinement of the mission to the Jews is not found in the other gospels, Professor Beare explains, is quite natural since they are more Gentile-Christian in orientation than Matthew. The initial hesitancy of the primitive Church to carry the gospel to the Gentiles is also more understandable if there was an early injunction against it.[20]

What is absolutely clear is that Paul views his reception of the gospel by revelation as being of primary significance for the Gentiles. In fact, Paul characterizes the gospel he received as "the gospel to the uncircumcised" (Gal. 2:7).

Even if Ephesians is not a genuine Pauline epistle, it must be noted that it accurately reflects Paul's thought on this point. Eph. 3:1-6 states that the mystery made known by revelation is that the Gentiles are partakers of the promise in Christ Jesus through the gospel, with special reference being made to the role of the Spirit in this revelation (3:5). Also, Acts 13:46, 47; 18:6; 22:21; 26:17 and 28:28 refer to Paul's special role in bringing the gospel to the Gentiles.

Paul by no means feels unopposed in his mission to the Gentiles. As the first two chapters of Galatians show especially, he was quite concerned about the success of his mission. His hope was that "the offering of the Gentiles may be acceptable, sanctified by the Holy Spirit" (Rom. 15:16), and that "in Christ Jesus the blessing of Abraham might come upon the Gentiles, that we might receive the promise of the Spirit through faith" (Gal. 3:14).

---

19   F. W. Beare, *The Earliest Records of Jesus* (Oxford: Basil Blackwell, 1962), 81.
20   Ibid.

Paul's stress on the gospel received through revelation with the involvement of the Spirit should in no way be interpreted as proof that Paul minimized the importance of the teaching of the pre-resurrection Jesus transmitted by way of tradition. All that can be said with certainty is that, in the face of opposition to his particular interpretation of the Gentile mission, Paul relied on the argument that none other than the resurrected Lord himself, who is the Spirit, had authenticated such a mission. This was essentially a new revelation. Paul did not, however, think that this new revelation contradicted the teaching of the pre-resurrection Jesus. Rather, it was viewed as a natural development of it.

Another factor which may have a bearing on Paul's apparent stress on the resurrected Lord who is the Spirit concerns Paul's right to be an apostle. As is indicated by 1 Cor. 9:2 there were some who cast doubt upon Paul's right to be called an apostle. What was at the basis of this controversy?

I would suggest that the clue to this issue lies in 1 Cor. 15:8. Having noted that the resurrected Christ appeared "to all the apostles" (15:7) Paul then is forced to differentiate between the appearance to these apostles and to himself: the appearance to himself was "as to one untimely born" (15:8). Of what significance is this qualification?

The resurrection tradition that is reflected in Acts 1:3 limits the resurrection appearances to the forty days between the resurrection and ascension. According to this criterion, Paul's experience would have taken place after the ascension and thus would have had a different character from the appearances to the other apostles. This might explain the "untimely born."

On the other hand, the possibility does exist that Paul was not aware of or did not adhere to the tradition reflected in Acts, but believed that there was a more extended period during which resurrection appearances might occur. In various Gnostic writings the appearances are not limited to forty days; for example, according to Pistis Sophia 1:1, "after Jesus had risen from the dead he spent eleven years speaking with his disciples."[21]

Another possible explanation for Paul's statement that he was "untimely born" could be that he was reacting against a tradition such as is reflected in Acts 1:21. The major qualification for the choice of an apostle to succeed Judas is a close acquaintance with Jesus during the period he was "among us." According to this criterion Paul was indeed "untimely born," that is, he could not point to an acquaintance with the pre-resurrection Jesus but only to the Lord who is the Spirit. Paul's stress on the importance of the Lord who is the Spirit could thus be an attempt to show that not only the pre-resurrection Jesus but also the resurrected Lord is important. Being acquainted with the latter in no

---

21 V. MacDermot, and C. Schmidt, *Pistis Sophia*, NHS 9 (Leiden: E. J. Brill, 1978), 3.

way excluded one from being a proper apostle. Naturally, the Lord who is the Spirit could only be known by means of the Spirit. Consequently, it is understandable why Paul stressed the concept of the Spirit in his relationship to Jesus Christ.

On the basis of the foregoing discussion it is evident that Paul insisted that the teaching of the Lord who is the Spirit was essential for gaining a proper understanding of the gospel. In essence there was room for revelation beyond that which the pre-resurrection Jesus had provided. The question that now arises is that of the finality of revelation: did Paul believe that the gospel of Jesus Christ which he had initially received from the Lord who is the Spirit was complete or was there room for ongoing revelation?

To gain a proper perspective on the question of the finality of revelation it may be instructive to look at this issue first of all in terms of various positions that developed in Christianity during the first two centuries.

According to Irenaeus the apostles received perfect knowledge at Pentecost through the mediation of the Holy Spirit (*Adv. haer.* 3.1.1).[22] There was no need for further revelation. Indeed, the perfect truth was passed on through the Church and the Scriptures, and through the guidance of the Holy Spirit it was kept pure. Nevertheless, Irenaeus does admit certain practical limitations as to the knowledge of truth. For example, parables are singled out as admitting of many interpretations (*Adv. haer.* 2.27.3). Man's partial understanding of the truth, however, is not to be viewed in a static fashion. There is the possibility of acquiring greater understanding of the truth. Specifically, with reference to the interpretation of Paul's writings, Irenaeus notes that man asks and the Spirit provides the answer (*Adv. haer.* 3.7.2). Thus, while the final revelation of the truth occurred at Pentecost, new understanding of the truth could be achieved through the Spirit-guided interpretation of Scripture, leaving the door open for finding solutions to new problems.

According to the Gnostic literature the majority view appears to be that the resurrected Saviour passed on perfect knowledge to selected disciples, who in turn were to pass on this secret tradition. Those who possessed this secret teaching had perfect knowledge. Thus any knowledge which might appear to be new, in actual fact was simply part of the secret tradition come to light.[23]

For the Montanists the term "new prophecy" was a significant self-designation.[24] Montanism purported to possess new revelation

---

22   Cf. *Adv. haer.* 3.12.5; 4.33.8; 4.35.2.
23   It is interesting to note that Gnostics pointed to 1 Cor. 2:7 to support the concept of a secret tradition.
24   Cf. G. N. Bonwetsch, *Die Geschichte des Montanismus* (Erlangen: Andreas Deichert, 1881), 127, with references to passages such as Eusebius, *Hist. Eccl.* 5.19.2; Tertullian, *Adv. Marc.* 4.22.4, *de Monog.* 14.

about the fulfillment of the kingdom of God and the criteria for participating in it. In turn, it was primarily the Montanist rejection of the theory of the finality of revelation that the Church opposed.[25]

Generally, the new revelations were concerned with ethics, especially the problem of second marriage. According to 1 Cor. 7:39-40, Paul, while not advocating second marriages, nevertheless allows them. The Montanists, on the other hand, condemned them. In essence, the Montanists believed that the Paraclete had the authority to change specific ethical teachings of the apostles.[26]

To substantiate the revelatory function of the Paraclete the Montanists appealed to various New Testament passages, chief of which was John 16:12-14.[27] What is the meaning of this passage? John 16:14-15 clearly states that the Father will take the truth which Jesus had and give it to the disciples. In 16:13 it is explicitly stated that this communication of the truth will be accomplished by means of the Spirit of truth. Finally, an actual example of this function of the Spirit is given, that is, the Spirit of truth "will declare to you the things that are to come" (16:13). While interpreters are divided on the exact interpretation of the phrase "things that are to come,"[28] it does appear that this statement refers to something that was not simply misunderstood by the disciples or brought to their remembrance,[29] but rather to something that was not revealed at all to them during the pre-resurrection ministry of Jesus.[30]

It should be noted that John 16:13 states that the Spirit of truth will not speak on his own authority. This explanation could very well have been meant as a safeguard in the sense that the Spirit of truth would in no way contradict anything which had been revealed by Jesus. Yet the possibility is left open that the Spirit could reveal additional facts, especially ones relating to things that are to come.

The foregoing overview shows that there was some diversity in early Christianity on the issue of the Spirit in relationship to the finality of revelation. Where would Paul fit into this spectrum of views?

Paul makes the general observation in 1 Cor. 13:9 that knowledge is imperfect. At least from a theoretical perspective this admission

---

25   E.g., Hippolytus, *Ref.* 8.12.
26   Tertullian, *de Monog.* 14. Cf. J. de Soyres, *Montanism and the Primitive Church* (Cambridge: Deighton, Bell, 1878), 58.
27   Cf. Didymus, *de Trin.* 3.41.2; Bonwetsch, *Montanismus*, 127-128.
28   E.g., R. Bultmann, *The Gospel of John: A Commentary* (Philadelphia: Westminster Press, 1976), 575, is against an apocalyptic interpretation of this passage. B. F. Westcott, *The Gospel According to St. John* (1881; rpt. Grand Rapids: Eerdmans, 1967), 231, suggests that this refers to the constitution of the Christian Church. G. H. C. MacGregor, *The Gospel of John* (London: Hodder and Stoughton, 1928), 299, claims that it is not a question of foretelling the future but of interpreting tendencies.
29   Cf. John 14:26.
30   Cf. J. H. Bernard, *A Critical and Exegetical Commentary on the Gospel According to St. John*, ICC (Edinburgh: T. and T. Clark, 1928), 2:511, "Prophecy in the sense of prediction is included here in the work of the Paraclete."

leaves the door open for new understanding and revelation. Indeed, a study of Paul's writings indicates that he thought in terms of three stages of revelation. As noted previously, Paul leaves room for a link with the teaching of the pre-resurrection Jesus by way of the mechanism of tradition (1 Cor. 11:23-25). Thus, the first stage of the revelation of truth is the teaching of the pre-resurrection Jesus. The second stage consists of Paul's reception of the gospel of Jesus Christ by revelation through the resurrected Lord. From Gal. 1:12-22 it is evident that this revelation took place before Paul embarked on his missionary activity in Asia Minor.

To what extent is the concept of the Spirit involved in these first two stages of the reception of the gospel? 1 Cor. 2:10-13 shows that Paul did not regard the gospel as being self-explanatory; the Spirit had to be involved in all mediation of truth. So in 1 Thess. 1:5 Paul notes that the gospel came to the Thessalonians "in power and in the Holy Spirit." This does not mean that the mediation of the truth of the gospel is altogether removed from Jesus Christ. For Paul, there is a close relationship between Jesus and the Spirit, for "the Lord is the Spirit" (2 Cor. 3:17).[31] Consequently, when in Rom. 9:1 Paul appeals to the Spirit as vouching for the truth, he is at the same time appealing to Jesus Christ.

That the Spirit plays a significant role both in guaranteeing and in interpreting the truth as revealed in the first two stages of revelation is thus clear. The question which remains to be answered is whether Paul leaves the door open for a third stage of revelation. I suggest that he does and that the third stage is characterized by revelation added to revelation.

According to 2 Cor. 12:1, 7, Paul experienced various visions and revelations. Indeed, at one point he claimed to have been caught up into paradise and to have heard things that he could not retell (2 Cor. 12:3-4).

More to the point for the purpose of our discussion, however, are those passages where Paul unequivocally admits that for some problems arising in the Church he had no command of the Lord. This is explicitly stated in 1 Cor. 7:25 and implied in 1 Cor. 7:12. It is interesting to note that not having a direct command of the Lord does not deter Paul from providing solutions to the problems at hand. The solutions, however, are not simply based on Paul's own authority. Rather, Paul concludes the discussion of these issues by pointing out that he has the Spirit of God (1 Cor. 7:40).[32] In other words, Paul infers that the Spirit provided a new revelation to a new problem.

---

31   Cf. Rom. 8:9; Gal. 4:6; Phil. 1:19.
32   Cf. P. Richardson, "'I say, not the Lord': Personal Opinion, Apostolic Authority and the Development of Early Christian Halakah," *Tyndale Bulletin* 31 (1980), 86.

Just as the reference to the Spirit in 1 Cor. 7:40 is seen as authenticating Paul's innovative teaching in 7:1-39, so the reference to the Holy Spirit in Rom. 9:1 should be seen as authenticating Paul's innovative ideas concerning the place of Israel in God's plan of salvation as outlined in 9:2-11:36.

Is the third stage of revelation completely open-ended? Paul does not provide us with the data to give a definitive answer to this question. What is clear, on the other hand, is that at least with reference to himself Paul appeals to the ongoing function of the Spirit to provide revelation. In instances where Paul has no direct command of the Lord, it is on the basis of the presence of the Spirit that normative solutions can be found to new problems. Thus Paul not only sees the Spirit as facilitating the way to the teaching of Jesus but also as providing the framework for going beyond this teaching.

"He who did not spare his own son . . .": Jesus, Paul, and the Akedah

ALAN F. SEGAL

It is a pleasure to contribute to a volume in honour of F. W. Beare, whose *The Earliest Records of Jesus*[1] had been a standard reference work for me before I came to the University of Toronto. The pleasure was quickened by an association with the man who, though in retirement, is still an active presence on Toronto's campus. The material which I want to evaluate here was first used in a colloquium at the University of Toronto and is an attempt to highlight the Jewish background of a Christian tradition, as was one of Professor Beare's recent papers at the Biblical Seminar of the Toronto School of Theology.

One of Professor Beare's most persistent emphases has been the necessity of being a good historian—bringing to bear form criticism, redaction criticism, and source criticism on every report.[2] Unfortunately, the effect of the principles on which New Testament scholarship is based cuts Jesus off from the Jewish environment by underlining his uniqueness. This is a necessary consequence of trying to discover what belongs uniquely to the Jesus-level of any tradition. But it should not keep us from also stressing Jesus' Jewish background to see the atmosphere in which he lived, his life, and the expectations of his disciples, even if we must remain ignorant of most of his intentions. For it cannot be that Jesus lived in the kind of isolation that as scholars we are forced to impose upon him. His own thought must have been formed within the social context of his pre-passion followers, though

---

1 F. W. Beare, *The Earliest Records of Jesus* (New York: Abingdon, 1962).
2 See, e.g., ibid., 16-17 (Introduction, sect. 2).

169

we have no reports which come unmediated from that period and
hence can only reconstruct it with difficulty.

In turning to the interpretations of the sacrifice of Isaac I would
like to deal not with Jesus' understanding of himself but the Jewish
understanding of martyrdom which emerges from the Isaac traditions
and with the transformations made in that tradition by the earliest
Christians because of their experience of Jesus.

The church, like Judaism, was interested in the story of Isaac
because it was an example of Abraham's steadfast obedience to God
that could also be understood as a story of martyrdom—the death of
the innocent to fulfill the will of God. My interest in the exegesis of the
Akedah will not be solely literary, nor will it be exhaustive, for there has
already been a good deal of criticism on the topic. Rather, I want to
recover what pre-Christian Jewish tradition had to say about the question of martyrdom, how that theme related to the story of Abraham's
sacrifice of Isaac and, in turn, how the question of the martyrdom of
Isaac affected Paul's version of Christianity. Of course, to the completely uninitiated, the story of the sacrifice of Isaac will seem of
dubious importance to Christianity. But those who know a little Jewish
tradition will know that occasionally Isaac was viewed by the rabbis as
being sacrificed and his ashes used to atone for Israel's sins.[3]

Though there have been dozens of studies of the Akedah, the
major methodological steps can be summed up with the three major
studies of the material.[4] The most influential contributor to the study
of the tradition of the Akedah is Shalom Spiegel, in *Meaggadot Ha-
Akedah*.[5] This is a delicate and disinterested literary study of the context
of the *Piyyut* of Rabbi Ephraim ben Jacob of Bonn, trying to show what
is assumed by the poet when he writes.

Part of Spiegel's genius is surely to have seen the importance of this
theme within Judaism and the need to make that theme explicit—
whether in its biblical version, as a model for the Maccabean martyrs, as
a model for the suffering messiah, or as a model for the Jewish martyrs
of the crusades. The martyrs of the mediaeval European pogroms saw
themselves as Isaacs prepared for the slaughter and even described the
knife as a sharpened instrument with no nicks, implying that the rules
for sacrifice (i.e., for appropriate dietary slaughter) had been observed.

---

3 For examples see *Mek.* de Rabbi Ishmael H-R, 24-25, 38-39; *Midr. Rab., ad loc.,* and
   the relevant chapters in Spiegel, *The Last Trial* (see n. 5 below).
4 See E. Yassif (ed.), *The Sacrifice of Isaac: Studies in the Development of a Literary Tradition*
   (Jerusalem: Makor, 1978), 34ff. in the Hebrew section; P. R. Davies and B. D.
   Chilton, "The Akedah: A Revised Tradition History," *CBQ* 40 (1978), 514-546; and
   J. Swetnam, *Jesus and Isaac: A Study of the Epistle to the Hebrews in the Light of the Akedah*
   (Rome: BIP, 1981). (Abbreviations in references are those used by the *Journal of
   Biblical Literature.* See *JBL* 95 [1976], 331-346.)
5 In the Alexander Marx Jubilee Volume (*Sefer Ha-yovel li-khvod Aleksander Marx*)
   Hebrew Section (New York: Jewish Theological Society, 1950); The English transla-
   tion is: *The Last Trial* (New York: Random House, 1967).

In the modern period the theme of the sacrifice of Isaac has continued to draw artistic attention when the problem of theodicy must be raised—from Britten's *Requiem* to Kierkegaard's concept of the "leap of faith" to Lipshitz's memorial to the fallen at Kent State. Apparently the frequent use of the model in discussions of theodicy points to its deep symbolic effect upon our sensibilities. The fact that Spiegel turned his attention to it when he did was surely influenced by the growing recognition of the horror of the European holocaust.

Even in the presence of such a masterpiece as Spiegel's work, however, hard questions about the adequacy of his method must be asked. We must take the force of Vermes' criticism of previous studies on the midrash.[6] Vermes himself defines two fundamentally different ways of approaching the midrash. The first can be represented in its best light by Louis Ginzberg's masterful *The Legends of the Jews*,[7] a giant anthology intending to collect all the available material from every possible source and "paying little attention to chronological data, to construct a synthesis of the various interpretations."[8] The second way, of course, is Vermes' description of his own approach: "To follow the development of exegetical principles by means of historical criticism,"[9] and thereby to identify the particular text read by a particular audience and to fill in the historical, social, cultural, and religious—or, in short, the entire semantic context of the time. At first one would think that Spiegel might fail this simple test while Vermes might succeed, since the latter identifies the methodological issue so well. Answers, however, are rarely as simple as they appear at first. Though Spiegel gives us a thematic (and hence by definition a homogenized) view of the theme of the sacrifice of Isaac in the Middle Ages, he does not entirely lose the possibility of defining a text. One must not forget that the purpose of Spiegel's book is to fill in the context of the *Piyyut* of Rabbi Ephraim ben Jacob of Bonn. Though he homogenized the tradition in the period of Jesus, he gives us an extremely well defined picture of the traditions that preceded Rabbi Ephraim ben Jacob, as well as a very informed reading of the poem itself.

Vermes, on the other hand, has given us not a literary so much as an historical argument—the background for a literary analysis—in which he attempts to show us that the midrash about Isaac in the first century became a paradigm to express the expectations of the disciples in Jesus' mission. We must take his arguments much more slowly, so as to see exactly what the tradition of the Akedah was just prior to the time of Jesus, to define what were the Christian additions to that text, and

---

6 G. Vermes, *Scripture and Tradition in Judaism* (2nd ed.; Leiden: Brill, 1974), 1-4. Spiegel's idea that the source of the story is entirely in pagan thought is probably Israeli romanticism and is certainly unfounded in evidence.

7 L. Ginzberg, *The Legends of the Jews* (Philadelphia: Jewish Publication Society, 1909).

8 Vermes, *Scripture*, 1.

9 Ibid.

finally to define what may have been the Jewish reaction to the Christian interpretation. That is a far less interesting task than to read, or even to reread, Spiegel. Nevertheless, it is quite necessary in light of the hard questions which Vermes has asked.

The first thing that must be said about Vermes is that his arguments are based upon a bold thesis—that the Palestinian Targum tradition contains a core of first-century tradition that can be isolated from the material that has entered the text much later. Vermes's conclusion, based on this hypothesis and his supporting evidence, is that the account of the sacrifice of Isaac and not the suffering servant of Isa. 53 may be the most important model of the early church in its understanding of Jesus' passion. According to Vermes the Jewish community had already begun to use the death and resurrection of Isaac as the model for the reward of the martyrs and so this naturally became the paradigm for the suffering of Jesus.

At the outset, the hypothesis seems rash, for there are only a very few references to Isaac in the New Testament and Isa. 53 is almost always assumed to lie behind much of the gospel tradition. But other scholars[10] have consistently reminded us that, in spite of the common assumption, Isa. 53 is rarely quoted in the New Testament and still more rarely is any use of it made to show vicarious atonement. Since one of the central aspects of the Isaac story in the midrash is vicarious atonement, or *zechuth aboth* as the rabbis put it, the story of the sacrifice of Isaac may well give us a source for vicarious atonement in Christianity.

Vermes' hypothesis of the early date of the Palestinian Targum (in its present shape) may one day be proved. We know that targumim were in use in the first century. But it has so far been almost impossible to develop consistent criteria for isolating the first century traditions in the targumim. In such a case, though we may appreciate the creativity of the targum and must come to some understanding of its method, we must bracket the targumic evidence of Vermes to bring the historical problem to the fore again: just what can be established as the commonly understood text of Gen. 22 in the first century? Vermes' methodological question about the meaning of the biblical text comes back to haunt

---

10   M. D. Hooker, *Jesus and the Servant* (London: S.P.C.K., 1959) represents the critical extreme of scholarship, while C. H. Dodd, *According to the Scriptures* (London: Fontana, 1965), 92-94, 103, 123-125, represents the more usual position. Vermes sees no relationship with Isa. 53, but I prefer to think that the martyrological tradition itself is the primary one, in which Isaac, and to a certain extent Isa. 53, figured. But one should also mention as important, e.g., the wonder tales in Dan. 2-3, and the woman and her seven sons in 1 Macc., as I will shortly outline. See the interesting study by Clemens Thoma, which claims too much for the targum but notes the importance of the martyr tradition: "Observations on the Concept and the Early Forms of Akedah Spirituality," in A. Finkel and L. Frizzell (eds.), *Standing Before God: Studies on Prayer in Scriptures and in Tradition with Essays in Honor of John Oesterreicher* (New York: KTAV, 1981), 213-222.

him when one takes away the targumic evidence on which he builds his own case.

The evidence against Vermes has been best summarized by our third example, in P. R. Davies and B. D. Chilton:[11]

We propose to deal with the poem of the four nights and the Targums to Genesis 22 after we have reconstructed the development of the Akedah from rabbinic sources. Our reasons for this approach are straight-forward, but the vogue for dating targums early is so strong that a word of explanation may be necessary. Daly, for example, cites Le Déaut and McNamara in asserting the antiquity of the targumic Akedah. In the light of the very strong objections to assuming the antiquity of targums raised by J. A. Fitzmyer and P. Grelot, it is necessary to look again at the arguments cited. McNamara is confident that the Akedah is in the main pre-Christian seeing that many of its themes are attested in the works of Josephus, Philo, in the Biblical Antiquities of Ps. Philo and the Mekilta. The last mentioned source is, of course, a rabbinic composition with a second century C.E. *terminus a quo*; its testimony is beside the point for this purpose. The first three documents cited are among those which we will deal with presently and in which we find no trace of the Akedah, so that McNamara's argument does not convince us. The same applies, *mutatis mutandis*, to Le Déaut's citation of Jubilees and G. Vermes's appeal to IV Maccabees.[12]

In other words, against Vermes, the position of Davies and Chilton is that the targums are not pre-Christian. But they go on to say that there is no mention of the Akedah in any other pre-Christian literature. This is an extreme position—one which has merit only in the literal sense of their words—for it is literally true that the term *"Akedah"* is not used in scripture. It occurs first in the rabbinic tractate *Tamid*, as a reference to the daily sacrificial offering. The use of the term *"Akedah"* is dependent upon a tradition that we cannot satisfactorily date before the second century. With this warning against anachronism, however, there is clear evidence for the hermeneutic interpretation of the sacrifice of Isaac as an example of martyrdom and as a temple sacrifice before Christianity. Davies's and Chilton's overly strict caution leaves out important parts of the evidence because they appear to want to preserve the integrity of the concept of atoning sacrifice in Christianity.

While it is true that the term *"Akedah"* is rabbinic, not all associations between sacrifice and the story of Isaac are post-Christian. The history of interpretation of the sacrifice of Isaac begins right in the Bible. In 2 Chronicles Mt. Moriah, scene of the sacrifice, is identified with the Temple Mount (2 Chron. 3:1); so an explicit connection between the story of the sacrifice of Isaac and the sacrificial cult in Jerusalem is established. Second, the criticism of Davies and Chilton to

---

11   Davies and Chilton, "Akedah," 514-515.
12   This short quotation shows how difficult it is to find agreement among scholars about the correct dating of targumic evidence. The correct method in such a case is to bracket the targumic evidence as unsure witnesses to the state of affairs in the first century.

the contrary, the book of Jubilees does contain an explicit connection between the sacrifice of Isaac (or *Akedah*, loosely speaking) and the Passover.[13] The fact that Jubilees also connects other events in the lives of the patriarchs with other holidays does not override the obvious fact that a significant connection between Passover and the sacrifice of Isaac has been made.

The passage is clearly the subject of much popular hermeneutical activity before Jesus. We have fragments of Philo the Elder,[14] Demetrius and Alexander Polyhistor,[15] as well as a passage from Sirach[16] devoted to the subject.[17] The Book of Judith[18] certainly links the sacrifice of Isaac with the trials which the Jewish community is facing, since it uses the same word (*peirazein*) as does the LXX in describing the testing of Abraham. But the focus of the event is Abraham's steadfastness rather than Isaac's. The testing of Isaac to which the text refers may be a reference to Rebekah's barrenness in Gen. 25:21.[19] The Greek version of the text, however, singles out Isaac as having been the object of God's testing, thus implying the martyrological analogy.

Philo does not give us many discussions of the sacrifice of Isaac. It is missing from his *seriatim* interpretation of the Pentateuch. However, he does give us some interesting traditions about the sacrifice of Isaac in *de Abrahamo*. There, the emphasis is on Abraham as priest officiating at a sacrifice (even though the sacrifice does not take place). The sacrifice that Philo has in mind must be the *tamid* offering: "perhaps too, following the law of burnt offering, he would have dismembered his son and offered him limb by limb."[20] He also clearly understands the concept of giving one's life for others' benefit.

Josephus' version of the sacrifice of Isaac appears in *Antiquities*, a work probably completed in 94 C.E.[21] For the most part, Josephus follows the biblical story closely. Like Philo, Josephus is interested in Abraham, rather than Isaac, and he takes special pains to show that Abraham's piety (*thrēskeia*) is tested, his piety rewarded. Josephus has Isaac greet the news of his impending sacrifice with great joy, rushing in anticipation to the altar. He is twenty-four or five when the event takes place, apparently an interpretation of *na'ar*, paralleled in the

---

13 See Jub. 17:15-18:19. The heavenly discussion takes place on the twelfth of Nisan. Three days later (Gen. 22:4) would bring us to Passover for the sacrifice itself. Jubilees also connects Noah's ark, Abraham at Shechem, and Jacob at Bethel. The sacrifice of Isaac is related to the liberation from Egypt and all future liberations as well.
14 See Eusebius, *Praeparatio Evangelica* 9.20.1.
15 Ibid.
16 Sir. 44:19-21.
17 See Swetnam, *Jesus and Isaac*, 29.
18 See Jdt. 8:25-27.
19 See Swetnam, *Jesus and Isaac*, 35.
20 *de Abr.* 198.
21 Josephus, *Ant.* 1.13.1-4, 222-236; also 20.12; 1.267.

story of Jephthah's daughter. In both cases the portrayal is designed to show that the victim was not a minor, rather a willing adult.

In other words, one may go too far to either extreme, as Vermes on the one hand, or Davies and Chilton on the other do, in evaluating the traditions which precede the Christian version of the Isaac legend. It is clearly wrong to say that there was no Jewish tradition of the sacrifice of Isaac before Christianity or that the exegesis of that biblical passage was not involved in martyrology or traditions of vicarious atonement. It is just as wrong to assume that there was a single paradigmatic tradition which could be picked up by the church as a type for Jesus, as Vermes does. Either is, as I will try to show, a misrepresentation of the literary quality of the texts.

Some reference to the broad context must be made before entering into a more detailed criticism of Davies and Chilton. Resurrection was still a new idea within Judaism in hellenistic times. It appears to enter the Bible in the book of Daniel (c. 165 B.C.E.) although there may be hints in parts of Isaiah and Ezekiel which are difficult to date.

Presumably the concept of resurrection is linked to the problem of theodicy raised by the Maccabean revolt. Thereafter, discussions of martyrdom are often associated with resurrection or eternal life.[22] Resurrection is first of all the reward of martyrs and only secondarily a general reward. In the time of Jesus the theme of resurrection was still hotly debated in the religio-political life of the Jews. Pharisees accepted it; Sadducees rejected it. Concomitant with the idea of resurrection the idea of ascension and heavenly exaltation developed in Judaism. Martyrs were thought to live with God in holiness. Now ascension itself was not originally a Hebrew idea of what happened after death. In fact, since Sheol, the abode of the dead, was underground, the only ascensions that took place in the early biblical period were those of figures like Elijah and Enoch who were supposed by the text to have avoided death completely by going to heaven while still alive. Originally ascension was a very special reward for extraordinary people. But since ascension became a favorite theme of late antiquity in general (for reasons that cannot be analyzed here) it also found a place in Daniel and other Jewish literature of the hellenistic period. These developments served to connect ideas of life after death with the apocalyptic idea of resurrection in extremely complex and varying ways. The one generalization about this complex constellation of material which still seems valid is that the Hebrew versions of the theme of ascension are almost always associated with the problem of theodicy.[23]

---

22 G. W. E. Nickelsburg, *Resurrection, Immortality, and Eternal Life in Intertestamental Judaism* (Cambridge, Mass.: Harvard University Press, 1972); H. C. C. Cavallin, *Life After Death: Paul's Argument for the Resurrection of the Dead in I Corinthians 15, Part 1: An Inquiry into the Jewish Background* (Lund: C. W. K. Gleerup, 1974).
23 See my paper, "Heavenly Ascent in Hellenistic Judaism, Early Christianity and their Environments," *ANRW* II 23:2 (Berlin: Walter de Gruyter, 1980), 1333-1394.

The problem of martyrdom—the man who dies a painful death precisely because he stays true to the commands of God—is a Hebrew expression of a broad ethical and moral question which was being debated actively in the hellenistic world. While the themes of martyrdom and resurrection are clearly connected and developed by the books of Daniel and 2 Maccabees, and especially by the addition of the story of Hannah and her seven sons to the text of 2 Maccabees 7, the motif of Isaac's sacrifice as the example *par excellence* of martyrdom does not appear until the first century—pre-eminently in the book of 4 Maccabees, dated to the early 30s but devoid of Christian influence.[24] This, not the targumim and not Jubilees, seems to me the best evidence supporting Vermes' general observations that some kind of tradition formed the basis of Christian view of Jesus as a type of Isaac. More interesting still is the occurrence of the concept of vicarious atonement in this book. Eleazar prays that his death may serve not only to atone for his own sins but also for the sins of the people as a whole:

Thou knowest God that though I might have saved myself, I die in fiery torment for the sake of the Law. Be merciful to thy people and let my punishment be sufficient for their sake. Make my blood an expiation for them and take my life as a ransom for theirs.[25]

Isaac's sacrifice is brought in later on as a paradigm of martyrdom. This work seems to me evidence of extraordinary importance, especially when one notes the absence of Isa. 53 as a significant part of martyrological discussion in the pre-Christian era. Instead, there are discussions of the paradigmatic value of the innocent sufferer, of which many could be adduced.[26]

---

24   Davies and Chilton, "Akedah," 517, do not see anything of importance in 4 Maccabees and note that the work has been variously attributed to dates in the first and second centuries. See U. Breitenstein, *Beachtungen zu Sprache, Stil und Gedankengut des Vierten Makkabäerbuches* (Basel/Stuttgart: Swabe, 1976); and A. Dupont-Sommer, *Le quatrième livre des Machabées* (Paris: H. Champion, 1939). They have their own reasons for accepting a late date in spite of the lack of evidence for Christian influence in 4 Maccabees. Their unsupported contention that it is of no importance to the development of the tradition is mistaken, as I will try to show below. For my part, I find the evidence of E. Bickermann, "The Date of IV Maccabees," in *Louis Ginzberg Jubilee Volume* (New York: American Academy for Jewish Research, 1945), 105-112, to be persuasive. The word *thrēskeia* is never used for religion until the period of Augustus, yet the book conceives of the Temple and its service as still existing, which naturally dates it before 70 C.E. Furthermore, the title of Apollonius in 4:9, "governor of Syria, Phoenicia and Cilicia," refers to an administrative arrangement that lasted only from 20 to 54 C.E. Splitting the difference, we can provisionally assign the book to the reign of Caligula, which was certainly a period in which Jews needed to consider the problem of martyrdom. See M. Hadas (ed.), *3 and 4 Maccabees* (New York: Harper, 1953), 95-96; and *EJ* "kiddush ha-shem" for an independent evaluation of the importance of 4 Macc. in the development of Jewish martyrology.

25   4 Macc. 6:27-28.
26   See J. J. Collins, and G. W. E. Nickelsburg (eds.), *Ideal Figures in Ancient Judaism: Profiles and Paradigms* (Chico, Calif.: Scholars Press, 1980).

It is fair to note, however, that even in the Greek paraenesis of 4 Maccabees, Isaac's sacrifice itself is never directly linked with vicarious atonement. Martyrdom is associated with vicarious atonement while Isaac is pre-eminent among the martyrs. 4 Maccabees may even imply that Isaac actually underwent martyrdom: *hypomenō*, the word used at that point, may mean "to suffer" or "undergo" or "await." This is in line with the editor's desire to use Isaac's example as a type of martyrdom, while yet preserving the blblical story intact. Since the editor wanted to keep the original biblical text, he could not link Isaac's sacrifice with vicarious atonement directly. Jewish tradition required that for atonement to be effected, sacrificial blood had to be spilt. All the ideas clearly come together in this work, but the explicit relationship depends on the scriptural passage under consideration. On the other hand, 4 Maccabees does not mention Isaac's death and subsequent resurrection—a very important part of the story from the Christian perspective.

From the Jewish exegesis of the Akedah, several conclusions are possible. First, the Akedah was heavily used in Jewish exegesis and had already gained a firm grip on Jewish sensibilities by the time of Jesus. Second, like all exegetical *cruces* it could be used in many ways, but this particular passage was used especially to clarify the meaning of martyrdom and encourage Jews in persecution. Associated concepts of death and resurrection are clearly present in 4 Maccabees, but they were not attracted to the Gen. 22 passage because of the biblical text itself. Third, although there are occasional references to the righteous character of the sufferer, the focus of the story is still on the trial of Abraham and his obedience. Finally, and this is the most important part, the story is nowhere used as a prototype of messianic suffering.

How different is the Christian material! Here, one finds that the identification of the martyred figure as the Messiah is absolutely central to the typology. Paul's use of the scripture immediately shows this distinction. Like the exegetes before him, Paul does not subject these traditions to systematic comparison. At most one can say that he is using the Isaac story with considerable exegetical functionalism. Possible references to Isaac come up only twice, and only in indirect ways in Paul: "He who did not spare his son but gave him up for us all"[27] clearly sounds the note of vicarious atonement, but it neither mentions Isa. 53 nor the temple service nor blood.[28] Paul appears to draw a kind of

---

27 Rom. 8:32.

28 It is possible that the language of this passage implies a direct relationship with Isa. 53, as both M. Hengel, *The Atonement* (Philadelphia: Fortress Press, 1981) and before him E. Lohse, *Maertyrer und Gottesknecht* (Göttingen: Vandenhoeck & Ruprecht, 1963) have implied. The evidence for this is the use of the terms *paradidonai* and *peri*. It appears to me that literary evidence based on this general use of language is very suspect. The general idea of vicarious atonement, however, is not extremely rare, nor is this language particularly rare in hellenistic-Jewish contexts. In any case, I

implicit analogy between God's action and the action of Abraham in sacrificing his son. Like Abraham, God recompensed mankind in a kind of "measure for measure" (*middah k'neged middah*) argument that is not unknown in the midrash. Of course, the understanding that Christ died for sins does not really need proof for Paul. It can be found in 1 Cor. 15:3b and frequently elsewhere. But only here in 1 Corinthians does he say that this saving death is in accordance with scripture. He does not explicitly tell us that Isa. 53 is the scripture he has in mind, although this is possible. Almost all scholars agree that he is using traditions which were taught to him by the community which he joined and which therefore antedate his entrance into Christianity.[29]

Note that in Rom. 8:32, in discussing the sacrifice of Isaac, the focus of the passage is Abraham, not Isaac, just as in the earlier Jewish interpretations. The "us" in Romans is left unspecified. But, by means of Gal. 3:13-14 the reference can be further clarified. "That the blessing of Abraham might come upon the Gentiles" is a paraphrase of Gen. 22:18, "and in your offspring shall all the nations of the earth be blessed." The expression "blessing of Abraham" may have been taken from Gen. 28:4, but "in Christ Jesus" has been substituted for the original "in your offspring."[30] Deut. 21:23 curses a man hanged upon a tree. But Paul, who applies the reference to Jesus, says that the curse has been turned into a blessing, perhaps thereby playing upon the Genesis story of the lamb caught in the thicket.[31] In this case, however, the analogy would be between the ram and Jesus, since both are seen as the sacrifice provided by God.

The novel aspect for Paul is a story of a crucified Messiah, the obvious aspect of the story missing from the pre-Christian Jewish exegesis, where Isaac is never understood as a type of the Messiah. It is very clear that Paul takes the crucified Jesus to be Messiah and Son of God because of his faith commitment, not because of a pre-existing development of the midrash. Only because of his prior faith can he say that as Abraham had offered up his son, so too God offered up his son for Isaac's children so that all the families of man would be blessed. It is a new idea totally absent from Jewish exegesis, even when Jewish exegesis stresses the vicariousness of the sacrifice.

At this point one wonders if the previous scholars' mistakes are not a bit more subtle than at first seemed evident. The hypothesis that the

---

would be prepared to concede some use of Isa. 53, although it would be much less explicit even than the figure of the sacrifice of Isaac, which itself is very allusive.

29   See Hengel, *Atonement*, 36.

30   This is the argument of N. A. Dahl, *The Crucified Messiah* (Minneapolis: Augsburg, 1974), 153, and it is very persuasive.

31   These themes are actually fairly common in the ancient Near East. See T. W. Doane, *Bible Myths and their Parallels in other Religions* (New Hyde Park, N.Y.: University Books, 1948), 94-95; E. O. James, *Sacrifice and Sacrament* (London: Thames & Hudson, 1962), 68-73; and R. Graves and R. Patai, *The Myths of the Hebrews* [in Hebrew] (Ramat Gan, 1967), 166-169.

targum must be early is one thing. But it is quite another thing to assume that, because many of the motifs which dominate Christian exegesis are present in Jewish exegesis, Christianity merely took them over, as Vermes sometimes appears to do. Rather, it seems to me that Christian exegesis was founded on various Jewish exegeses (*pace* Chilton and Davies) but the method was carried out with an entirely new understanding of what exegesis was meant to demonstrate. In other words, the method of Jewish midrash was brought to an entirely new purpose in Paul—the purpose of exposing the actual victory of an ostensibly failed messianic candidate.

When one looks carefully, the methodological mistake they all make is actually literary, one quite close to the implied methodological mistake which Vermes imputes to Ginzberg. Despite his respect for Ginzberg, Vermes complains that earlier studies had "homogenized" the text, destroying the historical context. Though he alone sees the role of the Jewish past in the tradition of the sacrifice of Isaac and may be blazing a new methodological trail, Vermes is in danger of "homogenizing" the text in a slightly different way. Although he notes where important themes are missing in each document, in sum he operates as if the whole constellation is always present once the parts of the tradition are attested. It seems as if Vermes describes a figure of Isaac the vicarious martyr which can merely be taken over into Christianity. Since this is clearly not the impression that the evidence gives, the criticism of Davies and Chilton has some validity. They note that the missing terms in the pre-Christian interpretation are just as important as the attested ones because they underline the thought processes of the Jewish interpreters before Jesus and emphasize the central aspect of the new Christian interpretation. I have tried to show, even in taking issue with Davies and Chilton's underinterpretation of the material, that the midrash is not a single text but an anthology made up of different interpretations of individual commentators. Each interpretation takes on some but not all the themes of later Christianity, while none interprets the Isaac passage messianically. Thus, we cannot identify a single text giving us a single sum of past experiences as Vermes does.

There is a corollary to this conclusion that there does not appear to be a figure with the title "suffering servant" whose identity could be described in the way that past Christian scholarship has implied.[32] There is no figure in Judaism approximating what scholars have called *THE* Suffering Servant. There is not even an overarching understanding of the referent of the servant songs in Judaism. The midrashic process (unlike the Christian interpretation in this respect) does not ask "Who is the suffering servant?" so much as "What can be further

---

32   W. Zimmerli and J. Jeremias, *"pais theou,"* *TWNT* 5, trans. as *The Servant of God* (London: SCM Press, 1957), or now *TDNT*.

known about the 'servants of God' from the passage under consideration?" By a process of analogy, Isa. 53 is often viewed in light of other
passages in which "servants of God" are mentioned. In various places in
the Bible, as the rabbis note, Abraham, Phineas, and pre-eminently
Moses are called "servant."[33] For our purposes it is important to note
that a targum to Job does identify Isaac as the servant of God on the
basis of a rather imaginative exegesis.[34] Although we know from Qumran fragments that a Job targum did exist in the first century, the extant
targum, the one linking Isaac with the servant, does not agree with the
Qumran fragments where it overlaps. Hence it is dubious evidence of
the identification of Isaac as a servant of God in pre-Christian times.

Some exegetical hints do exist about the various identities of servants of God in the first century. Another person who is called servant is
David.[35] This can be shown on the basis of Ez. 34:23 and 37:24-25.
David is called "servant" in Ps. 89 and in one place is called "the
branch,"[36] a messianic term. So there is some evidence that the Messiah
could have been thought of as one of God's servants.[37] In other words,
there is in Jewish exegesis an attempt to specify the meaning of a biblical
text by bringing other biblical texts with similar usage to bear upon them,
but there is no attempt to see any particular passage as a prophecy. This
looks rather like modern methodology, except for one glaring difference. No historical framework is developed for understanding the
two references; what is learned from one reference is simply inserted
into the second occurrence of the term. If one looks at the midrashic
enterprise from an overall perspective, one sees a constellation of associations of various figures and values rather than a system of pre-existent
titles whose identities were subject to constant identification.

This brings up another strand of the tradition under
consideration—the use of the word for "son." The normal Greek word
for son is *huios*, which is the term most used in the New Testament. In
Greek *pais* can mean either "son" or "servant." As "servant" *pais* can be
associated with the term "messiah" in Christianity. As "son" *pais* can
also pick up messianic interpretations. God calls the davidic king "son"
several times in the Old Testament.[38] In the Greek Old Testament

---

33 See D. Juel, "The Image of the Servant Christ in the New Testament," *Southwest
    Journal of Theology* 21 (1979), 7-22.
34 Here is the passage in Job 3:17-19: "There the wicked cease from troubling and
    there the weary are at rest. There the prisoners are at ease together; they hear not
    the voice of the slave driver. The small and the great are there; and the *SERVANT* is
    free from his master." Here is the targum to the passage: "Jacob, called the young
    one; and Abraham, called the old one; and Isaac, the servant of the Lord ('*abda
    deYHWH*), who was delivered from the bonds by his Master."
35 Zimmerli and Jeremias, "*pais*," say that this is "The Messiah," but they are mistaken.
    It is the historical personage of the King, who is so designated, not a future king.
36 It occurs four times in Ps. 89, and also at Zech. 3:8.
37 *THE* messiah is also a misnomer, since many different kinds of figures could be
    described as messianic.
38 J. Jeremias, "*pais theou*," *TDNT* 5, 664.

there is an interesting aspect of sonship, whose significance is unstressed by Vermes:[39] the term *yahid* in Hebrew ("only son") is translated as *agapētos* ("loved one").[40] It occurs in Gen. 22:2, 12, 16 speaking of Isaac's sacrifice and, interestingly, in Judges 11:34 of Jephthah's daughter, who was also a sacrifice. The other occurrences of the term—Amos 8:10; Jer. 6:26; Zech. 12:10—are metaphoric, comparing the grief at the destruction of the temple with the grief of the death of an only child. Jesus is called *agapētos* ("only" or "beloved son") at the baptism[41] and transfiguration.[42] Davies and Chilton to the contrary, it is impossible not to feel an implicit analogy between Isaac, other martyred children, and Jesus in these places. All this is especially important if one notes that the word for "servant," *pais*, is never used in Mark explicitly within the context of Isa. 53. It seems to me that one important aspect of the Gospels' use of the idea of sonship is the implicit analogy between Jesus and Isaac as only sone who were sacrificed. In this respect, the quotation of Isa. 42:1 in Matt. 12:18 may play an important role.

In other words, as we would expect from Jewish tradition, we can find many contexts which link some parts of this tradition together in Jewish thought. However, if one wants an explicit reference to the Messiah one does not find it until later in Christianity. The reason, it seems to me, is to be found not in exegetical tradition but in the events surrounding Jesus' life. This is what Vermes discounts but Davies and Chilton take too much in isolation. It makes no sense to begin the discussion of Christian exegesis in any place other than the Easter event accepted as fact by Christians—that Jesus, who was manifestly crucified as a messianic pretender by the Romans ("King of the Jews")[43] and taunted by that title in his execution, was believed to have merited the title ironically when his followers experienced what they took to be his resurrection. That experience justified the earliest Christian community in thinking, for the first time in Judaism, that there could be such a thing as a crucified Messiah. From this oxymoron everything else derives and, of course, all of it is post-resurrection in formulation. In other words, although it was theoretically possible for texts to be interpreted in this way, there is no historical evidence for an expectation of a crucified or suffering Messiah until the events of Jesus' life proved to the early church that this was the true and secret meaning of

---

39 See Davies and Chilton, "Akedah," 529, and esp. 530, n. 42. See also C. H. Turner, *"ho huios mou ho agapētos," JTS* 27 (1926), 113-129; W. Dekker, "De Geliefde Zoon in de synoptische Evangelien," *NedTTs* 16 (1961-1962), 94-106; and A. Scattolon, "L'*Agapētos* sinnotteco milla luce della traditione giudaica," *RivB* 26 (1978), 3-32.

40 Aquila has: *ton monogenē* (Ms. 135 reads *Monachos*, see J. Wevers, *Septuaginta 1: Genesis* [Göttingen: Vandenhoeck & Ruprecht, 1974], 213). Symmachus has *ton monon sou* (F. Field, *Origenis Hexaplorium* 1 [Oxford: Clarendon, 1875], 37). Otherwise in Greek the word is *agapētos*, used in Genesis, Amos, Judges, Jeremiah, and Zechariah, as specified below.

41 Mark 1:11 pars.

42 Mark 9:7 pars.

43 Dahl, *Crucified Messiah*.

scripture. All discussions of suffering in the Bible thereafter take on a new meaning—as prophecies of Jesus' suffering. But no Jew would have seen them in this way before Jesus' crucifixion. Rather, like a magnet, everything dealing with "sonship" or "messiah" or "suffering" or "servant" is attracted to Jesus.[44] When applied to Jesus all traditions combine into a single figure—in order to show how prophecy was fulfilled in the person of Jesus. One can see this at work in Paul's writings. Although his Christian commitment is evident, the strands of Jewish tradition are still intact. Paul talks about vicarious atonement and suffering but normally uses no scriptural references to demonstrate his point. In fact, he does not need them for vicarious atonement is a widely accepted understanding of the significance of the suffering of the martyrs. When he brings in the sacrifice of Isaac, it is to prove Jesus' sonship. He also knows why a crucified Messiah is a stumbling block to the Jews and folly to the Gentiles, in a way that would be incomprehensible only a few generations later, for instance to the readers of Acts.

Of course, Paul's use of the material represents only the beginning of the tradition. John's use of the Akedah in 3:16 provides another allusive reference to reinforce the concept of sonship. So do James and Hebrews, but they each develop the theme in new and interesting ways.[45]

In the church's later interpretation—the elaborate typologies comparing the three-day journey with the Easter event, the wood for the sacrifice with the cross—one need not look for any further influences than the New Testament. A word should also be said about the later Jewish material, although it too has often been reviewed in detail. It is easy to see that on the Jewish side in the first century the discussion of the Akedah was greatly elaborated after the destruction of the Temple. The placing of the Akedah at Rosh Hashanah rather than Passover, the motif of the *shofar* as the horn of the ram caught in the

---

44 Strangely, however, Isaiah 53 is brought in relatively late, as Hooker has shown us. Even then it is brought in to show that Jesus must suffer, not that suffering was vicarious, which was apparently in no need of proof to those that accepted it. See Hengel, *Atonement*, who notes the widespread hellenistic notion that dying for others is heroic. The context is fairly often one of sacrificial death to appease the gods, as well. So one must not get the idea that vicarious atonement was entirely a semitic idea. Hengel himself thinks that the particularly Hebrew aspect of the notion can be seen in Isa. 53, which is, in turn, used by the church—and even Jesus in his estimation—to understand Jesus' sacrificial death. Thus the Pauline use of the notion of vicarious atonement only reflects the pre-Pauline idea, which in turn, goes back to the earliest notions in Christianity. While I have my own ideas about the value of Isa. 53 to the early church, I think it safe to say, on the basis of Hengel and others, that the notion of vicarious atonement is quite widespread. Even Philo mentions it, polemically in *de Abrahamo*, using language which Hengel attributes to Isa. 53, but which is more likely just general vocabulary for describing a martyr's death for others' benefit.

45 See Swetnam, *Jesus and Isaac*.

thicket, the reading of Gen. 22 on the second day of Rosh Hashanah, with the first day being reserved for the biblical passage describing the sin-offering—all of these motifs make sense if one sees the Jewish community trying to understand the destruction of the temple by means of an Isaac martyrology and anything else at its disposal. The process starts as early as Johanan ben Zakkai with the *takkanah* about the blowing of the Shofar in the synagogue. This simple action of moving a Temple ritual to the synagogue is in many ways the ritual and symbolic equivalent of the Christian community's understanding of the crucifixion. Seemingly impossible events must be understood within the context of meaning available to the community. A new understanding of history had to be found on account of an anomalous event. Therefore, the scripture was re-read with new eyes until the event could be appropriated into a new web of meaning.

Rabbinic exegesis followed entirely different directions from Christianity, as the tradition about Isaac emphasizes. But this tradition-history also shows that they operated by very similar methods. From a methodological perspective, it is Christianity with its known history which serves as a model for the unknown but reconstructable rabbinic tradition-history. From my perspective, Isaac's relationship with the new-year festival of Rosh Hashanah is most appropriately dated to post 70 C.E. Judaism when a substitution, as it were, for Temple service had to be found. It is then, after the Temple is destroyed and sacrifice is only possible in a symbolic way, that the connection between Isaac and the word *akedah* through the agency of the *tamid* sacrifice is most likely to have been developed, although it is theoretically possible for the connection to have been formulated even earlier. It is beyond dispute that the midrashim stressing explicit sacrificial typologies developed more strongly at this time. It is also reasonable, however, to expect that the Passover tradition of Isaac's martyrdom in rabbinic midrash received further development at this time. Rabbinic exegesis, being a compilation of individual homiletics, need not be entirely consistent, as we all know, even when it is compiled into a single midrashic work. There is no reason why rabbis should not have continued to discuss this connection in competition with the Church father's use of Isaac as a *typos* for Christ. The amoraic traditions of the death and ashes of Isaac and his subsequent resurrection can be reasonably understood as an attempt to enrich Judaism with a figure that was as colourful as the one known to Christian exegesis. Considering the sure rabbinic knowledge of the central aspect of Christian doctrine, one does not even need to posit very much cultural contact between the two communities to allow for such a development.

In sum, then, we can outline two different routes taken by the two developing communities, in line with the events which shaped those communities and the traditions by which they attempted to explain their own founding events. Both the Christian and the rabbinic exegesis of Isaac's sacrifice are based upon the pre-Christian, Jewish exegetical tradition. But each community makes its own significance out of the event in its own terms—and also listens to some extent to what the other community is saying. The pattern is simple enough, but in order to see it one must give up ideas about hypothetical figures within Jewish tradition (so common in later times among the Church fathers). Instead, one is left with an appreciation of how the Jewish and Christian communities sought the meaning of its scriptures through hermeneutical reinterpretation.[46]

---

46   My thanks to Tom Boslooper for his advice and help in proofreading.

Musonius Rufus, Jesus, and Paul: Three First-Century Feminists

WILLIAM KLASSEN

When biblical theology flourished and scholars concentrated their work on the biblical materials themselves, one of the voices raised against such a narrow base for biblical studies was that of Frank Beare.[1] This paper will seek to heed that voice, to express gratitude for it, to repay a debt, and to apply that admonition to one specific issue— feminism. Three popular ethical teachers in the first century may be described as feminists: Musonius Rufus, Jesus, and Paul. While the precise interrelation among the three is complex, the similarities among them in their views and practices on the status of women are so striking that the matter deserves more attention than it has thus far received. Given the benign neglect that Musonius has suffered even among scholars who concentrate on the first century, it seems advisable to begin with a brief introductory survey of Musonius research. I then survey the positions which Musonius took on women, their education, their role in marriage, and the question of sexual morality, followed by a survey of the positions of Jesus and Paul on these issues. Finally, I draw some preliminary conclusions.

MUSONIUS RUFUS: THE STATE OF CURRENT RESEARCH

C. Musonius Rufus, a knight who lived in the first century C.E.—for a time in Rome—zealously embraced Stoic dogma and avidly pursued

---

1   See especially his "New Testament Christianity and the Hellenistic World," in *Theological Collections: The Communication of the Gospel in New Testament Times* (London: S.P.C.K., 1961), 57-73, esp. 71; and the dozen or so articles he contributed to *The Interpreter's Dictionary of the Bible* (New York: Abingdon, 1962), including a twelve-page article on "Religion and Philosophy in Greece."

Stoic philosophy. Judging by both the number and quality of the students whom he attracted and tutored,[2] but above all by the imprint he left on his contemporaries, he was an unusual man. If Stoics had canonized saints, he would have been one of them. Co-opted into the Christian church by men like Clement of Alexandria and called a model of the highest form of life by Origen, one might expect him to have enjoyed at least as good a reputation in the subsequent history of the church as Seneca. But such was not the case.

More baffling is the reception he has received from modern scholars who have described the variegated picture of Stoicism. Some have accorded him his place; for example, Martin P. Charlesworth in his five character studies from the Roman Empire selects Musonius to represent the philosopher. He finds "something noble and attractive in the figure of Musonius, a simplicity and strength of character . . . single-minded throughout . . . living hard and nobly. . . . It was a good life he lived, and he held before his pupils no low or light ideal."[3] Paul Barth and Albert Goedeckemeyer in their major book on Stoicism describe him as "a spirit whom certainly none excelled."[4]

In his lengthy treatment of Stoicism Pohlenz describes him as "a man cast in a unique mold who in the midst of a servile world went his own way—'Have you or anyone ever seen me cringing before anyone just because I am in exile or thinking that I am worse off now than I was before?'—and without following the doctrinaire approach of Cato he actualized Stoic philosophy in life. No wonder that he made a powerful impact on his contemporaries."[5]

More than one author has drawn a parallel between Musonius and Socrates, but apparently R. Hirzel first called him explicitly the "Roman Socrates."[6] This designation has achieved a certain popularity since it was used as a title for one of the two monographs ever published on Musonius in English in modern times.[7]

But is not the juxtaposition of these two names extravagant? Cora Lutz raises that question and answers it negatively by lamenting the

---

2 According to M. Pohlenz, *Die Stoa: Geschichte einer geistigen Bewegung* (3rd ed., Göttingen: Vandenhoeck & Ruprecht, 1964), 1:284, they include: Rubellius Plautus, Pliny the Younger, Minucius Fundanus, the teacher of Fronto, Athenodorus, Euphrates (an opponent of Apollonius), Timocrates, Artemedorus (future son-in-law), and above all, Epictetus.

3 M. P. Charlesworth, *Five Men: Character Studies from the Roman Empire* (Cambridge, Mass.: Harvard University Press, 1936), 60.

4 P. Barth, A. Goedeckemeyer, *Die Stoa* (6th ed., Stuttgart: Fr. Frommanns Verlag, 1946), 208.

5 Pohlenz, *Die Stoa*, 1:303.

6 R. Hirzel, *Der Dialog* (Leipzig: S. Hirzel, 1895), 2:239, according to Cora Lutz.

7 C. Lutz, "Musonius Rufus, 'The Roman Socrates,'" *Yale Classical Studies* 10 (New Haven: Yale University Press, 1947). Lutz provides a thirty-page summary of the life and influence of Musonius, translates all the fragments, and provides the Greek text. In view of the failure of the Loeb Classical Library to include him, her translation remains the only complete one available to the English reader and her Greek text is the only one relatively accessible to the serious student.

"obscurity which has dimmed the name and reputation of Musonius," which she designates as "one of the unfortunate accidents of historical record." What ancient writers said about him is fragmentary and meagre but it leads to the conclusion

that Musonius was a much more compelling personage than his surviving works permit us to suspect, in fact one of the most significant figures of his age.... His teachings were his own humanitarian interpretation of the fundamental principles regulating human conduct, truly the fruit of a good life and the expression of a great personality.[8]

Lutz notes that this coincidence of life and teaching has often been noted of Socrates as well. Both stood out in their age as individuals if not as individualists.

In the mere fact of standing forth as the spiritual and ethical leader and apostle of moral liberty (so Jaeger, *Paideia*, II, 13) to his own and succeeding generations, Musonius is rightly compared to Socrates. But the exactness of the comparison becomes vivid and impressive when one notes how numerous are the points of similarity suggested by a consideration of the life of Musonius, his aims and methods, and the content and temper of his teachings.[9]

A year after Lutz wrote those lines A. C. van Geytenbeek published a very important thesis on Musonius in Dutch (1948). Fortunately for Musonius research, his work was translated into English by a scholar working in Canada at the time, Ben Hijmans, Jr., and published in the series *Wijsgerige Teksten en Studies*.[10] Geytenbeek deals with an abundance of comparative materials, with all the important *topoi* in Musonius' teaching materials, with the relationships between the important fragments of Lucius and Epictetus, and with past scholarship. He concludes that we may have more authentic materials from Musonius than is sometimes supposed.

He recognizes that our judgment on Musonius' doctrine is a complex problem. Nevertheless, he argues that Musonius presents a considerable amount of material which deserves study.

The actual verdict will be dependent on the point of view one takes. If one judges Musonius as a philosopher, the judgement will have to be damning if one applies modern standards; unfavourable, too, if one starts from the Stoic point of view that ethics is the main part of philosophy, at least if one takes the concept of "ethics" in the exclusively theoretical sense. From a merely theoretical point of view Musonius' ethics has little value. It does not seem too bold to state on the evidence of the preserved fragments that Musonius probably added not one original thought to the theoretical foundation of Stoic ethics. However, it must be granted that according to the ancient—even the most

---

8   Lutz, "Musonius Rufus," 4.
9   Ibid.
10 A. C. van Geytenbeek, *Musonius Rufus and Greek Diatribe*, trans. by B. Hijmans (Assen: Van Gorcum, 1963).

"classical"—standard, the application of theory to praxis was an essential part of philosophy. Moreover, we must take into account that we are discussing discourses, diatribes, which do not admit of lengthy arguments, but which aim at striking the listener with a sudden impact.

If one compares Musonius with other authors of diatribes, he does not make a bad impression. . . . The discourses on equality of women, the problem of sex, and the one on exposure are of great value. Even if we possessed no other works of Musonius than these few treatises, his place in the history of Greek morality would have been guaranteed (159-160).

Geytenbeek explains the praise which was given Musonius in antiquity from the fact of his lofty character; that his wisdom was praised "can only be explained by a point of view which put the good example above the doctrine. . . . It is in this way that the striking difference between Musonius's fame and the relatively small value of the fragments will have to be explained."[11] After citing both praise and criticism of Musonius he states that "his significance should not be underrated."[12]

One of the factors which Geytenbeek considers to diminish Musonius' significance is his lack of originality. It may well be asked, however, what he means by originality. We understand "original" to apply not only to something never said nor done before, but also to something which takes already available elements and recombines them in a new way. Musonius placed example or life above doctrine without challenging the doctrine. Is this not "original" or creative? If this is indeed the case then there is an important reason to study him, precisely because it is generally agreed that this same thing held true for Jesus and Paul.

Lutz published her work more than a generation ago. In spite of the fact that for the first time the fragments of Musonius' teaching were readily accessible there is little evidence that Musonius is read today, or that his place within the history of Western thought is recognized.

Many scholars, for example, who work in the area of early Christian origins have not read him and know about him only vaguely. Such ignorance about Paul's contemporary is in part a result of an earlier obsession with biblical theology and a concomitant neglect of the surrounding culture in which the Bible came into being, and in part a result of trying to catch up in another area which has been seriously neglected, the relation of Judaism and Christianity.

But even scholars who write in the area of Stoicism generally refer to Musonius only in passing. In part, the explanation for this lies in Musonius' fascination with practical ethics. His comparative neglect of such matters as ethical theory, epistemology, logic, or metaphysics

---

11   Ibid., 158-161.
12   Ibid., 18.

would, in the judgment of many contemporary philosophers, seem to place him outside the pale of philosophy.

It should be conceded that Musonius is no philosopher of first rank. He is rather a popular moralist who spent most of his time dealing neither with metaphysical matters nor with theoretical ethical questions, but rather with concrete matters that could improve the quality of life of those who followed him.[13] Christian scholars who have had difficulty seeing either Jesus or Paul as theologians should welcome the opportunity to study Musonius, whose stance toward ethics is like theirs toward theology. One suspects that Musonius dealt primarily with wealthier people than did Jesus and Paul—although E. A. Judge has asked whether we have not stressed incorrectly the poverty of the early Christians.[14]

Whatever the assessment of Musonius be, our concern here is to look at the question of feminism—by which I mean someone who espouses or advocates the doctrine that women are equal to men, and practises that doctrine. Among the earliest and most articulate feminists are Jesus, Musonius, and Paul. None has received his due in this respect, although faint noises that Jesus and Paul deserve this recognition are being heard.

We will examine the question of freeing women from the bondage of being treated as second-class persons and, as closely related to this question, marriage and sexual ethics. On all of these matters Musonius deserves a hearing; some evidence will be provided that in fact he has been ignored. If the position of Musonius is taken seriously we might see certain historical issues in ethics more accurately.[15]

MUSONIUS AND THE ROLE OF WOMEN, MARRIAGE, AND SEXUAL ETHICS

Anyone who reads Musonius cannot help being struck by the prominence he gives to the equality of women and the consequences he draws from that basic position. He follows Plato to some extent in insisting that women have the same capacity for the classic virtues as men and also in insisting on equal opportunity for education.[16] Musonius rejected the teaching of the elder Cato that permitted a man to kill his

---

13   On popular ethics, see K. J. Dover, *Greek Popular Morality in the Time of Plato and Aristotle* (Oxford: Blackwell, 1975), and L. Pearson, *Popular Ethics in Ancient Greece* (Stanford, Calif.: Stanford University Press, 1962).

14   E. A. Judge, "The Early Christians as a Scholastic Community," *JRH* 1 (1960), 4-15, 125-137. (Abbreviations in references are those used by the *Journal of Biblical Literature*. See *JBL* 95 [1976], 331-346.)

15   See W. Klassen, "Humanitas as seen by Epictetus and Musonius Rufus," *Studi Storico Religiosi* 1 (Rom, 1977), 63-82; and W. Klassen, "'Child of Peace' (Luke 10.6) in First Century Context," *NTS* 27 (1981), 488-506. Cf. also F. Hock, *The Social Context of Paul's Ministry, Tentmaking and Apostleship* (Philadelphia: Fortress, 1980), chap. 4.

16   Plato, *Republic*, 5.451d.

wife without any legal process if he detected her in adultery, and he also insisted that since the female slave-owner was not permitted to have sex with her male slave neither should the male slave owner be permitted to have sexual relations with his female slaves (XII).

Not only in education and sexual ethics but also in the area of masculine and feminine roles, Musonius wrestled with the question whether women are not physically limited from doing certain tasks and more suited to others. In principle he rejects this; he is quite aware that *some* women are more suited to lift heavy objects than others, but then this is also true of men. With a slight lapse of accuracy in observation he suggests that "both [male and female] have the same parts of the body," but he redeems himself by adding that "one has nothing superior to the other" (III).[17]

He even allows for a man to do the spinning, and in fact sees all household duties as common tasks. What he expects of males, he expects as well of females, and vice versa. In this respect he is consistent, although at one point he uses a mildly ironic argument, in discussing whether it is allowed for a master/mistress to have sex with her/his slave: "And yet surely one will not expect men to be less moral than women, nor less capable of disciplining their desires, thereby revealing the stronger in judgement inferior to the weaker, the rulers to the ruled. In fact it behoves men to be much better if they expect to be superior to women, for surely if they appear to be less self-controlled they will also be baser characters" (XII).[18] He is aware that some people consider it "quite without blame" for a master to have sex with his female slave.

There is no question that Musonius is here borrowing heavily from the thought of his teacher, Antipater of Tarsus. His views of the equality of women in the marriage relationship were developed further by Hierocles the Stoic in Hadrianic times, and Epictetus followed his teacher here as well, although his view of marriage is less

---

17 Perhaps we have a mistranslation here. The word *homoiōs* may mean "equal" rather than "same," and *pleon* could mean "greater" not in number but "better." In any case it is a rejection of words of the anonymous poet *allos gunaikos kosmos, allos arrenōn* (Edm. III, A, 504).

18 This may be a case of what Lutz calls "studied innocence" ("Musonius Rufus," 26) which, I would argue, continues on to the end of that section. In any event it is clear that over against the concept of community of wives held by early Stoics like Zeno (see H. G. Baldry, "Zeno's *Politeia* . . . ," *JHS* [1959], 3-15) Musonius argues for monogamy and for faithfulness within marriage. In contrast to both Paul and Musonius, Metrodorus (a disciple of Epicurus) wrote to the young Pythocles troubled by his strong physical desires: "You tell me that the pricks of the flesh lead you to overdo the pleasures of love. If you do not break the laws or offend in any way against accepted good manners, if you do not annoy any of your neighbours, exhaust your strength or waste your substance, give yourself without worry to your inclinations. But it is impossible not to be halted by one at least of these obstacles: the pleasures of love have never profited anyone; it is a great thing if they do not harm" (cited by A. J. Festugière, *Epicurus and his Gods* [Oxford: Blackwell, 1955], 29).

enthusiastic. In both Musonius and Epictetus we have a clear rejection of the institution of pederasty, still widespread in the Roman Empire, and a vigorous and consistent rejection of the practice of infant exposure. Neither vacillated on these questions.

There is every reason to assume that Musonius had a happy marriage, something of a rarity among the philosophers of ancient times. It is particularly odd that he cites the case of Socrates on the advantages of marriage (XIV)[19]

When we turn to modern literature, however, it is surprisingly silent on Musonius' position on the role of women. An important contribution to the study of women in ancient times has been made by Sarah B. Pomeroy, yet she dispenses with Musonius in one line: "The Stoic Musonius Rufus asserted that women should be given the same education as men, for the attributes of a good wife will appear in one who studies philosophy."[20] While Musonius was primarily interested in women as wives, he does not confine himself to that; he was concerned that women be allowed the same freedom as men to realize their humanness.

One of the most extensive treatments of this theme is offered by Carl Schneider in his comprehensive study of the cultural history of Hellenism. As part of his treatment of the hellenistic image of the human he deals at length with the place of women in hellenistic society. He notes how Euripides' sympathetic treatment of the plight of women was picked up and how in actual fact women were allowed to rise to heights of political and artistic prominence not previously achieved. This in turn, since there are as many bad women as there are bad men, led to the first severe outbreak of misogyny. But Schneider is totally silent on Musonius. He concludes his treatment:

The hellenistic Stoics were the first to find it remarkable that the virtues as well as the vices could be personified as women by artists. From this they drew the conclusion, which became characteristic in general of the verdict of Hellenism concerning woman: There are more virtuous, as well as more vicious, women than there are men. The verdict was not quite incorrect for that epoch.[21]

The failure to deal with Musonius also emerges in the treatments of Stoicism *per se*. For example, in a recent major book on the philosophy of the Stoics there is only one passing reference to Musonius.[22]

---

19   The domestic life of Socrates was the object of many stories. Xanthippe is invariably depicted as a shrew, but there seems no historical basis for that except perhaps the desire to make a model of imperturbability out of Socrates.

20   B. Pomeroy, *Whores, Wives and Slaves: Women in Classical Antiquity* (New York: Schocken, 1975), 171.

21   C. Schneider, *Kulturgeschichte des Hellenismus* 1 (Münich: Beck, 1967-1969), 44-117; especially the section on "Die Frau und das Frauenbild des Hellenismus"; the quote is from 1:117.

22   J. M. Rist, *Stoic Philosophy* (Cambridge: Cambridge University Press, 1969), 45.

Others, however, do give him his place.[23] Ludwig Edelstein in his
attempt to get at the meaning of Stoicism recognizes the originality of
the first-century Stoics; they did not merely go back to the old Stoa. He
judges them to be more original than most modern scholarship is
willing to allow and with regard to Musonius says that "respect cannot
be denied him" for to his contemporaries he was a saint.[24]

The general neglect is, however, most serious when authors have
attempted to deal with such topics as women among the Stoics. An essay
by C. E. Manning on the equality of the sexes makes no reference
whatever to Musonius, allowing the author to conclude that "to talk of a
Stoic concept of the equality of the sexes requires so many reservations
in period and so lengthy a definition of its meaning that it is best to
dispense with the term altogether."[25] Such a conclusion can only be
drawn by ignoring Antipater of Tarsus (1st century B.C.E.), Musonius
Rufus (1st century C.E.), and Hierocles (2nd century C.E.).

Even Epictetus does not escape misrepresentation. There is, for
example, a fragment from Epictetus (Ench. 40) which describes the
way in which women are too often viewed by his society, and which
contrasts *that* view of women with the objectives of Stoic education. Yet
a modern commentator can see it as a normative description of the way
the Stoics regarded women and concludes that "whatever Paul thought
of the . . . ethical aspects of Stoicism, he met with an opinion which
conflicted with his general views on women."[26] Had the author taken
the trouble to study the teachings of Musonius, he would have been in a
better position to understand the similarities and differences between
the position of first-century Stoics and Paul.

The first to undertake a comparison of Musonius Rufus' teaching
with New Testament writers on such social problems as marriage and
the role of women was Heinrich Greeven. His book on social ethics
analyzes Musonius' views and puts him in the context of other first-

---

23   For example, F. H. Sandbach, *The Stoics* (London: Chatto and Windus, 1975),
     162-164.
24   L. Edelstein, *The Meaning of Stoicism* (Cambridge, Mass.: Harvard University Press,
     1968), 70, 94.
25   C. E. Manning, "Seneca and the Stoics on the Equality of the Sexes," *Mnemosyne* 26
     (1973), 170-177; quote from 176.
26   A. Cumming, "Pauline Christianity and Greek Philosophy: A Study of the Status of
     Women," *Journal of the History of Ideas* 34 (1973), 517-528. Not *all* writers on this topic
     ignore Musonius; for example, J. Donaldson, *Woman: Her Position and Influence in
     Ancient Greece and Rome and Among the Early Christians* (London: Longman, 1907),
     provides, two years after the Hense text was published, a translation by John Muir of
     an important part of that text and sees the influence of Musonius on subsequent
     legislation (135-138). J. P. V. D. Balsdon, *Roman Women: Their History and their Habits*
     (London: Bodley Head, 1962) also recognizes the enlightened position of Musonius
     (196, 214). But it is a particular disappointment not to find a Musonius text in that
     excellent collection of texts, M. R. Lefkowitz and M. R. Fant (eds.), *Women in Greece
     and Rome* (Toronto: Samuel-Stevens, 1977), nor in the anthology of texts, J. O'Fao-
     lain and L. Martines, *Not in God's Image: Women in History* (London: Fontana, 1974).

century writers.[27] He describes Musonius as the philosopher of the ideal marriage and accurately describes the contents of his teaching. It is a limitation in Musonius' view that he fails to take into consideration the harm done to the other party in extramarital sex; but one of his strengths, his concern for the other person—e.g., the poor slave girl— is lost.

Unfortunately Greeven does not place enough emphasis on the clearly stated objections which Musonius raises against extramarital sex. Musonius describes it as "shameful and unlawful" and, although Greeven is critical that he does not deal with it from the standpoint of the consenting partner, Musonius does indicate that "everyone who sins and does wrong, even if it affects none of the people around him, yet immediately reveals himself as a worse and less honourable person." Musonius also describes the act as an injustice (*adikia*, XII) and stays within the realm of absolutes or appeals to the standards of the wise man himself and to his self-esteem rather than to the consideration for the other partner, for this would be easily undermined by an assumption that the other partner may profit from the act or at least enjoy it. When criticizing Musonius one should attempt to do justice to his ethical standards and these should then be assessed by comparison with those of his contemporaries.

A similar example of a misreading of Musonius is found in an author who has distinguished herself in the careful reading of the sources, including the Greek sources. In an essay on Jesus' female disciples, Luise Schottroff says:

Even the enlightened philosopher, Musonius, who defends the thesis that daughters are to be educated in the same way as sons, imagines how the ideal woman, after she has studied philosophy, will be an especially competent housewife along Roman ideals: she serves her husband, manages the household, in brief, she sits at the spinning wheel.[28]

Few authors have seen as keenly as Schottroff into the role of women in the first century. Nevertheless she has not done justice to Musonius. To be sure, Musonius, like Xenophon (Oeconomicus VII-X) centuries before him, wants women to take major responsibility for being superintendents of the manor and to be fully trained for it. He assumes, furthermore, that there are times when the woman assists (*hypereteō*) the man. He does not expect that women "would neglect their appointed tasks" just in order to study philosophy, "any more than he would expect men to do so." He expects the woman in marriage

---

27 H. Greeven, *Das Hauptproblem der Sozialethik in der neueren Stoa und im Urchristentum* (Gutersloh: Bertelsmann Verlag, 1934), 117-119.

28 L. Schottroff, "Frauen in der Nachfolge Jesu in neutestamentlicher Zeit," in W. Schottroff and W. Stegemann (eds.), *Traditionen der Befreiung*, Vol. 2: *Frauen in der Bibel* (München: Christian Kaiser Verlag, 1980), 91-133; the quote is from 93; cf. also 113, 126.

to "assist her husband with her own hands, unhesitatingly doing things which some consider slave's work" (III). But since he views all tasks as common in marriage, by implication he says the same thing about what the husband does for the wife.

Musonius makes it clear that his system of education does not call for men to learn the art of spinning. He grants that women's nature is more suited to indoor work such as spinning and men's nature to hard outdoor work, but concludes:

Occasionally, however, some men might more fittingly handle certain of the lighter tasks and what is generally considered women's work, [spinning?] and again, women might do heavier tasks which seem more appropriate to men whenever conditions of strength, need, or circumstance warrant. For all human tasks, I am inclined to believe, are a common obligation, common to both men and women. None is necessarily appointed to either one exclusively, but some pursuits are more suited to the nature of the one, some to the other, and for this reason some are called men's work and some women's (IV).

For Musonius it is accordingly quite possible that the man will stay at the spinning wheel while the wife attends to philosophy. Was he first to do so? This reversal of the standard mores of his time is followed by Hierocles of Hadrianic times who also saw the man as helping in the rocking of the cradle or the making of the bed.

Musonius is not to be held accountable for the fact that the world was not ready for his radical position. Even contemporary historians are unable to see his radical views; we are too conditioned to thinking of set roles for women in ancient literature to see the light when it appears. For Musonius this view of marriage and the equality of the sexes is undergirded by a view of human nature which sees the relationship between the sexes as one of co-partnership in a common task. His major emphasis is the commonality of all human tasks and the partnership of male and female to get those tasks accomplished. The terms used describe a revolution in the relation between the sexes within marriage: *koinōnos biou* and *synergos*, which can best be translated as "life's partner" and "fellow worker." Both stress equality and commonality. Neither allows for the possibility that one is superior to the other (III).

Musonius displays an affinity with the early Jewish tradition, where man is alone until he has become united with an equal (so the expression "like unto himself" may be translated, Gen. 2:18, 20). The same emphasis appears also in Tob. 8:6-7, which breathes an atmosphere of deep respect for the marriage partner as a person in her own right who, far from being a sex object, is a sister and companion.[29]

---

29 This similarity does not mean that Judaism had any consistent teaching on the
    equality of women; it shows evidence of running counter to first-century develop-

Musonius, like Paul just before him (1 Cor. 7), insists that whatever applies to the man applies to the woman as well. With minor differences in emphasis both Paul and Musonius stress the fundamental equality of male and female,[30] although they have different grounds for doing so and draw different conclusions from it. It is one of the ironies of current scholarship that this similarity has not been observed and that the remaining differences likewise have consequently not been seen in perspective.[31]

One of the most able interpreters of Stoicism gave Musonius his full due. Max Pohlenz saw clearly that Musonius stood out as a striking and original figure. Pohlenz was also aware of the contribution that Antipater made in this area:

In a time period when a convenient arrangement with a young boy was praised as an experience fit for the gods (*ho ētheos bios isotheos*) he saw it as a symptom of decline. He repeatedly stressed that marriage and bearing children are duties one owes to the state and the fatherland. But he also placed a value on the common life with the spouse, in which even more profoundly than in a male friendship the truth of an alter ego could be expressed. It was the first time that

---

ments in its strengthening of misogynism and stressing the inferiority of women. Josephus is probably a valid spokesman for first-century Judaism when he says: "The woman, says the Law, is in all things inferior (*cheiron eis hapanta*) to the man. Let her accordingly be submissive (*hypakouō*), not for her humiliation, but that she may be directed; for the authority has been given by God to man" (*c. Apionem*, 2.201). Unfortunately he does not tell us what version of the "Law" he is citing. See L. Swidler, *Women in Judaism: The Status of Women in Formative Judaism* (Metuchen: Scarecrow Press, 1976).

30   Neither uses this precise formula, for they lived after all in the first century. The closest we come to this is among the Mystery Cults, where Isis is credited with having given to women power equal to that of men (*sy gynaixin isēn dynamin tōn andrōn epoiēsas*, Oxyrhynchus Hymn, 214-216; see S. K. Heyob, *The Cult of Isis among Women in the Graeco-Roman World* (Leiden: Brill, 1975), 52.

31   The article by J. B. Bauer, "Die Ehe bei Musonius und Paulus," *Bibel und Liturgie* 23 (1955-56), 8-13, presents the texts from Musonius in W. Cappelle's translation which he describes as the first translation of Musonius into German. He considers it "leicht denkbar" that Paul actually heard Musonius in Rome and concludes: "This ideal picture of marriage which Paul draws is in no way inferior to that of Musonius; on the contrary the Pauline ideal cannot be improved upon by anything" (13). But the matter is slightly more complicated. Paul is superior to Musonius in taking the bonding character of sexual intercourse more seriously and encouraging the sex act whenever *either* party feels like it. This takes a woman's personhood seriously and encourages her to take the initiative at least in making her wishes known. On the other hand, Musonius has a perception of marriage which stresses the commonality of work and the symbiosis of mind, soul and body. That is not present in Paul, or at least has to be inferred. One can see, however, why Roman Catholics are attracted to Musonius in view of his restriction of sex to child-bearing. More careful attention is given to Musonius by D. Balch in his essay, "I Cor. 7:32-35: To Marry or Not to Marry one's Equal," a paper read in 1980 at the IAHR Congress in Winnipeg, and also in his book, *Let Wives be Submissive: The Domestic Code in I Peter* (Chico, Calif.: Scholars Press, 1981). Musonius is also mentioned by W. Schrage, "Zur Frontstellung der paulinischen Ehebewertung in I Kor. 7:1-7" (appropriately dedicated to H. Greeven), *ZNW* 67 (1976), 214-234.

a Stoic played such a tune on marriage and for women, and thus he pioneered a new value placed on women in contrast to ancient Hellenism.[32]

Like Antipater, Musonius spends no time arguing whether love between an older man and a younger boy is to be preferred to heterosexual love (as in Plutarch's dialogue on love). He states quite unequivocally that the highest form of love known to humans is the love between a man and a woman: "To whom is everything judged to be common, body, soul, and possessions, except man and wife?" (XIV). Although he does not often use Antipater's term *symbiōsis* to describe the union of two lives in marriage it is clear that the description of marriage found in Musonius comes closest to that of Antipater.[33] His rejection of pederasty (he alludes to it only once) comes in a context where he assumes that a son will be congratulated for his disobeying his father when he—"so depraved"—sold him into a life of shame because of his youthful beauty (XVI).[34]

The contribution Musonius has made to Western sexual ethics is worthy of note. For even Epictetus' begrudging concession that marriage is allowed to the philosopher although it will surely interfere with his tranquillity or Paul's advice that marriage should serve as an anodyne to sexual passions (1 Thess. 4:3-7; 1 Cor. 7:1-7) do not come close to Musonius' insights about the way in which two lives can flow together enriching one another, yoked together in common work with all things held in common and both persons considered equal.[35]

Western thought, particularly the Roman Church, has taken from Musonius his least helpful insight: that sex should be restricted to procreation of children. Here he would seem to have been blinded by his fear of the ecstatic and the passionate. Paul's advice that married couples should have sexual intercourse whenever either one feels like it

---

32 Pohlenz, *Die Stoa*, 190.

33 Naturally the term is not confined to Antipater or restricted to sexual union in marriage, as the entries in Liddell-Scott show. The content Antipater put into the term seems to coincide with Musonius's view of marriage. Musonius used it in his discussion on "What is the Chief End of Marriage?" XIIIA.

34 Compare, however, J. J. Chapman, *Lucian, Plato and Greek Morals* (Boston and New York: Houghton Mifflin, 1931), chap. 4, and the two articles by W. Kroll "Knabenliebe," *RE* 21 (1921), 897-906; and "Lesbische Liebe," *RE* 23 (1924), 2100-2102. Although the illustrations in K. J. Dover's *Greek Homosexuality* (London: Duckworth, 1978) make it clear that there is usually a considerable age differential between the two partners, the text does not elaborate on this aspect. Kroll declines to enter into the moral question but sees the roots of the practice in the presence of "eines conträren Geschlechtsgefühles." Three factors contributed to it: climate, inequality of women, slavery. See also the spirited debate between Erich Segal and Milton Hindus after the former's review of Dover's book. Segal provides evidence of Jowett's doctoring the text of Plato in order to veil the fact that Plato's view of love is homosexual (*New York Times Book Review*, July 29, 1979).

35 I have made some preliminary comparisons between Paul and Musonius in this area in W. Klassen, "The Foundations of Pauline Sexual Ethics," *Seminar Papers for the Annual Meeting of the SBL* (Chico, Calif.: Scholars Press, 1978).

and that any restrictions on sexual activity should be mutually agreed upon (1 Cor. 7:5) seems much more in harmony with Musonius' view of a shared common life. Nevertheless that too deserves to be studied in Musonius' historical context and social context.[36]

Musonius is not to be ignored in this discussion. Many generalizations about the first century could be corrected by a careful reading of Musonius.

It should be clear that there can be no question of direct dependence between Musonius and the New Testament, in either direction. What is important is that both Paul and Musonius were addressing themselves to the same issues and of course to people of the same cultural background. Whether in Rome, Corinth, or Ephesus, these men attracted followers who must have met each other and interacted with each other. Both added pungent contributions to the cultural brew of the first century.

Both affirm in their own way the sanctity of marriage,[37] Musonius by saying that the gods are to be invoked in a special way in connection with marriage (XIV) and Paul by saying that the hallowing power of God is present in the union between two people so that even the children are sanctified (*hagioi*)[38] and that within such a marriage union lies great potential for the salvation of the unbelieving spouse.[39]

---

36 On Plutarch and his relation to Musonius see L. Goessler, *Plutarchs Gedanken über die Ehe* (Zürich: Buchdruckerei Berichthaus, 1962); she suggests that while Musonius rejects unfaithfulness in marriage because it contradicts the ideal of *sophos*, and since it is *akrasia* and *kakon*, Plutarch bases it on a socio-political (*staatspolitischer*) argument or consideration. This she sees as different from the Stoic who "derives his prescriptions from an absolute measuring stick, quite remote from reality. Plutarch derives his rules for life from an empathetic insight into the essence of humans, here of the woman and wife" (64).

37 Johannes Leipoldt is not convincing in his argument that Musonius believes that if the marriage partners have sex without intending to have children that they are committing fornication ("Es kann also Hurerei zwischen Ehegatten geben"); see *Die Frau in der Antike und im Urchristentum* (Gütersloh: Gerd Mohn, 1962), 44; cf. also E. Stauffer, "Copulatio ohne Communio ist Hurerei" (*TDNT* 1:648).

38 1 Cor. 7:14—the only place where Paul speaks of humans "sanctifying" other humans. In Eph. 5:23-31 the parallel is clearly drawn:

As Christ loved the church,   in the same way
                                     men are to love their wives

gave himself up for it,
consecrated it,
cleansed it by water, and word,   as their own bodies. . . .

But the author refrains from drawing the parallel with the verb *hagiazō* as Paul had done. Obviously it served no purpose here. Or was Paul engaging in a play on words? In Rabbinical circles *kadosh* may also mean to take a wife or to be espoused to someone. See J. P. Sampley, *And the Two Shall Become One Flesh* (Cambridge University Press, 1971), 42ff.

39 J. Jeremias, in "Die missionarische Aufgabe in der Mischehe, I Kor. 7,16," *Abba* (Göttingen: Vandenhoeck & Ruprecht, 1966), after a detailed comparison with Epictetus has convincingly shown that Paul expresses missionary confidence here and that he reckons with the distinct probability that the unbelieving partner will be saved.

Musonius stresses the place of *eros* in the marriage while at the same time he is fully aware of the way in which married partners live for each other.[40] While the gods they invoke are different, this rooting of a social institution in religious values is shared by Musonius and Paul.

JESUS AS A FEMINIST[41]

Whereas Musonius was motivated by the Stoic ideal of the breakdown of all social barriers and the unity of all mankind, the centre of the proclamation of Jesus was the announcement of the Kingdom of God. In that Kingdom the inclusion of women is unambiguous: they are treated equally, invited along with men, and never is any distinction made between male and female. To be sure, the Gospel narratives indicate that males dominate leadership of the disciple band. No woman is included in the Twelve. Yet women disciples follow Jesus: according to Mark they travelled with him from the early days of Galilee (Mark 15:40-41), and Luke also indicates that women were a constituent part of his entourage (Luke 8:1-3). He taught them (Luke 10:38-42), touched them (Luke 13:13; Luke 8:54), allowed them to touch him (Luke 7:38; 8:44), and travelled with them. It is to be taken for granted, then, that they were included in the commission to go forth and witness to the presence of the Kingdom. It would indeed seem that this is implicit in Luke's report that the disciples were sent out in "pairs" (10:1), and in the Emmaus account (Luke 24) where it is most logical to assume that Cleopas and his wife are the pair (cf. John 19:25) who share an encounter with the risen Christ, even though commentators and artists depicting the scene have usually assumed that we are dealing here with two males. The Fourth Gospel may very well be in touch with a genuine tradition when it portrays Jesus as commissioning women, in part because the Samaritan woman is more receptive to the message of Jesus than is the teacher of rank, Nicodemus (cf. John 3 and 4).[42]

---

40   His phrase *kai koina de hēgesthai panta kai mēden idion, mēd' auto to sōma* (XIIIA) surely implies that both male and female have given up autonomy over their bodies, and says the same thing Paul says in 1 Cor. 7:4: *hē gunē tou idiou sōmatos ouk exousiazei alla ho anēr tou idiou sōmatos ouk exousiazei alla hē gunē*. In any case Paul's view is surely the most radical feminist statement uttered in the first century and it is a profound irony that he has so often been painted with an antifeminist brush! And that the Stoic for whom autonomy of the self is so central can reject all Cynic pretensions of asceticism is a remarkable example of how it prepared the way by creating a "climate of thought congenial to the individualism, universalism and conception of brother-hood [and sisterhood?] of Christianity" (Beare, "Stoicism," *IDB* 4:445.)

41   See especially the essays by E. Schüssler-Fiorenza and L. Schottroff in Schottroff and Stegemann, *Traditionen*. An attempt was made to see the issue in sociological per-spective in my essay, "The Role of Jesus in the Transformation of Feminine Con-sciousness," in *Journal of Comparative Sociology and Religion* 7 (1980), 182-210.

42   R. E. Brown, "Roles of Women in the Fourth Gospel," *TS* 36 (1975), 688-699.

The gospel tradition was written down in a society which was deeply conscious of the efforts being made to give women a more nearly equal status. Surely it is not unlikely that Luke knew of the work and teaching of Musonius on this point. That Luke would have found it easy to highlight Jesus' liberating role for women in such a context is reasonable. That he would have freely invented stories about Jesus' relationship with women is harder to accept. It would seem more logical to assume that stories were suppressed in the face of so much evidence that Jesus related to women in a radically new way. The notion that all of this is an accommodation to a first-century movement to treat women equally simply has to be rejected.

Jewish ethics, with its high view of marriage and especially the rejection of two practices which victimized women most brutally—infant exposure and pederasty—still provides little evidence that women's role in the first century was anything but an insult to them. As indicated above, while Josephus alone states baldly that women are inferior and appeals to the Law, both he and Philo state that the Essenes could not tolerate women in their communities because the woman is the source of all discord.[43] The role of women among the Essenes is still not clear but it is significant that a lengthy poem has been found portraying evil in the guise of a wicked woman, specifically a harlot. Whether this is to be taken allegorically or not is debatable, but Swidler says: "Here is the fountainhead of misogynism."[44]

By contrast it is instructive that Jesus never depicts a woman as an evil person, never once tells a parable in which a woman is depicted in a bad light, and never warns his disciples of the temptations a woman may constitute for them. In short, Jesus breaks step with his Jewish colleagues and indeed with most of the popular religious teachers before him and after him, east and west. In doing so he ignores such anti-woman statements from his own scriptures as Eccl. 7:25-30; Wis. 19:2; 22:3; and 42:14. Joachim Jeremias pointed to the radical break with his liturgical tradition evident in the prayer life of Jesus. The fact that the prayer of blessing: "Blessed art thou, O Lord our God! King of the Universe; who has not made me a woman" is missing in Jesus is not without significance. At the same time he does not place women on a pedestal of unattainable attractiveness. Rather, he treats them as human beings.

The Jesus traditions are permeated by a non-patriarchal tone and it is this tone which allows us to speak of the early Christian community as a model of a community of feminism. Because it stressed the equality of all it was able to attract persons from all classes.[45]

43 Josephus, *Ant.* 18.1.5; Philo, *Apology for the Jews*; cf. Eusebius, *Praep. Ev.* 8.2.

44 See J. M. Allegro, "'The Wiles of the Wicked Woman': A Sapiential Work from Qumran's Fourth Cave," *PEQ* (1964), 53-55, and in *Discoveries in the Judean Desert* 5 (Oxford: Oxford University Press, 1968), 82-84. Also Swidler, *Women in Judaism*, 64.

45 Schüssler-Fiorenza, in Schottroff and Stegemann, *Traditionen*, 80.

Whatever the historical facts may be about the way in which Jesus dealt with women, it is clear that he did not look upon them as "imperfect men." He does not lump them together with the sick, the eunuch, the imbecile, the slave, the blind, the aged, and the cripple, excusing them from the need to appear at the Temple as the Babylonian Talmud (Hagigah 2a) does.[46] Jesus broke with the traditions of his contemporaries and went his own way, thus providing hope for liberation for any who wish to take the presence of the kingdom seriously.

PAUL AND FEMINISM

In the discussions of Christianity and the equality of women it is Paul who has been the favoured object of flagellation. His inconsistencies have often been noted; any consideration of this theme in Paul must, however, recognize the following.

(1) Paul must be studied in the context of his own century and the times in which he lived. This truism deserves repetition, for all too often in a most bizarre way he is expected to meet modern standards and he is judged in the light of values which did not emerge till centuries after he was born.

(2) A distinction must be drawn between Paul's statements of the principle and his advice concerning matters of church order. Clearly Paul himself does not make such a clear distinction but that does not excuse us. We do not follow his method of interpreting the Old Testament. Nor are we obligated to follow his accommodation to weaker members of the community.

(3) Statements of principle must be adapted to each situation. A statement of principle is not invalidated by a delay in its full implementation or an accommodation to human weakness.

(4) The fact that both Paul and Jesus affirmed the equality of women by their actions, if not in their words, nurtures the suspicion that Paul's practice derives from that of Jesus, although it is impossible to prove it. It seems likely that when Paul was introduced to the Jerusalem church he had his first encounter with female participation in public Torah discussion. According to Luke, the church as it expanded from Jerusalem increasingly found women playing a prominent role.[47] There was no need to invoke a special word from the Lord

---

46 J. M. Ford first noted this striking fact in her article: "The Apostolates of the Sick and Women in Pastoral Care," *Journal of Pastoral Care* 21 (1967), 147-162.

47 I see no reason to mistrust the author of Acts when he says that women were a part of the early group of disciples (1:14), or that they were added to the group (5:14); that Paul took men and women into custody (8:3; 9:2) and that Philip baptized both men and women (8:12). Nor do I see any reason to doubt that women of standing joined the church (13:50; 17:12). It is perfectly understandable why some scribe would like to think the standing of these women derived from their connections with their husbands (see 17:4 and the variant readings). There is no conflict between this evidence and that provided by the letters of Paul.

to justify this practice since it had been a hallmark of the ministry of Jesus right from the beginning. This surely is the ultimate basis for Paul's belief that "in Christ there is neither male nor female" (Gal. 3:28).

Paul expresses a basic statement of principle in Gal. 3:28.[48] It is necessary to see this formula—neither Jew nor Greek, neither slave nor free, neither male nor female—against its Greek background. Paul's classical roots have been too often neglected or seen too superficially. Some twenty years ago Professor Beare affirmed the conviction that the New Testament "reflects the outlook of the Hellenistic world . . . while it holds forth the vision of a community in which there is neither Jew nor Greek, barbarian nor Scythian, bond nor free—a true city of God whose citizenship is open to all alike; and in correlation with this, its concern with the individual—the person."[49] The work by H. G. Baldry demonstrates how widespread these stock categories were and their relevance for the issue of feminism.[50] Diogenes Laertius, for example, records the same threefold division used by Paul, and Hermippus in his *Lives* attributes to Thales the story which is told by some of Socrates, namely that he used to say there were three blessings for which he was grateful to Fortune: "First, that I was born a human being and not one of the brutes; next, that I was born a man and not a woman; thirdly that I was born a Greek and not a barbarian."[51]

As is well known there is a similar Jewish prayer that gives thanks that one is not born a woman. Schematically they look like this:

Greek	*Jewish*	*Pauline (Gal. 3:28)*
Human—not brute	Not heathen	Neither Jew nor Greek
male—not female	Not a slave	Neither slave nor free
Greek—not barbarian	Not a female	Neither male nor female

Although on the surface these look very similar, there are some important differences. To begin with, similar series are found elsewhere in Paul:

---

48 See especially K. Stendahl, *The Bible and the Role of Women* (Philadelphia: Fortress, 1966), 32ff.

49 Beare, "New Testament Christianity," 65. Also note the important article by E. A. Judge, "St. Paul and Classical Society," *JAC* 15 (1972), 19-36.

50 H. G. Baldry, *The Unity of Mankind in Greek Thought* (Cambridge: Cambridge University Press, 1965) lists many references to the status of women. Apparently Zeno first advocated a *politeia* where men and women would be equal members; only the foolish would be excluded (158).

51 R. E. Hicks (trans.), *Diogenes Laertius*, LCL (Cambridge: Harvard University Press, 1950), 351.

1 Cor. 12:13	*Col. 3:11*
Jew or Greek	Jew or Greek
	Circumcision or uncircumcision
	Barbarian or Scythian
Slave or free	Slave or free

In no Pauline case is there even a hint of a prayer of thanks that he does not belong to one category or the other. Rather, the emphasis falls on the fact that in Christ these distinctions have lost their force. These categories which humans have stressed to gain power and control over others and to congratulate themselves have been ended by Christ, for in him all are on an equal footing.

It is also worth noting that in all three original statements the male-female dichotomy is mentioned. While it does not occur in any other New Testament list, its presence in Gal. 3:28 serves to bind the Greek and Jewish series to the Pauline one.

In all instances there is an underlying affirmation of a spirit of thanksgiving for a new status achieved. In the Greek and Jewish affirmation that status is achieved by the way in which the one who prays stands out from others. In Paul gratitude is expressed for a changed condition brought about by Christ which brings everyone to the same position. Paul mentions those things which have been sources of gratitude and security for others and describes them as being no longer!

Finally, it is evident that of the Pauline list only one has any corresponding evidence from Jesus. According to the evidence from the Gospels, Jesus challenged only his contemporaries' rigid distinction of worth made between male and female. Slaves and Gentiles play a very small role in what he did and taught.

Paul's practice with regard to women co-workers is just as remarkable as his basic principle. George B. Caird concludes that Paul's great secret with his "fellow men was that all there was of him went into his friendships." Closely related was the fact that "Paul never had any assistants or underlings—only partners and colleagues."[52] This observation is true but does not go far enough, for writers on the apostle Paul have not been in the habit of noting that many of Paul's co-workers were women.[53] In the brief compass of his writings there are some fourteen references to women; eleven of whom are named. While it could be pointed out that he mentions some forty male co-workers by name, even that proportion is striking when compared with any other

---

52 G. B. Caird, *The Apostolic Age* (London: Duckworth, 1955), 117, 129.
53 Works by Deissmann, Nock and many others are not interested in this aspect of Paul's work. For a good treatment of the issue see P. Richardson, *Paul's Ethic of Freedom* (Philadelphia: Westminster, 1979), chap. 3.

ancient teacher, or virtually any ancient school of thought or literary source.[54]

It is illuminating to contrast Paul with someone like Billy Graham, who decided early in his work as an evangelist that he would meet "the threat of a moral downfall" by determining that he would "never walk alone with a secretary, never have lunch or ride in a car alone with her. And I never have."[55] From Paul's letters it is clear that he was willing to take the risk of working alongside of women and that he never singles out women co-workers as a particular source of temptation.[56] Nor does he ever specify any moral demands or clothing regulations for women solely so that they may not be a source for temptation. In this respect he consistently followed his master.

Paul's churches found this freedom too threatening. Thus Paul accommodates or compromises the freedom he had spelled out so clearly in Gal. 3:28 when he deals with the Corinthian situation. In 1 Cor. 11 specific dress instructions are given pertaining only to women—but these in no way inhibit the freedom of her participation in worship. Indeed, Paul is balancing two freedoms, the freedom to dress as one pleases and the freedom to prophesy and pray in public. He would rather give up the former in order to preserve the latter. To protect the freedom of the women to speak in public and to teach the church through the gift of prophecy and to allow that function to go unfettered by less important concerns, Paul instructs them to accommodate themselves to certain cultural practices. Likewise in chapter 14 he calls for women not to interrupt the service to inquire about matters which are obscure to them. They should rather ask their *own* husbands at home. For, like the ones given to ecstatic utterances and those given to prophetic utterances, the women have to learn the importance of silence in the assembly. Otherwise confusion will reign in the church and not order. In no way does Paul imply that women are not equal simply because there are stated times during the public worship service when they too must be silent.[57] Had he believed as other Greek thinkers that women are solely the property of their men, he would have urged

---

54 It has been pointed out that only one woman was mentioned by name in the Talmud, Beruria; but even in her case scandalous stories were added to discredit her. See Swidler, *Women in Judaism*, 96.

55 See M. Frady, *Billy Graham: A Parable of American Righteousness* (Boston: Little, Brown, 1979); this quote is from his article in *Esquire* (April 10, 1979), 36.

56 On the contrary, he uses an unusual term to refer to one of his female co-workers, in Phil. 4:3: *syzyge*, yokefellow. Its connotations are so warm and intimate that Clement and Origen took it as a reference to Paul's wife.

57 Although a major effort was made to show the unpauline character of this section, especially by G. Fitzer, *Das Weib schweige in der Gemeinde* (München: Kaiser, 1963), it seems to make more sense to see this in terms of church order. One notes the three groups to whom silence is recommended. Also, one might very well apply the principle of accommodation to this area of Paul's dealing with the church: see P. Richardson, "Pauline Inconsistency: I Cor. 9:19-23 and Gal. 2:11-14," *NTS* 26 (1980), 347-362.

the men to keep their women silent in church. As it is, he directs his appeal to the women to take their share of responsibility in church.

Perhaps the most difficult reference to female roles, also at times attributed to Paul, appears in 1 Tim. 2:9-15. In it the author rules out the possibility that women might teach in the church. It is also the only place where jewelry is proscribed for a woman and her role is seen as a "learner" and listener rather than a teacher.

The whole of that section has to be rejected as so blatantly contradicting Paul's clear teaching in 1 Corinthians and Galatians, flying so directly in the face of Genesis and Jesus that it cannot be seen as normative for early Christianity. To argue on the basis of God's creative sequence for the submissive role of the woman is out of character for Paul. Even though in 1 Cor. 11 he has also referred to the creation of male and female he concludes there: "In Christ's fellowship woman is as essential to man as man to woman" (11:11-12). Paul lived in the time of the restoration of the fall, provided by the death and resurrection of Jesus. There is clear evidence in Rom. 5 that Paul does not hold Eve responsible for the fall.

We have, therefore, no other option but to treat 1 Tim. 2:9-15 as the work of someone in the early church who could not come to terms with the freedom of Jesus and Paul on this matter. He consequently asserted a male chauvinism which was all too readily at hand for this use from either Greek or Jewish sources.[58] It must be considered a derailment from the track laid down by Jesus which Paul followed consistently in principle even when he had to make certain accommodations to it. It is hard to measure the damage it has done in the history of the church. Responsible exegesis demands that we come to terms with it.

Recent work on the person of Junia (Rom. 16:7) has shown how easily it became the standard for the early church to repress all evidence that women were equally treated in the church and given awesome responsibilities which they carried out with distinction. Bernadette Brooten has shown not only that women in Judaism played a much more important role, even as heads of synagogues, but also that male scribes and church fathers suppressed the evidence of that role. It is clear that Phoebe stands out as an appointed leader in her church, and also that Junia is described as an eminent apostle.[59]

When we look then at all the evidence, one cannot doubt that Paul would have felt comfortable claiming Junia as a fellow-apostle.

---

58   Among others one could cite the poem denigrating women written by Semonides of Amorgos (middle or late seventeenth century B.C.E.) which unfortunately has survived. For Judaism see Swidler's collection.

59   "'Junia . . . Outstanding among the Apostles' (Romans 16:7)" in L. and A. Swidler (eds.), *Women Priests* (New York: Paulist Press, 1977), 141-144, and her essay in the *SBL Seminar Papers* (Chico, Calif.: Scholars Press, 1981), on the same topic.

CONCLUSION

The views and practices with respect to women of three persons who lived in the first century can be summarized both with respect to similarities and differences. They are similar in the following ways:

(1) None of the three ever utters any words of warning against women or contempt for them.

(2) None of them ever gives specific moral instructions which apply only to women and not to men.

(3) In contrast to the Essenes and Mithraism the fellowships to which the three belong are open equally to men and women.

(4) All three have a positive outlook on marriage and the ensuing higher view of women which this entails, but they also give room for the achievement of women without marrying. None of them says that a woman achieves her life's goals only through the relationship with a husband or as a mother.

(5) For all three the role of women is only a part of a larger humanity which they believe is coming into being. Paul and Jesus are most explicit. In Musonius this can be inferred.

Significant as these similarities may be the differences are equally important. They are different in at least the following ways:

(1) Musonius may have taught courageously about the freedom of women to study philosophy, but we have no explicit evidence that he had female disciples or that he ever taught women. With Jesus and Paul the record is clear and very different. Women were an important part of their mission.

(2) Musonius attains depth in his understanding of marriage as a co-partnership between two people, male and female, which is missing in Paul and Jesus. In a strange way Musonius is reminiscent of the Genesis account of the reason for woman's creation. Jesus supports the idea that "the two shall be one flesh" but does so not in praise of marriage and the *symbiōsis* which two people can attain in marriage but in his instructions against divorce (Matt. 19:5; Mark 10:5). To be sure, part of his rejection of divorce had to do with the way in which women were being disadvantaged through the process, but a positive notion of marriage is not found in Jesus. For Paul the Jewish demonic view of marriage asserts itself. Marriage is basically seen as an anodyne for sexual pressures.

(3) Jesus does not address the question of sex and childbearing. Paul's Jewishness asserts itself when he refuses to restrict sex to childbearing. The later church took many aspects of social ethics from the Stoics and did not always note the differences between the Stoics and Christian ethics, thus it followed Musonius in prescribing that the goal of sex is to have children.

(4) One has the impression that Musonius speaks from a distinctly upper-class point of view. For example, he deals with the question of

sexual ethics from the standpoint of the female slave owner and not the
slave. Both Jesus and Paul seem to deal with sexual ethics from the
standpoint of the lower class, and their discussions of the issue seem to
be applicable to a larger group of people and to promise a larger group
of people some measure of self-respect.

While Jesus almost certainly heard about the world in which
Musonius was living, including intimations of feminism, it was Paul
who had to carry the freeing message of Jesus to the world in which
Musonius carried on his work. He, like Paul, was subject to persecution
and exile. Nevertheless, he held firm to his convictions and worked
untiringly for that time when humans would rejoice in each other's
freedom to recognize what binds us together in a common cause. While
recognizing the fascinating differences among individuals, all three
saw our life together on this earth as a partnership of such an intimate
nature that every effort must be made to keep the union among us. It is
to the credit of these three men that they saw that one of the most
debilitating human divisions is that which separates men from women
by conceiving of one as inferior to the other. Whatever differences
Musonius, Jesus, and Paul each had from the other, they were united in
refusing to pit male against female, and in their unanimous refusal to
consider women as inferior. Are we then not justified in calling them
feminists?[60]

---

60 Since writing the above it has been possible to work through D. Balch's work, *Let
Wives be Submissive: The Domestic Code in I Peter* (see n. 31 above). Although based on
1 Peter the work contains a wealth of material and engages in critical discussion with
all the major treatments of the role of women in the hellenistic age. He has shown
how statements on this subject may have been influenced by apologetic motifs; for
example, Josephus may have been trying to quiet fears about Judaism by saying that
women are kept in their place. Such a motive may lie behind some New Testament
statements as well. Balch has not paid close enough attention, however, to what
Musonius says and does not say. For example, Musonius never says that women are
to be submissive to men, and what he does say about roles of men and women can
only make sense when equality of men and women is assumed. He does not single
women out in warning them of extravagance, for what he asks of women he asks
equally of men (cf. Balch, 101). Here a detailed comparison with Areius Didymus,
the Stoic teacher of Augustus Caesar, would have been enlightening (see Balch,
40-41), in particular the statements, "For the deliberative faculty in a woman is
inferior" and "Rational household management, which is the controlling of a house
and of those things related to the house, is not fitting for a man" (Balch, 42). It is
surely striking that such statements are completely missing in Musonius. Balch's
conclusion that all the Roman moralists including Musonius "urged the subordination of wives" (147) would need to be supported with texts from Musonius, and it
cannot.

Marcion and the Critical Method

ROBERT M. GRANT

In an essay to honour Frank Beare there is certainly no idea of treating Marcion as a forerunner of twentieth-century biblical critics. On the other hand, it looks as though a remarkable silence has existed from the second century onward in regard to whatever method Marcion used in his search for the real Jesus and the real Paul. Even Harnack, with all his appreciation of Marcion as "der Kritiker und Restaurator,"[1] does not seem to have realized the necessity for putting him in the scholarly succession of those who dealt with the authenticity of documents.

Indeed, the silence may well be remarkable because it began as intentional. Not many early defenders of orthodoxy have anything to say about Marcion as biblical critic. Justin, who almost certainly wrote his *Apology* not long after Marcion had been expelled from the Roman church, makes no comment on this aspect of his work, even though Irenaeus, a generation later, was aware that he "circumcised" the Gospel of Luke and rejected other gospels (primarily Matthew, one must suppose) on the ground that the evangelists had mingled legal(is-tic) ideas with what the Saviour taught.[2] Origen does not seem to have spoken of Marcion as a critic; presumably it would have embarrassed him to do so since he was a critic himself. Eusebius, writing a *Church History* in which the real difficulties posed by heretics were never faced, makes use of Irenaeus on Marcion but does not discuss critical problems. He had not read Tertullian's books *Against Marcion* since he did not read Latin and the books were not at Caesarea anyway.[3]

---

1 A. v. Harnack, *Marcion: das Evangelium vom fremden Gott*, TU 45 (Berlin: Akademie Verlag, 1924), 35-73. (Abbreviations in references are those used by the *Journal of Biblical Literature*. See *JBL* 95 [1976], 331-346.)
2 Justin, *Apol.* 1.26; Irenaeus, *Adv. haer.* 1.27; 3.2.2.
3 Eusebius, *Hist. Eccl.* 4.11.1-2; 11.9; 18.9.

Yet Marcion was a critic, and his criticism, as we learn from the reports especially of Tertullian and Epiphanius, was exercised on various levels: textual, literary, historical, and theological. He presented a bold theoretical construct of the early history of Christianity in order to support his textual-literary and theological analyses. Apparently his starting point, as far as the New Testament was concerned, lay in Galatians, where he could read that there was only one gospel, which some perverted or contradicted (1:6-9; cf. 2 Cor. 11:4). It was no human gospel but derived from a revelation of Jesus Christ (1:12, 16). Paul fought over it with "false brethren" and did not yield to them for a moment (2:4-5; note that Irenaeus and Tertullian read that he did yield). He had no concern for "authorities" like Peter and James (2:6, 9), and he resisted Peter when he fell under James's influence (2:11-12). 2 Corinthians, too, presented Paul in conflict.

We have no evidence to show that Marcion rejected Acts, but if he used the first volume of Luke-Acts for his Gospel it would seem likely that he did look at the second. On his view the early apostles, notably at Jerusalem, set forth the gospel in such a way as to make it attractive to Jews, thus corrupting it. This is certainly the position reflected in the first half of Acts (without the idea of corruption). C. C. Torrey even argued that there was an Aramaic original for this part of the book. It is one in which Peter addresses his hearers as "men of Judaea" (2:14) or "men of Israel" (2:22, 3:12). It is one which reveals that until an experience depicted in Acts 10 Peter had "never eaten anything that was common or unclean" (10:14); thereafter he was criticized by "the circumcision party" at Jerusalem (11:3). This kind of evidence must have contributed to Marcion's picture of early Christianity. It led him to favour the notion that the gospel had been "interpolated by protectors of Judaism"; as Tertullian elsewhere put it, he "would rather call a passage an addition than explain it."[4]

The skeleton of Marcion's literary-historical theory was this: Jesus (or Christ) originally gave the true gospel to his apostles, but they perverted it in Palestine and its true meaning was lost until a fresh revelation was given to the apostle Paul; to be sure, his letters too were interpolated, but Marcion himself had been able to restore the authentic text of the epistles and the one gospel which he had preached. Ancient authors cited by Harnack supplied odd bits of flesh and blood. For instance, he held that the apostles originally preached the gospel orally (*agraphōs*) and did not ascribe any author to his gospel, i.e., the one he had recovered. We can see the sources he would use for both these points. 1 Corinthians tells how Paul "received from the Lord" what he also handed on to the congregation, an account of what "the Lord Jesus" did and said at the Last Supper (11:23-25). This account is

---

4 Tertullian, *Adv. Marc.* 4.4 and 7.

closely paralleled in the longer version of Luke 22:19-20, the version
read by Marcion. 1 Corinthians also tells how Paul handed down what
he had received (Marcion surely would have added "from the Lord"
except that he deleted "what he had received" completely) as central to
the gospel, the account of Christ's death, burial, resurrection, and
epiphanies (15:1-7; to Paul, 15:8). Marcion could not have assigned any
specific title or qualification to his *Gospel*. It must have been more or
less identical with what Paul called "the gospel of God" or "the gospel of
Christ" or even (though not for Marcion) "my gospel." From Tertullian
Harnack derived the sequence of letters in Marcion's *Apostle*.[5] As far as
one can tell, it was based on and modified from an arrangement
already in use. If we compare it with the usage (based on length) that
became traditional, we find that it is just the same, with two easily
explicable modifications. Marcion has exchanged the positions of Galatians and Romans because of the importance of Galatians in his
thought. In addition, he has exchanged the position of Colossians and
Philippians so that he can place Colossians next to Ephesians, which he
called "Laodiceans" because of the emphasis on letters related to
Laodicea in Col. 4:13-16. Everything else remained the same—except
that Marcion accepted as genuine neither the Pastoral Epistles (addressed to Paul's lieutenants Timothy and Titus) nor the Epistle to the
Hebrews. Certainly Marcion could have learned of forged Pauline
epistles from 2 Thess. 2:2 ("letter purporting to be from us"), and both
Clement and Origen suggest reasons for questioning 1 and 2 Timothy.
Clement mentions the reference to "the antitheses of what is falsely
called knowledge" (1 Tim. 6:20), which could look like a reference to
Marcion's book of *Antitheses* or to the subject-matter, while Origen
speaks of critics who disliked a reference to the secret book of Jannes
and Jambres (2 Tim. 3:8).[6] Once Timothy was excluded, the very
similar letter to Titus would go too.

But all this literary-historical material is secondary to the basic
literary criticism which served as its foundation and has now disap-
peared. In order to show that this was the case in Marcion's time we
turn to the well-trodden path of Papias of Hierapolis in an effort to
show that his statements, basically historical in intention, are supposed
to answer literary criticisms. Papias was a great collector of traditions,
and he had heard an important one from "the presbyter," whether
John or someone else. From this tradition we learn that Mark's gospel
had been criticized on the ground that it was not "in order," that it did
not contain something like a systematic compilation of the sayings of
Jesus (or the prophecies related to him), and that it was incomplete.[7]
Such criticisms could be based only on the comparison of Mark's gospel

---

5 Harnack, *Marcion*, 43*.
6 Clement, *Stromata* 2.52.6; Origen, *Matt. ser.* 117.
7 Eusebius, *Hist. Eccl.* 3.39.15.

with some other document or documents. In other words, a philologi-cal method was being employed by the critic(s) answered by the presby-ter. The presbyter's answer did not meet the question but supplied historical justifications. Mark was an accurate reporter of everything Peter told him, though he was not an eye-witness of Jesus' ministry. This does not answer the criticisms, though in passing their existence is noted.

Now if philological criticism was being employed on gospels in Papias' time, we can certainly infer that Marcion would have used it. Otherwise he would have had no foundation for his theory, and there is no reason to ascribe a special credulity to him or his disciples. Let us look at the early Christian criticism of Hebrews in the hope of finding analogies to what Marcion would have said. Here Eusebius supplies all the information we need. The oldest discussion is by Clement of Alexandria, who once more supplies historical explanations for philological problems. Obviously some critic(s) had noted that the epistle, unlike the genuine Pauline epistles, lacks the words "Paul an apostle" at the beginning. In addition, it gives the impression of being in the same style as Acts (conclusion: it was written by Luke?). Clement replies that Paul wrote for Hebrews in Hebrew and Luke translated. He did not give his own name to prejudiced Hebrews nor did he call himself an apostle to them.[8] Eusebius' own account of similar ideas is rather confused. First he states that many ideas and expressions are shared with Hebrews by Clement of Rome; this proves that Hebrews was not a recent product and made it reasonable to include it with the other Pauline epistles. On the other hand, Paul wrote for Hebrews in Hebrew; Eusebius or his source (more likely) is impressed by the similar style and thoughts of Clement (though others say Luke) and concludes that it was he who translated.[9] One may suppose that the original philological analysis indicated that Clement wrote, not trans-lated, Hebrews.

It appears that what we have suggested as the underlying argu-ment on Hebrews is reflected in Origen's comments in a homily (or perhaps a preface to a collection of homilies) on Hebrews: "the infor-mation (*historia*) that has reached us from some is that Clement, once bishop of the Romans, wrote the letter, from some that it was Luke, author of the Gospel and Acts."[10] Conceivably the suggestions origi-nated with Marcion, though no proof is possible. Origen's own discus-sion, as we should expect, deals directly with the philological subject. He differentiates diction and content in the epistle. First, the character of the diction does not have the "rudeness in speech" which Paul himself acknowledged (1 Cor. 11:6). Its diction is better Greek, "as

8   Ibid., 6.14.2-4.
9   Ibid., 3.38.1-3.
10   Ibid., 6.25.14.

anyone will admit who is capable of judging differences of this kind."
Therefore one should conclude that it was written by someone else—
God knows who he was. On the other hand, "as anyone will agree who
has paid attention to reading the apostle," the thoughts of the epistle
are "marvelous" and not inferior to Paul's. One could even say that they
are the apostle's. What conclusion can be drawn? Origen himself thinks
that "the style and composition belong to someone who remembered
the apostolic doctrines and, so to speak, made notes (*scholio-
graphēsantos*) on what was said by the teacher." This excerpt contains a
compromise between two views. First, those who rejected Hebrews
relied on its style (including the lack of the Pauline opening words).
Those who accepted it argued that its content was like that of the
Pauline epistles. Origen's theory is intended to combine the two views.
He adds that "if any church holds this epistle as being Paul's, let it be
commended even for this [apparently a reference back to something
not preserved by Eusebius]. For not without reason did ancient wor-
thies hand it down as by Paul."[11] Presumably the stylistic argument was
employed by Marcion and his followers.

Our conclusion as to Marcion's philological method is supported
by the content of the so-called Marcionite prologues to the epistles.
These deal with individual epistles and discuss authorship, destination,
and circumstances on the basis of the letters themselves, not traditions
about them.[12] Indeed, it could also be claimed that the famous first
sentence of the *Antitheses* should be interpreted in this context. "O
wealth of riches! Folly, power, and ecstasy!—Seeing that there can be
nothing to say about it, or to imagine about it, or to compare it to!"
Goodspeed commented that "it was evidently a book rich in paradox
and fraught with strong emotion."[13] The emotion, however, may have
been aroused in defence of the *Gospel* and the *Apostle* not only as unique
but also as requiring exegesis based only on their own texts.

If now we may turn to the presumed setting of Marcion's interpretations, we may hope to find it in the history of literary scholarship in
the world in which he lived, relying primarily on Rudolf Pfeiffer's
History of Classical Scholarship (Oxford, 1968) for guidance. Three
points deserve attention. First, the original head of the Alexandrian
school and library, Zenodotus, was a famous textual critic, well known
for his ability to ferret out interpolations in the text of Homer, partly by
using manuscripts, partly by relying on his sense of what was right
(105-122). Second, a century later the librarian was Aristarchus, to

---

11 Ibid., 6.25.11-13.
12 Text in J. Knox, *Marcion and the New Testament* (Chicago: University of Chicago
    Press, 1942), 169-170; cf. R. M. Grant, *Second-Century Christianity* (London: S.P.C.K.,
    1946), 90-91.
13 E. J. Goodspeed, *A History of Early Christian Literature* (Chicago: University of
    Chicago Press, 1942), 156, citing for Marcion F. C. Burkitt in *JTS* 30 (1929-30),
    279-280.

whom modern scholars have ascribed the exegetical rule "to explain
Homer out of himself" (225-227).[14] Pfeiffer says that the idea may
come from Aristarchus but the phrasing is from Porphyry. N. G. Wilson, however, found this "Aristarchean maxim" in Aelian, *Var. hist.*
14.13 ("Agathon out of Agathon"),[15] and indeed Clement of Alexandria tells us that the Saviour shows (Mark 10:17-31) that the "sayings
about the rich [in the gospels] are their own interpreters and reliable
exegetes."[16] This suggests that even something like the phrasing of the
rule could have been known to Marcion. And third, just as allegorism
arose at Pergamum largely under Stoic auspices, and in opposition to
the textual-literary criticism of Alexandria, as Pfeiffer makes plain
(234-242), so in Christian circles the efforts of Marcion provoked
exegesis such as that of the (other?) Gnostics, not to mention Justin and
the Alexandrians. Certainly Marcion as a philologist was opposed to
allegorization. The point is made especially clear by Origen, though
others also made it.[17]

By insisting on the primacy of Paul and a literal interpretation of
his genuine letters, Marcion was able to show that there was one gospel
of God or of Christ, preached by Paul (Gal. 1:6-9; 2 Cor. 11:4); Paul's
Jesus was the only one there was (2 Cor. 11:4); he was known to Paul by
revelation (Gal. 1:12, 16), lived in him (Gal. 2:20), spoke in him (2 Cor.
13:3). He was no longer known in a merely human fashion (2 Cor.
5:16), and it was this spiritual Christ whom Paul imitated (1 Cor. 11:1).
The gospel did not belong to Paul in such a way that he could call it "my
gospel," however, for Marcion did not read "my" in Romans 2:16 and
rejected 2 Timothy altogether (2:8).

What we have in Marcion's *Gospel*, then, is *the* gospel, not Paul's
and certainly not Luke's. Marcion had nothing to do with the snippets
of "information" handed down or invented by early Christians under
the guise of tradition. If he really was acquainted with classical scholarship, he must have viewed such items as on the level of the materials
transmitted in the various lives of Homer and other poets, often interesting, usually unverifiable, never useful for the exegesis of the
poems. (He thus did not resemble the church historian Eusebius,
whose early volumes of "history" are full of questionable traditions.) In
regard to the gospels, such traditions tended to flourish for Mark and
Luke, just because they had not been apostles and their works thus
needed a bit of explanation. Papias tells us that Mark wrote down accurately what he remembered from Peter; Irenaeus roughly repeats.[18]
Clement apparently gave two stories; Peter validated the gospel, or

---

14   See also A. Roemer, "Der exegetische Grundsatz... ," *Philologus* 70 (1911), 161.
15   *Class Rev* 21 (1971), 172.
16   *Quis div. salv.* 4.2.
17   Harnack, *Marcion*, 260*.
18   Eusebius, *Hist. Eccl.* 3.39.15; 5.8.3.

else he neither forbade nor recommended.[19] Of course in the *Letter to Theodore* he writes a public gospel, then at Alexandria a private one.[20] Origen says Peter instructed him to write the book.[21] It seems undeniable that this is the growth of legend, not the transmission of reliable tradition. As for Luke, Eusebius gives us nothing from Papias but cites Irenaeus for the idea that he was a follower of Paul who wrote down the gospel preached by him.[22] (We know that Irenaeus combined Col. 4:14, "Luke the beloved physician," with 2 Tim. 4:11, "Luke alone is with me.")[23] Eusebius himself, in a similar mood, refers to "my gospel" as validating Paul as Luke's source.[24] Origen more cautiously speaks of Luke as author of the gospel "praised by Paul"—evidently an allusion to 2 Cor. 8:18.[25] It is plain enough that in this case we are dealing with neither the growth of legend nor the transmission of tradition, but simply with a succession of teachers looking for an answer which they do not possess. There is therefore little reason to think of Eusebius' statement that Luke came from Antioch as anything but a guess.[26]

We mention these matters not for their own sake but in order to show one of the several ways in which reactions to Marcion's philology were expressed in church circles. The kind of reaction involved is the same as the one we noted earlier in regard to Hebrews. There is no attempt to meet the critical arguments. There is just a change of subject from literary criticism to historical information.

This is not to say that in Marcion's hands the method produced significant results. I have argued elsewhere that what ancient opponents considered his omissions from the Gospel of Luke can almost always be explained as due to his ideas about what was truly Christian.[27] Like the Homeric critic Zenodotus (whether or not he had good textual grounds for his deletions)[28] he kept what he thought was suitable, in the context he had decided upon. Here I propose to discuss only two examples of his method: first the beginning of the *Gospel*, second the Pauline prologues.

According to Harnack's reconstruction, Marcion began his *Gospel* with part of Luke 3:1 ("In the fifteenth year of Tiberius Caesar"), then skipped to 4:31 ("he came down to Capernaum"), identifying Jesus as "the Lord from heaven" (so Marcion read 1 Cor. 15:47) and as life-giving or salvific spirit (1 Cor. 15:45). What is missing? First of all,

---

19   Ibid., 2.15.1-2; 6.14.5.
20   M. Smith, *Clement of Alexandria and a Secret Gospel of Mark* (Cambridge, Mass.: Harvard University Press, 1973).
21   Eusebius, *Hist. Eccl.* 6.25.5.
22   Ibid. 5.8.3.
23   Irenaeus, *Adv. haer.* 3.14.1.
24   *Hist. Eccl.* 3.4.7.
25   Ibid., 5.25.6.
26   Ibid., 3.4.6.
27   R. M. Grant, *The Letter and the Spirit* (London: S.P.C.K., 1957), appendix.
28   Pfeiffer, *Classical Scholarship*, 108.

Luke's preface as a historian (1:1-4), next Jesus' conception, birth, and childhood narratives (1:5-2:52). It is obvious that items related to the Magnificat ("he has helped his servant Israel"; "Abraham and his seed forever"), the Benedictus ("Blessed be the Lord God of Israel"), and the Nunc Dimittis ("the glory of thy people Israel") had to go. The true Marcionite could not allow Jesus to speak of the Temple as his Father's house or, for that matter, to advance in wisdom and stature and favour with God and men. After that, Marcion left out the trivial historical details of Luke 3:1b-2, along with everything related to John the Baptist and, of course, the genealogy of Jesus, as well as his temptation. His going to Nazareth and speaking of the fulfillment of prophecy was most unsuitable, hence unlikely. What he did, then, was "go down" or "descend" (*katabainein*), a word which Marcion interpreted quite in the manner of the Fourth Evangelist or, for that matter, the Valentinian Gnostic Heracleon. None of this suggests either that Marcion relied on manuscript evidence or that his conjectures were in any way fortunate.

As for the Marcionite comments on the Pauline epistles (i.e., the *Apostle*), they too leave much to be desired. The method does not deserve rejection, but the Marcionite results are both twisted and trivial. The Marcionite author identifies the recipients of the various letters, usually relying on terms found in the letters themselves. Apparently "Greeks" for Galatians comes from a reference to Titus as a Greek (Gal. 2:3), while on the other hand the location of Rome in Italy, Colossae and Laodicea in Asia could come from a map or from very common knowledge. The information drawn from the epistles is presented in a highly stereotyped manner. After accepting the word of truth from the apostle, the Galatians and the Corinthians were tempted or perverted by false apostles; the apostle recalled them to faith or wisdom. The apostle did not visit the (Romans or the) Colossians, but false apostles reached them before he wrote; he recalled the Romans (and presumably the Colossians) to faith (or wisdom). The Thessalonians and the Philippians accepted the word of truth and did not receive false apostles or what they said but persevered either in persecution or in truth; the apostle praised them. To describe the situations in this way is to reveal the banality of whatever information Marcion or a follower derived from these epistles. (The preface to Laodiceans is lost but presumably it resembled the one to Colossians. Philemon is treated as a personal letter.)

What were the Marcionite prologues trying to say? They were trying to explain the differences among the epistles by providing three categories of classification. The basic problem was of course presented by false apostles; otherwise no letters would have been written, since in Marcion's view Paul was essentially a man of conflict. Therefore the letters could be classified by the reactions of the converts: Paul recalled to faith the Galatians, Corinthians, Romans, and Colossians, while he praised the Thessalonians and Philippians. A minor historical subdivision has to do with whether he had visited the churches or not. This looks to me like a drastic simplification of the sort of analysis discussed for example by Theon in relation to the *diēgēsis* or narrative.[29] The "elements of narrative" were these: person, event, place, time, manner, and the cause of these." Paul, the false apostles, and the converts are the persons,[30] the events are the conflicts, the places are those from which and to which the letters are sent, nothing is said about time or manner, and the cause is the conflict between truth and falsehood.

Why did the Marcionite author think that Galatians was sent from Ephesus? Perhaps it was because some ideas resemble those in 1-2 Corinthians, especially the latter. Romans was sent from Corinth because Phoebe came from nearby Cenchreae (16:1). Thessalonians apparently came from Athens because the city is mentioned in 1 Thess. 3:2. It is not clear why Colossians should have been sent from Ephesus, Philemon from Rome.

Details are not as important as the Marcionite method. However it may have been motivated (was Marcion a Gnostic or not?), we find in use a philological approach based on the idea of *scriptura* (limited) *sola*. For this reason he neglected and indeed had to reject the so-called traditions current in the churches of his time, as well as those among such Gnostics as Basilidians and Valentinians. It is hard not to sympathize with him. At the same time, if we have correctly reconstructed his method and results, it is equally hard to suppose that his philology really produced any valuable results.

If we return to the silence with which we began, we may venture the guess that it was due to the inability of critics of Marcion to attack his peculiar conclusions, which they rejected, without seeming to deny the validity of the method, which they were coming to accept as they had to deal with the flood of apocryphal apostolic literature. We see the method better employed in fragments of works by Serapion of Antioch, Origen, and Dionysius of Alexandria.

---

29   Theon, *Progymn.* 4.
30   The prologues incidentally mention Archippus (Colossians) and Onesimus (Philemon).

Notes on Contributors

ADRIEN M. BRUNET, O.P., is Professor of Theology at the Collège Dominicain de Philosophie et de Thèologie in Ottawa.

EUGENE R. FAIRWEATHER is Keble Professor of Divinity, Trinity College, University of Toronto. Among his many volumes are *The Oxford Movement* (New York: Oxford University Press, 1964).

LLOYD GASTON is Professor of New Testament in the Vancouver School of Theology, Vancouver, British Columbia. His main interest currently is Paul's letter to the Galatians. He has written *No Stone Upon Another* (Leiden: Brill, 1970), *Horae Synopticae Electronicae* (Missoula: SBL, 1973), and numerous articles.

ROBERT GRANT is Professor of New Testament at the Divinity School in the University of Chicago. His score of books have focussed on the New Testament, the Early Patristic period, and Gnosticism, with an excursion into U-boat intelligence.

JOHN C. HURD is Professor of New Testament in Trinity College, University of Toronto. His present preoccupations are 1 and 2 Thessalonians, and computer work with biblical materials. His work on *The Origin of 1 Corinthians* (London: S.P.C.K., 1965; Macon, Ga.: Mercer, 1983) is well known; he has also assisted in computerized concordances in Aramaic and Greek.

LARRY W. HURTADO is Associate Professor, Department of Religion, University of Manitoba. His primary concern is Christology with a specialized background in text criticism. He has recently published *Text-Critical Methodology and the Pre-Caesarean Text: Codex W in the Gospel of Mark* (Grand Rapids: Eerdmans, 1981).

GEORGE JOHNSTON, Emeritus Professor of New Testament, McGill University, Montreal, is well known for his interest on the Church and the Holy Spirit. He is the author, among other things, of *The Spirit-Paraclete in the Gospel of John* (Cambridge: Cambridge University Press, 1970).

WILLIAM KLASSEN was formerly Director of Resources at Simon Fraser University, Burnaby, British Columbia and is now Academic Dean at the Interfaith

Peace Academy in Jerusalem. His main interest is the relation between the Stoics and Cynics and the New Testament, an interest that he has explored in a number of articles. His book, *Peace in the New Testament* (Philadelphia: Fortress) is forthcoming.

BENNO PRZYBYLSKI, Associate Professor, North American Baptist Divinity School, Edmonton, Alberta, was for a number of years associated with the McMaster Research Project in the Normative Definition of Judaism and Early Christianity. He has recently published *Righteousness in Matthew and his World of Thought* (Cambridge: Cambridge University Press, 1980) and assisted in the editing of the McMaster seminar volumes.

PETER RICHARDSON, Professor of Religious Studies and Principal of University College in the University of Toronto, is primarily interested in Paul's ethics against the social and cultural milieux of his churches. He has written *Israel in the Apostolic Church* (Cambridge: Cambridge University Press, 1969) and *Paul's Ethic of Freedom* (Philadelphia: Westminster, 1979).

HANS ROLLMANN is Associate Professor in Religious Studies at Memorial University of Newfoundland, where he specializes in the history of nineteenth- and early twentieth-century New Testament scholarship. Soon to appear is a two-volume work, *William Wrede: Leben und Werk.*

ALAN F. SEGAL was previously Associate Professor in Religious Studies, University of Toronto, and is now Professor in the Department of Religion, Barnard College, New York. His main area of interest, worked out in his book *Two Powers in Heaven* (Leiden: Brill, 1977), is the relationship of Judaism, Gnosticism, and Christianity.

CHARLES H. H. SCOBIE is Professor of Religious Studies and Dean of Arts, Mount Allison University, Sackville, New Brunswick. After completing his book, *John the Baptist* (Philadelphia: Fortress, 1964) he has concentrated his attention on Samaritanism and Early Christianity, especially in the Gospel of John.

DAVID M. STANLEY, S.J., is Professor of New Testament at Regis College, Toronto. His books, reflecting his interest in Pauline spirituality, include *Boasting in the Lord* (New York: Paulist, 1973), *The Apostolic Church in the New Testament* (Westminster, Md.: Newman, 1967), and *Christ's Resurrection in Pauline Soteriology* (Rome: Pontifical Institute, 1961.

STEPHEN WILSON is Professor in the Department of Religion, Carleton University, Ottawa. His work has focused on Luke, and includes *The Gentiles and Gentile Mission in Luke-Acts* (Cambridge: Cambridge University Press, 1973), *Luke and the Pastoral Epistles* (London: S.P.C.K., 1979), and *Luke and the Law* (Cambridge: Cambridge University Press, 1983).

Index Nominorum*

Abbot-Smith, G.   122
Abel, E. L.   56
Abrahams, I.   153
Adnès, P.   132
Allegro, J. M.   199
Annen, F.   54
Arvedson, T.   99

Balch, D. L.   195, 206
Baldry, H. G.   190, 201
Balsdon, J. V. P. D.   192
Barclay, W.   153
Barrett, C. K.   149
Bartchy, S. S.   131
Barth, K.   116
Barth, P.   186
Bauer, J. B.   195
Baumann, R.   98
Baur, F. C.   3-5, 8-9, 63
Bavinck, J. H.   51, 54
Beare, F. W.   23, 52, 56, 61, 72, 73,
    91-94, 113-114, 117, 120, 128-129,
    138, 141, 143, 152, 158-159, 162,
    169, 185, 198, 201
Bernard, J. H.   165
Betz, H. D.   57, 63, 68
Beyer, H. W.   122
Beyschlag, W.   32, 39

Bickermann, E.   176
Black, M.   152-153
Blackman, E. C.   161
Blank, J.   24
Blauw, J.   51, 52, 54
Blevins, J. L.   32
Blythe, R.   1
Bonwetsch, G. N.   164-165
Bornkamm, G.   64, 132-133
Bosch, D.   54
Boslooper, T.   184
Bousset, W.   26, 34
Bovon, F.   68
Breitenstein, U.   176
Brooten, B.   204
Brown, J. B.   92
Brown, R. E.   198
Bruce, F. F.   2, 49, 158
Brückner, M.   4, 26
Bruners, W.   57
Buber, M.   24
Buck, C. H.   75
Bultmann, R.   1-3, 5-11, 13, 16, 18-20,
    24, 27, 29-30, 59, 69, 70, 116, 153,
    157, 165
Burkitt, F. C.   211

Caird, G. B.   156, 202
Campbell, T. H.   75

*   Index prepared by Peter D. Gooch.

Cassirer, E.   38, 39
Cavallin, H. C. C.   175
Chapman, J. J.   196
Charlesworth, M. P.   186
Chilton, B. D.   147, 170, 172, 175-176, 179, 181
Christ, F.   98-99
Clark, K. W.   55
Collange, J. F.   64
Collins, J. J.   176
Colpe, C.   117
Conzelmann, H.   50, 150
Corwin, V.   62
Creed, J. M.   154
Cullmann, O.   50, 51, 57, 160
Cumming, A.   192

Dahl, N. A.   70, 101-102, 125, 178, 181
Daniélou, J.   62
Davey, F. N.   58
Davies, P. R.   170, 172, 175-176, 179, 181
Davies, W. D.   17, 99, 120, 144
De Boer, W. P.   116, 120
Deichgräber, R.   119
Dekker, W.   181
de Lagarde, P.   29, 33-38, 42
de Soyres, J.   165
Dibelius, M.   81
Doane, T. W.   178
Dodd, C. H.   63, 151, 155-156, 157-158, 172
Donaldson, J.   192
Dover, K. J.   189, 196
Dungan, D. L.   3-4, 7-8, 11, 73, 82, 92
Dunn, J. D. G.   2, 11, 12, 119, 121, 158
Dupont, J.   49, 50
Dupont-Sommer, A.   176

Edelstein, L.   192
Eichhorn, A.   26
Enslin, M. S.   57, 120

Fant, M. R.   192
Faw, C. W.   77, 80
Fichte, J. G.   24, 29, 33, 36
Fiorenza, E. S.   198-199
Fitzer, G.   203
Fitzmyer, J. A.   127
Fjärstedt, B.   94-97, 100-101
Ford, J. M.   200

Frady, M.   203
Furnish, V. P.   3, 73, 120

Gadamer, H. G.   18
Garland, D. E.   55
Gasque, W. W.   49
Gaston, L.   52, 62-65, 93
Georgi, D.   64, 65, 117-118
Ginzberg, L.   171, 179
Goedeckemeyer, A.   186
Goessler, L.   197
Goodspeed, E. J.   211
Graf, F. W.   26
Grafe, E.   34
Grant, R. M.   211, 213
Graves, R.   178
Greeven, H.   192-193
Gressmann, H.   26
Grimm, W.   99
Grundmann, W.   50
Gunkel, H.   26, 37
Gunther, J. J.   75
Güttgemanns, E.   31, 33, 35

Hackmann, H.   29
Hadas, M.   176
Haenchen, E.   49, 151
Hahn, F.   51, 54, 55, 57, 60, 69
Hálevy, J.   57
Harnack, A. von   26-28, 41-44, 47, 94, 207-209, 212-214
Hawkins, J. G.   64
Heitmüller, W.   4-6, 9, 27
Held, H. J.   55
Hengel, M.   47-50, 52, 54, 177-178, 182
Herbert, G.   55
Heussi, K.   33
Heyob, S. K.   195
Hicks, R. E.   201
Hijmans, B.   187
Hill, D.   153
Hindus, M.   196
Hirzel, R.   186
Hock, R. F.   189
Hoffmann, P.   107
Holsten, C.   35
Holtzmann, H. J.   26, 27, 28, 32
Hooker, M. D.   101, 172, 182
Horsley, R. A.   95, 98
Hubbard, B. J.   55
Hunter, A. M.   87-88, 94

Hurd, J. C.   74-76, 78, 101-102
Hurtado, L.   65

James, E. O.   178
Jeremias, J.   2, 12, 19-20, 48, 52, 55,
   56, 59, 60, 66, 154, 179-180, 197
Jewett, R.   75
Johnston, G.   144
Judge, E. A.   189, 201
Juel, D.   180
Jülicher, A.   37, 43
Jüngel, E.   10, 12, 24

Käsemann, E.   2, 9-11, 17-20, 69-71,
   114-117, 119-126
Keck, L. E.   20, 64, 134-135
Kee, H. C.   99, 108
Keegan, T. J.   3
Kennedy, H. A. A.   87
Kippenberg, H. G.   58
Klassen, W.   189, 196, 198
Klijn, A. F. J.   62
Knox, J.   48, 211
Knox, W. L.   152
Koester, H.   92, 102, 111
Kraft, R. A.   62
Kramer, W.   67, 69, 71, 120
Kroll, W.   196
Kümmel, W. G.   2, 7, 10, 11, 13, 15,
   19, 24, 35, 60, 75, 80
Küng, H.   148

Larsson, E.   116, 120
Latourette, K. S.   47
Lefkowitz, M. R.   192
Légasse, S.   96
Leipoldt, J.   197
Lietzmann, H.   62
Lightfoot, R. H.   86
Linton, O.   102
Lohmeyer, E.   66, 114-115
Lohse, E.   64, 155, 177
Longenecker, R. N.   62
Lüdemann, G.   62
Lührmann, D.   108
Lutz, C.   186-187, 190

MacDermot, V.   163
MacGregor, G. H. C.   165
Mack, B. L.   98
MacKenzie, S.   23
Malina, B.   62, 64

Manning, C. E.   192
Manson, T. W.   54
Marshall, I. H.   57, 120
Martin, R. P.   114, 117, 119-120, 124-
   125, 155
Masson, C.   130, 134
Meeks, W. A.   58
Menoud, P. H.   50
Mertens, H.   99
Meyer, B. F.   20
Meyer, P. D.   93, 108
Meyer, P. W.   158
Michaelis, W.   120, 130, 136, 140
Miller, D. G.   51
Moffat, J.   160
Moule, C. F. D.   144
Munck, J.   48, 51, 52, 62-64, 101
Murphy-O'Connor, J.   66, 118, 121

Nickelsburg, G. W. E.   175-176
Nickle, K. F.   52, 65
Nipperley, T.   33

O'Faolain, J.   192
Ogg, G.   75

Paret, H.   4
Patai, R.   178
Pearson, B.A.   98
Pearson, L.   189
Peterson, E.   98
Pfeiffer, R.   211-213
Pfleiderer, O.   28, 42
Pluta, A.   69, 70
Pohlenz, M.   186, 195-196
Polag, A.   107
Pomeroy, S. B.   191
Popkes, W.   67
Purvis, J. D.   58

Quinn, J. D.   133

Radermakers, J.   58
Rahner, K.   129
Räisänen, H.   32
Rathje, J.   42
Regner, F.   3, 24, 29-30, 37, 41-42
Reischle, M.   37
Renan, E.   38-42
Renz, H.   26
Resch, A.   7-8
Rese, M.   24

Richardson, P.   92, 97, 107-108, 166,
    202-203
Ridderbos, H.   159
Riegel, S. K.   62
Rigaux, B.   128, 134
Rist, J. M.   191
Ritschl, A.   36, 41, 42
Roberts, C. H.   151
Robinson, J. A. T.   58, 75, 89
Robinson, J. M.   54, 108
Roemer, A.   212
Roetzel, C. J.   71
Rollmann, H.   24, 28, 29, 31, 42

Sampley, J. P.   197
Sandbach, F. H.   192
Sanders, E. P.   14, 15, 70
Sanders, J. A.   117-118
Sanders, J. T.   117-118
Scattolon, A.   181
Schäfer, R.   36
Schemann, L.   42
Schillebeeckx, E.   20
Schlier, H.   130
Schmidt, C.   163
Schmidt, K. L.   149
Schmithals, W.   19, 50, 63, 65-67
Schmitz, H. J.   44
Schneider, C.   191
Schoeps, H. J.   62, 71
Schottroff, L.   193, 198
Schrage, W.   195
Schulz, S.   99
Schütte, A. W.   33, 35-37, 42
Schütz, J. H.   139-140
Schweitzer, A.   10, 17, 27
Schweizer, E.   64, 69
Scobie, C. H. H.   53, 58
Scroggs, R.   50
Segal, A. F.   175
Segal, E.   196
Simon, M.   50
Smith, M.   213
Spiegel, S.   170-171
Stanley, D. M.   130, 133
Stanton, G. N.   116, 120
Stauffer, E.   197
Stendahl, K.   133, 140, 153, 201
Strecker, G.   62, 119, 161

Streeter, B. H.   93
Suggs, M. J.   94, 108
Sundkler, B.   52, 54-55, 66
Swetnam, J.   170, 174, 182
Swidler, L.   195, 199, 203-204

Taylor, V.   93, 110-111, 152
Thackeray, H. J.   98
Thoma, C.   172
Tinsley, E. J.   117, 120
Tödt, H. E.   107
Torrey, C. C.   208
Troeltsch, E.   26, 37, 39
Turner, C. H.   181

van Geytenbeek, A. C.   187-188
Verheule, A.   24, 26
Verkuyl, J.   51
Vermes, G.   171-173, 175-176, 179,
    181
Vielhauer, P.   66-69

Weiss, B.   32
Weiss, J.   5, 36, 99, 120
Weizsäcker, C.   27, 42
Wellhausen, J.   26-28
Wendt, H. H.   4, 5
Wernle, P.   26, 34, 42
Westcott, B. F.   165
White, J.   76
Wiefel, W.   24, 37, 41
Wilckens, U.   63, 68, 98
Wilckens, W.   69, 70
Williams, J. R.   23
Williams, S. K.   69, 70
Wilson, N. G.   212
Wilson, S. G.   49, 57
Windisch, H.   99
Worden, R. D.   93
Wrede, W.   3-6, 14, 24-45, 157
Wright, G. E.   51
Wuellner, W.   101

Yamauchi, E.   117
Yassif, E.   170

Zimmerli, W.   179-180
Zimmermann, H.   69

Index Locorum

Old Testament

Genesis
2:18   194
2:20   194
22   172-173, 177, 183
22:2   181
22:4   174, 178
22:12   181
22:16   181
22:18   178
25:21   174
31:14   147

Exodus
24:8   67

Numbers
18:20   147

Deuteronomy
21:23   178

Judges
11:34   181

2 Chronicles
3:1   173

Job
3:17-19   180

Psalms
37:11   147
72:11   51
89   180

Ecclesiastes
7:25-30   199

Isaiah
2:1-4   51
6:9-10   49
25:6-8   59
29:14   98, 100, 109
42:1-4   55
42:1   181
45:22-23   51-52
49:12   59
53   172, 176-179, 181-182
56:6-7   51
57:6   147
60:5-6   51
60:6   54
64:3   98, 100
65:16   98, 100

Jeremiah
6:26   181
30-31   53
31:31   67

Ezekiel
    33-37   53
    34:23   180
    37:15-23   53
    37:24-25   180
    45:1-8   53
    47:13-48:35   53

Daniel
    2-3   172
    7:14-27   147

Amos
    8:10   181

Zechariah
    3:8   180
    8:20-23   51
    12:10   181

Apocrypha and Pseudepigrapha

Tobit
    8:6-7   194

Judith
    8:25-27   174

Wisdom
    11-15   68
    19:2   199
    22:3   199
    42:14   199

Baruch
    3:9-4:4   98

2 Maccabees
    7   176

4 Maccabees
    6:27-28   176
    9:22   105

Jubilees
    17:15-18:19   174

New Testament

Matthew
    3:17   181
    5:1-16   95

5:5   146
5:6   84
5:9   154
5:13   135
5:20   146, 153
5:24   154
6:2-4   153
6:10   146
6:12   154
6:25-33   153
7:11   151
7:12   153
7:21   146
8:5-13   55
8:10   60
8:11   59, 84
8:28-34   55
10:5-6   48, 55, 56, 162
10:7   154
10:13   154
10:15   59
10:23   86
10:40-42   96
11:2-6   94
11:17-19   94
11:19   86
11:20-24   94
11:21-22   59
11:25-27   91-92, 98-101, 107-109
11:29-30   153
12:18-21   55
12:18   181
12:28   151
12:35   153
12:38-42   95
12:39   88
12:41   59
13:16-17   91-92, 97-101, 107-109
13:24-30   96
13:36-43   96
13:44   155
15:21-28   55
15:24   48, 162
16:4   88
16:17-19   64
18:3   146
18:13   155
19:5   205
19:23-24   146
19:28   59, 83, 103
19:29   147
20:15   153

20:25-28 122, 124
21:33-46 96
21:43 55
22:37 63
23:13 124
23:15 48
24:14 55
24:43 83
25:31-46 95
25:32 59
25:34 146, 147
25:46 147, 154
26:13 55
26:28 67
26:29 146
28:18-20 55, 56
28:19 162

Mark
1:11 181
1:15 154
3:29 151
5:1-20 54
5:34 154
7:24-30 54
8:12 88
9:7 181
9:35 124
9:43-47 154
9:50 154
10:5 205
10:17-31 212
10:17 147
10:19 153
10:43-45 122, 124
10:45 54
12:1-9 147
12:9 55
12:25 87
12:29-31 153
12:30 63
12:31 85
12:33 63
12:34 144, 153
13 148
13:5-27 83
13:10 54, 55
13:11 151
13:32 154
14:9 54, 55
14:22-25 67
14:24 54

15:39 54
15:40-41 198

Luke
1:1-4 214
1:5-2:52 214
1:51-55 147
3:1-2 214
3:1 110, 213
3:19-20 110
3:21 110
3:22 181
4:16-21 148
4:31 213
6:20-23 155
6:21 84
6:23 135
6:31 153
6:45 153
6:47-49 96
7:1-10 55
7:18-23 94
7:24-35 94
7:34 86
7:38 198
7:50 154
8:1-3 198
8:44 198
8:48 154
8:54 198
9:51-18:14 57
9:51-56 57
10:1-16 57
10:1 198
10:5-6 154
10:12 59
10:13-15 94
10:13-14 59
10:21-24 91-92, 95-96, 99-101,
   107-109
10:22 100
10:23-24 97, 100
10:25 147
10:27 63
10:30-37 57
10:38-42 198
11:4 154
11:13 151
11:20 151, 154
11:29 88
11:32 59
12:21-31 153

12:35-38   95
12:39   83
13:13   198
13:28-29   84
13:29   59
15:6   155
15:9   155
15:24   155
15:32   155
16:1-5   95
16:16   94
16:19   151
17:11-19   57
17:22-37   96
18:14   154
19:9   144
19:42   154
22:19-20   209
22:24-27   124
22:28-30   59
22:30   83, 103
23:43   151
24   198
24:46-47   57

John
    3   198
    3:3   147
    3:5   147
    3:15   147
    3:16   182
    4   58, 198
    4:39-41   57-58
    4:46-54   58
    7:35   58
    12:20   58
    13:5-17   124
    14:26   165
    16:12-15   161, 165
    16:25   160
    18:36   156
    19:25   198
    20:20   135

Acts
    1-12   48
    1-7   50
    1:3   163
    1:8   50, 56, 57
    1:14   200
    1:21   163
    2:14   208

2:22   208
3:12   208
5:14   200
8   50
8:3   200
8:12   200
9-12   50
9:1-22   49
9:2   200
9:15   49
10-11   49
10   208
10:14   208
11:3   208
11:19   50
11:20   49, 50
13-28   50
13:46-47   162
13:48   49
13:50   200
14:22   151
17:1-10   79
17:4   200
17:7   152
17:12   200
18:5   79, 81
18:6   162
18:24-19:10   106-107
18:28   109
19:8   152
20:25   152
22:3-16   49
22:14-16   132
22:21   162
26:9-18   49
26:17   162
28:28   162
28:29   49
28:31   152, 155

Romans
    1-15   64
    1:1   122, 131
    1:3-4   68, 155, 158-159
    1:3   7
    1:5   123
    1:14   97, 128
    1:16   131-132, 155
    2:1-11   148
    2:4   68, 71
    2:16   212
    3:21-26   147

3:24-26   69, 155
3:25   69
4:7-8   71
4:25   67-68, 71
5   204
5:1-5   147, 151
5:6-8   71
5:19   123
5:21   155
6:3-4   132
6:3   103
6:6-8   159
6:6   122, 132
6:8   132
6:11   155
6:16   88, 123
6:17   122-123
6:19   122
6:20   122
7:5   71, 158
7:6   122
7:25   122
8   11, 150
8:3   71, 158
8:4-9   158
8:4-5   158
8:5-8   150
8:6   151
8:9-10   159
8:9   166
8:11   126
8:12-17   145
8:13   158
8:14-18   155
8:14-17   148
8:14   158
8:17   126, 132
8:19-23   148
8:21   122, 150
8:23   130, 150
8:24-25   145
8:29   129, 152
8:32   71, 177-178
9-11   52
9:1-5   155
9:1   166-167
9:2-11:36   167
9:4   71
10:1   144, 155
10:9   67
10:10   144
10:14   134

11   93
11:11   144
11:13   47
11:25-26   52
11:27   71
12:11   122
12:14   7
13:9   7
13:11   144
14:14   7, 132
14:15   71
14:17   144, 152-155
14:18   122
15:2-3   7
15:3   120-128
15:8   48, 120, 122, 162
15:16   162
15:18   123
15:19   48
15:24   48
15:25-33   65
15:25-26   64
15:27   65, 72
15:28   48
15:31   64-65
16   64
16:1   122, 215
16:7   204
16:18   122
16:19   123
16:26   123

1 Corinthians
    1-4   92, 95, 102, 104, 107
    1-2   94-95, 97-98, 100, 109, 215
    1   97
    1:1-9   80
    1:8   149
    1:9   97, 139
    1:10-6:11   80
    1:10-4:21   91
    1:10-13   103-104
    1:10-12   151
    1:12-17   102
    1:12   64, 105
    1:13-17   103, 109
    1:13   71
    1:14-16   105
    1:16   102
    1:17-2:16   91, 95-96, 100, 139
    1:17-25   94, 103, 109
    1:17-21   97

1:17   102, 106, 130, 149
1:18-31   98
1:18   94, 104, 130, 149
1:19   98, 100, 103, 104, 109
1:20-21   100
1:20   92, 103
1:21   149
1:22-25   147
1:22-24   102
1:23-24   94, 106
1:23   159
1:24   152
1:26-29   92, 96
1:27-28   96
2:1-5   100, 103, 147
2:2   7, 132, 159
2:3-4   150
2:4-14   106
2:4-5   94
2:5   149
2:6-3:4   98-99
2:6-16   103
2:6-10   97
2:6   100
2:7   164
2:8   106, 132
2:9   98-100
2:10-16   96
2:10-13   160, 166
2:11   96
2:14-3:4   100
3:1-4:21   139
3   96-97
3:1-4   97
3:1-3   103
3:1   102
3:3-9   104
3:4-6   106
3:5-15   105
3:5-9   106
3:5   122
3:6   103
3:10-15   104, 106
3:15   109
3:18-23   100, 104-105
3:18-19   105
3:19   109
3:21-4:2   104
3:22   64, 105-106
4   95
4:1-14   131
4:1-13   103

4:1-5   105
4:5   103
4:6-8   109
4:6-7   104, 106
4:6   101, 105
4:8-13   150
4:14-20   103
4:15   135
4:16-21   101
4:16-17   102
4:16   104, 128, 130
4:17   127
4:19-20   94, 102, 109
4:20-21   149-152
4:20   144
5-16   101
5-6   101
5:1-5   109
5:3   103
5:4-5   150
5:6   78
5:9-11   80
5:10   150
6:1   84, 150
6:2-3   82, 103
6:5   97
6:9-11   151
6:9-10   147-148
6:12-20   80
6:12   85
6:13-24   80
7:1-16:12   80
7   195
7:1-39   167
7:1-7   196
7:2-4   87
7:4   198
7:5   197
7:10-13   7-8
7:10   87, 132, 147
7:12   87, 166
7:14   197
7:18   66
7:25   87, 166
7:39-40   165
7:40   166-167
8:1-11:1   140-141
8   85
9   95
9:2   163
9:3-18   136
9:4-5   64

9:14   7-8, 87, 132, 147
9:15-18   7
9:16-18   130
10:2   103
10:11   150
10:23   85
10:25   85
10:27   85
11   203-204
11:1   120, 128, 130-131
11:2   88
11:5-10   87
11:11-12   204
11:17-27   109
11:20-21   84
11:23-26   8, 84
11:23-25   7, 67, 160, 166, 208-209
11:23   87, 132, 147
11:25   71, 155
11:26   152
12   106, 151
12:3   158
12:13   103, 109, 202
13   85
13:9   165
13:12   7
14   106
14:33-35   203
15   7, 80, 109
15:1-8   209
15:1-3   132
15:1-2   131
15:3-11   147
15:3-8   136
15:3-7   66-67
15:3-5   67
15:3   71, 87, 178
15:5-8   131
15:5   7, 64
15:7-8   163
15:11   65-66, 71
15:12-28   148
15:12-19   109
15:17   71
15:20-24   159
15:24-26   82
15:24-25   156
15:24   152
15:28   97
15:29-34   109
15:29   103
15:45   130, 150, 152, 213

15:47   213
15:50   147-148
15:57   64
16:1-11   109
16:1-9   102
16:1-4   65
16:1   64
16:10-12   102
16:12   104, 107, 109

2 Corinthians
1-9   78
1:6   144
1:14   144
1:17-20   131, 133
1:19   104
1:20   155
3:1-7:16   150
3   64
3:6   71, 122, 150
3:14   71
3:17-18   158, 160
3:17   166
3:18   129-150
4:4   130, 152
4:5-6   122
4:5   127, 131, 159
4:6   131
4:7-12   150
4:7-11   133
4:8-11   120
4:14   144, 150
4:16   150
4:17   144
4:18   150
5:2   151
5:7   151
5:10   148
5:14   120
5:16-17   157, 159
5:16   8-9, 110, 132, 212
5:17   129, 131
5:18-6:1   149
5:19   150
5:21   71
6:1   151
6:2   52, 149
6:4   122
7:3   132
7:9-11   71
7:10   144, 151
7:15   123

7:29-31   150
8-9   65
8:4   64
8:18   213
9:1   64
9:12   64
10-13   64, 78
10:1   7
10:3-6   131
10:5-6   123
11:1   212
11:4   208, 212
11:7-10   136
11:7   123
11:9   81
11:13-15   105
11:14   132
11:16-12:13   150
11:22-23   64
11:24   136
12:1-10   147
12:1   133, 166
12:3-4   166
12:7-9   141
12:7   166
12:21   71
13:3   212
13:12   7

Galatians
1:4   67-68, 71
1:6-9   65, 208, 212
1:7-12   162
1:7-9   136
1:7   132, 160
1:10   122, 131
1:11-17   8
1:11-12   132
1:12-22   166
1:12   160, 208, 212
1:15-16   47-48, 72, 131
1:16   65, 127, 208, 212
1:18   64, 132, 136
1:19   7, 64
1:22-23   65
1:22   64
2:1-10   65-66, 71
2:1-2   136
2:1   64
2:2   132
2:3   214
2:4-5   208

2:6   208
2:7-9   64
2:7   162
2:9-10   65
2:9   208
2:11-12   64, 208
2:14   64
2:16   68
2:19   132
2:20   71, 129, 147, 212
3:1   7
3:3   158
3:13-14   178
3:13   71
3:14   162
3:15   71
3:17   71
3:18   147-148
3:23-4:7   148
3:26-27   130
3:27   103
3:28   201-203
4:3   122
4:4   7, 158
4:6   159, 166
4:7-9   122
4:17   64
4:24   71, 122
4:25-31   64
4:25   122
5:1   122
5:3   66
5:10-12   64
5:13   122
5:16-18   158
5:21   147-148
5:22-23   150
6:6-10   65
6:12-13   64
6:15   129, 131

Ephesians
1:14   147
1:18   147-148
3:1-6   162
5:1   127
5:2   71
5:5   147-148
5:23-31   197
5:25   71
5:26   103

Philippians
  1:1   122, 131
  1:7   137
  1:10   130
  1:12-20   131
  1:19   159, 166
  1:21-28   147
  1:21   129
  1:24   151
  1:27   137
  1:28   144
  2:1-11   137
  2:3   123, 137
  2:5-11   15, 113-126, 158
  2:6-11   52, 66, 128, 130, 137, 141
  2:8   158
  2:10-11   155
  2:12   123, 144
  2:16   148
  2:22   122, 139
  3   64
  3:2-16   137
  3:2   136
  3:9   138
  3:10-11   133, 138
  3:12   137-138
  3:13-15   138
  3:16   88
  3:17   128, 130, 138
  3:18-19   105
  3:20   137, 152
  3:21   105, 123, 126
  4:3   203
  4:5   130
  4:8   150
  4:9   132
  4:12   123
  4:15-16   81

Colossians
  1:7   122
  1:12   147-148
  1:13-14   144
  1:13   156
  1:15-20   15
  1:15   130, 152
  1:18   152
  1:23   122
  1:25   122
  1:28-29   147
  2:12-13   132
  3:11   202

  3:12   123
  3:24   122, 147-148
  4:7   122
  4:10-11   155-156
  4:12   122
  4:13-16   209
  4:14   213

1 Thessalonians
  1:1-10   80
  1:2-3:13   133-136
  1:2-8   133-135
  1:2-3   145
  1:3   85
  1:5   130, 166
  1:6-8   79, 86
  1:6   84, 120, 127, 130, 146
  1:9-10   51, 68, 145
  1:9   122
  1:13   132
  1:15   132
  2:1-3:10   80
  2:1   88
  2:11-12   139, 145-147
  2:12   146
  2:13-16   135-136
  2:13   132
  2:14   64, 65, 84, 130
  2:19-20   146
  2:19   145
  3:2-6:13   145
  3:2   122, 215
  3:3   88
  3:7   130
  3:8-10   146
  3:9   130
  3:11-13   80
  4:1-5:11   80
  4:1-2   132
  4:2   88
  4:3-12   145
  4:3-7   196
  4:4-8   146
  4:9   85, 88
  4:13-18   79, 81, 146
  4:14-15   7
  4:14   136
  4:15   87, 132
  5:2-3   146
  5:2   83, 88
  5:6   145
  5:8-9   144

5:8   85
5:9   146
5:10   71
5:12-28   80
5:12-22   145
5:13-15   146
5:14   84

2 Thessalonians
1:5-12   145
1:5   145
1:6-7   84
1:8   123
1:12   145
2:2   209
2:3-4   83
2:9-10   83
2:13   144-145
2:14   145
2:15   88, 147
2:16   145, 147
3:6-9   133, 136-137
3:9   128
3:10-12   84
3:13   145
3:14   123
3:18   145

1 Timothy
2:9-15   204
3:16   159
6:20   209

2 Timothy
2:8   212
2:12   126
3:8   209
4:11   213

Philemon
10   139
21   123

Hebrews
5:8-9   124
6:2   71
6:12   127
13:7   127

James
4:10   123

1 Peter
2:1-12   96
5:6   123

2 Peter
1:4   63

3 John
11   127

Jewish Sources

Philo
  de Abrahamo
    198   174

Josephus
  Antiquities
    1.13.1-4   174
    1.13.222-236   174
    1.267   174
    18.1.5   199
    20.12   174
  Against Apion
    2.201   195

Mekilta of R. Ishmael
    H-R,24-25   170
    H-R,38-39   170

b. Hagigah 2a   200

Early Christian Sources

Apocryphon of John
    (II,1)1:2-3   161
    31:28-31   161

Clement of Alexandria
  Quis div. salv.
    4.2   212
  Stromata
    2.52.6   209

Didymus
  de Trin.
    3.41.2   165

Eusebius
  Hist. eccl.
    2.15.1-2   213
    3.4.6-7   213
    3.38.1-3   210
    3.39.15   209, 212
    4.11.1-2   207
    5.8.3   212-213
    5.19.2   164

5.25.6   213
6.14.2-4   210
6.14.5   213
6.25.5   213
6.25.11-13   211
6.25.14   210
11.9   207
18.9   207
Praep. ev.
8.2   199
9.20.1   174

Hippolytus
Ref.
8.12   165

Irenaeus
Adv. haer.
1.27   207
2.27.3   164
3.1.1   161, 164
3.2.2   207
3.7.2   164
3.12.5   164
3.14.1   213
4.33.8   164
4.35.2   164

Justin
Apol.
1.26   207

Origen
Matt. ser.
117   209

Pistis Sophia
1:1   163

Pseudo-Clementines
Rec.
6.4   161
8.59   161
Hom.
3.20   161
11.19   161

Tertullian
Adv. Marc.
4.4,7   208
4.22.4   164

de Monog.
14   164-165

Greco-Roman Sources

Aelian
Var. hist.
14.13   212

Epictetus
Ench.
40   192

Musonius Rufus
Dis.
iii   190, 194
iv   194
xii   190, 193
xiiia   196, 198
xiv   191, 196-197
xvi   196

Oxyrhynchus Hymn
214-216   195

Plato
Rep.
5.451d   189

Pliny
Epistulae
10.96   47

Suetonius
Vita Claudii
25.4   47

Tacitus
Annales
15.44   47

Theon
Progymn.
4   215

Xenophon
Oeconomicus
vii-x   193